Information Environmentalism

This work is dedicated to my beloved Catherine Atoms.

'Work', said Kahlil Gibran, 'is love made visible'.

Information Environmentalism

A Governance Framework for Intellectual Property Rights

Robert Cunningham

Assistant Professor, Faculty of Law, The University of Western Australia

Edward Elgar

Cheltenham, UK • Northampton, MA, USA

Published by
Edward Elgar Publishing Limited
The Lypiatts
15 Lansdown Road
Cheltenham
Glos GL50 2JA
UK

Edward Elgar Publishing, Inc.
William Pratt House
9 Dewey Court
Northampton
Massachusetts 01060
USA

A catalogue record for this book
is available from the British Library

Library of Congress Control Number: 2014937811

This book is available electronically in the ElgarOnline.com Law Subject Collection, E-ISBN 978 0 85793 844 2

ISBN 978 0 85793 843 5

Typeset by Columns Design XML Ltd, Reading
Printed and bound by CPI Group (UK) Ltd, Croydon, CR0 4YY

Contents

Acknowledgements

> Writing a book is an adventure. To begin with it is a toy and an amusement. Then it becomes a mistress, then it becomes a master, then it becomes a tyrant. The last phase is that just as you are about to be reconciled to your servitude, you kill the monster and fling him to the public.
>
> Winston Churchill

Writing a book has been a long-standing goal of mine. Upon reflection the ambition is strange in some ways. Alone the goal does not mean a great deal. Why bother? Surely the answer lies in actually having something to say. In the beginning I was not altogether sure what I wanted to 'fling to the public'. I had a few intuitions and some leftover political/economic/philosophical grievances from my days as a student activist. Yet I was often plagued by the question of whether intuitions and grievances were enough.

As a student, my passion for ideas made engaging with politics at university, and in the environmental movement, slightly awkward at times. I despised the notion of toeing the party line. However, some good did come of my political engagement. Occasionally I was confronted with the question of why it was I cared so much about the state of the natural world. It was a probing question that always made me think a little. Was it the destruction of that creek bed at the bottom of my street when I was seven years old? I liked playing with the tadpoles and frogs in that creek as a kid. Or was it the influence of that teacher I had in Year 4, Mr Meadows. He played a VHS (not Beta) video to the class once about nuclear issues. I remember being scared out of my wits for weeks after that. Or was it when I witnessed those blue-green algae formations growing on the shores of the Hawkesbury River near Sydney when I was ten? Or that documentary screened at primary school in Year 6 by Mr Watson about ozone depletion and greenhouse gases? Or was it the time I saw my first clear-felled forest with my own eyes as a late teenager? Or when, a few years later, I caught a bus from Sydney to the world heritage-listed Kakadu National Park in the Northern Territory to visit the planned Jabiluka uranium mine? Or was it that all of the environmentally friendly inventions showcased on that TV programme

'Beyond 2000' never seemed to come to fruition? Maybe it was all of the above. Accretion works like that. One thing was for sure; I came to care intensely about the state of the natural world. And as time passed, I wanted to do something about it. In the end, this book is a manifestation of that concern.

There are indeed many people to thank for the creation of this book. Some of them – like Mr Meadows and Mr Watson – have slipped into my subconscious, only to be thought of when strolling down memory lane. However, there are many others who sit firmly at the forefront of my mind. In the first instance, there are five people who truly believed I could successfully undertake this project and, more importantly, told me so. First, my loving wife Catherine Atoms. She is a beautiful, intelligent, powerful, spirited woman who kept me on track even during the dark hours. I thank her from the bottom of my heart for her unwavering support. She holds the power to make me laugh and cry – simultaneously. Second, my mother Joanne Lang. She initially sparked my interest in the written word and the world of ideas. On many occasions, my mother affirmed a belief in my ability to realise this work. She is a great, loving woman and an excellent mother. Third, my father David Cunningham. He taught me lots of things, but above all else to never be 'a half-jobber'. If a job's worth doing, it's worth doing properly (he'd say). A handy lesson indeed. Fourth, Professor Brian Fitzgerald, previously based at the Queensland University of Technology and now at the Australian Catholic University, was an early supporter of my project. I thank him for his foresight in appreciating the merit of undertaking blue-sky theoretical research within the cultural environmental domain. Professor Fitzgerald is a man of copious energy and encouragement. Fifth, Professor Peter Drahos at the Australian National University. A better supervisor a doctorate student could not imagine. He is passionate about ideas, has a sharp intellect and a good sense of humour, is an excellent communicator, abundantly encouraging, and an all-round charming human being.

Along with my mother and father, I am exceptionally grateful to the rest of my direct family kin. Politically speaking, we sometimes differ. But I now realise that disagreement has been a great motivator for me to sharpen my intellect and develop my thoughts regarding the 'art of the possible'. So thanks earnestly to my two brothers Sean Cunningham and Jason Cunningham for everything over the years (including those political arguments). As it turns out, disagreement can be a powerful gift – a gift that keeps on giving. I love and care for each one of you more deeply than you could ever know. And I suspect the feeling is mutual. This love also extends to my sisters-in-law, Nelly Cunningham and Paula Cunningham, as well as my awesome nieces and nephews: William Cunningham,

Casey Cunningham, Bridgette Cunningham, Charlotte Cunningham and Harper Cunningham. I look forward to witnessing the growth and evolution of each of you in the years to come.

My extended family has also been an important anchor throughout the course of writing this book. To his credit, Geoff Lang has often asked me to justify my philosophical and political claims. A skill particularly pertinent in the scripting of this work. Geoff is a fun person who mostly refuses to grow up; and I mean that in the kindest of possible ways. Rani Sharma, Varsha Sharma and Neha Cunningham have all pushed and prodded me along this curious journey we call life. Also, for all of the immense love and great support over the years, I express my deep gratitude to Ken and Elaine Dwyer, David and Sarah Dwyer, Michelle and Glen Turner, Kevin and Belinda Dwyer, and my amazing extension of nieces and nephews for all of that spontaneous amusement and life-affirming distraction: Emily Dwyer, Madeline Dwyer, Georgia Dwyer, Alexander Turner, Elizabeth Turner, Gabrielle Turner, Victoria Turner, Bernadette Turner, Jacob Turner, Felicity Turner, Lucinda Turner, Isaac Dwyer, Bede Dwyer, and Kiara Dwyer. Stay fun – all of you!

The composition of this book began at the Queensland University of Technology. As foreshadowed, Professor Brian Fitzgerald was an important inspiration during the initial stages. Between 2008 and 2011 I was most glad to be part of the Margaret Street QUT scholars. I visited there on several occasions and I always left feeling inspired. Through these visits I came into contact with Professor Anne Fitzgerald, Neale Hooper, Dr Nic Suzor, Kylie Pappalardo, Benedict Atkinson and Dr Rami Olwan. Each of these scholars motivated me, in their own distinct way, to progress my research. I remain particularly indebted to Dr Nic Suzor who gave me very valuable feedback on earlier drafts of this work.

In putting the book together, I visited several universities as a research fellow. The Faculty of Law at the University of New South Wales was most hospitable in January and February of 2011. I am grateful to Dr Catherine Bond for facilitating this stay, and to the other UNSW colleagues such as Professor Kathy Bowrey and Professor Graham Greenleaf who made me feel very welcome. I am also grateful to Professor David Brennan at the Faculty of Law, Melbourne University who facilitated my research fellowship at that university in January and February 2012. Professor Megan Richardson and Dr Chris Dent – likewise based at Melbourne University – provided valuable feedback.

It was the Dean of the Faculty of Law at The University of Western Australia, Winthrop Professor Stuart Kaye, who was kind enough to grant me the time, by way of sabbatical in 2012, to complete this project. For that I am grateful. The opportunity of sabbatical provided the requisite time along with the possibility of fruitful research fellowships and visitations. To this end, during March and April 2012 I had valuable interactions with Professor Pamela Samuelson, Professor Molly van Houweling and Assistant Professor Jason Schulz at the University of California, Berkeley. I thank each of them for their time and insights. Lloyd Bonfield was a gracious host during my research fellowship at the New York Law School between April and June 2012. I also remain indebted to Professor Dan Hunter and Professor James Grimmelmann who likewise hail from NYLS.

The scholarship of Professor James Boyle from Duke University was the initial and ultimate springboard for this project. It was a great pleasure to discuss my research ideas with him in person during my short stay at Duke University in May 2012. I thank him enormously for that discussion along with the intellectual inspiration that he has provisioned more generally. The words of wisdom from Professor Laurence Helfer, Professor Jerome Reichman and Andrew Rens, also at the Faculty of Law of Duke University, were very gratefully received.

During my research fellowship at Queen Mary College, University of London during June/July 2012, Malcolm Langley (IP Librarian) proved to be an informational resource beacon. I thank him.

I travelled a lot during 2012 in order to gather ideas and stimulus for this project. Yet as it turned out the most conducive intellectual environment was at my doorstep (relatively speaking). The Regulatory Network Institutions (RegNet) at the Australian National University in Canberra was an excellent place and space to integrate thoughts and material I had collected along the way. So often I fail to realise I am standing knee deep in treasure. Professor Peter Drahos and Julie Ayling made me feel extremely welcome, as did the rest of the RegNet team. In particular, I am most thankful to Professor Veronica Taylor, Professor Neil Gunningham, Dr Miranda Forsyth, Dr Mamoun Alazab, Dr Imelda Deinia, Dr Emma Larking, Dr Kyla Tienhaara, Dr Jeroen van der Heijden, Kamalesh Adhikari, Shane Chalmers, Ibi Losoncz, Budi Hernawan, Kate Macfarlane and Rhianna Gallagher. Also at ANU, Professor Tom Faunce, Professor Geoffrey Brennan, Professor John Dryzek, Dr Hazel Moir, and Dr Rebecca Monson proved to be generous with their time and thoughts.

Since 2008 I have been greatly assisted by many colleagues at my home institution, the Faculty of Law at The University of Western Australia. In relation to the project at hand, I am particularly beholden to Professor Michael Blakeney, Professor Ana Vrdoljak (now at the University of Technology, Sydney), Professor Sharon Mascher (now at the University of Calgary), Associate Professor Greg Carne (now at the University of New England) and Professor Tony Buti (now Member of

Parliament, WA). I thank each of you. I also thank Dr Volker Oschmann and Anke Rostankowski who visited UWA in 2010 and proved to be excellent guests (and later amazing hosts in Berlin, Germany).

The idea of actually publishing this work in book format was consolidated during a meeting with Edward Elgar himself in October 2010 at UWA. The meeting confirmed all my prior suspicions that Edward Elgar would be a true 'English gentleman'; and it also confirmed my resolve to write the book. I thus thank Edward Elgar. From little things, big things grow. Needless to say, the Edward Elgar Publishing team have been a great pleasure to work with. In particular, I thank Ben Booth, John Paul-McDonald, Megan Ballantyne, Sue Sharp, Jane Bayliss, and David Fairclough for their proficiency and professionalism. I also acknowledge the good work of Carolyn Fox and I thank her for it. Last, but not least, I thank Dale Mackie (and the rest of KB) for providing conceptual inspiration for the cover design – who said you should never judge a book by its cover?

There are many others who could be thanked. However, with a core claim of this book in mind – that creativity and innovation can only flourish within a *social context* – it would be particularly remiss if I failed to acknowledge the collective shoulders upon which I have stood. I therefore respectfully thank society at large.

Dr Robert Lee Cunningham
December 2013
The University of Western Australia

Acronyms

A2K	Access to Knowledge
ACF	Australian Conservation Foundation
ACTA	Anti-Counterfeiting Trade Act
CC	Creative Commons
CSS	Content scrambling system
Cth	Commonwealth
DRM	Digital Rights Management
DVD	Digital Versatile Disc
EFF	Electronic Frontier Foundation
EIS	Environmental Impact Statement
ETS	Emission Trading Scheme
FLOSS	Free (Libre) and Open Source Software
FSF	Free Software Foundation
GATS	General Agreement on Trade in Services
GATT	General Agreement on Tariffs and Trade
IBM	International Business Machines Inc
ICRs	Information Commons Rights
iEDO	Information Environmental Defenders Office
iEIS	Information Environmental Impact Statements
IP	Intellectual Property
IPRs	Intellectual Property Rights
NSW	New South Wales
PIPA	Protect IP Act
PK	Public Knowledge
PPP	Public Private Partnerships
SOPA	Stop Online Piracy Act
TK	Traditional Knowledge
TPMs	Technological Protection Measures
TRIPS	Trade-Related Aspects of Intellectual Property Rights Agreement
WTO	World Trade Organization

1. Introduction: [Enter Stage] Information environmentalism

How difficult it is for a people accustomed to live under a prince to preserve their liberty.

Niccolò Machiavelli

1.1 INTRODUCTION

Information environmentalism is a normative discourse that seeks to protect and nurture the information commons. Protecting the information commons is important because within the information age it provides critical raw material for, among other things, creativity and innovation. As James Boyle has insightfully argued, there are strong similarities between the struggles to secure the integrity of the physical environment and efforts to preserve the integrity of the information environment. One similarity is the struggle to protect the commons – both physical and informational. In a seminal article, Boyle points out that the protection of the information commons will require 'a successful political movement'.[1] According to Boyle, this movement is to be founded upon 'a set of (popularizable) analytical tools which reveal common interests around which political coalitions can be built'.[2]

This book concurs with Boyle, but rather than seeking to solely construct a politic, the core focus is to begin the task of constructing an *information environmental governance framework*. In doing so, the book builds upon four environmental analytical frameworks: (i) welfare economics, (ii) the commons, (iii) ecology, and (iv) public choice theory. Drawing on these analytical frameworks, the book probes whether the principles of environmental governance hold lessons for the construction of a governance framework for the information environment. In the twenty-first century it is Intellectual Property Rights (IPRs) that have become the primary regulator of information. Contemplating IPRs through an environmental governance framework spawns several important questions. For instance, is there something to be learned from the application of the precautionary principle that is missing from the current evaluations of the use of IPRs? Does ecology, with its focus on managing complexity, help us reach a better understanding of the dangers of IPR intervention?

The objective (and arrangement) of this introductory chapter is threefold. First, after a brief historiography of IPRs, the chapter outlines the structure of the book using the four environmental analytical frameworks. Explaining the unifying relationship between the respective analytical frameworks and the information commons is important in this regard. Second, the chapter will explain the tensions between IPR maximalism and IPR minimalism with reference to the authorial (inventive) romance that underpins IPR incentivisation discourse. As we will see, IPR maximalism generally supports the expansion of IPRs whereas IPR minimalism argues the opposite. Third, after reinforcing that IPRs are indeed a type of property, the chapter briefly discusses how theories of property validation relate to IPRs. It is argued that property exhibits self-reinforcing characteristics; is often complicit in the concealment of ethical considerations; and is typically built upon a 'negative community' conception of the commons. These characteristics of property will be further revealed throughout the course of the book.

1.2 INFORMATION ENVIRONMENTALISM

The contemporary relationship between human beings and the environment is problematised with reference to a plethora of statistics and studies concerning climate change, biodiversity, deforestation, overfishing, pollution, and the list continues. The causes of these environmental detriments are complex and numerous. However, over the last several decades political movements built implicitly on analytical frameworks have emerged in response to underlying environmental concerns. Institutionally, the global rise of the Greens political party symbolises the political currency associated with local, regional and international environmental issues.[3] Naturally, political parties do not emerge in isolation, but rather are built upon relatively broad-based, grassroots consensus within at least discrete aspects of society. In this respect, we could speak of an institutional ecology that has emerged in direct response to contemporary environmental concerns.

At the dawn of the twenty-first century, beside the continuing evolution of contemporary environmentalism, developed Western societies have steadily transitioned into the information age. Accompanying this transition is the global harmonisation of the *so-called* intellectual *property* rights system.[4] Recording the political history of IPRs alongside the emergence of contemporary environmentalism provides an early clue as to the nexus between the physical environment and the information environment. The transition into the information age has been long in the making. As noted by Ruth Okediji, it has co-evolved alongside mercantile and colonial expansionism:

> IP law was not merely an incidental part of the colonial legal apparatus, but a central technique in the commercial superiority sought by European powers in their interactions with each other in regions beyond Europe. The early period of European contact through trade with non-European peoples thus was characterized predominantly by the extension of IP laws to the colonies for purposes associated generally with the overarching colonial strategies of assimilation, incorporation and control. It was also characterized by efforts to secure national economic interests against other European countries in colonial territories.[5]

A brief historiography of IPRs supports Okediji's perspective. The story begins with the first IPR grant issued during the first half of the 1400s in either Berne or Milan.[6] During this era exclusive rights to practise printing were also granted in Venice for a period of five years;[7] and in 1507 the Venetian council granted a 20-year patent for a secret process of mirror making.[8] Such IPR grants were replicated later in the 1500s in other European countries such as France.[9] In support of Okediji's viewpoint, from the early days of IPR grants there has been a commingling between two ancient tools of state power, being information control and economic monopoly.[10] This is partly evidenced by the charter to the Stationer's Guild, which granted the Stationers a monopoly on 'the art or mistery [sic] of printing'.[11] The rationale for this grant was reflected in the preamble to the charter thus:

> Know ye that we, considering and manifestly perceiving that certain seditious and heretical books rhymes and treatises are daily published and printed by divers scandalous malicious schismatical and heretical persons, not only moving our subjects and lieges to sedition and disobedience against us, our crown and dignity, but also to renew and move very great and detestable heresies against the faith and sound doctrine of the Holy Mother Church, and wishing to provide a suitable remedy in this behalf.[12]

Under this charter, the right to print 'copy' was restricted to members of the Stationers' Company, who were in turn restricted in what they could print by the Stationers' register.[13] The right to 'copy', or 'copy rights', were owned by the Stationers not the authors of the relevant work.[14] This system, which operated between 1557 until the Statute of Anne in 1709, was both 'closed' and 'private' operating to a large extent outside the formal legal system.[15] The rationale underpinning copyright was not so much legal or economic, but rather political.[16]

The political history of IPRs has been alluded to by many scholars, none less than Foucault who spoke of the 'forensic' and 'warranting' attributes of authorship.[17] Foucault reminds us that '[i]n our culture (and doubtless in many others), discourse was not originally a product, a thing, a kind of goods; it was essentially an act – an act placed in the bipolar field of the sacred and the profane, the licit and the illicit, the religious and the blasphemous'.[18] One of the primary traditional functions of regulating authorship was identifying who should be punished when literature violated social, legal or moral norms.[19] This perspective is as relevant now, if not more relevant, than it has been throughout history.[20] This is because copyright law not only provides financial benefits to its holders, but it also facilitates cultural control and the amassing of political power.[21] A parallel narrative can be transcribed in relation to patents.[22]

Many of the themes related to environmental degradation and preservation evident in the nineteenth and twentieth centuries map to the twenty-first-century 'information environment'.[23] Given the success (albeit limited) of the environmental movement in raising the profile and political currency of environmental concerns, one response is to reflect on how *environmental analytical frameworks* might apply to the information environment.

1.2.1 Environmental Analytical Frameworks

James Boyle, in his seminal article *A Politics of IP: Environmentalism for the Net?*, implicitly identifies four environmental analytical frameworks underpinning the environmental movement, being the commons, ecology, welfare economics and public choice theory:

> A successful political movement needs a set of (popularizable) analytical tools which reveal common interests around which political coalitions can be built. Just as 'the environment' literally disappeared as a concept in the analytical structure of private property claims, simplistic 'cause and effect' science, and markets characterized by negative externalities, so too the 'public domain' is disappearing, both conceptually and literally, in an intellectual property system built around the interests of the current stakeholders and the notion of the original author. In one very real sense, the environmental movement invented the environment so that farmers, consumers, hunters and birdwatchers could all discover themselves as environmentalists. Perhaps we need to invent the public domain in order to call into being the coalition that might protect it.[24]

The four environmental analytical frameworks inherent within this passage are implicit rather than explicit. To elaborate, the analytical structure of private property claims relates indirectly to *the commons* to the extent that the commons can be dichotomised with private property. The discipline of *ecology* that emerged during the nineteenth century can be thought of as a counter-reaction to the reductionist, Baconian-inspired 'cause and effect' science that prevailed prior to the evolution of ecological science. Reference to 'markets characterized by negative externalities' relates to the broader discipline of *welfare economics*, which ultimately seeks to include social and private costs within its analysis when seeking to determine the overall costs and benefits associated with economic activity. And finally, the idea that there is a need to 'reveal common interests around which political coalitions can be built', along with the notion that IPRs are 'built around the interests of the current stakeholder', infers the applicability of *public choice theory*. This theory is traditionally concerned with how private interests trump the interests of the public at large and, more contemporaneously, how fragmented interests can respond to this tendency.

In contemplating the four analytical frameworks of environmentalism, it is clear that relevant regulatory and governance structures struggle to fully take into account:

i. the true costs associated with production and consumption (welfare economics);
ii. historically diverse interactions between human beings and land (the commons);
iii. the complex relationship between living ecosystems (ecology); and
iv. the rent-seeking effect of concentrated interests on regulatory frameworks (public choice theory).

A critical function of the environmental movement has been to underscore these failings. Based on this aspect of the environmental movement, the book seeks to determine whether there is any utility in the theoretical application of the four environmental analytical frameworks to IPRs. To this end, the core research question of the book becomes: Is there utility in applying environmental analytical frameworks to Intellectual Property Rights (particularly copyrights and patents)?

We will see throughout the book that there are indeed analytical gains that flow from this application.

1.2.2 Information Commons

The information commons is an important unifying theme when applying the four environmental analytical frameworks to the information environment.[25] Part II will provide a more detailed definition of the information commons. For now, it can simply be noted that there is a complex interrelationship between the 'public domain', the 'intellectual commons' and the 'information commons'; but that there is also considerable overlap between each term such that very loosely speaking the terms can be collectively conceptualised as 'the opposite of private property'.[26] The crux at this stage is that *the information commons is a unifying theme when applying the four environmental analytical frameworks.* The connection between the information commons and each respective theoretical foundation is as follows.

First, with reference to *welfare economics*, the information commons linkage stems from the fact that the private property dimensions of IPRs are, to a large extent, the opposite of the information commons. In Part I of the book a welfare economic analysis of IPRs underscores the exclusivity costs associated with the propertisation of information. The exclusivity costs include efficiency costs, administration costs, externality costs and distributional costs. In highlighting the exclusivity costs, we will see that the true costs of property are often concealed behind the 'veil of property'. A corollary being that the propertisation of information becomes more attractive than allowing that information to reside in the information commons.[27] This is despite the fact that it may well be more efficient and less costly to *not* propertise information in discrete circumstances.[28] By revealing the exclusivity costs associated with the monopolistic characteristics of IPRs, the welfare economic analysis highlights the opportunity costs that flow from removing information from the information commons.

Second, with respect to *the commons* analytical framework, the nexus between the information commons and the commons is mostly self-evident. By way of synthesising commons tragedy discourse, we will observe within Part II of the book that the contrast between the 'tragedy of the commons' and the 'tragedy of the anticommons' gives birth to the 'tragedy of ignoring the information semicommons'. As the semicommons relates to the dynamic interaction between private property and the commons, it stands to reason that within the information environment there is no semicommons of which to speak unless the information commons exists in the first instance. Contemplating the role of fair use within copyright is useful here because it facilitates dynamic interaction between private and commons usages of information. Naturally an important aspect of this dynamic interaction is clear demarcation of the information commons. This is a central task of Chapter 4.

Third, the *ecology* analytical framework relates to the information commons by virtue of the 1970s environmental jurisprudential scholarship that sought to allocate rights to nature. Building upon ecological governance principles, Part III of the book argues that one method of fostering a resilient information environment is to allocate rights and provision standing to the information commons through the creation and maintenance of information commons rights (ICRs). After debunking some of the criticisms that potentially stem from this emergent argument, Part III suggests that the ICR notion is to be built upon the criterion of 'rational truths' (i.e. a threshold level of technical expertise), 'reasonable arguments' (i.e. sound and credible legal arguments), and 'rhetorical imagination' (i.e. innovative rhetorical methods). By way of illustration, the public trust doctrine provides an example of a *reasonable argument* that can be employed to realise the creation and maintenance of ICRs.

Fourth, in relation to the application of the *public choice theory* to the information environment, Part IV of the book illustrates that the information commons is an important prerequisite to social production such as Free (Libre) and Open Source Software (FLOSS). Social production arises in the context of public choice theory because it holds the potential to simultaneously counteract regulatory capture and overcome collective action problems. Specifically, Part IV contends that social production inadvertently fosters competitive tension between the productive forces. This in turn serves the 'constitutional' function of separating (economic) power. This perspective is founded upon the economic efficiencies of social production, alongside public choice theory and its constitutional economic derivative. As indicated, the information commons is a critical prerequisite of social production.

Hence, while each of the four environmental analytical frameworks proffers a distinct perspective, it is the *information commons* that unifies their application. This is reflected in Figure 1.1.

1.2.3 Information Environmental Governance Framework

A further explanation of the information commons will appear in Part II of the book. At this stage, a clearer account of the normative phrase 'information environmentalism' is necessary. This is particularly because the scholarship of James Boyle and others is often placed under the alternate banner of 'cultural environmentalism'. Although the book seeks to build upon established cultural environmental discourse, the phrase

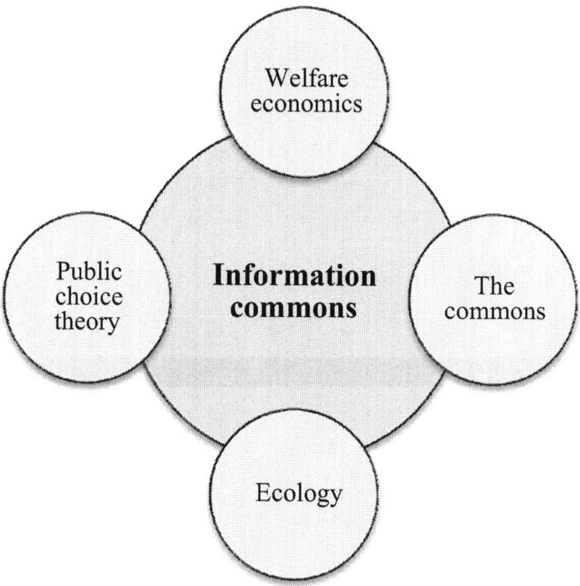

Figure 1.1 The information commons as unifier

'information environmentalism' is nevertheless deployed.[29] This is primarily because the 150 formal definitions of 'culture' speak to a lack of definitional consensus among sociologists.[30] Fortunately, the word 'information' has a more settled definition being 'facts provided or learned about something or someone; what is conveyed or represented by a particular arrangement or sequence of things'.[31] Building upon the definition of 'information', the 'information environment' can be thought of as encompassing those systems that relate to the processing, production, consumption, communication, distribution and diffusion of information.[32]

Although the provision of a working definition of 'information' and the 'information environment' is a useful starting point, information environmentalism is perhaps best understood through description rather than definition. In short, information environmentalism stems from Boyle's argument that those who seek to protect the information commons are working towards a similar end as environmentalists who seek to protect the physical environment.[33] Like many socio-political movements and discourses, information environmentalism is simultaneously reactive and proactive. It has *reacted* by exposing the harms caused by a relentlessly maximalist programme of IPR expansion; and it has *pro-acted* through the creation and maintenance of private ordering social production initiatives such as FLOSS and Creative Commons (CC).[34]

At its core, information environmentalism seeks to promote information regulation that simultaneously facilitates efficiency and distributional justice.[35] It does this by highlighting that the information commons preserves the health and diversity of the information environment. In this sense, the information commons becomes a rallying point for a diverse range of information environmental interests. As Boyle states:

> Right now, it seems to me that, in a number of respects, we are at the stage that the American environmental movement was at in the 1950s or 1960s. At that time, there were people – supporters of the park system, hunters, birdwatchers and so on – who cared about what we would now identify as 'environmental issues'. In the world of intellectual property we now have start-up software engineers, libraries, appropriationist artists, parodists, biographers, biotech researchers, and others.[36]

The idea that 'the environment' exists has allowed for the establishment of a coalition around a reframed conception of common interest, which allows the duck-hunter and the bird-watcher to recognise their commonality. That is, both the duck-hunter and the bird-watcher rely on the functioning of the wetlands and the accompanying ecosystem services.[37] Boyle explains:

> The invention of the concept of 'the environment' pulls together a string of otherwise disconnected issues, offers analytical insight into the blindness implicit in prior ways of thinking, and leads to perception of common interest where none was seen before. Like the environment, the public domain must be 'invented' before it is saved. Like the environment, like 'nature,' the public domain turns out to be a concept that is considerably more slippery than many of us realize. And, like the environment, the public domain nevertheless turns out to be useful, perhaps even necessary.[38]

Note that Boyle refers to the 'public domain' rather than the 'information commons'. This will be further explored in Part II. Whereas the environmental movement illuminated the effects that social decisions can have upon ecology, information environmentalists seek to illuminate the effects that IPRs can have upon culture and society. Such illumination requires a set of analytical tools that can be relied upon to advance the profile of the information commons. For this reason, the four environmental analytical frameworks of welfare economics, the commons, ecology, and public choice theory are applied to IPRs. A central aspect of this application is to contribute to the building of an *information environmental governance framework*. The 'invention of the information commons' is critical to this project.

Despite the rich philosophical and scientific history of environmentalist thought, the 'invention of the environment' has been no slight task.[39] The 'invention of the information commons' is also likely to be a considerable challenge. Beyond refining the parameters of the information commons in Part II, Part III of the book argues that the protection and nurturance of the information environment generally, and the information commons specifically, will require strategic reliance upon a combination of rational truths, reasonable arguments and rhetorical imagination. This combination is an important aspect of the information environmental governance framework project.[40] We will see throughout the book that the rationale underpinning this framework is to develop a language and geography of experience that can be relied upon to coalesce information environmental interests that might otherwise fall dormant.[41]

1.2.4 Authorial (Inventive) Romance and Incentivisation Discourse

Along with applying the four environmental analytical frameworks to IPRs discussed above, and the general project of building an information environmental governance framework, countering authorial (inventive) romance is also a crucial component of information environmentalism.[42] Such romance underpins many of the incentivisation arguments that pervade IPR maximalist discourse.[43] There is no need to discuss at length, within this book, the natural consequences of IPR maximalism. Whether the subject matter is peanut butter and jelly sandwiches or Mr John Moore's spleen, the point has been satisfactorily made within IPR scholarship that the propertisation of information can be taken too far.[44]

As implied, authorial romance applies not just to authors but also to inventors.[45] Reflecting upon authorial (inventive) romance and the associated IPR-related incentivisation arguments provides a useful springboard in appreciating the tensions between IPR maximalism and IPR minimalism. This tension is a persistent theme within both IPR discourse and throughout this book. While propertisation of information is *sometimes* necessary to secure incentivisation, there are also inherent limitations such that, beyond a certain point, more propertisation does not necessarily equate to more incentives.[46] When it comes to IPRs there are instances where less is more. Moreover, the end purpose of providing incentives via IPRs (in order to encourage the production of information) is to provide the public with benefits. As Breyer J states in relation to the intellectual property clause within the US Constitution:

> The Clause exists not to 'provide a special private benefit', but to stimulate artistic creativity for the general public good ... The 'reward' is a means, not an end. And that is why the copyright term is limited. It is limited so that its beneficiaries – the public – 'will not be permanently deprived of the fruits of an artist's labors'.[47]

Within a liberal economic framework it is difficult to rally against the proposition that, economically, society is obliged to reward persons to the extent that they have produced something useful in accordance with the dictum 'as one sows, so should one reap'; and morally, there are strong arguments which suggest that a person has a natural right to the product of her brain.[48] Moreover, some types of innovation patents are likely to induce more innovation, particularly where innovation is independent, or non-cumulative, which is to say that one invention is essentially separate from another.[49] And further still, even where innovation is cumulative, if the use of the patent is obvious then it is possible that the original patent holder will be compelled to license a patent to follow-on innovators.[50]

Yet despite the seductive nature of the theoretical arguments correlating IPRs and incentivisation, IPR minimalists underscore that IPR maximalist incentivisation arguments are usually *theoretical* rather than *empirical*.[51] On the empirical front, Lerner's study concerning the economics of innovation is thought provoking. He considered amendments in intellectual property law in 60 countries over a time frame of 150 years, examining nearly 300 intellectual property policy changes.[52] His study found that investment in research and development decreases slightly when patent law is strengthened.[53] The inference is that when a country strengthens its patent protection, it marginally reduces the level of investment in innovation by local firms.[54] As Drahos highlights: 'the connection between intellectual property, science and economic development is contingent and local rather than necessary and universal'.[55]

Significantly, IPR minimalist scepticism towards incentivisation arguments is not confined to academe. For instance, Justice Breyer voiced ambivalence in relation to the incentivisation arguments that underpin copyrights when he stated in *Eldred v Ashcroft* (537 US at 254) that: '[n]o potential author can reasonably believe that he has more than a tiny chance of writing a classic that will survive commercially long enough for the copyright extension to matter.'[56] This perspective was founded on empirical studies, which suggest that only approximately 2 per cent of copyrighted works maintain commercial value between 55 and 75 years after they are created.[57]

Empirical evidence referred to by Lerner and Justice Breyer serves to consolidate IPR minimalist propositions, an example being that IPRs operate more as a lottery system than as an incentivisation mechanism.[58] But regardless of empirical evidence, questioning the incentivisation function of IPRs remains a challenging task.[59] This is because such arguments are deeply embedded within IPR scholarship, stemming back to the early days of the IPR system. The plea made by Giacop Acontio in 1559 exemplifies what has more contemporaneously become the Lockean rights tradition as it relates to creation and invention: 'Nothing is more honest that those who by searching have found out things useful to the public should have some fruit of their rights and labors, as meanwhile they abandon all other means of gain, are at much expense in experiments, and often sustain much loss.'[60]

The following description of IPRs by Francis Bacon in Parliament on 20 November 1601 is also insightful:

> If any man out of his own wit, industry, or endeavor, find out anything beneficial for the commonwealth, or bring any new invention, which every subject of this realm may use; yet in regard to his pains, travail, and charge therein, her Majesty is pleased (perhaps) to grant him a privilege to use the same only to himself, or his deputies, for a certain time: this is one kind of monopoly.[61]

The IPR minimalist response to the assumptions inherent within these historical submissions is that scant homage is paid to the *social context* in which the inventors reside.[62] This is significant because notwithstanding the dual objectives of the IPR system – private incentive and public benefit – IPRs are typically granted to individual economic agents rather than communities.[63] Furthermore, as IPR minimalists are quick to point out, IPRs exhibit strong *monopolistic characteristics*, which is a theme that pervades the history of IPR minimalist discourse. The following plea in 1735, from an anonymous pamphleteer protesting against the legislative push by booksellers to extend the copyright term, is an early exemplar:

> I see no Reason for granting a further Term now, which will not hold as well for granting it again and again, as often as the Old ones Expire; so that should this Bill pass, it will in Effect be establishing a perpetual Monopoly, a Thing deservedly odious in the Eye of the Law; it will be a great Cramp to Trade, a Discouragement to Learning, no Benefit to Authors, but a general Tax on the Publick; and all this only to increase the private Gain of the Booksellers.[64]

Correspondingly, Benjamin Franklin pronounced patents immoral in his autobiographical account in 1793, and Mertonian norms (although subject to considerable contestation), have lingered in science since time immemorial.[65] Even within the contemporary context, avid supporters of the IPR system have expressed latent scepticism. Bill Gates, for instance, wrote the following memo to Microsoft executives in 1991: 'If people had understood how patents would be granted when most of today's ideas were invented and had taken out patents, the industry would be at a complete standstill today.'[66]

Inherent within the IPR minimalist perspective is the view that IPR maximalists discount the debt that present authors (inventors) owe to prior authors (inventors) for their raw material.[67] This is founded upon the truism that all creators and inventors begin as users to the extent that they combine or reform new material with old material drawn from the information commons.[68] When the social dimensions of creativity and innovation are considered, it is no great surprise that IPR minimalists are caustic in their assessment of IPR maximalist incentivisation arguments. For instance, it has been suggested, within the context of copyright, that 'author-centered IP is a sham promoted by publishers to conceal their economic power behind a façade of moralism'.[69] In this vein, Drahos has intimated that the incentivisation function of IPRs is an 'ideological fairytale designed to hide the systematic exploitation of creative labour in the capitalist mode of production'.[70] And Waldon has echoed these concerns when he suggests that the tendency to commodify information through the IPR system 'shatters the connection between author and work, no less effectively than modern capitalism shatters the connection between the individual labourer and the product commodity that emerges from an assembly line'.[71]

Although authorial (inventive) romance (and the accompanying incentivisation arguments) is all pervasive within IPR scholarship, it represents merely one method of fleshing out the tensions between IPR maximalism and IPR minimalism. Another effective method is to contemplate the *validating theories of property.*

1.3 INTELLECTUAL PROPERTY RIGHTS AND THE VEIL OF PROPERTY

Given that property is a fundamental aspect of IPR characterisation, it is useful within the introductory context to briefly explore the nature of property validation.[72] Although there is some controversy as to whether IPRs are best characterised as property, monopoly or some other alternate such as a state subsidy, the truth is that these categories are not mutually exclusive. IPRs are a type of property with monopolistic characteristics, which operate in many instances akin to a state subsidy. If the state explicitly allocates private property rights to a given resource then it is difficult to argue outright that the resource is not private property. Of course, from a normative perspective it is possible to argue that a given resource should not be private property. But that is different to the positivist argument that the resource is not private property. As all World Trade Organization (WTO) member states essentially regard IPRs as property, IPRs should be thought of as a property right, albeit different from real property.

When IPRs are perceived through the property lens, a credible theory of validation is imperative. Historically, validating theories of property stem from the foundational narrative of colonial and imperial sovereignty.[73] In adopting this narrative, the first point of call is usually Blackstone's famous definition of property being 'that sole and despotic dominion which one man claims and exercises over the external things of the world, in total exclusion to the right of any other individual in the universe'.[74] Inherent within this definition, along with complementary sources such as John Locke's *Two Treatises of Government* (1689), is a set of value judgments that describe a vision of human nature, meaning, the past and the future.[75] The Blackstonian and Lockean perspectives of property are foundational because, as Blackstone himself suggested, 'property came first among institutions, and all else followed'.[76] Within this frame, Blackstone surmised:

> Necessity begat property; and, in order to ensure that property, recourse was had to civil society, which brought along with it a long train of inseparable concomitants; states, governments, laws, punishments, and the public exercise of religious duties. Thus connected together, it was found that a part only of society was sufficient to provide, by their manual labor, for the necessary subsistence of all and leisure was given to others to cultivate the human mind, to invent useful arts, and to lay the foundation of science.[77]

The social contractarian foundations of Blackstonian narratives are appealing. However, critical realists remind that although property is often construed as a noun, the truth is property is not really a *thing* but rather a 'verbal announcement that certain traditional powers and privileges of some members of society will be vigorously defended against attack by others'.[78] A corollary of perceiving property in this way is that the self-reinforcing nature of propertisation becomes evident.[79]

1.3.1 Property is Self-reinforcing

According to the Lockean 'labour theory of value' tradition, if a person applies their labour to a given piece of land, this in turn gives the person a valid legal claim to that land through the legal protection afforded by real property rights.[80] Once real property rights are allocated, the value of the relevant land is represented not just by the labour inherent within it (among other things), but also the value inherent within the legal protection afforded by the real property rights. Thus, real property rights instil an inherent value which, once applied, becomes self-reinforcing.[81] This self-reinforcing dynamic of property rights is an important aspect of the 'veil of property'. As we will see in Part I, this dynamic applies just as much to the information environment as it does to the physical environment. Felix Cohen, for example, underscored the self-reinforcing dimension of IPRs by relaying the validation of trademarks in this way:

> There was once a theory that the law of trade marks and trade names was an attempt to protect the consumer against the 'passing off' of inferior goods under misleading labels. Increasingly the courts have departed from any such theory and have come to view this branch of law as a protection of property rights in divers economically valuable sale devices ... The current legal arguments runs: one who by the ingenuity of his advertising or the quality of his product has induced consumer responsiveness to a particular name, symbol, form of packaging, etc, has thereby created a thing of value, a thing of value is property; the creator of property is entitled to protection against third parties who seek to deprive him of his property ... The vicious circle inherent in this reasoning is plain. It purports to base legal protection upon economic value, when, as a matter of actual fact, the economic value of a sales device depends upon the extent to which it will be legally protected ... The circularity of legal reasoning ... is veiled by the 'thingification' of property.[82]

Aside from the self-reinforcing nature of the foundational narratives of property, when such narratives are stripped to their essence it also becomes clear that property rights regularly serve to conceal ethical considerations.

1.3.2 Property Conceals Ethical Considerations

The following excerpt from Locke neatly exemplifies the way in which property can foster the concealment of ethics:

> God gave the World to Men in Common; but since he gave it them for their benefit, and the greatest Conveniences of Life they were capable to draw from

> it, it cannot be supposed he meant it should always remain common and uncultivated. He gave it to the use of the Industrious and Rational (and Labour was to be his Title to it;) not the Fancy or Covetousness of the Quarerelsom and Contentious.[83]

According to this Lockean perspective, the 'Quarerelsom and Contentious' should be left out of the property validation equation with the underlying legitimiser to the title of property being the labour of the 'industrious and rational'. Once this perspective is adopted, the foundation has been established to argue by extension that for Indigenous peoples to 'deny Europeans the right to occupy and cultivate land would be a naked denial of another's natural right to acquisition'.[84] That is, the denial of European colonisation by Indigenous peoples would be an attempt to occupy more land than they could make use of and in this respect Indigenous peoples become 'liable to be punished' like a man who 'invaded his Neighbour's share, for he had no right, farther than his Use called for'.[85]

Beyond Locke, the concealment of ethical considerations facilitated by property rights was also a critical dimension of Aldo Leopold's classic *A Sand County Almanac*. In that work, by drawing upon Charles Darwin's lesser-quoted perspectives in *Descent of Man*, Leopold argued that while the general tendency of humanity is ethical expansionism, private property often serves to mutate and stifle this tendency to the extent that private property relations prioritise expediency over ethics.[86] Leopold made this point by recounting the history recorded in the myths of Homer:

> When god-like Odysseus returned from the wars in Troy, he hanged all on one rope a dozen slave-girls of his household whom he suspected of misbehavior during his absence ... This hanging involved no question of proprietary. *The girls were property. The disposal of property was then, as now, a matter of expediency, not right and wrong.*[87]

In recounting the myths of Homer, Leopold sought to draw a link between private property and ethics, or the lack thereof, by contrasting the treatment of female slaves with the treatment of females with a different social station such as wives. Though the ethical structure of Odysseus' Greece encompassed wives; it had not yet been extended to human chattels such as slaves. According to Leopold's analysis, it was the veil of property that led to ethics being trumped by expediency.[88] It is within this context that Leopold's attempt to establish a clear nexus between private property relations and ecological ethics is most noteworthy: 'There is as yet no ethic dealing with man's relation to land and to the animals and plants which grow upon it. Land, like Odysseus' slave-girls, is still property. The land-relation is still strictly economic, entailing privileges but not obligations.'[89] In arguing that it is necessary for the ethical structure of humanity to further expand so as to encompass land as a whole, including animals and plants, Leopold succinctly articulated his often-quoted land ethic: 'A thing is right when it tends to preserve the integrity, stability, and beauty of the biotic community. It is wrong when it tends otherwise.'[90]

In advancing his land ethic, Leopold emphasised that the penetration of private property has fundamental consequences for the physical environment.[91] Leopold's sentiments were similarly reflected within the views of religious communities during the Middle Ages, who likewise sought to highlight the ethical concealment function of property. According to religious tradition, in a similar vein to usury, 'to have "property" of goods (or goods "in proper") was a sin, and monks in particular found guilty of this vice were denounced as "properietaries" or "owners"'.[92] Saint Francis of Assisi, for instance, rejected property by proclaiming that his brothers would not claim ownership over anything and in doing so would live in 'true apostolic poverty'.[93] The Franciscans made an important distinction between usage and ownership. As individuals and as an order the Franciscans claimed to have no property at all, instead arguing that: 'all the property of the order was available for them to use, but that they did not have the right to alienate it or engage in financial transactions regarding it'.[94] The crux of the Franciscan perspective was the claim that commons use is conceptually and ethically distinct from appropriation.[95]

While the 'sin' of private property was predominantly linked to monastic communities, the contentious nature of private property was definitely not confined to the monastery. Within the history of Western thought, there are a plethora of non-religious figures that exemplify historical philosophical struggles that relate intimately to private property. Symbolical thinkers include Gerrard Winstanley, Jean-Jacques Rousseau, and Pierre Proudhon. Each thinker, in their own distinct form, gave voice to the political contestations of their day concerning private property rights. Thus, remnants of the Franciscan perspective can be found in the practical initiatives of Winstanley and his 'diggers' in the mid-1600s, along with the theoretical work of Rousseau and Proudhon.[96] For instance, Winstanley's message to 'those who call yourselves lords of manors and lords of the land' was simple and direct:

> The earth was not made purposely for you to be the lords of it, and we to be your slaves, servants and beggards; but it was made to be a common

> livelihood to all, without respect for persons; and that your buying and selling of land and the fruits of it, one to another, is a cursed thing.[97]

The oft-quoted passage of Rousseau reflects similar sentiments:

> The first person who enclosed a piece of land and be-thought himself to say, 'This is mine,' and found people foolish enough to believe him, was the real founder of our social system. What crimes, wars, murders, what miseries and horrors would have been spared to mankind, if somebody had torn down the stakes or filled up the ditch, and had warned his fellows, 'Beware of listening to this impostor; you are lost if you forget that the produce is for all, and the earth for no one'.[98]

And Proudhon spoke in a corresponding vein:

> If I were asked to answer the following question: What is slavery? and I should answer in one word, It is murder!, my meaning would be understood at once. No extended argument would be required ... Why, then, to this other question: What is property? may I not likewise answer, It is robbery!, without the certainty of being misunderstood; the second proposition being no other than a transformation of the first?[99]

Historically, many of the critical issues in relation to property ultimately flow from concerns about the private appropriation of resources from the commons. The most potent examples in this respect fall within the ambit of the colonisation process. The first enclosure movement in England during the 1500s is a case in point.[100] The application of the *terra nullius* doctrine as it purportedly pertained to Australia in 1788 provides a slightly more recent example.[101] Within this context, it is useful to refer to the positive community/negative community dichotomy. In doing so we will see that property validation, more often than not, is built upon the notion of 'negative community'.

1.3.3 Property Validation is Typically Built Upon Negative Community

Theoretical support for the private appropriation of the commons is most often founded upon the simplification of complex historical periods of humanity. This simplification, in turn, generally fosters the negative community view of the commons. To explain, colonial and imperial narratives of property typically reduce the history of humanity into four distinct activities, being hunting, pasturage, farming and commerce.[102] According to this 'four stages of history' lens, property becomes a somewhat clear-cut construct.[103] For hunters property begins and ends with possession, whereas the shepherd extends the idea of property further, and the agriculturalist further still.[104] Once cities began to be built, and commercial activities ingrained, property then becomes well instilled within civil society as a practical method of embedding a foundation of sociability, or, perhaps more accurately, a particular brand of social contract.[105]

Inherent within this four stages of history perspective is a particular view of the commons. Boyle's discussion of both the first enclosure movement and second enclosure movement reminds that everything ultimately begins in the commons until it becomes subject to (private) propertisation.[106] This is true for the physical environment and the information environment. Part II of the book will demonstrate that theories of property validation relate intimately to the positive community/negative community dichotomy. Specifically, the tendency of the IPR maximalist perspective is to adhere to a negative community conception of the information commons (i.e. *res nullius*).[107] This is to say that resources can be perceived as belonging to no one and are therefore unclaimed and for the taking.[108] In contrast, the tendency of the IPR minimalist perspective is to subscribe to a positive community conception of the information commons (i.e. *res communis*).[109] This means that resources are considered to belong to everyone and therefore any use of such resources is required to be for the benefit of the public at large. The choice adopted with respect to positive community and negative community is vital. This is because the penetration of private property within any given population has fundamental consequences for individuals and society.[110] And most importantly, within the context of this book, the choice has fundamental consequences for the information environment and the information commons.

1.4 PRINCIPLES OF INFORMATIONAL ENVIRONMENTAL GOVERNANCE

Before concluding the chapter, it is worth specifying in concise form the key principles that the book derives from its application of environmental analytical frameworks to IPRs. Table 1.1 summarises the relevant principles with reference to the respective analytical frameworks.

Table 1.1 sets out the governance principles that flow from the arguments in the chapters that follow. As is clear, the distilled information environmental governance principles are derived directly from the respective analytical frameworks. The principles within the table form the basis of an integrated approach to the governance of the information

Table 1.1 Principles of information environmental governance

Analytical frameworks	Information environmental governance principles		
Welfare economics	1. Account for costs of IPRs and benefits of information commons	2. Avoid internalising positive externalities where costs exceed benefits	3. Support initiatives that foster free flow of information
The commons	4. Apply 'positive community' principle to information commons	5. Delineate parameters of information commons	6. Neutralise 'tragedy of ignoring the information semicommons'
Ecology	7. Build a resilient information environment by facilitating diversity and modularity	8. Allocate rights and provision standing to information commons	9. Protect information commons by deploying 'rational truths', 'reasonable arguments' and 'rhetorical imagination'
Public choice theory	10. Guarantee equitable access to information commons and critical hardware infrastructure	11. Deploy social production to foster resilience, diversity and modularity within information environment	12. Leverage social production to separate economic power

environment. This approach is supported by the arguments of the book as a whole. The integrated approach takes various forms. For instance, principle 1 is foundational to principle 6; principle 10 is a fundament of principle 12; and principle 4 supports the enactment of principles 7, 10 and 11. Likewise, in order to enact the rhetorical imagination aspect of principle 9 (by establishing informational national parks), principle 5 must be fulfilled. Shared themes deepen the integration of the principles. By way of example, principles 7 and 11 are tied together by the notion of resilience; and principles 4 and 8 are connected through a positive community perspective of the information commons. Throughout the book we will see that a variety of tools will be required in order to operationalise the principles. The *social net product analysis* conducted in Part I is exemplary in that it satisfies principles 1 and 2. As the book unfolds, further interrelationships and tools will be revealed.

1.5 CONCLUSION

The core research question of this book is as follows: Is there utility in applying environmental analytical frameworks to Intellectual Property Rights (particularly copyrights and patents)? The book will answer this question in the affirmative by applying the four environmental analytical frameworks of welfare economics, the commons, ecology and public choice theory to IPRs. We will see that the information commons is a crucial unifying theme for information environmentalism. As James Boyle has emphasised, struggles seeking to secure the integrity of the physical environment have relied upon the 'invention of the environment'.[111] Likewise, securing the integrity of the information environment requires the 'invention of the information commons'. But the inherent tension between the IPR maximalists and the IPR minimalists poses significant challenges with respect to inventing, protecting and nurturing the information commons. In this regard, the information commons is a 'site of struggle'.[112] Just as colonial powers throughout history have built empires upon the shaky theoretical foundations of private property validation, so too the IPR system is often built upon questionable propositions that flow from authorial (inventive) romance and incentivisation arguments inherent within IPR maximalist discourse. In applying environmental analytical frameworks to IPRs this book will contribute to the building of an information environmental governance framework. Such a framework will prove useful in fostering a language and geography of experience that can be adopted when seeking to protect and nurture the information environment (generally) and the information commons (specifically).[113]

PART I

Welfare economics

The introductory chapter argued that the veil of property facilitates a dynamic whereby expediency trumps ethical considerations. As Aldo Leopold underscored, this dynamic has spawned significant implications for individuals, societies and the physical environment alike. Extending this Leopoldian theme, Part I argues that the veil of property is also implicit in concealing a range of exclusivity costs within the information environment.[1] Exclusivity costs are a corollary of relying upon property to overcome market failure.[2] In the context of the information environment, examples of market failure include lack or asymmetry of information (and the accompanying information paradox), public goods, externalities and monopolies.[3] Each of these market failures, in one way or another, relate intimately to IPRs.[4]

We will see in Part I, particularly with respect to externalities, that there is an underlying paradox in relying upon property (and related market activity) to overcome market failure. It is for this reason that Part I begins by exploring the nexus between property and markets. Although propertisation and related market activity works extremely effectively in many instances to mediate production and consumption, there are clear instances where the market does fail.[5] By drawing out the interaction between market failure and the propertisation of information, the exclusivity costs of IPRs are revealed. To this end, Chapter 2 shows that the information paradox underscores efficiency costs of IPRs, and the public goods market failure highlights the administration costs of IPRs.[6] In Chapter 3 the externalities analysis emphasises the externality costs that stem from IPRs, and the monopoly market failure speaks to distributional costs. Transaction costs that flow from the propertisation of information will also be canvassed.

Part I does not seek to establish a complete catalogue of exclusivity costs related to IPRs. Nor is there an attempt to place a numerical value on these costs. Rather, the kernel is to highlight the need to take particular categories of costs into account when engaging with a social net product assessment of IPRs. The essential inference of Part I is that ignoring IPR-related exclusivity costs has the effect of skewing the social net product equation of IPRs away from the information commons and towards the propertisation of information.

2. Information paradox and public goods

> One must not think slightingly of the paradoxical ... for the paradox is the source of the thinker's passion, and the thinker without a paradox is like a lover without feeling: a paltry mediocrity.
>
> Soren Kierkegaard

2.1 INTRODUCTION

Welfare economics concerns weighing up the costs and benefits – private and public – inherent within the economic system. One way of engaging with this equation is to apply what Pigou referred to as a social net product analysis. This analysis is particularly useful when applied to the market failures inherent within the information environment. Doing so draws out costs that might otherwise be obscured when using a pure neoclassical economic market analysis.[1] The social net product equation will be explained more fully in the next chapter. For now it can simply be thought of as a type of cost-benefit analysis that takes into account private and public costs and benefits.[2]

The chapter begins by discussing the nexus between property and markets from a welfare economics perspective. This will be followed by a discussion of the information paradox, which gives rise to efficiency costs. The public goods provisioning problem, and the accompanying administration costs of propertisation will follow. We will begin to see in this chapter that although there are several options available when seeking to overcome market failure (e.g. state- or social-based production), propertisation has come to dominate. This domination is a corollary of ignoring, concealing or understating the costs of property. By revealing certain categories of costs associated with property, this chapter prepares the way for the post-Part I exploration of alternate information environmental governance options.

2.2 PROPERTY AND MARKETS: A WELFARE ECONOMICS PERSPECTIVE

Building upon Leopold's 'property trumps ethics' perspective discussed in the introduction, this chapter argues that the veil of property often serves to conceal the exclusivity costs associated with the propertisation of information. Property is central to economics. Economics, as Adam Smith underscored, is riddled with ethical quandaries.[3] The fundamental question of economics – 'who gets what?' – is ultimately an ethical question.[4] Although the focus of Part I relates to the unaccounted exclusivity costs that flow from the propertisation of information, we will see that economic costs and ethical considerations are, at times, intimately intertwined. For instance, with respect to the physical environment, there is an unspoken ethical component to the imposition of negative externalities upon third persons that are not a party to a contract. Thinking about the social effects that result from negative externalities such as carbon pollution is a case in point. Similarly, as we will see in Chapter 3, the distributional costs that flow from monopoly rights within the information environment also bring to the fore ethical questions.[5] This is particularly evident in relation to the distribution of pharmaceutical medicines. Just as Leopold argued that property trumps ethics, we will see over the next two chapters how the propertisation of information conceals the exclusivity costs associated with IPRs. And how this concealment, in turn, gives rise to ethical implications.

Reliance upon welfare economics is particularly useful when simultaneously fleshing out concealed costs and ethical considerations inherent within the information environment. This is because welfare economics concerns, among other things, weighing up the costs and benefits inherent within the economic system. In doing so, it unsurprisingly concerns itself with welfare – both private welfare and social welfare.[6] The work of Pigou is often cited as the formal beginning of welfare economic discourse. However, there were many earlier writers who covered issues that today would be considered to fall under the welfare economics banner. The writings of Adam Smith, J.S. Mill, Karl Marx, David Ricardo and Alfred Marshall provide but a few examples.[7]

The welfare economic perspective of Adam Smith stresses that he was actually a moral philosopher not a political economist.[8] In this regard, Smith's 'invisible hand' passage was primarily deployed to illustrate that self-interest often trumps good intentions when it comes to promoting the interests of society as a whole.[9] But strictly speaking, Adam Smith was not discussing allocative efficiency, as the oft-quoted invisible hand passage has come to be interpreted by neoclassical economists.[10] Rather, the point that Smith was making is that in discrete circumstances the market can facilitate an alignment of private welfare and the welfare of society.[11] This is a different proposition than stating that private interests will always align with public interests. In fact, one of the central aspects of externalities (as discussed in Chapter 3) is the precise scenario where reliance upon the market leads to a misalignment of private and public interests.

In building an information environmental governance framework, the primary rationale of applying welfare economics to IPRs is to reveal certain categories of costs. Contemporaneously the environmental movement has done a relatively good job of revealing and popularising hidden environmental costs (e.g. carbon pollution). A parallel project is required with respect to the information environment. A central reason as to why exclusivity costs are obscured within the IPR system is that the property characteristics of IPRs are often accentuated at the expense of the monopolistic characteristics.[12] This tension between property and monopoly partly maps to the IPR maximalist/IPR minimalist dichotomy discussed in the introductory chapter. In essence, it is the IPR maximalists that tend to emphasise the property characteristics of IPRs, whereas the IPR minimalists tend to highlight the monopoly characteristics of IPRs. This tension between property and monopoly also loosely relates to the distinction between allocative efficiency and dynamic efficiency.

In general terms, allocative efficiency tends to be associated with 'the market' (and therefore property), whereas dynamic efficiency is usually connected with monopoly. More specifically, allocative efficiency is concerned with making the best use of society's scarce resources in order to produce the greatest-value combination of goods and services.[13] This type of efficiency is realised when resources allocated to produce a combination of goods and services maximise the value of society's output. In contrast, dynamic efficiency refers to the situation where an economy finds an appropriate balance between short-run considerations and long-run considerations.[14] For instance, investment in education, research and innovation may lead to short-run losses, but over time such investment should theoretically lead to an increase in overall economic efficiency.

While it is generally understood that IPRs foster dynamic efficiency at the expense of allocative efficiency, this understanding depends partly on how IPRs are perceived.[15] For example, when IPRs are thought of through the property lens, then it is possible to argue that IPRs facilitate informational markets just as real property rights facilitate real estate markets. According to this perspective, IPRs may have a positive allocative efficiency effect, at least to the extent that they foster markets in information. However, when IPRs are perceived through a monopoly lens, the popular argument is that IPRs produce long-term creativity and innovation benefits at the expense of short-term costs (such as monopoly pricing, or intense price discrimination activities that capture consumer surplus). As we will see below, the inherent tension between allocative efficiency and dynamic efficiency manifests within the information paradox. Clearly, as IPRs exhibit property *and* monopoly characteristics, the inherent allocative/dynamic efficiency tensions are ongoing.

Just like exclusivity costs, the nuances between allocative efficiency and dynamic efficiency are generally obscured behind the veil of property. When IPR maximalists focus on the property characteristics of IPRs (as they often do), there is an implicit reliance upon real property Coasian/Demsetzian arguments related to incentivisation and the allocative efficiency of the market.[16] In other words, by emphasising the property characteristics of IPRs, the IPR maximalists tend to implicate the benefits of the market. As the theory goes, the market is an economic instrument that relies upon the price mechanism to 'efficiently coordinate productive activities and allocate resources to their most productive use'.[17] In short, the market is generally said to be allocatively efficient. As property rights facilitate corresponding markets, and as markets generally foster allocative efficiency, the chain of reasoning leads to a simple conclusion: property rights must be efficient.[18] But the difficulty with this reasoning – at least from an efficiency point of view – is that a dominant characteristic of IPRs is monopoly.

It is true that for many products, and in many areas of the economy, the market does deliver incentivisation and allocative efficiency – and this is a fact that should not be forgotten. However, the market is not perfect and in some areas, and in some circumstances, the market simply fails. Even pure neoclassical economists, including the late Milton Friedman, would admit the same.[19] It is here that the nexus between property and markets is most noteworthy. Where there is a market failure, it may also be the case that there is a 'property failure'. This is to say that neither the market nor property will be effective in resolving the problem at hand. The dominant market failure in relation to the physical environment is that of negative externalities. When applying the market failure analysis of welfare economics to the information environment, a broader range of market failures can be considered. Doing so is useful because it underscores the costs associated with relying on property.

This book focuses on four relevant market failures within the information environment: (i) lack or asymmetry of information (and the related information paradox), (ii) public goods, (iii) monopolies, and

(iv) externalities.[20] The present chapter will focus on the two former market failures, whereas the next chapter will concern itself with the latter two market failures.

2.3 INFORMATION PARADOX

The information paradox is important for two reasons. Firstly, it emphasises that each property right granted to ensure production of information – as per the incentivisation arguments inherent within IPR maximalism – becomes an efficiency cost within the economic system.[21] Secondly, the information paradox is useful in fleshing out inherent tensions between the IPR maximalists and the IPR minimalists. The initial task in advancing these claims is to clarify the nature of the information paradox. This will be done with reference to efficiency costs.

2.3.1 Efficiency Costs

One of the many assumptions made within neoclassical economic discourse is that economic agents (e.g. human beings or firms) have perfect or near-perfect access to information in the marketplace. This assumption relates to perfect competition. Whether or not an economic agent has perfect information in any given circumstance is an empirical matter that lies beyond the scope of this book. However, even in the absence of empirical knowledge, the information paradox underscores the difficulties of the perfect information assumption.[22] The nature of the paradox is that while economists assume that the free flow of information is a prerequisite for economic activity within the economic system, economists equally assume that information is a commodity to be treated as private property within that same economic system.[23] With respect to the latter assumption, it is generally IPRs that operationalise the propertisation of information.

Hence, the economic analysis of information is riddled with an internal paradox. Information is a freely available component of the perfect market and a good that must be produced within that market.[24] As a consequence of this paradox, each property right granted to ensure production of information ultimately becomes an efficiency cost within the economic system. This is especially the case as a result of transaction costs and other related costs that transpire as a corollary of propertisation.[25] As a consequence there is an inherent conflict between the efficiency with which markets spread information and incentives to produce that information.[26]

The information paradox underscores inherent tensions between IPR maximalists and IPR minimalists because the paradox can be relied upon in various ways to support differing arguments. This is a point well made by Boyle, who has argued that the 'commodification of information can always be portrayed either as a time-consuming and unjust impediment to, or a necessary prerequisite for, the free flow of information'. Boyle further explains:

> The analytical structure of microeconomics includes 'perfect information' – meaning free, complete, instantaneous, and universally available – as one of the defining features of the perfect market. At the same time, both the perfect and the actual market structure of contemporary society depend on information being a commodity – that is to say being costly, partial, and deliberately restricted in its availability. Our concern with market efficiency pushes us toward information flows that are costless, general, and fast. Our concern with incentives for the producers of information pushes in exactly the opposite direction – toward temporary monopolies that delay the release of information, limit its availability, and raise its price.[27]

Grossman and Stiglitz implicitly referred to this problem in their seminal article *On the Impossibility of Informationally Efficient Markets*. In that article the authors emphasise that an efficient market assumes information is distributed at zero cost, yet at this cost information producers will have no incentive to produce.[28] In contrast, if information producers charge for their information production then information is no longer costless. Therefore decisions made within the market context that rely upon that information could not be perfectly efficient.

Grossman and Stiglitz are often credited for bringing the information paradox to the fore. However, it was actually Kenneth Arrow who initially brought this issue to the attention of economists.[29] At the heart of the information paradox is a core question: What is the best method of encouraging information production? On the one hand, Arrow believed without IPRs not enough information would be produced since information producers would not be able to capture its true value.[30] This perspective is ultimately built upon a combination of incentivisation and dynamic efficiency considerations. In this regard, Arrow stated: 'in a free enterprise economy the profitability of invention requires a suboptimal allocation of resources'.[31] On the other hand, scholars such as Hirshleifer espouse a more ambivalent position by questioning, in relation to patent law for instance, whether IPRs are an 'unnecessary legal monopoly in information that overcompensates an inventor who has already had the opportunity to trade on the information implied by his or her discovery'.[32] This latter position implies that the first-mover advantage is real, the incentivisation effects of property are overstated, and the costs of monopolisation are understated.[33] According to this view it may be better in some instances to reduce obstacles to information flow. This perspective is reflected in principle 3 of Table 1.1.

The information paradox is especially significant within the IPR domain, not just because IPRs concern information, but also because information is a major input of creative and inventive activity (aside from the talent of the creator/inventor).[34] Building upon the work of Kenneth Arrow, Robert Merges discusses the connection between the information paradox and IPRs by relaying the bind of an intellectual property licensor: 'if in trying to strike a deal she discloses her idea (e.g., the technology she invented), she has nothing left to sell, but if she does not disclose anything the buyer has no idea what is for sale'.[35] Patents (and to a lesser extent trade secrets) protect the licensor's property so she can confidently negotiate the sale of the property by attempting to strike a 'Coasian bargain'.[36] It is in this connection that the focus within IPR scholarship tends to subtly move away from the monopoly characteristics of IPRs and towards the property characteristics of IPRs. That is, by facilitating a 'Coasian bargain', IPRs allow inventors to rely upon property and by implication the market.[37]

In light of this discussion, we can see the information paradox spawns interesting political economic tensions. How should an economic libertarian perceive IPRs? For example, do IPRs represent a state interventionist approach to the regulation of information, or is the creation of IPRs by the state an essential element of the free market?[38] Political economics is not the only discipline which has a stake in resolving, or at least reconciling, the information paradox. Information is also an important aspect of deliberative democracy. If a nation has narrowly controlled information it usually follows it will also have narrowly controlled politics.[39] This issue will be further developed in Part IV of the book with reference to public choice theory. For now, further elaboration on the tension between IPR maximalism and IPR minimalism is warranted.

2.3.2 IPR Maximalism vs. IPR Minimalism

Although the information paradox cannot be resolved (as by definition a paradox is irresolvable), it does provide a conceptual framework upon which to understand the different arguments on either side of the 'propertisation of information' ledger. When IPR maximalists argue that information must be propertised so that a person can disclose their idea in order to strike a (Coasian/Demsetzian) deal in relation to that idea, we can observe the argument stems from the fact that the propertisation of information is a necessary prerequisite for the production and free flow of information.[40] Divergently, when IPR minimalists argue that creative and innovative activity is likely to occur regardless of the IPR system, then we can note such arguments are built on the premise that the propertisation of information is a time-consuming and unjust impediment to the free flow of information. Thus, the information paradox highlights crucial tensions within IPR discourse between the incentivisation of information production (i.e. information producer rights) and access to information which is produced (i.e. information user rights).

The tension between producer rights and user rights is encapsulated within the IPR maximalist/IPR minimalist dichotomy. In short, the IPR maximalists highlight that property rights can overcome the public goods provisioning problem through the internalisation of positive externalities (discussed below). In contrast, the IPR minimalists place emphasis on the benefits that stem from access to, and the sharing of, information. The minimalists also underscore the costs associated with monopolistic characteristics of IPRs. As each camp is situated to overcome one dilemma or another, and because the dilemmas stem from the information paradox in the first instance, the chasm between the two camps remains mostly intractable. For this reason, the aim of this book is not to resolve the paradox as such, but rather to think about methods of reconciling the private and public aspects of information production and consumption which the paradox gives rise to. Semicommons theory, discussed at length in Chapter 5, is one useful approach in this regard.[41]

As might be expected, IPR maximalists and IPR minimalists adopt different positions in relation to market failures inherent within the information environment. The information paradox is beneficial here as it exposes inherent tensions associated with propertising information. However, these tensions are not confined to the information paradox. The discussions below in relation to public goods, externalities and monopolies will further demonstrate that the information environment is in fact peppered with internal dilemmas and paradoxes. At each turn there are different methods of perceiving and interacting with these challenges. For instance, in the following section of this chapter we will see public goods (such as information) can be perceived through the lens of either the public goods provisioning problem, or as a positive externality which should be allowed to flow freely for the benefit of the public at large.[42] Within this context the public goods market failure will now be explored.

2.4 PUBLIC GOODS

The public goods problem inherent within information production is well-trodden ground within IPR discourse.[43] The problem provides powerful arguments in favour of IPRs generally. The cost of creating information goods is high, the cost of reproducing them is low, and once created, the works may be reproduced at large without depleting the original.[44] Seemingly, it is the power of this public goods reasoning, accompanied with inventive (authorial) romance, which has led to the constant expansion of IPRs over the last few centuries. By way of example, the initial Copyright Act of 1790 in the US was restricted to protection of books, maps and charts, but subsequent legislation has continued to protect new creative works: ‘prints in 1802, music in 1831, photographs in 1865, dramatic works in 1870, paintings, drawings and sculpture in 1870, movies in 1912, sound recordings in 1971, dance in 1976, computer programs in 1980, architectural works in 1990, and boat hull designs in 1998’.[45] At the same time, the US has expanded copyright by extending the term of copyrights in 1831, 1909, 1976 and 1998.[46] Along with copyright, the scope of patentable material has also been subject to similar IPR maximalist tendencies.[47] In the last several decades, patent protection has extended to plant varieties, organisms, software, genes and surgical procedures. Yoga stances and athletic manoeuvres are perhaps next in line.[48] The accompanying anticommons- or patent-thicket-effect of IPR maximalism (further discussed in Part II of the book) is well documented within IPR scholarship.[49]

Similar to the information paradox, the public goods market failure is significant for two reasons. First, it highlights the fact that propertisation involves a host of administration costs: the most obvious being that of registration and enforcement costs. Such costs are often left out of the social net product analysis of the IPR system.[50] Second, in parallel to the information paradox, the public goods market failure provides yet another framework upon which to appreciate the tension between IPR maximalists and IPR minimalists. Understanding this tension will allow us (later within the book) to move beyond the dichotomous thinking that pervades IPR scholarship, towards a more synthesis-oriented approach.

2.4.1 Non-rivalry/non-excludability and the Provisioning Problem

The public goods provisioning problem is an important aspect of information environment public goods. The problem is a core constituent in ongoing IPR discourse because, at least in the absence of IPRs, information is a *pure public good* in that it is both non-rival and non-exclusive.[51] Non-rivalry essentially means that two or more persons can use a good simultaneously without depleting the good.[52] The non-exclusive characteristic means that it is either difficult or impossible to prevent persons from using a good even when they do not pay for it.[53] The following table exemplifies, in simplified form, various classifications of resources based on rivalry and exclusion.

Table 2.1 Goods classification based on rivalry and exclusion

		EXCLUDABILITY		
		Non-exclusive	Exclusive	Hyper-exclusive
RIVALROUS-NESS OF CONSUMPTION	Non-rival	Pure Public Good (e.g. idea, fact, language, lighthouse)	Roll or Club Good (e.g. country club)	Public Good (e.g. snow ski field)
	Congestible	Non-pure Public Good (e.g. road, beach, lakes, rivers, ocean, air, national park)	Roll or Club Good (e.g. golf club or day care centre)	Non-pure Public Good (e.g. Rottnest Island)
	Rival	Limited Commons Property Regimes (e.g. irrigation systems, libraries, grazing areas)	Pure Private Good (e.g. apple, computer)	Pure Private Good (e.g. Rolls Royce)

Sources: Derived partly from Frischmann B., *An Economic Theory of Infrastructure and Commons Management*, American Law & Economics Association Annual Meetings, 2006, paper 18 at 942; and Hess and Ostrom (2003), *Ideas, Artifacts and Facilities: Information as a Common Pool Resource*, 66 Law and Contemporary Problems 111, at 120 [hereafter *Ideas, Artifacts and Facilities*].

A public goods analysis highlights that if a resource is non-rivalrous and non-exclusive then the challenge relates to provisioning rather than depletion/congestion. This is because the key task with public goods lies in providing enough incentive to produce the good (i.e. provisioning problem) rather than ensuring that the good is not overburdened by demand (i.e. depletion/congestion problem).[54] With reference to Table

2.1, the provisioning problem is most relevant to pure public goods (e.g. idea, fact, language, lighthouse), and the depletion/congestion problem is most relevant to non-pure public goods (e.g. road, beach, ocean, air, national park). A rivalrous/congestible non-pure public good such as a road is potentially simultaneously subject to both the provisioning problem and the depletion/congestion problem.[55] In relation to private goods, generally speaking, property rights accompanied by the market forces of supply and demand tend to militate against the applicability of both the provisioning problem and the depletion/congestion problem.[56]

The axes of rivalry and excludability (and related notions such as non-pure public goods and the commons) are best thought of in spectrum terms rather than as absolutes.[57] For instance, even within the non-pure public good sphere there is a large spectrum of 'congest-ability'. Obviously a beach in the inner city of Sydney during summer is more liable to congest-ability than the ocean at large. But even here, overfishing underscores the fact that a very expansive 'environmental good' such as the ocean is still subject to the depletion/congestion problem. This point is well made by the environmental movement, and the contemporary issue of climate change highlights the point in relation to air, which is of course yet another example of a non-pure public good (as per Table 2.1).[58]

Correspondingly, even within what might be loosely referred to as 'the commons', the parameter of exclusion differs intensely.[59] The 'open commons', for instance, can be distinguished from 'limited-access commons'. Examples of open commons include the oceans, the air and highway systems. In contrast, irrigation regions in Spain or Swiss villages, where access is limited only to members of the village or association that collectively 'owns' some defined irrigation system or pastureland, exemplify limited-access commons.[60] As Carol Rose notes, these later examples are better labelled as limited common property regimes, rather than commons.[61] This is because they behave as property vis-à-vis the entire world except members of the group who together hold them in common (i.e. exclusive community). Reflecting upon the commons in this way stresses that goods that lie within an open commons will generally be categorised as public goods, whereas goods which lie within limited common property regimes have a fuzzier relationship with the public goods classification.

2.4.2 Public Goods Dilemma and Sidgwick's Lighthouse

Contemplating the field of all possible ideas prior to the formation of IPRs, it can be reasoned such a field is closer to 'Locke's commons' than an unclaimed wilderness.[62] A prerequisite for Locke's commons was practical inexhaustibility. One person's extraction from the commons should not prevent the next person from extracting something of the same quality and quantity.[63] This type of extraction is often referred to as the 'spoilage principle'. Locke articulated this principle eloquently:

> A Man can take as much as they can make of to any advantage of life before it spoils; so much he may be his labour fix a Property in. Whatever is beyond this, is more than his share, and belongs to others. Nothing was made by God for Man to spoil or destroy.[64]

Logistically Locke's inexhaustibility prerequisite requires a large supply, at least within the context of the physical environment. However, in the information environment the inexhaustibility principle becomes easier to satisfy.[65] This is because each idea can be used by an unlimited number of individuals. Formally speaking, the inexhaustibility principle reflects non-rival and non-exclusive characteristics of information just described.[66] Grotius was keenly aware, at least implicitly, of non-exclusive and non-rival characteristics when he pronounced in the early 1600s that:

> If any person should prevent any other person from taking fire from his fire or a light from his torch, I should accuse him of violating the law of human society, because that is the essence of its very nature, as Ennius has said: 'No less shines his, when he his friend's hath lit.' Why then, when it can be done without any prejudice to his own interests, will not one person share with another things which are useful to the recipient, and no loss to the giver? These are services which the ancient philosophers thought ought to be rendered not only to foreigners but even rendered for nothing. But the same act which when private possessions are in question is jealously can be nothing but cruelty when a common possession is in question. For it is most outrageous for you to appropriate a thing, which both by ordinance of nature and by common consent is as much mine as yours, so exclusively that you will not grant me a right of use in it which leaves it not less yours than it was before.[67]

If this natural law proposition of Grotius is accepted – that it violates the law of human society to refuse to share a non-rival, non-exclusive good when such sharing would not prejudice the use of that good by the person who is in possession of it – then it must also be accepted that those non-rival, non-exclusive goods which can be shared without loss, should be shared.[68] In the IPR context, the key contention here relates to the notion of 'without loss'. This contention, in turn, concerns the public goods provisioning problem, along with the inherent tensions between allocative efficiency and dynamic efficiency.

With implicit reference to the public goods provisioning problem, Sidgwick once noted: '[I]t may easily happen that the benefits of a well-placed light-house must be largely enjoyed by ships on which no toll could be conveniently levied'.[69] Of course, the principal concern of this book is the information environment. But it is useful at this stage to briefly think about the role of property rights and technology in securing exclusivity in relation to public goods within the physical environment. Sidgwick's lighthouse provides one example.[70] This reflection is valuable because the same principles generally apply in both the physical environment and the information environment, at least as far as exclusivity is concerned.[71] Also, in abstract terms, Sidgwick's lighthouse can be partly thought of as an early example of an information good.[72] This is because the light projected by a lighthouse essentially provides information to seafarers.

When contemplating Sidgwick's lighthouse from a welfare economic perspective, a key question is: should the lighthouse be perceived as a public goods provisioning problem (with the accompanying challenges related to incentives and free-riders), or should the lighthouse be perceived as facilitating positive externalities for the benefit of the world at large (with related benefits such as network effects)?[73] For ease of reference, the tension inherent within this question will be referred to as the 'public goods dilemma'. Simply put, the dilemma can be thought of as a situation whereby property rights (along with technology) can theoretically incentivise production of a public good; yet public goods should generally be readily accessible because such goods facilitate the operation of the economic system and by extension the market. Put in this way, the public goods dilemma partly corresponds to the information paradox. And like the information paradox, the public goods dilemma is another pivotal issue that polarises IPR maximalists and IPR minimalists.

The public goods dilemma focuses attention on whether information should be subject to exclusivity (e.g. IPRs), and if so, to what extent? An important aspect of exclusivity as it relates to public goods is the internalisation of positive externalities.[74] Externalities will be discussed at length in the next chapter, but for now we can caricature IPR maximalists and IPR minimalists. To this end, IPR maximalists tend to underscore the public goods provisioning problem associated with the lighthouse. As a consequence they argue, based on Coasian/Demsetzian principles, that it is necessary to establish exclusivity through propertisation (or technology, or a combination of both).[75] This exclusivity is said to incentivise production of the public good by facilitating the internalisation of positive externalities.[76] In other words, stylistically speaking, IPR maximalists seek to partly rely upon the market to overcome the public goods provisioning problem by establishing property rights in information (i.e. light) that the lighthouse provides. In contrast, IPR minimalists would perceive the lighthouse as a positive externality (i.e. spillover) which should generally flow uninhibited to seafarers and society at large. In direct response to IPR maximalists, IPR minimalists would argue that the incentivisation benefits of internalising positive externalities via IPRs are overstated.[77] Minimalists might also argue that there are various ways to provision public goods other than property (e.g. state- or social-based production) and allocating monopoly rights to the lighthouse owner leads to exclusivity costs.

To be sure, the above depiction of the polarisation between IPR maximalists and IPR minimalists is heavily stylised. However, the depiction does draw attention to the key point: the perspectives of IPR maximalists and IPR minimalists respectively contain their own internal challenges.

2.4.3 Propertising Sidgwick's Lighthouse: Administration Costs

When Sidgwick's lighthouse is perceived as a public goods provisioning problem, the Coasian/Demsetzian solution of propertisation (and related market activity) gives rise to a series of administration costs. These costs relate to the creation and maintenance of propertisation.[78] The most obvious type of cost is enforcement costs. If the lighthouse is propertised (or more specifically if the light that the lighthouse projects is propertised) it will be necessary to collect a toll from those seafarers that make use of the lighthouse. As technology evolves more options become available in this respect.[79] Therefore, propertisation becomes increasingly seductive. However, technology is not necessarily a cheap fix. Whichever toll collection option is adopted there will be administration costs that must be taken into account when determining the overall social net product of propertisation.[80] In this respect the costs of enforcement technology can be thought of as an important subset of the overall administration costs.

As implied, given the state of contemporary technological advancement, it may be theoretically possible for lighthouses to apply a toll. Yet there are many examples scattered throughout society where the expense associated with overcoming non-excludability is simply not worth the cost. The facts in the case of *Victoria Park Racing and Recreation Grounds Co Ltd v Taylor*[81] provide a tangible example. Here, the plaintiff company facilitated horse racing and the defendant owned a property nearby to the racecourse. On the nearby property, the defendant constructed a raised platform so he could view the horse racing in order to publicly broadcast the races.[82] The happenings of the horse racing were a non-excludable resource. This is because the costs of enclosing the racecourse or alternatively erecting a high fence were prohibitive. In other words, the administration costs associated with propertising the viewing dimension of the racecourse were greater than the benefits that would ensue from this propertisation.[83]

Aside from highlighting the administration costs associated with propertisation, the significance of the lighthouse example is to underscore the theoretical and practical tensions that result from using property (with monopolisitic characteristics) to overcome the public goods provisioning problem. On the theoretical front, there is the question of whether property operates as a pure incentivisation mechanism. In this regard, IPR minimalists suggest the incentivisation function of property (and related market activity) to overcome the public goods provisioning problem is generally overstated. This is because throughout history, in both the physical environment and the information environment, an abundance of developments have occurred in the public goods space without reliance upon strong property rights.[84] The development of law, music, science and language are examples. The provisioning of blood through donors is yet another case in point.[85] As we will see in Part IV, similar claims can also be made in relation to social production initiatives within the information environment such as FLOSS and Wikipedia.

On the practical front, even if a public good is subject to property rights the administration costs associated with enforcing those rights can outweigh the benefits which ensue from propertisation. The role of technology is critical in this context since propertising public goods will almost always rely upon a technological fix of some description. For example, with the racecourse it was the technology of fencing that would provision exclusivity. The 'tolling technology' which propertises the light of the lighthouse would be more advanced than the technology of a fence, but the principle remains the same. The crux being property rights alone are usually not enough to secure exclusivity, especially with respect to public goods. Such rights will usually need to be supplemented with technology and this in turn spawns a range of administration costs.[86]

Of course, in a similar vein to the lighthouse and the racecourse, an information good such as a book, movie, song or computer software program has non-exclusive characteristics.[87] The cost of reproducing the work in practical terms is usually very low. Moreover, with the advent of the digital age and new media such as the Internet, information becomes closer and closer to a pure public good as a consequence of the virtually costless nature of information reproduction.[88] To this extent, the theoretical and practical challenges associated with the propertisation of the light projected by the lighthouse are also reflected within the information environment. The contemporary IPR accompaniment of Digital Rights Management (DRM) and Technological Protection Measures (TPMs) cements this claim. Lawrence Lessig has made this point neatly in *Code 2.0*.[89]

2.4.4 Private Property vs. The Commons

Over the last several decades there has been a strong tendency to rely upon propertisation as a governance tool when seeking to incentivise the production of public goods. This is despite the fact that propertisation is just one of many governance options. As we will see in Part IV, state- or social-based production also proffer legitimate methods of provisioning public goods. As Carol Rose has aptly pointed out the private propertisation propensity has come to dominate, even though 'our legal doctrine has strongly suggested that some kinds of property should not be held exclusively in private hands, but should be open to the public'.[90] Rose has pointed to this tension by implying that the traditional rules concerning public acquisition of streets and roads do not sit comfortably with private property assumptions of classical economic theory:

> Indeed, public acquisition of roadways by long usage seems a particularly striking illustration of the imperviousness of practice to theory: the doctrines by which the public acquired roads over private property, without purchase even through eminent domain, flourished side by side with the popularization of classical economics and burgeoning of privately owned commerce and industry.[91]

The 'propertisation propensity' can be prefaced by the ongoing tussle between private property rights and the commons. In this way, the information commons becomes a 'site of struggle'.[92] The propertisation propensity, as it concerns the information environment, is built upon a series of thematic arguments that relate to authorial (inventive) romance, incentivisation and the internalisation of positive externalities. All of these elements serve to implicitly conceal the inherent exclusivity costs inherent within the monopolistic characteristics of IPRs. A critical task of the next chapter is to further expose the veil of property as it relates to the information environment by underscoring the externality costs and distributional costs that flow from IPRs.

2.5 CONCLUSION

The power of welfare economics as it concerns the information environment stems from its ability to reveal concealed or understated costs. This is significant because much IPR maximalist discourse has a tendency to understate the costs associated with market failures, property and monopoly. Building upon the perspectives of Aldo Leopold, the chapter argued that many economic costs associated with propertisation are concealed behind the veil of property. The stated benefits of propertising information generally stem from incentivisation along with the purported benefits that flow from the internalisation of positive externalities. These benefits are well documented within IPR (maximalist) discourse. Nevertheless, Pigou's social net product analysis reminds that when property is relied upon to overcome market failures there are both costs and benefits. The market failure of lack or asymmetry of information and the related information paradox (which speaks to efficiency costs) and the market failure of public goods (which speaks to administration costs) provide cogent examples. As we saw throughout the chapter, the costs and benefits of propertising information largely underscore the tension between IPR maximalists and IPR minimalists. Exploring the information paradox and the public goods provisioning problem, and related costs and benefits which stem from reliance on propertisation to overcome these market failures, brings the tension between IPR maximalists and IPR minimalists to the fore. Rather than seeking to resolve this tension the chapter has argued for the need to take into account private and public costs and benefits of IPRs when evaluating the effectiveness of propertisation of information. This advocacy, which is also reflected in principle 1 of Table 1.1, will be further advanced in the following chapter.

3. Externalities and monopolies

Every solution to a problem creates new unsolved problems.

Karl Popper

3.1 INTRODUCTION

Consciously or unconsciously the environmental movement has relied upon welfare economics as a theoretical foundation for the following key claim: the economic system largely ignores environmental costs.[1] Within economic theory environmental costs are usually referred to as 'negative externalities'. Pollution is a prime example. Building upon the work of Adam Smith, the welfare economist A.C. Pigou clearly articulated the concept of externalities in his classic *The Economics of Welfare*.[2] This chapter begins by discussing externalities as a source of market failure. Just as there is an intimate relationship between property rights and markets, so too there is an intimate relationship between property rights and externalities. In the physical environment context Coasian/Demsetzian reasoning is often used to argue that the internalisation of externalities through property rights (and corresponding markets) can overcome the externalities of market failure. Yet property rights entail costs, both private and public. Transactions costs are a private cost example and externality costs are an example of public costs. The latter arise from what will be termed the 'externalities paradox'. After engaging with externalities the chapter will then turn to a discussion of monopolies with the view of revealing another type of public cost – distributional costs associated with the monopolistic characteristics of IPRs. This discussion will invoke price discrimination activities, which are often deployed by IPR holders. Finally, the inherent tension between efficiency and distribution in the IPR context will be covered through the frame of the 'monopoly dilemma'. The concluding inference of Part I is that when the full costs of IPRs are taken into account, propertisation becomes less attractive than it might otherwise be. This inference, in turn, fosters the exploration of alternate governance options, which is a core task of the book post-Part I.

3.2 EXTERNALITIES

Continuing the reliance upon welfare economics, this chapter reinforces the theme of the last: many benefits associated with the IPR system are overstated and many of the exclusivity costs associated with the IPR system are understated.[3] A corollary of the overstatement of benefits and understatement of costs is that profits related to IPRs tend to be privatised and costs socialised.[4] That is, just as the public bears the cost of environmental degradation (as related profits flow privately), so too many of the benefits within the information environment are privatised through monopoly rights (with the costs associated with IPRs being socialised).[5] Initially, the 'privatization of profits and socialization of costs' perspective might appear to overreach, particularly as the public benefits in a whole host of ways from the IPR system.[6] Furthermore, the Internet has arguably made more information available to more people than at any time throughout the course of human history. Further still, significant dynamic efficiencies have resulted from IPRs (at least within some industries). Despite these advances many of the costs associated with the benefits of the IPR system remain ignored, understated or concealed. Accordingly IPR costs are often borne by the public at large. The preceding chapter advanced this perspective with respect to efficiency costs and administration costs, and it will be further advanced in this chapter with respect to externality costs and distributional costs. When the exclusivity costs implicit within the IPR system are highlighted, as Part I of this book seeks to do, the argument that many IPR benefits are privatised while the costs are socialised begins to strengthen.

3.2.1 Demsetzian Property Rights and Internalising Externalities

There is naturally some truth to the incentivising effect of propertisation. However, incentivisation benefits tend to be overstated within IPR maximalist discourse. This overstatement is partly built upon the Coasian/Demsetzian 'internalization of externalities' function of property.[7] According to the Demsetzian perspective of property rights, one of the strengths of relying upon property is that it is a low-cost method of internalising externalities:

> [a]n increase in the number of owners is an increase in the communality of property and leads, generally, to an increase in the cost of internalizing … The reduction in negotiating cost that accompanies the private right to exclude others allows most externalities to be internalized at rather low cost.[8]

Henry Smith synthesises the Demsetz perspective by describing property as a 'shortcut over all the bilateral contracts (or regulations) that would have to be devised for every pair of members of society in all their various interactions'.[9] That is, A's right to grow corn on Blackacre as against B's trampling, same against C, etc; A's right to park a car on Blackacre as against B, C, etc.[10] This Demsetzian standpoint is underpinned by two precepts. First, property owners are required to take responsibility for the potential third-party costs. And second, property owners are entitled to capture third-party benefits.[11] Building upon these precepts, Demsetzian theory suggests property owners' interests will align with the interests of society, and in turn allocatively efficient social welfare-maximising decisions will be made.[12] In other words, according to Demsetzian theory, internalisation of externalities is the economic instrument that aligns private and social welfare based on allocative efficiency considerations.[13] This standpoint is purportedly built upon Adam Smith's 'invisible hand'.

The essence of the Coasian/Demsetzian perspective is that it is possible to solve many problems by internalising externalities through strong property rights.[14] In the physical environment, negative externalities such as pollution are of key consequence. In the information environment, it is the treatment of positive externalities which dominates. In distilling the notion of externalities in the 1930s, A.C. Pigou referred to both negative and positive externalities:[15]

> It might happen ... that costs are thrown upon people not directly concerned, through, say, uncompensated damage done to surrounding woods by sparks from railway engines. All such effects must be included – some of them will be positive, others negative elements – in reckoning up the social net product of the marginal increment of any volume of resources turned into any use or place.[16]

A negative/positive externality is a cost/benefit realised by one person as a result of another person's activity without compensation/payment.[17] In essence, negative externalities lead to a situation where resources are directed at the production of Product X even though citizens do not value the product as much as the cost of all the resources needed to produce the product.[18] With respect to positive externalities, resources are not devoted to producing Product Y even though citizens value its production more than any of its alternatives.[19] Consequently, too many/few resources might be allocated to those activities that cause negative/positive externalities.[20] This is because the resource allocation decision makers do not account for the full gamut of costs/benefits.

The market generally fails in relation to externalities to the extent that the existence of externalities within an economic system decreases allocative efficiency. Put another way, externalities are said to have distorting effects on market coordination and the general allocation of resources.[21] Interestingly, a common response in overcoming externalities is to establish new property rights and corresponding markets. For example, in relation to the negative externality of carbon pollution, a prevalent 'solution' is to establish property rights in carbon. A corresponding carbon market is a corollary of these property rights.[22] The reasoning underpinning this approach is that property rights 'capture' the relevant externality and in doing so improve allocative efficiency.[23] But as we will see below, it can be somewhat paradoxical to rely upon the market to overcome the market failure of externalities (i.e. externalities paradox).

The internalisation of externalities perspective is not only prevalent with respect to negative externalities within the physical environment. It is also common with respect to the information environment. The approach is not new. As early as 1901, Sidgwick implicitly drew attention to the internalising function of IPRs thus:

> External economies [i.e. externalities] are an important aspect of the production of knowledge. The greater the externality, the more inefficient is the final equilibrium. If inventions are completely inappropriable, no profit-maximizing competitor will produce an invention because increases in productivity would be instantaneously erased by a fall in price, and the firm would suffer losses to the extent of its research outlay.[24]

Many contemporary IPR scholars have continued Sidgwick's theme.[25] Wendy Gordon, for instance, exemplifies the internalisation perspective as it applies to the information environment when she surmises: 'most of IP law is concerned with internalizing positive externalities'.[26] Harrison also argues that the internalisation of positive externalities is a core function of IPRs. Relying upon US copyright law as an exemplar, he states:

> When it comes to copyright, the key concept is 'positive externality' – the benefits to others resulting from the activity of another. There are also good economic reasons to permit those who create positive externalities to be compensated by those who enjoy the benefits of those efforts. Thus, the composer of a song that is performed by others is permitted to recover. This, too, is internalization. In fact, *intellectual property law*, including its Constitutional authorization, *has internalization as its principal focus*.[27]

Clearly, the internalisation of positive externalities perspective is closely related to the incentivisation arguments inherent within much IPR scholarship (discussed in the introductory chapter). The reasoning flows that if an inventor is unable to capture the full social benefit of her innovation then she will not have enough incentive to produce information.[28] According to this outlook, IPRs vest with the information producer so as to enable that producer to internalise at least part of the positive externality that accrues from the information production.[29] Although not all of the social value of information production is captured, the granting of an exclusive property right allows the information producer to leverage much of its social value.[30] A corollary being in the absence of IPRs there is leakage in relation to investment guidance and management decisions.[31] This in turn is to the detriment of information production. In other words, if there is no exclusivity in relation to information then underproduction of information will ensue because the producer is not fully rewarded for productive effort.[32]

We saw in the last chapter that the incentivisation function of property is often promoted as a method of overcoming the public goods provisioning problem. In this context the public goods dilemma spoke of tensions between incentivising production of public goods via property rights (on the one hand) and allowing public goods to flow freely (on the other hand). Although there are alternate methods of overcoming the public goods provisioning problem (e.g. social production methods discussed in Part IV), propertisation via IPRs has become the dominant method advanced. This default reliance on IPRs tends to implicitly overstate the benefits of property and understate the costs of monopoly. Conducting a social net product analysis of property rights is one way of reconciling the benefits and costs of the IPR system.

3.2.2 The Social Net Product of Property Rights

Pigou referred to social net product as 'the total net product of physical things or objective services due to the marginal increment of resources in any given use or place, no matter to whom any part of this product may accrue'.[33] Casting aside the question of whether an informational good is a physical thing or objective service (or neither), Pigou's definition of social net product is inherently useful because it underscores not just private costs and benefits but also public costs and benefits.[34] In doing so Pigou implied that if the social costs of production are ignored then the true cost of providing a good or service is skewed. This is one of the key points that welfare economics generally, and the analysis of externalities more specifically, has proffered in relation to the physical environment.

The same message is also intensely applicable with respect to the information environment.[35]

When conducting a social net product analysis in relation to positive externalities, the first question is whether the positive externality exceeds the cost of ensuring those externalities are internalised by the information producer.[36] This query is based on Coase's argument that property rights will be created or altered depending on whether the social gains from internalising an externality exceed the costs of doing so.[37] As we have already begun to see, Demsetz further developed the Coasian perspective by espousing a theory of property rights evolution such that 'private property rights should emerge, evolve, and extend to enable internalization of externalities only when the benefits of doing so exceed the costs'.[38] Demsetz supports this claim by relying upon several examples of commons that were transformed into private property rights once the problem of overhunting prevailed.[39] When negative externalities related to hunting became sufficiently large, the transaction costs associated with internalising those externalities were justified so as to enable the establishment of a property rights regime.[40]

Demsetzian theory concerning the evolution of property rights is deployed in a (simple) normative sense and in a (complex) positivist sense.[41] The normative usage of Demsetzian property rights theory amounts to the proposition that: property rights should exist, full stop. The positivist perspective is more complex, suggesting: in a given range of circumstances property rights naturally evolve because it is less costly to create property rights than to not create them. Inherent within Demsetz's more complex positivist perspective of property rights evolution is Pigou's social net product analysis.[42] Relying upon this analysis underscores that within the IPR context the objective is not necessarily to maximise total gains resulting from creativity and innovation. Such maximisation relies upon protection, which in turn results in exclusivity costs.[43] Rather, the objective is to maximise the social net product. If it costs more to internalise benefits that accrue from a creative or innovative process than the worth of the benefits, then the costs should not be incurred and the creation or innovation should not be internalised.[44] In other words, if the social net product to propertise a given piece of information is negative, then the information simply should not be propertised. This is the essence of principle 2 in Table 1.1.

While it is difficult (or perhaps impossible) to place a numerical value on all of the costs associated with IPRs, there are two important costs typically left out of the equation. These costs are transaction costs and externality costs. The former costs are private and the latter costs are public. These costs will now be examined respectively.

3.2.2.1 Private transaction costs

As information is different to real property, Demsetzian reasoning cannot be easily transposed to the information environment. Far from increasing allocative efficiency, IPRs are in many ways allocatively inefficient. This being said, Demsetz is not entirely redundant when it comes to the information environment. For example, a Demsetzian analysis is useful in highlighting transaction costs (and other such costs) which are often ignored when evaluating IPRs. When espousing his propertisation theories, Demsetz relied upon zero transaction costs, stating when such conditions exist the establishment of a well-defined property right results in the internalisation of costs and benefits of the owner's activities.[45] This in turn facilitates the sale of that right to others who may place a greater value on the property. Demsetz did, however, at the same time, acknowledge that there are transaction costs related to the internalisation of externalities and therefore externalities will persist as long as the cost of a transaction outweighs the gains from internalisation.[46]

In the real world zero or even low transaction costs are difficult or indeed impossible to realise.[47] This is particularly the case where economic activity relates to property rights and even more so in relation to IPRs where high transaction costs are the norm.[48] In other words, to ignore transaction costs when determining the effectiveness of property rights in overcoming the public goods provisioning problem (for example) skews the equation in favour of propertisation.[49] This is especially true in the information environment where transaction costs are generally higher than they are in the physical world. Janet Hope has reinforced this perspective by arguing that high transaction costs related to multiple IPR holders is one of the primary reasons for oligopolistic industry structures within information-based industries.[50] Thus, far from being a marginal issue, transaction costs have a considerable influence over the efficacy of IPRs.

When determining the effect of transaction costs as they relate to the efficacy of IPRs the work of Calabresi and Melamed is critical.[51] Rather than ignoring transactions costs, Calabresi and Melamed construct a property/liability framework indicating that transaction costs can have a *determining influence* on whether a 'property rule' is more appropriate than a 'liability rule'. According to this framework, some resources such as real property are best regulated by the property rule whereby a party has an absolute property right that can be enforced *ex ante*.[52] In contrast, the liability rule may be more appropriate for resources such as *information* whereby courts set the price in a proceeding that takes place after the right has been infringed as it does with legally enforceable contracts.[53] Importantly, the decision as to which rule to apply depends largely on the nature and degree of the transaction costs,[54] with the liability rule being the entitlement of choice when transaction costs are high such as they are in the information environment.[55]

We will see in the next chapter the commons is generally regulated by a liability rule rather than a property rule. In this regard, the high transaction costs that flow from propertising information mean information is often best regulated through a commons framework rather than a property framework.[56] The other side of the coin is when transaction costs are taken into account, *there are strong economic reasons to be suspicious of the effectiveness of propertising information.* This is because high transaction costs undermine the efficiency of propertisation. Many of these ideas are embedded within principles 1, 2 and 3 of Table 1.1.

Although transaction costs are generally borne by private parties, the same cannot be said in relation to costs that stem from the externalities paradox. We will now explore this paradox along with the related (public) externality costs.

3.2.2.2 Public externality costs and the externalities paradox

Contemplating (public) costs as they relate to the physical environment highlights that costs can be immensely significant yet remain unaccounted for.[57] Consideration of the global costs of pollution is a case in point. Indeed, if the claims of ecological economists are to be taken seriously, negative externalities very much extend to the health and well-being of the planet at large.[58] This was an issue forcefully advanced by Rachel Carson in *Silent Spring* and further extended by Christopher Stone in his classic *Should Trees Have Standing?* As Stone states:

> Every well-working legal-economic system should be so structured as to confront each of us with the full costs that our activities are imposing on society. Ideally, a paper-mill, in deciding what to produce – and where, and by what methods – ought to be forced to take into account not only the lumber, acid and labor that its production 'takes' from other uses in the society, but also what costs alternative production plans will impose on society through pollution. The legal system, through the law of contracts and the criminal law, for example, makes the mill confront the costs of the first group of demands. When, for example, the company's purchasing agent orders 1000 drums of acid from the Z Company, the Z Company can bind the mill to pay for them, and thereby reimburse the society for what the mill is removing from alternative uses.[59]

The crux is there are both *private* and *public* costs associated with production. The legal framework (through the law of contract, criminal law, etc.) ensures that economic agents are held to account in relation to private costs. Yet accountability in relation to the social or public costs described become much fuzzier within the legal framework. This is principally because the market fails with respect to externalities. Where this is the case, and the state fails to intervene by way of regulation, social costs will often be borne by the public at large. In other words costs are unlikely to be fully taken into account.

Although propertisation is often used to internalise externalities it is not always the most effective means of overcoming externality problems. This is because internalisation of one brand of externalities through property may in fact lead to externalisation of (new) externalities. Where this is the case society will generally be lumbered with (new) externality costs. This point is perhaps best understood by considering the concrete example of an Emission Trading Scheme (ETS). As reported elsewhere an ETS creates property rights and corresponding markets in the 'right to emit carbon' so as to reduce carbon emissions over time.[60] While there are a variety of possible legal and economic ETS-related structures, an effective ETS system will discourage activities that are carbon emission intensive and encourage the opposite. This is a beneficial consequence which ultimately flows from the internalisation of externalities. But an ETS may also spawn a variety of environmental problems. For instance, it may encourage the planting of trees (for carbon sequestration) such that precious water resources are wasted and/or biodiversity is degraded. The question then arises as to whether more property rights need to be allocated to water and/or biodiversity so as to overcome related negative externalities. This questioning process can continue ad infinitum. Within this context Demsetz's observations concerning the evolution of markets in relation to externalities are noteworthy:

> [J]ust as the market dictates that there will be no good X if the cost of producing X exceeds what people are willing to pay for it, so the market dictates that there will be no market if the cost of producing the market exceeds what people are willing to pay for it.[61]

According to this view whether or not a market evolves in relation to a particular brand of externality is an issue to be determined by the market itself. This Demsetzian reasoning is somewhat paradoxical because in order to overcome the market failure of externalities, the market (and corresponding property rights) is given as the answer. This paradox is referred to henceforth as the 'externalities paradox'.[62] To elucidate the paradox, although it is possible the internalisation of externalities through property rights may overcome a given externality, it is equally possible that establishing property rights (and therefore creating a corresponding market) in order to internalise externalities establishes a new range of externalities. It is true that, from the outset, it may be difficult to define the new externalities in question. It may also be the case the new externalities are considered 'irrelevant'. After all, environmental pollution and degradation were considered 'irrelevant' for most of ancient and modern history combined. However, within the general economic frame there are no free lunches.[63] As a given externality intensifies (e.g. pollution) alongside the intensification of property and markets, the externality in question becomes less and less concealed and more and more relevant.[64]

Also, reliance upon propertisation to internalise externalities often amounts to privatisation of benefits and socialisation of costs. This is primarily because collective action problems dictate (public) costs that are spread over a large number of people (i.e. the public) will remain outside the social net product equation. Intriguingly, and perhaps slightly ironically from the Demsetzian tradition perspective, this is a point acknowledged by Demsetz himself:

> The reduction in negotiating cost that accompanies the private right to exclude others allows most externalities to be internalized at rather low cost. Those that are not are associated with activities that generate external effects impinging upon many people. The soot from smoke affects many homeowners, none of whom is willing to pay enough to the factory to get its owner to reduce smoke output. All homeowners together might be willing to pay enough, but the cost of their getting together may be enough to discourage effective market bargaining. The negotiating problem is compounded even more if the smoke comes not from a single smoke stack but from an industrial district. In such cases, it may be too costly to internalize effects through the market-place.[65]

Collective action problems are inherent within this Demsetz passage. These problems dictate that public costs, which are spread over a large number of people, will essentially remain unaccounted for. This is a theme further advanced in Part IV with reference to public choice theory. For now we can simply note the soot resulting from the factory or the industrial district is a negative externality imposed on the public (i.e. a public cost). The Coasian/Demsetzian response to this externality cost is most often to establish property rights in relation to that negative externality so the market can then mediate the cost. Yet as the Demsetz quote indicates above, even Demsetz himself implicitly questions the applicability of this process without qualification.

Although property owners may be able to negotiate with each other so as to secure the most efficient allocation of resources in accordance with Demsetzian theory, the definition of efficiency tends to exclude environmental and social costs. This means any leakage associated with the negotiation process (due to high transaction costs, for example) is usually soaked up by the environment and/or the public at large. In other words both the environment and the public become sinks that are filled with fragmented interests and unrepresented damage claims.[66] This is at least partly because the economic system does not account for the benefits provisioned by the environment and other public goods.[67] It is also because, as Drahos underscores, 'the efficiency of property presupposes uncoerced bargaining among equals, but the logic of collective action points to the possibility of dominant interest groups and unequal contests'.[68]

Of course in strict economic terms the inability to appropriately value the environment and the interests of the public at large is a key exemplar of market failure.[69] This is as true in relation to the information environment as it is with respect to the physical environment. While the internalisation of externalities through propertisation is the theoretically dominant method of incentivising production, there is a paradox inherent in overcoming the market failure of externalities through property and corresponding markets. This is because new property rights and corresponding markets are likely to establish a new externalities cost-set, which will in turn need to be overcome.

Obviously further empirical research in this domain is required so as to identify the specific externalities that are likely to result from relying on property to internalise externalities in a given circumstance. Such empirical research might focus on externalities apparent within a secondary market. For instance, in the information environment context, internalisation of positive externalities via IPRs leads to new externalities that flow from informational markets. The IPRs of Google and Facebook are a case in point. Negative externalities that flow from such IPRs include privacy violation. These violations spawn private costs for the individual and public costs for society at large. Yet these costs are rarely taken into account when the effectiveness of IPRs is being evaluated.

Hence reliance on property rights within the information environment and accompanying informational markets to overcome (positive) externalities gives rise to the externalities paradox. The essence of this paradox is that propertisation is more likely to shift or mutate externality costs rather than erase costs all together. For this very reason it may be better in some instances to allow information to reside in the information commons. Principle 3 in Table 1.1 flows from this perspective.

We have thus far seen that perceiving IPRs as an internalising instrument serves to understate private and public costs associated with IPRs. Another important public exclusivity cost is the 'distributional costs' that flow from the monopolistic characteristics of IPRs.

3.3 MONOPOLIES

In allocating property rights to information the IPR system seeks to overcome or at least diminish the market failure relating to the public good provisioning problem. Yet in doing so the IPR system falls into the trap of another market failure, being that of monopoly rights. For ease of reference henceforth this book will label this scenario as the 'monopoly dilemma'. This dilemma is often obscured within IPR scholarship. One reason is IPR maximalists tend to focus on property characteristics of IPRs rather than monopoly characteristics. IPR minimalists in contrast emphasise the monopolistic characteristics of IPRs.[70] By thinking about IPRs as both property and monopoly we can ensure costs of monopoly fall within the ambit of any social net product analysis of IPRs.

While IPRs such as copyrights and patents definitely grant a monopoly in information (albeit temporary and limited) the truth is that IPRs can be classified into a variety of different categories including monopoly rights, property rights, and/or some other alternate such as a state subsidy.[71] The classifications are not necessarily mutually exclusive to the extent that IPRs can be catalogued as a hybrid of two or more of these categories.[72] As all WTO members effectively refer to IPRs as property it is problematic to argue outright that IPRs are not property. However, while IPRs can be defined as property strictly speaking, this does not mean IPRs are the same in all respects as all other types of property. There are both similarities and differences between various forms of property, examples of which include securities, real property and IPRs (to name but a few).

We saw in Chapter 2 that one of the chief distinctions between real property and an information good is that the former is rivalrous whereas the latter is non-rivalrous. An important consequence which flows from this distinction is that in the case of real property it is the market which determines the price. In contrast, in the case of an information good an IPR owner is often able to escape pure market forces as they possess a monopoly right.[73] Monopolistic characteristics of IPRs are not pure in that informational goods are often substitutable. However, IPRs do possess monopolistic characteristics and it is these characteristics that foster distributional costs.

3.3.1 IPRs and Distributional Costs

Distributional costs encompass costs borne by certain entities or societal groups as a consequence of the imposition of a policy or regulation.[74] For example, within the context of the so-called US Great Recession of 2007–2009, particular groups of people (e.g. the less educated) were more greatly affected by the bursting of the US housing bubble than others. Thus various financial regulations relating to housing pre-2007 led to distributional costs.[75] These costs are not marginal but rather are fundamental to any economic system. Economics is, or at least should be, concerned with 'who gets what?'.[76] For this reason when conducting a social net product analysis of the IPR system distributional costs must be considered.[77] In the information environment context, distributional costs are not just limited to the division of surplus between information producers and information consumers.[78] There is also the question of distributional costs for users of information, who might be information producers or information consumers (or both).[79]

In Chapter 2 the issue of excludability was discussed within the context of the public goods provisioning problem. We saw, at least in the absence of IPRs, information is a pure public good due to its non-exclusive and non-rival characteristics. Yet in practice information is often exclusive. This is primarily because the IPR system makes it so (subject to various IPR exceptions and time limitations). Moreover, exclusivity stems not just from the law (e.g. IPRs) but also from technology (e.g. TPMs) and/or physicality (e.g. hidden information such as trade secrets).[80] Through IPRs, exclusivity in the information environment is most often delineated through the price mechanism. As price (along with income) makes informational resources exclusive to some, yet not to others, excludability via monopoly rights generates distributional costs.[81] This chapter fleshes out this claim by discussing price discrimination activities and income discrepancies respectively.

3.3.1.1 Price discrimination

While economists and IPR maximalists generally support property rights as these rights facilitate development of markets, in the information environment context property rights foster various cross currents.[82] On the one hand IPRs facilitate information markets through licensing mechanisms.[83] On the other hand IPRs undermine the functioning of markets due to the monopolistic characteristics of IPRs.[84] Price is a critical aspect of this equation because often the monopolistic characteristics of IPRs means the price mechanism is not mediated by supply and demand, but rather through price-discriminatory activities.[85] If IPRs just fostered monopolies without price discrimination, then IPRs would be necessary to establish informational markets in order to facilitate dynamic efficiency gains. But when IPRs are accompanied by price discrimination, as they usually are, then dynamic efficiency gains of IPRs are to be offset against distributional costs.[86] In discussing the relationship between price discrimination and IPRs, Wendy Gordon states:

> Patent law permits a potential inventor to distinguish between someone who wants to use her widget-making machine to make widgets, and someone who wants to use the machine as a prototype for manufacturing identical widget-making equipment. Similarly, copyright enables a potential novelist or song-writer to effectually distinguish between readers or listeners on the one hand, and publishers or record companies on the other. That is because any person who buys a copy of a book or song or machine has a legal duty to refrain from copying it without the creator's permission.[87]

While price discrimination is not inevitable with respect to IPRs there are a plethora of examples of price discrimination within the IPR domain.[88] Understanding the relationship between price discrimination and IPRs becomes particularly important within the digital environment where the ability to segment markets is amplified. DRMs and TPMs are an important part of this equation.[89]

In order to fully understand price discrimination (and related distributional costs), it is first necessary to be abundantly clear about the role of price in a functioning market. As already implied, from a practical perspective it is price (along with the coercive forces of the state and perhaps a dose of technology) that reinforces the exclusivity characteristics of property. In a regular market, economic theory informs that price is established and maintained through the market forces of supply and demand. However, if the producer is a monopolistic producer, then the supply and demand equation breaks down because, by definition, supply is limited to one firm. It is the monopoly firm that decides the question of supply rather than the market. Therefore, the market fails in the context of a monopoly since in the absence of competition the price mechanism is unable to efficiently allocate resources by mediating production and consumption. In other words, rather than the price mechanism of the market allocating resources, within the monopoly context it is monopolists that ultimately govern production. Moreover, the monopolist is likely to capitalise on their economic power through capturing the maximum amount of consumer surplus. This is made possible by relying upon various tactics of which price discrimination is an important example.[90] To be sure, distributional costs are generally lower when monopoly is coupled with price discrimination (as compared to a monopoly situation where there is no price discrimination).[91] But distributional costs are lower still where there is no monopoly of which to speak (i.e. where there is perfect competition).

Price discrimination occurs where a producer charges a different price to different groups of consumers for an identical good or service for reasons not related to the cost of production. According to the textbook example of price discrimination, a producer will maximise profits by determining the price in segmented markets based on local demand elasticity.[92] Generally, the greater the size of the market and the more inelastic demand, the higher the price. It follows that when the market is small and demand is elastic price is likely to be lower. Boyle describes price discrimination with reference to a 'Furbies' example.[93] According to this example, a monopoly exercising price discrimination will target various markets depending upon the willingness and ability of consumers within those markets to pay. A poor child might be able to pay $15 for a Furby, a middle class child could pay $25, and an upper class child could pay $85. Boyle explains in the absence of price discrimination the monopolist is likely to tend towards producing for rich children only. This in turn would lead to an allocatively inefficient social deadweight loss whereby poor and middle class children will remain Furby-less. However, if the monopolist can price discriminate then all children will obtain a Furby and the monopolist will make an extra profit over and beyond what they would make if they just sold Furbies to rich children.[94] By relying upon this reasoning a monopolist can effectively argue for the allocative efficiency benefits of price discrimination and accompanying market segmentation.[95]

A separate but nonetheless related issue to price discrimination is that of differential pricing.[96] This is the norm within the travel industry where there are different classes of travel such as economy, business and first class. Although differential pricing does not precisely equate to price discrimination (as the good or service provided differs in either quality or quantity), the rationale underpinning differential pricing is similar to that of price discrimination. That is, the monopolist is seeking to capture as much consumer surplus as possible. Similar to price discrimination, price differentiation is part of a broader strategy of market segmentation. Boyle relates differential pricing by reliance on an introductory quote by Jules Dupuit:

> It is not because of the few thousand francs which would have to be spent to put a roof over the third-class carriages or to upholster the third-class seats that some company or other has open carriages with wooden benches ... What the company is trying to do is to prevent the passengers who can pay the

> second-class fare from travelling third class; it hits the poor, not because it wants to hurt them, but to frighten the rich ... And it is again for the same reason that the companies, having proved almost cruel to third-class passengers and mean to the second-class ones, become lavish in dealing with first-class passengers. Having refused the poor what is necessary, they give the rich what is superfluous.[97]

The reason price discrimination and price differentiation are both relevant to IPRs is because such practices speak to the market segmentation inherent within the information environment.[98] Also both practices rely to various extents upon the monopolistic characteristics of IPRs. In the IPR context, an IPR-holder will generally argue since an IPR has monopolistic characteristics the only efficient market will be one that relies upon price discrimination (or aggressive price differentiation).[99] It is true that once a monopoly is established, price discrimination (or differential pricing) can assist in producing a Pareto optimal result.[100] It is for this reason Meurer argues that price discrimination can have 'negative as well as positive effects on social welfare'.[101] However, perfect competition produces a Pareto optimal result without the need for a monopoly accompanied by price discrimination and therefore without the associated distributional costs.[102] Thus, price discrimination is often anti-competitive in that it allows producers to dictate the price according to market power in differing markets.[103]

A Pareto analysis highlights that the central difference between perfect competition and monopoly accompanied by price discrimination is *distributional*.[104] That is, the monopolistic characteristics of IPRs lead to distributional costs. This is because when monopoly is coupled with price discrimination the consumer surplus that would otherwise flow to the consumer under perfect competition will ultimately flow to the producer.[105] This consumer surplus capture by the monopolist creates a deadweight loss, which consists of two components: first, the amount of lost satisfaction encountered by each consumer who is unable to buy the product in question as a corollary of the monopolistic price; and second, the total number of consumers who suffer such loss.[106] Clearly these costs are distributional.[107]

Alongside price discrimination, the issue of income discrepancy is a key determinant when analysing distributional costs associated with IPRs.

3.3.1.2 Income discrepancies

In contrast to neoclassical economics, welfare economics has a long history of analysing distributional costs by exploring the marginal utility of income. It is distribution of income that is a central determinant in relation to resource allocation. If people generally desire what they need and if needs are more urgent when people are poor then it follows additional income has greater utility to the poor than it does to the rich.[108] This is because the marginal utility of income tends to diminish as additional income is used to fulfil needs that become less pressing as a person's income increases. Pigou drew attention to the relationship between income distribution and welfare when he wrote:

> It is evident that any transference of income from a relatively rich man to a relatively poor man of similar temperament, since it enables more intense wants to be satisfied at the expense of less intense wants, must increase the aggregate sum of satisfaction. The old 'law of diminishing utility' thus leads securely to the proposition: Any cause which increases the absolute share of real income in the hands of the poor, provided that it does not lead to a contraction in the size of the national dividend from any point of view, will in general, increase economic welfare.[109]

Distribution is important not just for increasing welfare generally, but also in assisting in facilitating the proper functioning of the market.[110] A simple example proves the point. If all income in the world flowed to one person and the remainder of the population had no income, then production would be entirely skewed towards the whims of the sole income earner at the expense of society at large and the market as a whole. Accordingly, if the bulk of the population has no income their needs would have to be met outside of the market. It follows that a more egalitarian distribution of income broadens the operation and functioning of the market. Within this context, when the international IPR regime is analysed through a distributional cost lens the outcome becomes problematic, because IPRs tend to transfer wealth from poorer countries of the world to richer countries.[111] Emphasising the distributional costs of IPRs, James Boyle writes: 'Curare, batik, myths, and the dance "lambada" flow out of developing countries ... while Prozac, Levis, Grisham, and the movie Lambada! flow in ... The former are unprotected by intellectual property rights, while the latter are protected.'[112] There are various mechanisms relied upon by IPR holders to operationalise this distributional imbalance. The restrictions on parallel importing in the US are exemplary.[113] And indeed some IPR minimalist scholars would argue that a central function of the Trade-Related Aspects of Intellectual Property Rights (TRIPS) Agreement is to maintain and deepen this distributional imbalance.[114]

The over-emphasis of incentivisation benefits that accrue from internalising positive externalities through propertisation of information, and the under-emphasis of distributional costs that flow from monopolies, is particularly evident in relation to patents and pharmaceutical products.[115] It is often reported that pharmaceutical companies spend significantly more on lifestyle remedies (e.g. hair-growth) than on life-saving cures (e.g. medicine targeting life-threatening diseases such as malaria).[116] This is despite the fact that contemporaneously life-threatening disease is an enormous and growing problem.[117] A similar story can be told in relation to agricultural biotechnology.[118] Moreover, Harrison has underscored analogous distributional concerns in relation to copyright legislation, arguing it 'is less about maximizing social welfare and more about determining how the profits from protected works are to be distributed'.[119]

Extending Harrison's theme to the IPR system as a whole, we can reason that IPRs are more concerned with the distribution of profits than maximising social net product.[120] This claim stems from the welfare economic premise that the distributional costs of IPRs largely countenance the dynamic efficiencies of IPRs.[121] Moreover, although the market is reasonably efficient at allocating resources by responding to consumer preferences measured by consumers' willingness and ability to pay for goods and services, demand recognised by the market is only demand supported by income.[122] In the terms of Drahos and Braithwaite:

> When knowledge becomes a private good to be traded in markets the demands of many, paradoxically, go unmet. Patent-based R&D is not responsive to demand, but to ability to pay. The blockbuster mentality of the large pharmas takes them to those markets where there is the ability to pay. Drugs for mental illness, hypertension and erectile dysfunction are where the [pharmaceutical] blockbusters are, not tropical diseases.[123]

And as Boyle states:

> The market measures the value of a good by whether people have the ability and willingness to pay for it, so the whims of the rich may be more 'valuable' than the needs of the destitute. We may spend more on pet psychiatry for the traumatized poodles on East 71st Street than on developing a cure for sleeping sickness, because the emotional wellbeing of the pets of the wealthy is 'worth more' than the lives of the tropical world's poor.[124]

In other words, when the dynamic efficiency and propertisation benefits of IPRs trump distributional costs associated with IPRs, then information production tends to become skewed in perverse ways. Given that distributional costs are difficult to measure it is no great surprise this is the case. But rather than relying upon the proposition that the production of information is to be incentivised by internalising positive externalities, it would perhaps be more intellectually honest if the IPR system acknowledged that borrowing from various cultures is permissible in some circumstances because: 'that is what people do, and ... allowing people to do what they do has produced, over the centuries, artistic and intellectual expressions of breathtaking variety, beauty, and power in cultures the world over'.[125]

*****

It is difficult to calculate the efficiency costs, administration costs, externality costs and distributional costs which flow from the propertisation of information via IPRs. This is one reason why these categories of costs are often left out of the social net product equation when determining the efficiency of IPRs. Yet when these costs are taken into account the benefits of propertising information are significantly diminished. This is not to say property is never useful when seeking to incentivise production of information. Clearly it will be. But propertisation is merely one governance tool for overcoming market failures such as the public goods provisioning problem or externalities. The opportunity costs that flow from reliance upon propertising information must also be considered. What might transpire if propertised information otherwise remained accessible within the commons? Principles 3 and 4 of Table 1.1 are concerned with this question, as is Part II of this book.

3.4 CONCLUSION

This chapter extended the theme of the preceding chapter by highlighting the understated costs associated with the propertisation of information. In particular, beyond the efficiency costs and administration costs discussed in the previous chapter, a welfare economic analysis of externalities and monopolies stresses that the propertisation of information spawns externality costs and distributional costs respectively. This position is built upon Pigou's social net product analysis, which seeks to take into account private and public costs and benefits of a given regulatory/economic framework.

Unpacking the evolution of property rights is a complex task. A dominant justification of property is premised on Coasian/Demsetzian arguments, which espouse the benefits of internalising externalities.[126] As with all economic theory, this justification relies upon a number of assumptions, one of which is zero transaction costs. This is significant within the context of the information environment because it is well known that IPRs generate such costs. Accordingly, the internalisation of externalities theory used to justify propertisation within the physical environment does not map neatly to the information environment. Moreover, the externalities paradox discussed throughout the chapter emphasised that although propertisation is often deployed to internalise externalities, IPRs do not necessarily eradicate externality costs. Rather, IPRs often serve to shift or conceal such costs.

With respect to monopolies, we saw that the market fails because a monopoly producer is able to dictate supply, which in turn undermines the market forces of supply and demand. Although monopoly represents only one characterisation of IPRs, the monopoly dilemma discussed within the chapter underscores an important aspect of the overall social net product equation of IPRs. That is, within the monopoly context, price discrimination practices and universal income discrepancies lead to substantial distributional costs. These costs ultimately lead to perverse production trends within the information environment such that the whims of the wealthy are considered to be much more valuable than the needs of the poor. For this reason equitable access to the information commons, discussed in Part IV of the book and espoused in principle 10 of Table 1.1, is fundamental to information environmentalism.

PART II

The commons

The information commons has thus far been loosely conceptualised as 'the opposite of private property'.[1] By contrasting the terms 'public domain', 'intellectual commons' and 'information commons', Part II will provide a more nuanced perspective. As was suggested in the introductory chapter, the information commons lies at the heart of information environmentalism. In particular, the information commons is a unifying theme of the four environmental analytical frameworks: welfare economics, the commons, ecology, and public choice theory.

Boyle has been at the forefront of scholarship underlining the significance of the information commons.[2] He argues strengthening it is a healthy antidote to the IPR maximalist impulse. According to this view the information commons should be construed in a broad sense to include all aspects of informational works that are open to access and use. So conceived, the information commons is to be thought of in positive definition terms rather than as a place for 'left-overs'.[3] Throughout Part II we will see the information commons is in many ways as critical to innovation and creativity as the environment is to the physical world.[4] For this reason Part III advocates theoretical and practical methods of protecting and nurturing the information commons. Part of this advocacy is recognising that the information commons is to be thought of not necessarily as a force of either liberation or enslavement but rather as a 'site of struggle'.[5]

The aim of Part II is twofold: (i) to delineate the parameters of the information commons, and (ii) to stress the importance of the dynamic interaction between the private property dimensions of IPRs and the information commons. With respect to the first issue, one of the reasons why the information commons is difficult to protect is because of the challenges inherent in defining its parameters. To this end, Chapter 4 establishes an information commons definitional matrix that comprises narrow and broad definitions of the intellectual commons and the public domain respectively. The purpose is to survey and clarify the parameters of the information commons as per principle 5 in Table 1.1. With respect to the second issue, Part II demonstrates that any given community is ultimately confronted with decisions about how private property and the commons are to be defined and constructed. The positive community/negative community matrix alluded to in the introduction and discussed in Chapter 4 is a useful starting point. Once private property is accepted as a legitimate form of governance, the key question then becomes: how does private property interact with the commons? In pursuing this line of inquiry, Chapter 5 seeks to apply semicommons theory to the information environment. We will come to appreciate there are mutual symbiotic benefits stemming from the dynamic interaction between the private property dimensions of IPRs and the information commons. To ignore this dynamic interaction is a tragedy – 'the tragedy of (ignoring) the information semicommons'. Principle 6 in Table 1.1 advocates the neutralisation of this tragedy.

4. Information commons

If particulars are to have meaning, there must be universals.

Plato

4.1 INTRODUCTION

Part I underscored the exclusivity costs associated with the IPR system such as efficiency costs, administration costs, externality costs and distributional costs. There will be instances where benefits of propertisation may outweigh costs, and instances where this will not be the case, although it may be difficult to make this determination with absolute certainty. Here, a social net product analysis supported by empirical evidence becomes a vital project of information environmentalism. The inherent risk, particularly evident within IPR maximalist discourse, is that incentivisation arguments and purported benefits associated with the internalising of positive externalities trump the exclusivity costs of IPRs.

To a large extent, the exclusivity costs inherent within the IPR system are acknowledged by the system itself as evidenced by the leaky nature of IPRs that flow from doctrines such as fair use and the requirement to disclose information about an invention as a *quid pro quo* for a patent right. The IPR system contains leaks and exceptions because it implicitly recognises the information environment relies upon access to and use of information so that more information can be created. To this extent, the IPR system is, like most property systems, a mixed system of private property and commons, although it is not often perceived in this manner.[1] A central rationale as to why IPRs implicitly rely upon the information commons is because the latter contains its own in-built efficiency mechanisms. For instance, the information commons evades many exclusivity costs associated with the property system (discussed in Part I).[2]

While it is perhaps too late in the day to entertain fundamental questions concerning the application of property to the information environment (as per the property interrogations of St. Francis of Assisi and Rousseau discussed within the introductory chapter), we can still consider how propertisation of information is to be reconciled with the information commons. Naturally, an important part of this project is to understand the precise nature of the information commons. This task lies at the heart of the present chapter. In so doing, there are a number of important distinctions that must be engaged with. For instance, we must distinguish between concepts of positive community and negative community; and it is also necessary to distinguish between the intellectual commons and the public domain. This in turn provides the foundation for the information commons definitional matrix and related information commons terminology.

The chapter begins by advocating reconciliation between private property and the commons. A discussion of the positive community/negative community matrix will follow. Intellectual commons and public domain will then be contrasted so as to consolidate the information commons terminology. The information commons consists of the bundling of narrow and broad definitions of intellectual commons and public domain respectively. In operationalising various aspects of the information commons definition, the chapter will conclude by exploring distinctions between access, use and ownership.

4.2 POSITIVE COMMUNITY VS. NEGATIVE COMMUNITY

As was stressed in Part I, whether or not private property is the optimum method of overcoming the market failures inherent within the information environment is a moot point to be resolved with reference to a thorough empirically based social net product analysis of IPRs.[3] In practical terms this is a task that lies beyond the scope of this book. However, regardless of contentions in this respect, propertisation of information has become well entrenched within the global economic framework as exemplified by the WTO TRIPS Agreement. Indeed, as the nexus of WTO agreements ensures that TRIPS is inexorably bound within the international trade framework, it is difficult to conceive of a reversal of this state of affairs, at least in the foreseeable future.[4]

As we have seen, although there are some important exceptions, information is often subject to propertisation. As a corollary it becomes essential for any theory of property to provide some explanation concerning the relationship between individual property rights and those rights relating to the commons.[5] That is, within a given economic system, one must either abandon the commons as an explanatory construct, or alternatively find a method of reconciling commons rights with individual rights.[6] As the information commons is already inherent within the

IPR system, and indeed within the economic system more generally, it is the latter task of reconciling private property rights and commons rights that is most appropriate.

There are many possible approaches when discussing reconciliation of private property and the commons. A postmodern perspective, for instance, might build on the private/public dichotomy following thinkers such as Heidegger and Sartre.[7] These thinkers respectively argued that human reality is essentially constituted by the mutually disclosing presence of the self and others. According to this perspective, in order for an individual to have a subjective existence it is necessary that 'private' and 'public' are complements.[8] Hannah Arendt draws out this latter distinction in *The Human Condition* where she indicates that although the 'public' is a human construct, not necessarily synonymous with 'the earth or with nature', it is nevertheless vital the construct is maintained. In this context, she claims:

> The public realm, as the common world, gathers us together and yet prevents our falling over each other, so to speak. What makes society so difficult to bear is not the number of people involved, or at least not primarily, but the fact that the world between them has lost its power to gather them together, to relate and to separate them.[9]

Arendt argues that in the 'world of things' it is the *table*, at least in a metaphorical sense, that 'relates and separates men at the same time'.[10] If we move from the physical environment to the realm of IPRs the question lingers: what is the equivalent of 'the table' within the information environment?[11] Various answers have been given in this respect, the most prevalent being the intellectual commons, the public domain and/or the information commons. We will discover below there are actually important nuances between these terms, but generally each term draws upon the physical commons. This in turn necessitates the contrast of negative community and positive community as initially discussed by natural law theorists.[12]

Pufendorf was one such natural law theorist. He sought to distinguish between private and public through the prism of property: 'the oak tree was no one's, but the acorns that fell from it became his who gather them'.[13] Pufendorf's distinction between the oak tree and the acorns brings to light the Lockean spoilage principle (discussed above in Chapter 2), which relates not just to what is taken but also to what is left. According to Locke, consumptive use is consistent with the commons provided that the person who takes from the commons leaves 'as much and as good' for other commoners.[14] Discerning the commons in these terms gives rise to an important distinction between positive community and negative community. This distinction was in fact initially discussed by Pufendorf but has been more recently popularised within IPR scholarship by Peter Drahos.[15]

As implied in the introductory chapter, positive community largely maps to the Roman law concept of *res communis*. This is to say that resources are considered to belong to everyone and therefore any use of such resources is required to be for the benefit of the public at large. On the other hand, negative community maps to the Roman law concept of *res nullius*. This means that resources can generally be perceived as belonging to no one and are therefore unclaimed and for the taking.[16] Locke generally subscribed to a negative community perception of the commons in that the commons was largely there for the taking provided that labour could be attached to it. But his spoilage principle indicates he believed there were some important limitations to privately appropriating the commons.

While Locke's spoilage limitation principle may have some utility in the physical environment (although even here Locke implied that the advent of money changed the equation), the non-rival nature of information discussed in Chapter 2 means information is generally not subject to the depletion/congestion problem.[17] Accordingly, the spoilage principle has restricted application in the information environment. The principle does, however, point to another important question: what are the circumstances whereby the commons can be validly propertised in a private sense? It is difficult to answer this question in the abstract because both the commons and private property are culturally contingent constructs.[18] As discussed in Chapter 2, the parameters of exclusion differ intensely across geography and cultures such that the commons can be delineated in a number of ways.[19] This is evidenced by the contrast between open commons and limited-access commons.[20] Yet despite the fact that the physical environmental commons is grounded in geography and culture, it is nevertheless possible to universalise the discussion of the commons and the information commons by drawing further upon the positive community/negative community dichotomy.

As Drahos underscores, Pufendorf considered the distinction between positive community and negative community by exploring different approaches of interacting with the commons.[21] In essence, negative community refers to a 'community of all things' in which 'all things lay open to all men, and belonged no more to one than to another'.[22] At first glance, it may appear this conception of the commons would prevent persons from owning it, as things are to belong 'no more to one than to another'. However, it has quite the opposite effect in that it represents a state where anybody can seek to attach exclusive belonging to the relevant subject. In contrast, positive community refers to the situation where a group jointly owns things that lie within the commons. That is, a positive community is one in which the commons is owned by everybody. This conception of the commons 'would make the acquisition of property by an individual heavily dependent upon the consent of others, since the individual is trying to acquire something that belongs to all'.[23]

Importantly, neither positive community nor negative community preclude ownership. The distinction relates to how a community interacts with the commons and how the construct of propertisation penetrates that community. Determining what is meant by 'a community' is primarily dependent upon the parameters of inclusivity and exclusivity.[24] The terms inclusivity and exclusivity are relatively self-explanatory and are perhaps best understood within the context of the following matrix (Table 4.1).

Table 4.1 Positive community/negative community matrix

	Positive community	Negative community
Inclusive	Broad vision of human community that includes all humans. Hence, there is only one community of which to speak in which all have the right to use the commons for their individual welfare.	Encompasses all individuals, but it is a community in which the acquisition of things lies open to all.
Exclusive	Represents ownership of things in the commons by a particular group. If a person falls outside of this group, then they are excluded.	Ownership of things in the commons is open to the members of a particular group, rather than to everybody.

Sources: Derived from Drahos, *A Philosophy of IP*, at 58; and Tully, *A Discourse On Property*, at 126–129.

While neither positive community nor negative community preclude ownership of private property per se, the perspective of property does differ considerably. For instance, according to the inclusive positive community concept it is possible for individuals to acquire property rights in things that are created through resources of the commons, but the commons itself cannot be appropriated.[25] On the other hand, under an exclusive negative community conception, anyone within a specified group may seek to subject part or all of the commons relating to that group to property ownership. Thus, the particular option adopted within the above matrix will determine the nature of property as it relates to the commons within any given community. According to negative community, property can be perceived as the right of exclusive possession to objects that are ultimately taken from the commons.[26] In contrast, according to positive community, property rights refer to a type of usufructory right whereby the user of the commons gains property rights in things made from the commons, but not in the commons itself.[27]

Drahos implies that thinking about the commons through the lens of the matrix in Table 4.1 may be overly reductionist in that there might be other methods of perceiving the interaction between property and the commons.[28] However, it does seem that any community is ultimately required to make a choice about the commons which accords, at least in general terms, with one of the four matrix options. The questions of how property and the commons are defined and constructed are to be resolved by the relevant communities. Yet one way or another the choices presented by the matrix must be engaged with. The position in this book is reflected in principle 4 of Table 1.1 – that is, positive community should be applied to the information commons. Choices related to inclusivity/exclusivity are mostly contextual.

As we have seen, Locke generally adopted the negative community perspective of the commons.[29] In practical terms this means that provided labour can be mixed with the possession of land (that would otherwise fall within the commons) then ownership of that land will be forthcoming subject to certain limitations such as the spoilage principle.[30] When the evolution of property ownership is seen in these terms, the legitimising philosophy underpinning the process of colonisation becomes readily apparent. For instance, as highlighted in the introductory chapter, Locke's application of negative community meant the denial of European colonisation by Indigenous peoples the world over would be an attempt to occupy more land than Indigenous peoples could make use of.[31] Locke was not alone in his negative community perceptions of the commons.[32] Grotius also implicitly defended negative community (although he did not refer to this concept in the way Pufendorf did), which essentially became the basis of his appeal to ensure that the oceans remained free for all to use.[33]

Whether or not negative community or positive community promotes universal principles such as freedom is context contingent. Also, it will depend on whose freedom is actually being measured. Negative community may have been generally more freedom-enhancing than positive community in the respective eras of Grotius and Locke, at least as far as the oceans are concerned, and at least as far as certain groups of persons were concerned. However, in the contemporary context the negative community conception tends to turn the commons into 'a hunting ground for the economically strong and the technologically capable'.[34] Here, Drahos explains that generally speaking the developed world prefer a negative community definition so they can exploit resources that are deemed to lie within the commons such as the ocean sea-bed.[35] In contrast, Lesser Developed Countries prefer a positive community definition so those that seek to exploit the commons in question must first seek the consent of the relevant group. By extension, Drahos argues: 'Linking positive community to the intellectual commons would have the effect of reducing predatory moves against the commons by individuals. The cooperation of other individuals would be necessary before individuals could make any such moves.'[36]

Within the context of preserving the intellectual commons, there are two inherent dangers which flow from applying negative community. First, negative community allows for raids of appropriation to be carried out; and second, strategic behaviour is fostered to the extent that individuals find ways and means of preventing resources from entering into the commons in the first place.[37] Certainly the history of colonisation speaks volumes to these hazards, but as we will observe below this dynamic is also intensely relevant within the information environment. To further develop the information environmental application of the positive community/negative community matrix it is necessary from the outset to engage with the distinction, or lack thereof, between the intellectual commons and the public domain.

4.3 INTELLECTUAL COMMONS AND PUBLIC DOMAIN

When seeking to reconcile individual property rights and commons rights within the information environment, we must be clear about how the (information) commons is in fact delineated. In IPR discourse the commons is discussed with reference to a number of different terms, the most prominent being the intellectual commons and the public domain.[38] Although Andreas Rahmatian suggests 'there is no qualitative difference' between these two terms, there is in fact a meaningful contrast.[39]

Seemingly, there are several reasons why Rahmatian would suggest there is no difference between the intellectual commons and the public domain. First, within IPR scholarship the terms have become considerably intertwined in that the terms are used interchangeably. Second, the meaning of each term morphs depending upon the commentator and the context.[40] Third, both terms can be presented as a contradistinction to property and in this respect the terms are often conflated alongside the physical commons.[41] And fourth, both the intellectual commons and the public domain speak to the creation of commons rights such that the public can obtain access to particular resources.[42]

Putting aside the similarities between the intellectual commons and the public domain, there are some distinctions. The most important of these is that the intellectual commons excludes from its frontier those works that are restricted as a consequence of non-property law, technology and/or physicality. In contrast, the public domain does not necessarily subscribe to these limitations. As to further distinctions, this depends largely upon whether narrow or broad definitions of the respective terms are being referred to. Before elaborating upon these narrow and broad definitions, the commons must be defined.

4.3.1 The Commons

The distinction between negative community and positive community ultimately relates to how communities interact with the commons. Naturally, this begs the question: what is the commons? *The Australian Oxford Pocket Dictionary* defines the commons as 'for joint use, shared; land belonging to the community'.[43] The shared attributes of a common resource mean the resource is free (libre) to the community in that the resource is subject to usage without the permission of anyone else, or if permission is granted it is done so neutrally.[44] As Reichman and Lewis put it, common resources are protected by a liability rule rather than a property rule.[45] It is not that no control exists, but rather the type of control is different from the control granted by property law.[46] A key attribute of the commons is that no single person or organisation has exclusive control over use or disposition of a particular resource. Rather, resources governed by commons may be used or disposed of by anyone (within a relevant community) in accordance with rules that may range from 'anything goes' to quite crisply articulated formal rules that are effectively enforced.[47] In the contemporary landscape the most evident (regulated) commons are the footpaths, roads and highways that facilitate the ability to move from one place to the other.[48]

As Drahos highlights, it is important to recognise the relationship between the commons and the legal framework in which the commons is situated.[49] For instance, when Locke referred to the commons he was referring to the English law definition of the concept relevant to that geography and era.[50] At that time the commons ultimately referred to a bundle of rights such as the right to fish and the right to pasture.[51] These rights were specific to groups of people in accordance with the *inclusive* positive community/negative community definition. Importantly, the commons did not represent public ownership of land but rather the land was often privately owned.[52] Notwithstanding the fact commoners maintained common rights to use land specifically in relation to the allocated rights, there was 'no general right of access by commoners and no general right of access by members of the public'.[53] It is noteworthy that Locke's commons underscores the distinction between 'use rights' and 'access rights', a theme further developed below. For now, it is necessary to contrast narrow and broad definitions of intellectual commons and public domain respectively.

4.3.2 Intellectual Commons

Intellectual commons derives its meaning from the concept of the commons as it relates to the physical environment. Within the physical world, footpaths, roads and highways provide obvious and explicit examples of the commons. The intellectual commons is a subtler concept, at least in terms of presence, yet it is just as important as the physical commons, particularly within the contemporary information age. Twenty-first-century society would mostly grind to a halt without a robust physical commons and intellectual commons. The latter includes virtually all pre-twentieth-century knowledge and culture, a majority of scientific knowledge from the first half of the twentieth century, and the lion's share of contemporary science and academic learning.[54] Einstein's theory of relativity sits alongside the local beach, park or nearest footpath since the (relevant) community can access these resources without the permission of anyone else.[55]

In pursuing a formal definition of the intellectual commons, Drahos indicates that it encompasses 'those abstract objects which remain open to use'.[56] He elaborates by stating that the intellectual commons consists of '[t]hat part of the objective world of knowledge which is not subject to any of the following: property rights or some other conventional bar (contract, for instance); technological bars (for example, encryption) or a physical bar (hidden manuscripts)'.[57] This definition raises several questions. What is the distinction between access to and use of informational resources? And, does the intellectual commons include those informational resources that are actually protected by IPRs, and if so, to what extent? Before addressing these questions, it is necessary to distinguish between narrow and broad applications of the intellectual commons definition. Drahos's definition above is a narrow intellectual commons definition because it arguably excludes those works that are protected by IPRs (i.e. property rights). On the other hand, scholars such as Deazley deploy intellectual commons in a broad sense such that it includes works in which IPRs subsist. In particular, Deazley's broad perspective of the intellectual commons seems to implicitly (and perhaps unconsciously) borrow from Locke's commons. This is because the commons of Locke's era did not necessarily represent public ownership of land, but rather commoners maintained common rights to use specific land (that may have been privately owned) with respect to particular allocated rights.[58] In the broad definition of intellectual commons, rather than use being the key criterion as it was in Locke's day, the key determinant seems to be that of access. That is, provided information can be accessed, according to Deazley it generally falls within the broad definition of intellectual commons. In contrast, Drahos's narrow intellectual commons requires not just access rights, but also use rights.

4.3.3 Public Domain

Like the intellectual commons, the public domain can also be distinguished along narrow and broad lines. Despite the fact that the public domain is now principally equated with IPRs, the term initially related to public land. Relevantly, in discussing the politics of privatisation, Cohen argues that the public domain within the public land context 'served largely as a holding device for land destined for privatization'.[59] The public domain, as it relates to IPRs, originates from the *French Decree* of 1791 (*domaine public*).[60] According to this Decree, the protection and enlargement of the public domain was considered to be of equal importance to the protection of the author's dramatic work. In the US, the notion of public domain was not part of the IPR lexicon until the turn of the twentieth century, although the term was deployed occasionally in the nineteenth century.[61] The 1896 Supreme Court case involving the Singer sewing machine is an example.[62] In that case the Court indicated that upon expiry of a patent the public obtained the right to make use of the technology as 'the invention fell into the public domain'.[63]

The meaning of the public domain is confusing because the phrase is used in different ways depending upon the context and commentator. In simplified terms, in parallel with the intellectual commons, there is a narrow and broad definition of the public domain.[64] Obviously both definitions need to be understood if the public domain phrase is to have any import. In the *narrow* sense, which was the traditional meaning, the public domain simply refers to those works in which the IPR has expired as a consequence of the termination of the relevant IPR term.[65] According to this understanding, the narrow public domain term would extend to works that have never attracted IPR protection along with those works to which the author or inventor has renounced all claims.[66] This aspect of the public domain is sometimes referred to as the 'structural core'.[67] The narrow definition of the public domain seems to accord with the meaning adopted in *Black's Law Dictionary*. Here, the public domain is defined with reference to 'information artifacts' including works subject to expired copyrights and patents but excluding subcomponents of the public domain such as ideas and unprotected information.[68]

Contemporaneously, however, the meaning of public domain tends to equate to a broad, expansive usage that embraces all types of 'public rights' to use IPR-related works.[69] For example, in the domain of copyright, any usage related to 'fair dealing', 'fair use' or 'compulsory licensing' would fall within this broad definition.[70] Work that makes use of FLOSS and CC licences would also fall within the broad definition of public domain.[71] Hence, the public domain in the broadest sense encompasses all types of public rights relating to the use of information.[72] In other words, the public domain consists of those things not subject to IPRs. Examples include those works where the relevant copyright or patent has expired, facts, and other critical aspects of culture that are not subject to ownership, the most obvious exemplar being language.[73] Under this broad definition, some scholars simply equate the public domain with a particular brand of the commons such that a person can make use of a relevant resource without asking permission.[74] This broader definition encompasses the 'structural core' of the public domain, along with what is sometimes referred to as the 'functional portion'.[75]

4.4 ACCESS, USE AND OWNERSHIP

We have begun to see there is an intricate relationship between the narrow intellectual commons, the broad intellectual commons, the narrow public domain, and the broad public domain. By way of amalgamation, the terminology of 'information commons' will be adopted as a bundling term to refer to all of the distinct definitions collectively. There are occasions when it might be necessary to distinguish between the various distinct terms presented, in which case one or more of the specific terms will be deployed. However, where the point being made is of a more general nature, the term 'information commons' suffices. The various distinct definitions covered above are represented in the following information commons definitional matrix:

Table 4.2 Information commons definitional matrix

	Narrow	Broad
Intellectual commons	Includes those informational resources that are 'open to use' but excludes those informational resources that are subject to property rights or restricted by some other limitation such as non-property law (e.g. contract), technology (e.g. encryption), and/or physicality (e.g. hidden manuscript).	Same as narrow intellectual commons but includes informational resources where IPRs subsist provided that persons have access to these works.
Public domain	Includes those informational resources that never attracted IPR protection, those works where the relevant IPR has expired, and those works where the creator/innovator has renounced all claims.	Same as narrow public domain, but includes all types of public rights related to the use of IPR-related works such as fair use, fair dealing, compulsory licensing, and works subject to an open licence such as FLOSS or CC.

Now the landscape of the information commons has been surveyed, the nuances between the various aspects of the information commons can be further detailed. We have seen one of the issues that arises when fleshing out the distinction between the intellectual commons and the public domain is the access/use dichotomy.[76] Within the information environment, as with the physical environment, it is possible that property can be accessed but not used. Generally access is a prerequisite for usage, but just because property can be accessed it does not necessarily follow it can be used.[77] Hence, the access/use distinction is one of the means of contrasting the various definitions of the intellectual commons and public domain as per the above definitional matrix.

Generally speaking, the narrow definition of intellectual commons requires access and use, whereas the broad definition of intellectual commons requires access only. Contrarily, the narrow public domain does not require access or use. This is because an informational resource can theoretically fall within the narrow public domain but not be accessible or open to use (e.g. a secret diary). Similarly, like the narrow public domain, the broad public domain does not necessarily require access or use. This is because the broad public domain definition rests on public use rights. Such rights do not necessarily require that the information resource is available or open to use in a practical sense. For example, a computer software program may be subject to the General Public License and therefore fall within the broad public domain. Yet the program might require a specific form of computer hardware that is only to be found in a hidden vault. In this unlikely circumstance, the computer program is technically in the broad public domain, but it cannot be accessed or used in any meaningful sense and so it would fall outside the narrow intellectual commons.

As the definition of the narrow intellectual commons encompasses use rights the question of whether or not a resource is accessible (as per the broad intellectual commons) does not necessarily have a bearing on whether it falls within the narrow intellectual commons. For example, an information resource may be accessible yet subject to an IPR that prevents use and therefore the resource would fall outside the narrow intellectual commons. A book that is subject to copyright is an example – although this is arguably to be qualified by the fact that the issue of usage of the book is governed to some extent by copyright exceptions (e.g. the fair use doctrine and/or the idea/expression dichotomy).

Correspondingly, an information resource may be inaccessible because of a physicality restriction, yet the resource would otherwise theoretically fall within the public domain definition (narrow or broad) if the resource were not the subject of a physical restriction. A secret diary is one such example. At some point in the future the contents of the secret diary may theoretically fall into the public domain (narrow and broad).[78] However, if the resource continues to be subject to a physical restriction then although the work may theoretically fall into the public domain, it will not reside within the intellectual commons in a practical sense unless the work becomes no longer secret. In other words, it is possible for a resource to fall into the public domain, but fall outside of the intellectual commons. It is the issue of accessibility that is the determining factor.

Aside from accessibility, another definitional determinant, particularly with respect to the narrow intellectual commons, is whether or not the resource is 'open to use'.[79] Even if an informational resource is accessible, it may not be 'open to use' to the extent that the resource requires technology or knowledge in order for the resource to be used. An alternate method of conceptualising this 'open to use' characteristic would be to relate the issue of capacity. A language is exemplary.[80] While a language may fall within the broad intellectual commons because it can be accessed, it does not necessarily follow that it will fall within the narrow intellectual commons. This is because unless we know how to speak or read the relevant language then accessibility per se has scant bearing on whether the language is 'open to use', at least in a practical sense. This example could be extended to the language of computer software, which may import technology requirements such that the computer software is not 'open to use' unless access to particular forms of technology (e.g. computer hardware) is forthcoming.[81]

The access/use distinction is not just important within the realm of intellectual commons. It is also important in maintaining distinctions between intellectual commons and the public domain. This is reinforced through a concrete example of a resource subject to IPRs such as a book governed by copyright. As a result of the copyright, we can say that the book falls outside the definition of the narrow public domain. However, it is also true that parts of the work fall within the broad public domain as a consequence of certain copyright exceptions such as the fair use provisions and the idea/expression dichotomy. Accordingly, a person has access to the book as a whole, yet that person can only make use of the book in specific ways in harmony with the relevant copyright law. Of course, it is possible the book is subject to an open licence such as one of the six CC licences, in which case the licence itself will mostly stipulate how the book can and cannot be used.[82] Any public rights flowing from such an open licence would generally fall within the ambit of the broad public domain.

If this is how the broad public domain relates to the book, how then does the intellectual commons relate? As persons generally have access to the book (subject to, for example, the exclusivity of price and/or access to a library) the book clearly falls within the broad intellectual commons definition. In relation to the narrow intellectual commons definition the situation becomes fuzzier because the question arises as to what content within the book persons have not just access to, but use of. This query concerns not just the law, but also other restrictions stemming from technology and/or physicality. With respect to the law, fuzziness arises because it might be argued that ideas presented in the book (for example) are not actually subject to IPRs and therefore the ideas fall fairly and squarely within the narrow intellectual commons definition. This perspective accords with the spirit of the definition of the narrow intellectual commons in that the said definition refers to 'those abstract objects which remain open to use'.[83] If the book is subject to a CC licence, we can query whether the open licensing arrangement could be considered to be a 'non-property law restriction'? While there are some restrictions relating to FLOSS and CC licensed works, on balance these licensing arrangements tend to foster greater access to and use of informational resources. For this reason, those works that rely upon open source licensing generally fall within the narrow intellectual commons definition, albeit it is recognised there may be some important exceptions in this regard.

Hence, at least so far as the book example is concerned, there is largely a collapse in the distinction between the broad public domain and the intellectual commons (broad and narrow). When returning directly to the question of how the book relates to the intellectual commons, the starting point is 'ditto' as per the broad public domain discussion. However, this is not the end of the story because both the narrow and broad intellectual commons definitions also consider whether or not the book is subject to other limitations stemming from non-property-law restrictions (e.g. contract law or licensing arrangements), technology (e.g. encryption) or physicality (e.g. hidden manuscript). If the book is subject to one or more of the said limitations then this will affect whether the book falls within the intellectual commons (broad or narrow).[84] It is possible that an informational resource (or part thereof) falls within the broad definition of the public domain but that that resource is not within either the narrow or broad intellectual commons because of one or more of the said limitations.

Beyond the access/use dichotomy, there is also the question of ownership. As we have already seen, the power of incentivisation arguments, coupled with the benefits of internalising positive externalities through property, have provided powerful rhetorical foundations for the IPR maximalist impulse within the information environment. When Locke's implicit perspective of negative community is thrown into the mix, it is no great surprise there are continual propertisation pressures on the information commons. As Drahos argues, a pure Lockean perspective indicates that the information commons simply does not exist: 'Abstract objects, whether discovered or created, are always the product of individual intellectual labour and, therefore, the property of the intellectual worker responsible for their generation. Intellectual property legislation that sets limits on the private ownership of such objects invades the natural right of the owner.'[85]

Notwithstanding the power of such arguments, they have not entirely trumped within the IPR system to the extent that IPRs continue to recognise the role of the information commons in facilitating ongoing creation and innovation. Naturally, within the context of the information environment, if information is subject to an IPR then strictly speaking that information, or at least parts of it, will fall outside of the narrow intellectual commons. The earlier discussion concerning positive community/negative community ultimately relates to the ownership of the commons. There are a number of possibilities within any given community relating to the justification or otherwise of commons ownership. The focus of the next chapter is not so much where the IPR line is drawn as it relates to the information commons (although this question is critically important), but rather once the line is drawn how then does the private property dimension of IPRs relate to the information commons?

4.5 CONCLUSION

Without the commons a radical breakdown of the physical environment would likely ensue. A similar story can be told with respect to the information environment, which without the information commons would be seriously compromised. For this reason, the chapter has laboured over the parameters of the information commons. This labour has been a manifestation of principle 5 of Table 1.1. That is, a prerequisite of relying upon the information commons as a governance tool is to clearly delineate its parameters. This challenge was confronted within the chapter with reference to a definitional matrix. The matrix encompassed the narrow and broad public domain and the narrow and broad intellectual commons. In doing so, the general terminology of the 'information commons' was posited as a bundling term.[86]

Throughout the chapter we saw that all resources essentially begin in the commons. As a result it is necessary for any community to make choices about how resources can validly transition from the commons into the domain of private property. The positive community/negative community matrix provides an effective framework for exploring the options in this regard. As reflected in principle 4 of Table 1.1, this book advocates the application of the positive community principle to the information commons. But regardless of the matrix position adopted, once private property is established a crucial consideration becomes how private property is to interact with the commons. This theme is the core focus of the ensuing chapter.

5. Tragedy of (ignoring) the information semicommons

That which is essential is invisible to the eye.

The Little Prince (Antoine de Saint-Exupéry)

5.1 INTRODUCTION

The preceding chapter sought to clarify the parameters of the information commons and related terminology. The present chapter builds upon this discussion by introducing the information semicommons.

The interrelationship between the information commons and the information semicommons is important to the extent that the former provides the foundation for the latter. Put simply, without an information commons there is no information semicommons of which to speak. The information semicommons can be thought of in terms of the dynamic interaction between private and commons usages of information. With reference to popular tragedy discourse, namely the tragedy of the commons and the tragedy of the anticommons, this chapter seeks to hazard against the tragedy of ignoring the information semicommons. In so doing, the chapter underscores the contentious nature of the commons as it relates to the physical environment and the information environment. On the one hand, environmentalism has grappled with the tragedy of the commons with respect to natural resources: oceans, rivers, forests and air. On the other hand, information environmentalism has wrestled with the tragedy of the anticommons, particularly in relation to innovation: computer software, agriculture and medicine. By contrasting these tragedies the relevance of the information semicommons is revealed.

The central theme of the chapter is that ignoring the dynamic interaction between private and public concerns creates a great tragedy that, like all tragedies, is best avoided. This perspective is embedded within principle 6 of Table 1.1. The chapter begins by discussing the tragedy of the commons, which will be followed by a discussion of the tragedy of the anticommons. By way of synthesis, the chapter then outlines the tragedy of ignoring the information semicommons.

5.2 TRAGEDY OF THE COMMONS

Hardin's well-known tragedy of the commons arises when too many people have a privilege to use a resource and no one user has a legal right to exclude any other user, with the end result being over-consumption and the depletion of the resource.[1] Hardin used the notion of a 'pasture open to all' to make the point that each herdsman has an incentive to add more cattle than the pasture as a whole can bear, since the costs of the cattle are socialised and the benefits of the cattle are privatised in favour of the herdsman.[2] Under this tragedy each herder is motivated to add more and more animals because she receives the direct benefit of her own animals and bears only a share of the costs resulting from over-grazing. As Hardin describes the consequences:

> Therein is the tragedy. Each man is locked into a system that compels him to increase his herd without limit – in a world that is limited. Ruin is the destination toward which all men rush, each pursing his own best interest in a society that believes in the freedom of the commons. Freedom in a commons brings ruin to all.[3]

Of course, Hardin was not the first to become aware of the tragedy of the commons. Aristotle long ago observed: property that is common to many has the least care conferred upon it.[4] The *bellum omnium contra omnes* as described by Hobbes is yet another variation of this theme: people seek their own good and end up killing one another.[5] In the nineteenth century, Lloyd outlined a theory of the commons that foresaw careless use of property owned in common.[6] Contemporary scholarship concerning resource economics also postulates that where a number of users have access to a common-pool resource, the cumulated resource units withdrawn from the resource will be more than the optimal economic level of withdrawal.[7]

It is true there is a diverse range of instances where the tragedy of the commons has eventuated. Examples include various famines, firewood provision crises, and climate change.[8] Nevertheless, as many scholars have discussed, it is equally true that not all commons situations have fallen into the trap of the commons dilemma.[9] In response to the popular argument that the commons is an unviable means of effective resource management, Nonini argues:

> Various kinds of commons have long existed as viable and durable arrangements for providing for the needs of human survival. This is best documented in … hundreds of case studies of long-term stable arrangements for the use of common-pool resources, such as land, waterways and irrigation works, forest

> stands, fisheries, and game and wild food plant catchment areas … This research shows that Hardin's (1968) supposed situation of the 'tragedy of the commons,' in which users compete with one another to appropriate commons resources, thus beggaring one another and so exhausting the commons, is far from inevitable.[10]

Ostrom hypothesises that the difference between those who fall victim to the commons dilemma trap and those who do not may relate to factors internal to a given group.[11] The participants may not have the ability to communicate with each other (as per the prisoner's dilemma), no means to foster trust, and no sense they are to share a common future.[12] Moreover, even where a commons dilemma has become entrenched, the predicament may be rectified through strategic external assistance measures such as the provision of a government subsidy.[13]

One of the great ironies of the tragedy of the commons discourse is that Hardin's thesis originally aimed to explain why private incentives would lead firms to pollute their environment even against their own long-term interest, and thereby to justify pollution controls.[14] The tragedy of the commons thesis has since taken on a life of its own, coming to stand for the proposition that all commons are tragic, and property rights are a necessary precondition to efficient, or even sustainable, resource management. In this way the tragedy has come to validate the arguments discussed in Part I of the book, being that strong property rights are required to overcome public goods problems. Robert Smith, for example, voiced what might be referred to as the 'privatise or perish perspective' with respect to environmental conservation in 1981: 'Both the economic analysis of common property resources and Hardin's treatment of the tragedy of the commons [means that] the only way to avoid the tragedy of the commons in natural resources and wildlife is to end the common-property system by creating a system of private property rights.'[15]

Although the commons dilemma is not fait accompli, the notion 'the whole world is best managed when divided among private owners' has principally dominated public debate over the last several decades.[16] As a corollary, the prevailing tendencies have been to divide as many resources as possible among private owners so as to better manage the world. Indeed, the coupling of the tragedy of the commons arguments with the Demsetzian notion that such 'tragic' situations give rise to solutions grounded in exclusionary property rights regimes has provided a strong foundation of support for the neoliberal privatisation propensity.[17] However, as stressed in Part I, this propertisation propensity is not uncontested. IPR minimalists in particular argue that rather than property overcoming the tragedy of the commons, property may indeed compound the problem by simply shifting externalities rather than diminishing them.

Drawing upon the externalities paradox in Chapter 3, although the creation of property rights may go some way towards minimising carbon emissions, such rights may also foster new externality cost-sets. This is because whenever a market is established the market failure of externalities is likely to arise.[18] That is, the creation of property rights and corresponding markets do not necessarily overcome the market failure of externalities; and in some circumstances property rights and related markets can simply lead to the shifting of costs and benefits from one place to another. The sentiments of Drahos in the following passage implicitly reflect this thinking:

> [Property rights] allow owners of those rights to escape the true costs of the negative externalities generated by various production processes. For example, while mining companies operate under many environmental constraints, the true costs of the exercise of their mining rights – in terms of atmospheric pollution and biodiversity loss – are still not being met. Even if we devise property-based schemes to help internalize the externalities (e.g. emission trading schemes), all models of economic growth underpinned by property rights eventually hit the wall of natural resource finitude. Property rights do not save us from the tragedy of the commons. Instead, under the cover of false dawn of natural resource management they unleash in owners of the means of production a much deeper and more aggressive assault upon the biospheric commons.[19]

An extension of this critique is that the tragedy of the commons only arises in the first instance because the cows are actually owned privately by individuals.[20] On this account, private property (and the related markets in cows) actually causes the tragedy because if the cows were not privately owned, then there would be no reason for each herder to introduce an extra cow in that the benefit would not accrue to the individual alone. This is especially the case where the common land is already at carrying capacity since the extra cost of putting cattle on the common land does not outweigh the corresponding benefit.[21] In other words, where the land is at carrying capacity the social net product of an additional cow is negative. The tragedy is that each herder is motivated to add more and more animals because she receives the direct benefit of her own and bears only a share of the costs resulting from overgrazing. In this respect it becomes clear that propertisation can be used as a method of privatising the benefits of the cattle, but yet socialising the related costs of those cattle. This dynamic was a vital theme in Part I; and it is also implicit within principle 1 of Table 1.1, which advocates accounting for the social costs of IPRs (and the social benefits of the information commons). The crux is that costs associated with the cattle are often not fully taken into account because they are generally borne by the public at large.

In relating the tragedy of the commons to the prisoner's dilemma (along with the issue of scale), Fennell drives home the argument that the individual ownership of Hardin's cows is an important part of Hardin's commons equation:

> The problem for Hardin's herders is only partly about the fact that grazing is pursued at a large scale and on commonly owned ground; it can be equally attributed to the fact that the raising of cattle is pursued through individual ownership of the animals. Furthermore, the mix of ownership types occurs under circumstances that permit private ownership to be used as a platform for offloading costs onto the commons, and that allow access to the commons to be used for the benefit of private property (the roving cattle).[22]

The crux here is that although the tragedy of the commons is a real and proper consideration in some circumstances, it is not always resolved through the allocation of property rights and corresponding markets. Aside from the welfare economics discussion in Part I, engaging with the tragedy of the anticommons is another method of progressing this argument.[23]

5.3 TRAGEDY OF THE ANTICOMMONS

Within the domain of property-based ironies and the privatisation predilection generally, Rose advances an argument (adopted by Lessig and Benkler) that the under-utilisation of resources might be as tragic as their exhaustion. This, of course, is the tragedy of the anticommons.[24] By contrast with the tragedy of the commons, the tragedy of the anticommons points to the quandary of where 'too many owners hold rights of exclusion, the resource is prone to under use'.[25] The anticommons tragedy is, in many ways, the mirror image of the commons tragedy. Anticommons property exists where multiple owners have a right to exclude others from a scarce resource, and no one has an effective privilege of use.[26] As others had already hypothesised that anticommons property might exist in theory, Heller's contributions were more nuanced.[27] First, to demonstrate how a limited number of exclusory rights would suffice to generate anticommons property; and second, to provide actual physical-world examples of anticommons property.[28]

An important differentiator between Hardin's tragedy of the commons and Heller's tragedy of the anticommons is the 'right to exclude'. As Aoki explains, in the commons tragedy, part of the problem is no one has the right to exclude, thereby giving rise to the possibility of over-utilisation and depletion.[29] By contrast, under the anticommons tragedy, too many parties independently possess the right to exclude, which gives rise to under-utilisation amounting to the tragedy of the anticommons. As the commons is defined as 'for joint use, shared; land belonging to the community', most theorists assumed the anticommons could only come into existence if every member had the right to exclude.[30] Since 'member' in this context meant any person, the requirement was thought to mean an anticommons would only occur if every single individual could prevent other uses. As a consequence, practically speaking, the anticommons under these preconditions would be virtually impossible. Given such difficult prerequisites, theorists were simply unable to conceptualise a physical world equivalent and hence did not develop the argument.[31]

Heller's insight regarding how a limited number of exclusory rights would suffice to generate anticommons property was used to demonstrate that a small number of individuals could effectively frustrate a more efficient use by others.[32] The classic example used by Heller to exemplify this phenomenon is that of the post-1989 Moscow storefronts, which remained empty while at the same time flimsy metal kiosks proliferated.[33] Kiosk vendors were required to sell goods in the cold, rather than using the empty enclosed shops behind them, as a direct consequence of the complex bundle of property rights that had been established in the transition from a socialist to a market economy. The convoluted set of divided and coordinated entitlements meant someone could always inhibit the efficient usage of the relevant property. As Heller notes: 'Once anticommons property is created, markets or governments may have difficulty in assembling rights into usable bundles. After initial entitlements are set, institutions and interests coalesce around them, with the result that the path to private property may be blocked and scarce resources may be wasted.'[34] Heller argues that in the digital information era the anticommons poses a more serious threat than the post-1989 Moscow shop fronts because the digital brand of anticommons simultaneously averts better uses of resources and conceals the recognition that better uses exist.[35] While the empty Moscow shop fronts advertise the existence of the anticommons, in the digital information anticommons the new product which might have been generated through novel use of gene fragments, for instance, is never realised.[36] In a similar vein to the tragedy of the commons, the tragedy of the anticommons makes explicit the inefficiencies of the property system whereby all can end up worse off.[37] This is particularly the case in the information environment where propertisation can actually increase transaction costs related to negotiating with multiple proprietary interests.[38] Note this is contrary to Demsetzian analysis as it relates to the physical environment.

Of course, we could theorise that *if* Adam Smith's perfect information were to exist, and *if* Coase's transaction costs were to disappear, and *if* all economic actors were perfectly rational, and *if* economic actors did not engage in strategic behaviour, then it may be possible to simply reassemble the various property entitlements into efficiently usable bundles. However, as one of Diderot's famous characters exclaimed when confronted by his master's relentless *if* questions: 'If, if, if ... if the sea boiled, there would be a lot of cooked fish!'.[39] In the physical world (with less than perfect information, real transaction costs, irrational economic actors and active strategic behaviour) the anticommons is difficult if not completely impossible to rebundle.[40]

Importantly, the tragedy of the anticommons does not suggest property will always be a tragedy. As Fennell underscores, it may be the case there are no great benefits to be had by rebundling property entitlements.[41] Unassembled pieces might be more efficient than when they are assembled, or it may simply be not worth bundling for one reason or another. The most likely scenario where a tragedy of the anticommons will eventuate is where there is a difficulty in substitution in relation to bundled property rights. To this extent, the tragedy of the anticommons can principally be perceived as an 'assembly problem'.[42]

Though the tragedy of the commons and the tragedy of the anticommons are often stylised within IPR scholarship such that property is characterised as either good or evil, the discussion above reveals the situation is more complex. Sometimes propertisation will be effective in bundling information into usable form, and sometimes the information commons will be more effective at doing so. Answering the question of when private property is effective and when it is not is fraught with difficulty. Beyond the requirement for a social net product analysis (stressed within Part I of the book) one certainty remains. A nuanced approach is required. Discussion of the semicommons is productive here because this approach seeks to move away from the pure dichotomy between private property and the commons by concerning itself with how private property and the commons *interact*. To ignore this interaction is to facilitate the tragedy of ignoring the information semicommons – a tragedy, as with all tragedies, that is best avoided.[43]

5.4 TRAGEDY OF (IGNORING) THE INFORMATION SEMICOMMONS

As we saw in Part I, information is significantly different from most tangible commodities because of its non-rival and, at least in the absence of property rights or technological measures, non-exclusive traits. Accordingly the legal structures and policy discourse surrounding information should also be different.[44] As information is a critical raw material for production in the digital information age, questions concerning the ownership of information have dramatically increased in importance.

We have previously noted there are generally two opposing viewpoints with respect to information ownership. On the one hand, IPR maximalists concentrate on private ownership (and thus private control) of information in frameworks drawn primarily from property theory.[45] On the other hand, IPR minimalists pay homage to common ownership (and thus common control) of information and highlight monopolistic characteristics of IPRs.[46] For the most part, the viewpoints of IPR maximalists and IPR minimalists are presented as a contradistinction, where private use exists at the expense of commons use and vice versa. Various themes are employed such as incentivisation through internalising externalities or exclusivity costs related to propertisation to support relatively entrenched positions.[47] IPR maximalists tend to advocate more private control, longer ownership terms and more rights in relation to information, whereas IPR minimalists generally argue the opposite.[48]

The result of this dichotomisation is that IPR debates progress from the initial understanding that commons and private usages of information are intrinsically at odds. For instance, granting longer copyright protection for information is seen as having the effect of removing that information from the information commons. Accordingly copyright protection and the information commons are perceived in mutually exclusive terms.[49] A critical thread within this debate, as evidenced by Boyle's second enclosure movement critique, is the way in which private property displaced the commons so as to purportedly make more efficient use of the resource in question.[50] The benefits of semicommons theory become apparent within this general frame: to reduce the dichotomous tendencies between private and commons-based interests and to move the focus onto the dynamic interrelationship between these interests.[51]

5.4.1 Semicommons

Heverly's arguments concerning the semicommons are built upon the respective insights of scholars such as Henry Smith and Carol Rose that all types of property contain rudiments of private and common ownership, albeit often one or the other dominates.[52] As Smith explains, a person possesses quasi-private rights to that moving spot on the highway which her vehicle occupies when driving, yet a highway is accepted as a commons because that is its more significant feature.[53] Likewise a parcel of land subject to an easement for emergency services is generally thought of as private. It is this dynamic interaction between private and common uses of resources which lies at the heart of semicommons theory.[54] Within a semicommons, property is owned and used in common for one chief purpose; however, in relation to some other crucial purpose private interests obtain property rights to separate pieces of the commons. Smith exemplifies the semicommons thus:

> The archetypal example of a semicommons is the open-field system of medieval and early modern northern Europe. In the open-field system, peasants had private property rights to the grain they grew on their individual strips of under 1 acre, which were scattered in two or three large fields around the central village. However, during certain seasons, peasants would be obligated to throw the land open to all the landowners for grazing their animals (especially sheep) in common, under a common herdsman. This enabled them to take advantage of economies of scale in grazing and private incentives in grain growing (with no important scale economies).[55]

Traditionally under the open-field system a peasant grain grower engaged in strategic behaviour by influencing, coercing or bribing the shepherd to graze flock on other private users' plots during the day (so as to avoid detrimental impact on soil from grazing) and to pen up the flock on his property at night (so as to capture benefits of fertilization from sheep droppings). To avoid this strategic behaviour, a private owner's lands were scattered throughout the designated area of the whole grazing land. The rationale of this approach was to increase the cost of engaging in strategic behaviour.[56] This occurred by making it very difficult, if not impossible, for the grazing shepherd to work out whose land the flock was either grazing upon in the day or enclosed in for the evening.[57] Since scattering created property demarcation challenges for the shepherd, agreement between the shepherd and the private user concerning strategic grazing or enclosure of the flock involved considerable transaction costs.[58] As a corollary, scattering had the effect of minimising strategic behaviour while simultaneously capturing the dynamic benefits which flowed from using the land for both private and common purposes.[59]

Although scattering may appear prima facie inefficient due to peasant farmers being required to farm in varied locations, this apparent inefficiency was in fact a source of efficiency when costs of strategic behaviour were taken into account.[60] As Smith explains, scattering of private plots, and thus private uses, was part of the overall design used to prevent strategic behaviour.[61] In this sense, it was an economically efficient, and indeed rational, method of property ownership. This is particularly the case as semicommons property ownership maximised wealth to an extent not possible under either a purely common or a purely private ownership scheme.

5.4.2 Information Semicommons

In adapting semicommons theory to the information environment, Heverly employs the 'fair use' copyright doctrine to draw attention to the dynamic interaction of private and common uses of information. The example of a standard book review within the information environment demonstrates the benefits of an information semicommons property scheme.[62] Heverly submits that a book reviewer often relies upon fair use provisions within the IPR regime to quote a book author's words for the purposes of critiquing and reviewing the book.[63] This is a classic example of an information semicommons since clearly private and common uses are interacting. This interaction is dynamic because private use affects commons use and vice versa. The benefit lies in the exposure to the public that the author receives of her book. In this regard, the fair use provisions within IPRs might be thought of as the equivalent of an easement in real property since both private and common uses are better off for the existence of the other. As Heverly states: 'If we imagine that, from its inception, Copernicus's *De Revolutionibus* was subject to pure private control to the point where all common uses were prohibited, then we begin to understand the importance of the dynamic interplay between private and common uses of information.'[64]

Examples of laws which combat the strategic behaviour of information producers include the requirement that IPRs are not automatically perpetual; and the use of definitions which set the boundaries of information protection, such as where copyright law protects particular expressions of information fixed in a tangible medium without allowing ideas to be copyrighted.[65] Fair use provisions inherent within copyright law provide yet another example of averting the strategic behaviour of information producers, since these provisions protect commons users' rights to use information to criticise information owners, even in the face of the information owners' explicit objection. Fair use provisions are in fact so fundamental to the semicommons perspective of information that Heverly suggests, at least in the US context, that information is in fact a natural semicommons.[66] This is because too much change in the landscape of fair use, and the Supreme Court may reject the changes based on the needs of the First Amendment.

Once it is accepted that the property regime of IPRs contains a host of leaks and exceptions, the application of the semicommons theory to the IPR regime is readily achieved. The application of semicommons theory to information does, however, entail a more detailed exposition of the dynamic nature of the private and common uses of information than was required for Smith's account of the semicommons in the open-field system.[67] This has typically been lacking since the efficiencies of the dynamic interaction between private and commons uses have largely been left out of debates concerning information ownership and regulation. Although a thorough social net product analysis concerning private and public costs and benefits of the information semicommons is beyond the scope of this book, it is important to recognise, as Heverly does, that in many instances information does fall within a semicommons framework. And, in at least some instances, the information semicommons is wealth maximising in that the private uses benefit the commons uses and vice versa. It is for this reason the tragedy of ignoring the information semicommons must be neutralised (as per principle 6 of Table 1.1).

The final task of the present chapter is to draw a bridge between Heverly's insights concerning the semicommons and Lessig's 'code as law' principle. Lessig's principle essentially states that controls and liberties of the information environment are governed not just by the legal framework, but also by the architecture of the digital environment.[68] By coupling Heverly's semicommons with Lessig's code-as-law perspective, it can be reasoned when regulation of information moves from the law (i.e. IPRs) to digital architecture (e.g. DRM) the possibilities of realising the efficiencies associated with a semicommons structure are diminished.[69] Accordingly if the IPR maximalist position is adopted wholesale it follows that efficiencies related to the dynamic interaction between private and commons usages are at risk of disappearing. For this reason the perpetual struggle between rights of information producers and rights of information users is best anointed through semicommons theory.[70]

Of course, Lessig's code as law principle – reflecting the idea of governance by (technological) architecture – is not new.[71] Even under the traditional open-field system of medieval Europe the semicommons was governed not just by law but also by architecture and technology. We can recall from Part I (when we discussed exclusivity and public goods) that even a fence can be conceived of as technology. However, the fact that the digital environment is fully embedded within a technological landscape potentially amplifies the effect of technological architecture.[72] DRM technology such as Digital Versatile Disc (DVD) 'content scrambling system' (CSS) encoding exemplifies this technological architecture paradigm. In deploying a variety of technological fixes, TPMs create absolute bars against (so-called) strategic behaviour by consumers.[73] But the latent risk here is that the focus remains on the avoidance of (so-called) strategic behaviour of would-be consumers (e.g. illegal downloading) without any acknowledgment of benefits which flow from the dynamic interaction between private and commons usages.[74] It is precisely in this way the semicommons efficiency equation often becomes unjustly skewed towards private property. And this skew, in turn, fosters the tragedy of (ignoring) the information semicommons.

5.5 CONCLUSION

Application of environmental analytical frameworks such as the commons to the information environment assists with the conceptual resolution of challenges arising within the IPR regulatory framework. By engaging with commons tragedy discourse, this chapter has promoted the idea that IPR dialogue move beyond a private property/commons dichotomy towards a more nuanced dialogue which recognises the efficiencies arising from the dynamic interaction between private and commons usages of informational resources. Differing ways of using information need not be mutually exclusive and can in fact spawn mutual benefits. This is why, wherever possible, it is important to neutralise the tragedy of ignoring the information semicommons (as per principle 6 of Table 1.1). To be sure, it is difficult working out whether particular information resources should be private or public; free or controlled; or rather whether information should be governed through a combination of ownership and/or regulation traits. However, one thing remains clear – the information environment would be massively depleted of exchanges if a society did not make some arrangement for an information commons. The remainder of the book will discuss some alternate governance options available in this respect. But we should bear in mind that a critical prerequisite when considering these options is the neutralisation of the tragedy of (ignoring) the information semicommons. This tragedy is by no means inevitable. Indeed, Carol Rose suggests if appropriate institutional arrangements are struck with respect to the information environment the results can be truly 'comedic' ... in the classic sense of a happy outcome.[75] It is this ongoing search for 'appropriate institutional arrangements' that underpins the integrated information environmental governance framework project (outlined in Table 1.1 and elsewhere). The chapter has demonstrated the importance of breaking down the dichotomy between private and commons usages of information. Another aspect of this ongoing search for appropriate institutional arrangements is exploring alternative governance options other than propertisation, which is a core remit of Part III.

PART III

Ecology

When thinking about how ecology relates to the information environment there are numerous approaches that could be adopted. On the practical front, Article 27 of TRIPS and the 'patenting of life' provides rich terrain for scholars interested in the interface between IPRs and ecology through exploration of biotechnological initiatives. The Convention on Biological Diversity also provides an important springboard to discuss the relationship between IPRs, particularly technology transfer, and ecology.[1] Moreover it would be possible to explore how IPRs interface with 'green technology', which holds promise to improve environmental outcomes.[2] In this book, however, we are not concerned with practical linkages between IPRs and ecology so much as theoretical linkages. This approach is built upon the Kurt Lewin premise that 'there is nothing quite as practical as good theory'.[3] 'Good', of course, being the operative word. On the theoretical front we have already seen the dominant method of regulating the information environment is propertisation. However, private property represents just one method of regulation/governance.

When observing IPRs through a broader governance frame the limitations of private property as a governance mechanism become apparent. For example, the welfare economic analysis in Part I highlighted the exclusivity costs associated with private property; and the discourse in Part II concerning the information commons reminded that the private propertisation of information must be situated within an information commons landscape. In Part III, by applying the ecology analytical framework to the information environment, we will see the utility of broadening the governance options of the information environment. To this end, Chapter 6 will distil ecological governance principles such as resilience, diversity and modularity. Chapter 7 will build upon the ecological governance approach by wrestling with the normatively fuelled rhetorical question of whether the information commons should have standing. And Chapter 8 will traverse the information environmental governance framework imperatives of rational truths, reasonable arguments and rhetorical imagination.

We will see in Part III that the theoretical application of ecology to the information environment is part of a broader project of developing an integrated information environmental governance framework. This framework, which is summarised in Table 1.1, is useful in expanding the governance and policy options concerning the regulation or otherwise of the information environment.

6. The social ecology of information environmental governance

The thinking for the future has to be loyal to nature.

Arne Naess

6.1 INTRODUCTION

Just as ecologists recognise that minor changes in the physical environment may produce effects that reverberate through species, food chains and habitats, ultimately disrupting larger patterns of sustainability, changes in the regulatory framework of the information environment may lead to large disruptions in the ecology of creative culture and innovation.[1] As both the physical environment and the information environment can be perceived as macro systems, it follows that each respective system can move to new equilibriums as a consequence of feedback mechanisms.[2] By drawing upon ecological governance principles this chapter explores the interaction between equilibrium and feedback.

The chapter begins by situating ecology within an information environmental context. Defining ecology and exploring the 'methodological interrelational' dimensions of ecological thinking is part of this discussion. The chapter will then explore an empirically based information environmental discipline, which is referred to as 'information ecology'. This will be followed by the application of the precautionary principle to the information environment. More often than not principles such as the precautionary principle are founded upon an ethical foundation. For this reason the chapter seeks to build information environmental governance principles upon the foundation of an 'information environmental ethic'. This ethic imports the ecological governance principles of resilience, diversity and modularity. The application of these principles to the information environment will be contextualised with reference to the FLOSS production mode. The chapter will conclude by addressing the question of whether IPRs are diversifying or homogenising.

6.2 *OIKOS LOGOS*: STUDY OF LIFE AT HOME

At first glance destruction of the physical environment may seem much more serious than degradation of the information environment. Yet deeper contemplation reveals the dichotomy between the physical environment and the informational environment is not so neat.[3] The root cause of physical environmental destruction and information environment degradation is the failure of social and legal institutions to mediate an appropriate balance between private and public concerns.[4] Furthermore, in the contemporary information age, the health of the information environment is likely to have significant impacts upon the physical environment. In this way, the information environment can be thought of as a critical corrective springboard upon which to preserve the physical environment. This interrelationship between the physical environment and the information environment is ignored at our peril.

Although the interrelationship between the physical environment and the information environment is significant, the linkage has a strong metaphorical component. In this regard Justice Cardozo once hazarded that 'metaphors in law are to be narrowly watched, for starting out as liberators of thought they end often by enslaving it'.[5] Along with narrowly watching metaphors in law, it is also imperative within Part III that we narrowly watch the application of ecology to social systems such as the information environment. This is because, relying upon ecology to advance political claims – such that the state should be mindful of overreaching in its provision of IPRs – brings with it inherent dangers. In particular, ecology is an ideological battleground which has been employed across the political spectrum to advance a variety of ideologically fuelled assertions.[6]

Everyone from Charles Darwin to Pyotr Kropotkin to Adolf Hitler has relied upon ecology in one form or another to support a particular view of both individuals and society.[7] Contemporaneously, the politically heated nature of ecology is particularly apparent within the climate change issue where the ecology discipline has been deployed to advance political agendas across the ideological continuum. In many respects these ideological tensions within ecology reflect older, broader tensions inherent within jurisprudential natural law discourse.[8] In light of these age-old tensions, the present chapter concentrates on the ecological governance dimensions of ecology rather than the pure politics of the ecology discipline. Defining and outlining ecology is a prerequisite of this ecological governance discussion.

6.2.1 Ecological Science and Ecological Ethics

The word ecology stems from the convergence of two Greek notions being those of *oikos* (relating to household) and *logos* (relating to study).[9] Hence, literally speaking, ecology is the study of 'life at home'. This accords with its contemporary usage provided that an expansive perspective of 'home' is adopted (i.e. earth). More formalised definitions of ecology, along with prevailing ecology scholarship, tend to implicate two broad streams: ecological science and ecological ethics.[10] For example, the *Collins English Dictionary* defines ecology as 'the set of relationships of a particular organism with its environment' (roughly equating to ecological science).[11] This definition sits alongside the following complementary definition: 'the study of the relationships between human groups and their physical environment' (equating generally to ecological ethics).[12]

Ecological scientists have traditionally been concerned with the interrelationship between living things as they appear within the 'economy of nature'. In contrast, ecological ethicists have been primarily interested in espousing how human beings should live as part of nature (rather than simply describing it).[13] In discussing the history of ecology, and referring to ecological ethicists as 'romantics', Bate suggests that '[s]cientists made it their business to describe the intricate economy of nature; romantics made it theirs to teach human beings how to live as part of it'.[14] In this sense, ecological scientists have tended towards objectivity and positivist thought whereas ecological ethicists have tended towards subjectivity and normative thought.

Dichotomising ecological science and ecological ethics underscores that ecological thinking involves not only the study of the 'real' or tangibly physical environment, but also how different groups and individuals *perceive* that environment.[15] Typically such perception is coloured by economically, socially and culturally based presuppositions.[16] The relationship between humans and nature is defined not by what is 'out there' so much as how humans perceive it. As David Pepper has noted the perception of humans is a function of their 'cultural filter' and the associated assumptions:

> Man consciously responds to his environment as he perceives it: the perceived environment will usually contain some but not all of the relevant parts of the real environment, and may well contain elements imagined by man and not present in the real environment … The real environment … is seen through a cultural filter, made up of attitudes, limits set by observation techniques, and past experience. By studying the filter and reconstructing the perceived

> environment the observer is able to explain particular options and actions on the part of the group being studied.[17]

Both 'ecological science' and 'ecological ethics' can be thought of as 'cultural filters' that colour perception of the natural world. Contrast between these respective cultural filters is best thought of in terms of tendencies rather than absolutes. Each school of thought overlaps and intertwines with the other.[18] Kropotkin's *Mutual Aid*, for example, can be classified within either an ecological science or ecological ethic perspective.[19] Moreover, on a purely practical level, it was not unusual during the eighteenth and nineteenth centuries for artists (who were often motivated by an ecological ethic or Romantic concerns of the day) to accompany ecological scientists such as geologists, botanists and phytogeographers into the wilderness to record and discover discrete aspects of nature.[20]

6.2.2 Interrelationalism and Systems Theory

Along with ecological science and ecological ethic components of ecology, the *Collins English Dictionary* also defines the term with implicit reference to *interrelational* dimensions of the physical environment by stating that ecology is 'the study of the *relationships* between living organisms and their environment'.[21] Interrelationalism, and the corresponding understandings of systems, is a key insight of ecology. This is particularly so when applying ecology to social systems such as the information environment.

Contemporary understandings of interrelationalism principally stems from ecological scientific insights of the physical environment developed over the last several centuries.[22] Throughout this timeframe the natural world came to be seen as a set of interrelated environments. While indigenous knowledge of the natural world stretches back to time immemorial it was only during the seventeenth and eighteenth centuries that the physical environment became an object of Western scientific discovery.[23] During this era a science of natural history evolved such that a unique and universal language for ordering form was developed. This language fostered the growth of taxonomical methods, which in turn led to the cataloguing of potentially useful discoveries.[24] Scientific division of the world into global vegetation zones by scientists such as Darwin and Humboldt was a hallmark of this discovery process.[25] The result, by the end of the nineteenth century, was an abundant collection of observations and descriptions of the physical environment. The evolving phytogeographical terminology and language, coupled with the cataloguing of exotic organisms, fostered a nuanced appreciation of the natural world as a set of interrelated environments.[26]

An important aspect of interrelationalism is the interaction between natural systems. Formal study of this interaction is often referred to as 'systems theory'.[27] This theory embodies an anti-reductionist, holistic approach to the physical environment. Theoretical thinking in relation to systems formally emerged during the 1960s through a confluence of ecology and economic theory alongside emerging understandings of population dynamics.[28] Implicitly or explicitly, ecologists tend to draw upon systems theory when studying how individual parts of an ecosystem relate to each other and how one ecosystem relates to another ecosystem.[29] Bramwell has discussed the dynamic interplay between ecology and systems theory with reference to 'energy flows within a closed system':

> The normative sense of the word [ecology] has come to mean the belief that severe or drastic change within that system, or indeed any change which can damage any species within it, or that disturbs that system, is seen as wrong. Thus ecological ideas have come to be associated with the conservation of specific patterns of energy flows. These patterns can be relatively small in scale, such as a one acre wet-land site; or it can be the weather pattern resulting from the Amazon rain forests, or larger patterns that affect the continuity of human existence.[30]

A crucial aspect of systems theory is moving beyond the exploration of various component parts of a system as they operate in isolation, rather focusing on how the system works together as a whole.[31] In this respect, the principle of interrelatedness and the accompanying systems theory pervade most aspects of ecological thinking.[32] This was evident from the early days of ecology at which time there was a systematic focus on how populations and communities relate to each other and the environment.[33] Such holistic, interrelational approaches were to a large extent a reaction to the reductionist and empirical scientific methods which developed between the fifteenth and nineteenth centuries. Pertinently this reductionist approach severed the relationship between humans and nature, enabling humans to exploit nature more voraciously than they could in the past.[34]

6.2.3 Methodological Interrelationalism

As the information environment is a social system, this book is primarily concerned with how interrelationalism applies to the social domain.

Although understandings of interrelationalism within Western thought stem primarily from the study of the natural world over the last few centuries, there is a long tradition of applying the concept to the social realm. Aristotle referred to a variant of interrelationalism to argue that it could form the basis of a stable social life where persons are bound together through webs of mutual reliance that constitute economic activity.[35] Pufendorf also drew upon this aspect of Aristotle's thinking within his work.[36]

In applying ecology to social systems, Carter stylises the interrelational aspect of the physical environment by contrasting individualism, collectivism and interrelationalism.[37] This contrast is built upon 'methodological interrelationalism', which is an effective approach in overcoming what Carter refers to as the 'individualist fallacy' and the 'collectivist fallacy':

> The methodological individualist is in error when he or she omits relevant relational features. I shall call this error 'the individualist fallacy'. At the other extreme, the illicit attempt to explain certain facts about social individuals in terms of their relations to the totality of which they are a part, I shall call 'the collectivist fallacy'.[38]

Appreciating the effect of these fallacies is an important part of understanding interrelationalism. With respect to the physical environment, the individualist fallacy can be portrayed with reference to the reductionist tendencies of Baconian 'cause and effect' science. According to this brand of science, ecosystems are understood through studying individual members of a species outside of their relations to others within their wider environment. On the other hand, the collectivist fallacy correlates with the tendency to make false connections between wholes and their parts.[39]

In applying Carter's methodological interrelationalism to the information environment, we can map the individualist fallacy to authorial/inventive romance. As we saw in the introductory chapter, this romance underpins the IPR maximalist position by ignoring or understating the social dimensions of creativity and innovation. In parallel the IPR minimalist position is sometimes guilty of the collectivist fallacy when it seeks to rely on social production methods (such as FLOSS) to draw out conclusions about the information environment as a whole. While some forms of creativity and innovation can be explained with reference to social production methods, these explanations cannot necessarily be conflated across the entire information environment without committing the collectivist fallacy.

Thus, application of methodological interrelationalism to the information environment simultaneously hazards against both conflating the role of authorial (inventive) romance and assuming all informational production can take place within a social production framework. The strength of methodological interrelationalism and the accompanying understandings of systems theory is that the individual fallacy and collectivist fallacy can be circumvented. This is because methodological interrelationalism focuses on how individual parts of a system relate to each other while also simultaneously recognising these relations constitute a system.[40] Semicommons theory, discussed within Part II, implicitly adopted this methodological interrelationalist perspective by focusing on both private property and the commons, along with the dynamic efficiencies that exist between them.

More could be discussed with respect to the application of ecology to social systems but the focus here is on the implications of applying ecological governance to the information environment.[41] To this end, one of the key insights revealed when applying methodological interrelationalism to the physical environment is the symbiotic relationship between empirical knowledge and the development of governance principles. That is, as ecological science and related fields of knowledge such as interrelationalism and systems theory have evolved, so too have related governance principles relating to the physical environment.[42] This insight is further explored below with reference to the proposed information environmental discipline of 'information ecology', which in turn is framed within the broader context of information environmental governance.

6.3 INFORMATION ENVIRONMENTAL GOVERNANCE

A critical aspect of information environmentalism is the development of an information environmental governance framework. By reflecting upon ecology, we can note empirical knowledge within ecological science has been established through a range of methodologies and techniques. For instance, at times the focus has been on species across geography and timeframes (e.g. bees or ants) and at other times ecology has studied ecosystems confined to a specific geographical location (e.g. forest or lake). Through these studies, critical understandings about biodiversity (or the lack thereof) have led to the enactment of generalised governance principles related to, for example, 'threatened species'. The precautionary principle discussed further below is one of many exemplars.

Thinking about applying ecology to the information environment in these terms underscores several intertwined themes. First, it is imperative to develop an empirically based discipline related to the information environment. This discipline might be akin to ecology as it concerns the physical environment. It will be referred to as 'information ecology'. Second, the information environment requires governance principles, an example being the precautionary principle. Such information environmental governance principles would stem from empirical foundations of information ecology. Third, by way of providing a springboard for information environmental governance principles, there is a need for a coherent 'information environmental ethic'. We will now discuss these three themes respectively so as to advance the project of constructing an integrated information environmental governance framework.

6.3.1 Information Ecology: A Discipline

Just as ecological science and related sub-disciplines have advanced the study of the physical environment, it is also normatively necessary to develop a parallel discipline to ecology that focuses on the information environment. The role of this discipline – henceforth referred to as 'information ecology' – would be to provide a foundation of empirical knowledge concerning the health and well-being of discrete systems within the information environment and of the information environment as a whole.[43] This appeal for a sturdier empirical foundation to IPRs is not new. Over two decades ago, Ricketson put forth a strong case for more empirical evidence with respect to copyright policy development:

> [W]hat is required, therefore, are national and international studies that seek to ascertain, on a factual basis, the appropriate term for copyright protection, a kind of cost/benefit approach that seeks to evaluate the public and private costs and benefits of different terms of protection.[44]

Ricketson's plea has not been ignored to the extent that in recent years there has been a burgeoning of empirical studies related to IPRs.[45] However, it is still the case that much of the empirical evidence related to IPRs is established on a piecemeal basis. Also, there is a lack of systemisation in ordering the evidence which is collated. The information ecology discipline would thus serve not only to advance the empirical study of the information environment but it would also assist with ordering and systemising knowledge in a more coherent and usable form. When IPRs textbooks initially emerged the discipline was considered somewhat novel.[46] Now is the time to contemplate the creation of an information ecology discipline, which would also spawn its own disciplinary textbooks.

Of course, there is no one approach to the systemisation of empirical knowledge relating to the information environment. Numerous methods could be adopted in deciphering subsystems which constitute the information environment as a whole. It would be possible to speak of the IPR subsystems of patents, copyrights, trademarks, design, etc. but equally possible would be to divide the IPR domain into industries such as computer science, biotechnology, pharmaceuticals, film, music, etc.[47] Various attempts have already begun in this respect within IPR scholarship, particularly in relation to the public domain.[48] These attempts suggest the embryo of a formalised information ecology discipline is already in the making.

It lies beyond the scope of this book to resolve precisely how the information environment might be systematically studied and analysed within the formalised information ecology discipline. This is a task for a future research project. But in some ways the study of IPR as a whole implicitly engages with this project already and no doubt various approaches will continue to evolve over time akin to the manner in which ecological science has developed. The point here is that a discipline needs a name and a body of systemised knowledge. Information ecology is a feasible suggestion.

6.3.2 Precautionary Principle and the Alchemy of Risk

Methodological interrelationalism underscores that there is a symbiotic relationship between empirical knowledge and governance principles. Along with the requirement for a more formalised information ecology discipline, there is also a need for the development of distinct governance principles that would apply to the information environment. To explain, even with the advent of information ecology (which would ultimately seek to systemise and further empirical studies of the information environment) it would remain either difficult or impossible to make firm determinations about the effect of particular forms of information regulation in all circumstances. Thus what is required is not just systemised empirical evidence, although this is vital to evidence-based decision making, but also a set of information environmental governance principles which can be relied upon when formulating IPR policy.

To be sure, principles can change as empirical evidence amasses and becomes further systemised. But in light of the fact that empirical knowledge will always be somewhat incomplete, governance principles can at least provide a policy compass suggesting the correct direction in which to travel.[49] The precautionary principle as it relates to the physical environment has been critical in this regard. As a legal construct the precautionary principle stems from a notion found in German administrative law known as 'Vorsorgeprinzip', which literally translates as the 'principle of prior care and worry'.[50] Although the precautionary principle meandered into several international environmentally related institutional mechanisms during the 1980s it did not gain prominence until the Rio Earth Summit in 1992 at which time it was embodied in Principle 15 of the so-called Rio Declaration: 'In order to protect the environment, the precautionary approach should be widely applied by States according to their capabilities. Where there are threats of serious and irreversible damage, lack of full scientific certainty shall not be used as a reason for postponing cost-effective measures to prevent environmental degradation.'[51]

The precautionary principle has often taken centre stage within negotiations concerning international environmental agreements. However, from a governance perspective its greatest influence is perhaps on the practical front where it has had the effect of shifting the burden of proof. This shift ensures persons taking action have the onus of proving that the action itself is not harmful. A practical manifestation of the precautionary principle is Environmental Impact Statements (EIS) where developers are required to provide concrete evidence of the potential effect of development on the physical environment.

When applying the precautionary principle to the information environment, it might operate by mandating that IPRs be generally avoided in the absence of clear evidence confirming IPRs will not inflict undue damage on the information environment and/or the information commons. In practical terms, this could involve the development of an information Environmental Impact Statement (iEIS) process.[52] Such a process would require a patent holder, for instance, to submit an independently audited iEIS along with a patent application.[53] An iEIS would be particularly relevant to 'sensitive subsystems' of the information environment (e.g. patenting of life, research databases, etc).

The purpose of an iEIS would be to shift the onus on to the patent holder to explicitly demonstrate the patent in question is not detrimental to the information environment and/or the information commons.[54] Obviously, the manifestation of an iEIS process would involve the identification of 'sensitive areas' of the information environment. While such identification may appear overly conjectural it would not differ greatly from the procedures which have emerged to identify sensitive ecosystems within the physical environment. The adoption of the iEIS process would rest upon the formal discipline of information ecology along with an accompanying iEIS audit profession that would be constructed along the lines of the accounting profession.[55]

Putting aside the more practical consequences of applying the precautionary principle to the information environment, the question remains as to whether the principle has any governance insights on the theoretical front. In governance terms, and in one word, the precautionary principle is ultimately concerned with 'risk'. Rutherford explains that it is risk which allows for the physical environment to become 'thinkable' and therefore subject to political deliberation.[56] In this context, he states: 'the relationship of society to the natural environment is conceived in terms of the language of security and risk; ecological hazards and insecurity must be addressed by putting in place behaviours that minimise risk'.[57] The work of Ulrich Beck in relation to the alchemic characteristics of risk is particularly insightful in this connection:

> Risk opens the opportunity to document statistical consequences that at first were always personalized and shifted onto individuals. In this way risk de-individualizes. Risks are revealed as systematic events, which are accordingly in need of general political regulation ... A field for corresponding political action is opened up: accidents on the job for instance, are not blamed on those whose health they have already ruined anyway, but are stripped of their individual origin and related instead to plant organization, the lack of precautions, and so on.[58]

According to Beck's analysis, although risk is a corollary of scientific and technological expansion, considerations of risk are influenced 'not only by recognised scientific expertise but also by the "counter-expertise" of citizen activists and ecologists who have developed a sustained critique of the application of technology and the potential devastation of the environment'.[59] In many respects the 'counter-expertise' in relation to IPRs has begun to play an important role in militating against real and perceived risks within the information environment. Recent responses by 'counter-experts' to initiatives such as the Stop Online Piracy Act (SOPA) and the Protect IP Act (PIPA) in the US provide a case in point.[60] But such counter-expert claims give rise to a fundamental question: What are the actual *risks* inherent within the information environment? Though the information environment would exist even in the absence of regulation, many of the risks associated with the information environment actually stem from the regulation itself (i.e. IPRs).[61] In order to determine the inherent risks within the information environment it is therefore necessary to recall the purpose of IPRs, which underpin the regulatory framework of the information environment.

The core objective of IPRs, alongside the incentivisation and reward for creativity and innovation, is the facilitation of creativity and innovation for the benefit of the public at large.[62] Hence, simply put, the risk associated with IPRs is that the regulatory framework moves the information environment to a new equilibrium such that creativity and innovation are no longer facilitated for *public benefit*. As implied at the beginning of this chapter, although the concept of risk may seem more serious as it relates to the physical environment than it does with respect to the information environment, risk within both respective environments stems from a common failure of social and legal institutions to mediate an appropriate balance between private and public considerations.[63]

Building upon Leopold's land ethic alluded to in the introductory chapter, one method of counteracting the inherent risks within the information environment would be to construct and subscribe to an information environmental ethic.[64]

6.3.3 Information Environmental Ethic

Symbiosis between empirical knowledge and governance principles with respect to the physical environment largely maps to the interrelationship between ecological science and ecological ethics. To elaborate, as ecological science developed, these new scientific understandings of the natural world fed into the ecological ethic perspectives concerning how human beings should relate to the physical environment. To this extent when Aldo Leopold pronounced his 'land ethic' in *A Sand County Almanac* in 1949 he was building upon a rich body of ecological science that preceded him. While Leopold's land ethic was embedded within a complete work, it will be recalled from the introductory chapter that it is most often condensed in the following terms: 'A thing is right when it tends to preserve the integrity, stability, and beauty of the biotic community. It is wrong when it tends otherwise.'[65] Much can be relayed concerning Leopold's land ethic. To begin with, in its stated form, it is very short and extremely general. However, it has come to symbolise a vast array of literature relating to the physical environment. To this end the rhetorical and practical power of it should not be underestimated. Within the context of the present discussion there are three distinct observations to note about Leopold's land ethic. First, the land ethic was foundational in supporting claims for more empirical knowledge in relation to the physical environment. To this end, the ethic actually initiated a new 'science of wildlife management'.[66] This standpoint supports advocacy of the information ecology discipline above and little more will be said about this but for a short passage in Chapter 8 concerning rational truths. Second, the land ethic provided rhetorical support, along with other key subsequent publications such as Rachel Carson's *Silent Spring*, for the rights movement as it relates to nature. This in turn contributed to the philosophical foundation of environmental law (as it came to be known).[67] We will discuss this in Chapter 7 with reference to a thought experiment relating to the allocation of rights and the provisioning of standing to the information commons (i.e. ICRs). Third, Leopold's land ethic can be thought of as a precursor to the more formalised, institutionally embedded precautionary principle, which has had a significant influence over ecological governance during the last several decades. Extending this theme as it relates to the information environment, an information environmental ethic is a prerequisite for a more formalised institutional mechanism for protecting the information commons in the future.[68] For the sake of argument such an information environment ethic might read as follows: A thing is right when it tends to preserve the resilience, diversity, and modularity of the information environment. It is wrong when it tends otherwise.

Exploring resilience and the related concepts of diversity and modularity is the selected method of further advancing this proposed information environmental ethic.

6.3.3.1 Resilience, diversity and modularity

Resilience reflects the capacity of a system to absorb new entrants and retain its basic function and structure or perhaps recover after disturbance.[69] Thus resilience relates to the information environment because it speaks to the level of disturbance that can be sustained and absorbed before a change in system control or structure occurs.[70] The nexus between interrelationalism and resilience is governed by the fact that the former speaks to connections between things, whereas the latter speaks to the strength of those connections. Numerous studies of social-ecological systems indicate there are several important elements relating to maintenance of resilience within systems, the most important being diversity and modularity.[71]

The essence of diversity relates to the numerical variety of species, people and institutions which operate within a social-ecological system.[72] The more diverse a system is the more likely that the system will be stable over time and therefore resilient.[73] Of course, as with any principle, there are exceptions. So, for example, with reference to the physical environment if a thousand different species are artificially introduced into an ecosystem overnight then theoretically that ecosystem becomes more diverse in the short term by virtue of the introduced species.[74] Yet it may be that the introduction of these species over time reduces overall diversity within the ecosystem. If this is so then the effect of the introduction of the new species is homogenising. The real question is, from varying temporal and geographical perspectives, whether the introduction of new species within an ecosystem leads to a tendency towards diversification or homogenisation within the related system.

Thinking about agriculture, which is coincidentally highly related to IPRs such as patents and plant breeding rights, is one method of conceptualising the significance of *diversity* within social systems such as the information environment.[75] As Carson underscored in *Silent Spring*, prior to modern intensification of agriculture the farmer generally had few insect problems.[76] As agriculture intensified the general inclination was to move towards single-crop farming whereby large tracts of land were dedicated to the one type of crop. From an ecological perspective this trend is problematic in that nature has historically gone to great trouble to introduce significant diversity into natural landscapes. By homogenising nature through agricultural practices humans have either consciously or unconsciously set about undermining the 'built-in checks and balances by which nature holds the species within bounds'.[77] Carson explained:

> One important natural check is a limit on the amount of suitable habitat for each species. Obviously then, an insect that lives on wheat can build up its population to much higher levels on a farm devoted to wheat than on one in which wheat is intermingled with other crops to which the insect is not adapted.[78]

Useful insights in relation to diversity can also be garnered from mature ecosystems such as the Appalachian forests. One of the features of such ecosystems is that high level of diversity leads to high levels of organisation, which in turn minimises entropy within the system.[79] Because mature ecosystems contain an abundance of species, more niches within the system are occupied. Therefore the system as a whole has a greater capacity when contrasted with immature ecosystems to 'capture matter and slow down energy dissipation'.[80] In this sense there is a strong nexus between diversity and stability. Diverse systems inherently contain greater resilience in the event of changing environmental influences. That is, the correlation between diversity and stability implies a high level of organisational efficiency and a tendency towards temporal equilibrium.[81]

There are various methods of incorporating understandings of diversity within social systems. For example in the economic domain the principle of diversity manifests to some extent within competition policy, which generally looks disfavourably upon economic organisation that homogenises rather than diversifies. However, the question remains: how does this discussion of diversity relate specifically to the information environment? Based on the understanding that monoculture within agriculture facilitates homogenisation, the key query with respect to diversity is whether IPRs have a similar effect in relation to the information environment.[82] The discussion in Part I concerning the internalisation of positive externalities through IPRs, and more specifically the monopolistic characteristics of IPRs, highlights that there is some cause for concern in this respect.

The crux is that although efficiency is seductive, especially in the short term, ecology underscores that the more one seeks to optimise elements of a complex system, whether that system relates to nature or social systems such as the information environment, the less resilient the relevant system becomes.[83] The drive for an 'efficient optimal state outcome' leaves a system vulnerable to shocks and disturbances.[84] It is for this reason that Gunderson and Holling in their exposition of cycle phases of systems state: 'the cost of efficiency is a loss in flexibility'.[85] Although their conclusion may initially seem counterintuitive – efficiency is almost always perceived as a positive characteristic – it is the central deduction of numerous studies that have sought to explore how social-ecological systems transform over time.[86] If ecology teaches nothing else it is that uniformity and homogeneity are ultimately unstable in the long term.[87] To reinforce the point, the fixation of IPRs on internalising positive externalities, alongside the monopolistic characteristics of IPRs, implies that IPRs may be seeking an efficient optimal state outcome that will undermine resilience and foster inefficiency and instability over time.

The 'just-in-time' inventory approach, which is often advocated within managerial economics, provides a practical example of this tension between resilience and efficiency within the social-economic domain.[88] The core idea underpinning just-in-time is that ensuring parts and supplies arrive at the factory or retail outlet at the precise time in which they are required will reduce storage costs. While this *modus operandi* stemming from efficient optimal state outcome can reduce costs in relation to inventory it is also considerably vulnerable to shocks and disturbances.[89] This in turn can lead to severe industry dislocations when problems emerge along the supply chain. Thus, we can see the drive for efficiency can indirectly undermine resilience and foster significant inefficiencies and instability from a temporal perspective. Exploration of diversity raises a key question: What shocks and disturbances might result from the homogenisation of the information environment?[90]

The question of diversity will be further explored in Part IV within the context of public choice theory. For now the book turns to a discussion of modularity. Before doing so, however, a quick summary of the content covered in the chapter thus far is likely beneficial. Early in the chapter the discussion turned to the interrelational aspects of ecology. We saw that interrelational thinking is often coupled with systems theory. Together these methodological interrelationalist attributes of ecological science provide the foundation for a body of empirical knowledge, which in turn led to governance principles that flow from and interact with this knowledge.[91] An ethic of one description or another typically underpins governance principles. For instance, in the context of the physical environment Aldo Leopold's land ethic was foundational to the precautionary principle. As both Leopold's land ethic and the precautionary principle have played an important role with respect to the physical environment, the chapter has briefly explored metaphorical application of equivalent principles within the information environment. For the sake of argument, the chapter has posited an information environment ethic, a core aspect of which is resilience and the related notions of diversity and modularity. The fundamental lesson stemming from diversity is that homogeneous systems are generally unstable in the long term. So what is modularity and how might it apply to the information environment?

Reflecting upon earlier discussions of interrelationalism and resilience, we can note that interrelationalism does not of and by itself facilitate resilience. Rather, resilience stems from related characteristics such as diversity and modularity. Thus, along with diversity, modularity is also an important component of resilience. Modularity refers to the manner in which the components of a given system are linked to one another.[92] If a system is highly connected (that is, interrelational) it stands to reason disturbances within one part of the system are likely to affect the system as a whole.[93] On the other hand, if a system is modular it means the system can generally function effectively even when modules within that system fail. On a spectrum a modular system is less interrelational than a non-modular system. In this regard there is a tension within systems between interrelationalism and modularity. This is because interrelationalism is concerned with the connection between things, whereas modularity refers to the situation where part of a system can function even when other parts of the system fail.

The core features of a modular system are decentralisation, self-organisation and strong feedback loops.[94] These features give a modular system a greater capacity than a non-modular system to absorb shocks and disturbances. This is because the decentralised nature of a modular system, coupled with the accompanying self-organisation and feedback characteristics, mean that any latent risks that emerge with respect to the system violating a 'relevant threshold' are fed back into the system allowing for the system to 'self-correct'.[95] In contrast, centralised governance is inherently non-modular and exhibits weaker feedback loops.[96] This means that a centralised governance system is more likely to cross a relevant threshold without the risk of such being fed back into the system in a timely fashion. The implication being 'system failure' will result from violations of the relevant threshold.

In other words when a system is centralised and therefore less modular it is more likely it will violate relevant thresholds without corresponding feedback. This in turn increases the risk of system failure. The extinction of a 'key species' exemplifies the crossing of a relevant threshold within the physical environment because the removal of a key species within an ecosystem poses system failure risk such that the ecosystem in question may collapse.[97] Hypothetically speaking, with respect to the information environment, system failure might equate to collapse in public benefit-inspired creativity and innovation.

6.3.3.2 FLOSS

One method of explicitly applying resilience to the information environment is to contemplate the FLOSS production mode, because FLOSS embeds the resilience characteristics of diversity and modularity.[98] Moreover, FLOSS remains central to the imaginary landscape of information environmentalism. Abundant discussion of FLOSS takes place elsewhere.[99] For now we can think of FLOSS as a type of software production that evolved during the mid-1980s in direct response to proprietary, closed source software production methods. A key contrast between closed source and open source is the release of code, which is the programming language that computer software engineers rely upon to create software products.[100]

As will be explored in Part IV, FLOSS facilitates diversity because it relies upon an unbounded access of agents to resources and agents rather than limiting possibilities through the binding nature of contract and property.[101] Modular aspects of FLOSS require a lengthier explanation. The starting point here is that modularity is generally present within FLOSS projects because unless it exists in some shape or form then FLOSS production methods are unlikely to manifest in the first instance.[102] In other words, one of the reasons why FLOSS works is that it divides projects into asynchronous components.[103] This in turn allows individuals to choose independently from each other how and when they contribute to the project in question. If we extend the application of modularity to the information environment we find that there are three modular-related characteristics inherent within FLOSS: *decentralisation, self-organisation and strong feedback loops*. These characteristics of FLOSS need to be further elaborated upon.

Decentralisation is the first port of call. In the context of proprietary software, enhancements and the fixing of software bugs are entirely dependent upon the schedule and employees of a single centralised firm such as Microsoft. To the contrary, under the FLOSS model a plethora of decentralised software development communities, connected via the Internet around the world, are available to freely and willingly provide enhancements and bug fixes.[104] If these communities are not satisfied with the pace or performance of the production in question they have access to the code so they can improve or rectify as is seen fit.[105] Activity occurs primarily through decentralised convergence of wills rather than centralised command and control.[106] This perspective of FLOSS was emphasised by Eric Raymond in *The Cathedral and the Bazaar* with reference to the following decentralist sentiments of Kropotkin:

> Having been brought up in a serf-owner's family, I entered active life, like all young men of my time, with a great deal of confidence in the necessity of commanding, ordering, scolding, punishing and the like. But when, at an early stage, I had to manage serious enterprises … I began to appreciate the difference between acting on the principle of command and discipline and acting on the principle of common understanding. The former works admirably in a military parade, but it is worth nothing where real life is concerned, and the aim can be achieved only through the severe effort of many converging wills.[107]

Secondly, with regard to the related notion of self-organisation, FLOSS projects are generally facilitated via the original software developer or a small group of interested programmers who typically act as a de facto project manager.[108] Although the project manager exerts considerable influence over a FLOSS project by determining what new code will be incorporated into the evolving software program, this process is dominated by self-organisation to the extent it is a decentralised network of interested programmers that are generating the new enhancements, extensions or improvements.[109] This *modus operandi* is to be distinguished from closed source software production where, as indicated above, the schedule of work is dominated by the hierarchical governance structure inherent within the firm. It is not that no organisation exists within FLOSS, it is rather the nature of the organisational form differs from closed source in terms of who leads the organisational structure and how. To this end, FLOSS is essentially built upon self-organisation.

Thirdly, with respect to feedback, one of the reasons why FLOSS continually evolves and improves is because it is easy to access source code. This in turn fosters an accompanying feedback loop, which facilitates efficient detection of bugs and security problems and therefore enhances positive evolution of a FLOSS product.[110] Feedback is an important part of this process because under the FLOSS development model the typical arrangement is for a community of developers to engage with source code so as to create extensions, enhancements and improvements.[111] These are in turn fed back freely into the community so as to be further enhanced, extended and improved.[112] Therefore, strong feedback is an essential element of FLOSS production.

6.3.4 Intellectual Property Rights: Diversifying or Homogenising?

Reflecting upon the information environment through the ecological governance lens of resilience leads to important follow-on questions. For instance, does the IPR system facilitate diversity or homogenisation? True, such a question is difficult to answer in the abstract because of the various subsystems within the information environment which flow from the different types of IPRs and the numerous IPR-related industries. Also, there are a plethora of exceptions in relation to each relevant IPR. The advent of the Internet has also made the information environment more complex.[113] But the point is, as a matter of principle, if the information environment is to be resilient it must seek to foster diversity and modularity wherever possible.[114] This perspective is embedded within principle 7 of Table 1.1.

The fixation of IPRs on internalising positive externalities, alongside the monopolistic characteristics of IPRs discussed in Part I of the book, underscores considerable risks.[115] Moreover, the nature of the WTO framework and the corresponding TRIPS Agreement, together with the various bilateral free trade TRIPS-plus agreements, arguably has the effect of centralising control of the information environment. This centralisation potentially undermines resilience, diversity and modularity.[116] From an ecological governance perspective, the question arises as to how this risk should be managed. The next chapter explores this question by turning to a 'thought experiment' concerning the allocation of rights and provision of standing to the information commons. The rationale for this thought experiment relates to a significant unifying theme of this book: *the information commons is critical to the information environment*. We must nurture and protect the information commons if we are to facilitate resilience within creative culture and innovative activity.

6.4 CONCLUSION

The chapter applied ecological governance principles to the information environment. We saw that ecology is an amorphous and complex discipline, which is often deployed within the political context to support claims across the ideological spectrum. For this reason the focus remained on ecological governance rather than the pure politics of ecological discourse. An example of an ecological governance principle is interrelationalism and related concepts stemming from systems theory. Discussion of these ecological principles led to the advancement of methodological interrelationalism. By applying methodological interrelationalism to the information environment, it became possible to mediate between the individualist fallacy inherent within IPR maximalist discourse and the collectivist fallacy evidenced within IPR minimalist discourse. To this end, methodological interrelationalism is an important fundament of an integrated information environmental governance framework.

In exploring information environmental governance the chapter discussed the imperative of an empirically based discipline within the information environment. This discipline, which is akin to ecology as it relates to the physical environment, was referred to as 'information ecology'. Information environmental governance also involves the application of ecological principles such as the precautionary principle to the information environment. This application leads to initiatives such as information Environmental Impact Statements (iEIS), which would serve to shift the burden of proof within the information environment to IPR holders. We saw the iEIS would ultimately be built upon an information environmental ethic. Such an ethic seeks to militate against risks inherent within the information environment by ensuring the IPR regulatory framework preserves the resilience of the information environment. Resilience encompasses diversity and modularity; and together these ecological principles were applied to the information environment through a discussion of FLOSS.

It is true that not every single aspect of ecology translates neatly to the information environment. Yet on the whole, as we have seen throughout this chapter, there is utility in applying ecology to the information environment.[117] This application is further advanced in the subsequent chapter when we engage with the rhetorical question of whether the information commons should have standing.

7. Should the information commons have standing?

> Those who lack the courage will always find a philosophy to justify it.
>
> Albert Camus

7.1 INTRODUCTION

In the last chapter Leopold's 'land ethic' provided a foundation for ecological principles. In particular, we have seen how the land ethic provided rhetorical support, accompanied by other key publications such as Rachel Carson's *Silent Spring*, for the rights movement as it relates to nature. This movement in turn contributed to the philosophical foundation of environmental law (as it came to be known). The present chapter seeks to elaborate on this theme as it concerns the information environment. In the process, we will see the central normative claim is that the information commons should be allocated rights and provisioned with standing. This claim is built upon parallel submissions made in the 1970s, which were founded on ecological thought.

The underlying inquiry of this chapter is: If intellectual property is to be allocated rights why not also contemplate the allocation of rights to the information commons? An alternate framing of this inquiry, grounded in both the commons and ecology analytical frameworks, gives rise to the rhetorical question: Should the information commons have standing? The affirmative answer posited advocates the development of ICRs as a governance tool. ICRs serve to operationalise the allocation of rights and the provision of standing to the information commons (as per principle 8 of Table 1.1). Structurally, after outlining ICRs and reinforcing the economic efficiencies inherent within the information commons, the chapter considers several possible criticisms to the emergent ICR notion along with potential responses.

7.2 INFORMATION COMMONS RIGHTS

Drawing upon ecological thinkers such as Aldo Leopold and Rachel Carson, a host of American lawyers during the 1970s sought to 'bestow legal rights of existence on animate and inanimate objects' within nature.[1] For example, in 1970 Joseph Sax sought to revitalise the 'public trust doctrine' as a legal instrument for citizens to protect the environment.[2] In 1972 Christopher Stone published his original work *Should Trees Have Standing?* arguing for the application of rights to nature.[3] And in 1974 Laurence Tribe wrote *Ways Not to Think about Plastic Trees*, probing the foundations of environmental law.[4] A core idea in each work was the value of the physical environment and how law symbolises and interacts with this value.[5] Although such innovative approaches to rights discourse relating to the physical environment (as proffered by Sax, Stone and Tribe) were certainly not accepted wholesale within the legal fraternity or elsewhere, there were some noteworthy judicial pronouncements in response to these claims. For example, in the early 1970s Supreme Court Justice Douglas in the US stated, in a dissenting opinion concerning the Sierra Club's attempt to prevent increased access to some National Forest:

> Those who like it [the Forest], fish it, hunt it, camp it, or frequent it merely to sit in solitude and wonderment are legitimate spokesmen for it … Those who have that intimate relation with the inanimate object about to be injured, polluted or otherwise despoiled are its legitimate spokesmen.[6]

The question of standing and the corresponding question of who is a 'legitimate spokes[person]' for the physical environment is crucial because the answer has significant implications for the information environment generally, and the information commons more specifically. While the issue of determining who is a legitimate spokesperson for the physical environment relates more to the issue of standing than the allocation of rights, there is nevertheless an intimate nexus between rights and standing. The basic point flowing from standing is that until something (or someone) has been made the subject of law there is simply no legal right to be asserted.[7] If something (or someone) has no rights then the thing or person is not valued by the law and it is therefore possible to impinge upon the thing or person in any which way, whether it be a forest, the air, the right of a person to practise their chosen religion, or indeed the information commons.[8] In a distinct sense something does not really exist unless the law deems it to exist.[9]

Through the confluence of Christopher Stone's original work *Should Trees Have Standing?* and James Boyle's influential work *The Politics of IP: Environmentalism for the Net?* this chapter argues that the information commons should be allocated rights and provisioned with standing so the public might speak on its behalf. Hereafter, the bundling of rights allocation and the provision of standing as it concerns the information commons is referred to as 'Information Commons Rights' (ICRs). These rights would be established in contradistinction to IPRs.

ICRs are not a completely new idea. David Lange submitted in his influential 1981 article *Recognising the Public Domain*: 'recognition of new intellectual property interests should be offset today by equally deliberate recognition of individual rights in the public domain'.[10] The central rationale of ICRs is they would serve to foster the public interest aspects of the information environment as a counterbalance to the private interest claims of IPRs. Despite the dual objectives of IPRs, the IPR system operates such that it primarily creates and defends property rights.[11] This is particularly apparent within the patent system where 'conquistador claims' in relation to emerging technology serve to obstruct entry of other claimants into the market.[12] Whereas in the 1940s and 1950s it was somewhat difficult to obtain a patent, by the 1980s it had become significantly easier.[13] As one US patent attorney explained with reference to the contemporary patent landscape: 'you get utility if you can spell it'.[14]

Though the recent *Prometheus Case* in the US demonstrates that the IPR maximalist trend is not set in stone and expansion of IPRs is subject to the vagaries of legal, political, economic, social and cultural landscapes, it remains imperative to establish an informational environmental governance framework that would serve to protect public interest concerns relating to the information environment.[15] ICRs would be one important tool within the information environmental governance framework toolbox. By way of grounding the ICR notion, patent oppositions systems reflected in patent legislation of many countries, as exemplified by section 25 of the Indian Patent Act, provides one tangible example of how ICRs might be operationalised in practice.[16] To create a notion of 'essential intellectual property' in parallel with the 'essential facilities' doctrine inherent within competition law provides another practical alternative when seeking to realise ICRs.[17] Further theoretical considerations concerning the realisation of ICRs will be explored in Chapter 8 with reference to rational truths, reasonable arguments and rhetorical imagination.

As the ICR claim is unorthodox, it is necessary to address possible criticisms and potential responses that might flow from ICR advocacy.

Before doing so, however, the economic efficiencies of the information commons must be reinforced so as to bolster inherent justifications of protecting the information commons.

7.2.1 Information Commons and Economic Efficiency

The central rationale for why the information commons should be protected is that creators and inventors alike build their work to a large extent from materials within it. In this sense the information commons is a vital complement to IPRs. Copyright and patents would be mostly intolerable without a corresponding information commons.[18] If we imagine a situation where IPRs were permanent and hermetic, then nothing would ever flow back into the information commons and it would therefore become less and less useful as a starting point.[19] Both authors and inventors build their work from materials drawn from the information commons.[20] As Litman suggests, it is virtually impossible to argue that any given work is thoroughly original.[21] No work is created *ex nihilo*. For this reason, the information commons is in many ways as vital to the world of creativity and innovation as ecosystems are to the physical world.[22] Over and above activity related to creation and innovation, the information commons provides the foundation for a wide range of undertakings including learning, experiencing, imagining, speaking and engaging.[23] Referring to the (broad) public domain, Pamela Samuelson lists eight functions: '[a]s building blocks for the creation of new knowledge, enablers of competitive imitation, enablers of follow-on innovation, enablers of low cost access to information, enablers of public access to cultural heritage, enablers of education, enablers of public health and safety, and enablers of deliberative democracy.'[24]

When the information commons is seen through this broader lens, it becomes a prerequisite not just for creativity and innovation but also 'an essential precondition for cultural, social and economic development and for a healthy democratic process'.[25] To this end, Cohen has argued the information commons is analogous to a 'pervasive infrastructure for cultural interchange, a sort of *lingua franca* without which proprietary forms of content could neither exist nor be received by their intended audiences'.[26] For now the focus is not so much concerned with broader functions of the commons but rather the economic efficiencies of the information commons. This approach is adopted because many of the arguments employed to support enclosure of the information commons through IPRs are economically based. By highlighting economic efficiencies of the information commons it is possible to simultaneously undermine enclosure arguments and provide a positive rationale for protecting the information commons.

There are many methods of discussing economic efficiencies related to the information commons. One option is to discuss the social production methodology, which we will do in Part IV. For now the economic efficiencies of the information commons will be engaged with by revisiting the public goods dilemma referred to in Part I. This dilemma describes a situation whereby property rights (coupled with technology) may theoretically incentivise production of a public good (e.g. information); yet public goods should generally be readily accessible as these goods facilitate operation of the economic system and by extension the market. The dilemma ultimately speaks to inherent tensions between propertising public goods so as to incentivise production and allowing public goods to flow freely so as to facilitate the proper functioning of the economic system. Bearing in mind information is a type of public good, one method the IPR system employs to resolve the public goods dilemma is to provision IPR leaks and exceptions. Although internalisation of positive externalities through propertisation is an important IPR maximalist hallmark, it is equally the case, as emphasised by IPR minimalists, that the IPR system was designed to promote the free flow of positive externalities.[27] As Giovanni Ramello emphasises: '[T]he main function of intellectual property is ... to cause information to be created and disclosed, thereby facilitating a more complex dynamic connected with the special attributes of knowledge. In a sense, the existence of information externalities is the statutory goal of intellectual property.'[28]

The patent system promotes positive externalities by ensuring works and ideas that would otherwise be kept secret are widely disseminated.[29] Fair use provisions and the idea/expression have a comparative function within copyright law. These leaks and exceptions within the IPR system are a fundamental aspect of the information commons.[30] It is true the IPR system grants private rights but the system also provisions leaks and exceptions so as to sustain common access to and use of information resources. The IPR system is leaky for a reason. Leakage allows information producers and information users alike to access the raw material of creative and innovative activity.[31] The information commons facilitates this access. Thus we can reason society benefits from the free flow of positive externalities in the information environment and this in turn fosters a positive social net product equation with respect to information production and consumption.[32]

When the free flow of information is perceived through a positive externalities lens it becomes abundantly apparent that any IPR protection of information beyond a default minimum essentially undermines social benefits and increases exclusivity costs.[33] This point has been well made by Lemley and Frischmann who argue what is required within the information environment is a 'sufficient' incentive but not a 'perfect' incentive:

> [I]nventors do not need to capture the full social value of their inventions in order to have sufficient incentive to create. Indeed, we have abundant innovation despite the fact that they virtually never do so. Society needs merely to give them enough incentive to cover the fixed costs of creation that their imitators will not face. Any greater return is wasteful – it doesn't encourage any more innovation in the field, and it may actually interfere with innovation and distort behavior in the market … Thus, while we need some ex ante incentive to innovate, we don't need (and don't particularly want) full internalization of the benefits of an invention. As long as we get enough incentive, the fact that other benefits aren't captured by the innovator doesn't impose any real cost on innovation, and may even contribute to innovation.[34]

While the 'sufficient incentive not perfect incentive' maxim has rhetorical appeal, the challenge of demarcating between sufficiency and perfection remains. It is here Buchanan and Stubblebine's analysis concerning 'relevant' and 'irrelevant' externalities is insightful.[35] These authors make this distinction by examining 'the impact that the external costs or benefits have on decision making by relevant agents'.[36] Relevant externalities constitute those costs and benefits whereby internalisation would change behaviour and in doing so affect resource allocation decisions.[37] In contrast, irrelevant externalities constitute those costs and benefits whereby internalisation would not have an effect on behaviour and therefore resource allocation decisions.[38] In other words, some externalities affect resource allocation and others do not. The problematic truth, however, is that even with the benefit of Buchanan and Stubblebine's analysis it remains difficult if not impossible to make this distinction with any certainty.

Interestingly, the difficulty of distinguishing between 'relevant' and 'irrelevant' positive externalities provides an insight as to why the information commons is efficient. Lemley and Frischmann consolidate this perspective in their article *Spillovers* where they argue positive externalities 'do not necessarily or generally undermine incentives to invest' and, counterintuitively, in some cases 'actually drive further innovation'.[39] Leakiness is desirable within IPR systems, not just in the context of (re)distributional considerations but also to promote creativity and innovation generally.[40] As Frishmann states:

> Plugging the leaks by increasing copyright duration, shrinking fair use, extending copyright to ideas, and so on, may have superficial appeal as intellectual resources increase in value and the costs of managing rights with

> technology and contract decrease, but ... there are strong economic reasons to question the Demsetzian impulse in copyright law.[41]

As we saw in Part I, rather than becoming fixated on capturing positive externalities the IPR system would be much more effective if it focused on maximising social net product.[42] A critical requirement in this regard is ensuring equitable access to the information commons.[43] Doing so, in turn, fosters free flow and broad distribution of those positive externalities that stem from information production. This facilitates further creation and innovative activity. In this way, a positive cycle of creativity and innovation is generated. This positive cycle provides a strong motivation to nurture and protect the information commons. Yet despite a sound rationale, nurturance and protection is not automatically assured. It is within this context the tool of ICRs can be relied upon as part of a broader integrated information environmental governance framework. We will see in the next chapter that the realisation of ICRs will require strategic reliance on a combination of rational truths, reasonable arguments and rhetorical imagination. However, before we directly engage with these criteria, it is first necessary to raise and debunk possible criticisms that might be directed at ICRs generally.

7.2.2 Possible Criticisms and Potential Responses

When discussing the possible criticisms of ICRs and consequent responses, the intention below is not to draw an exhaustive list. Rather, the purpose is to engage with representational concerns so a foundation can be laid for the ideas advanced in Chapter 8. The possible criticisms and potential responses of ICRs are as follows:

7.2.2.1 Mechanisms to protect information commons already exist

Of course, there are already built-in mechanisms within the IPR system, which implicitly operate to protect the information commons. Classic examples include the idea/expression dichotomy within copyright law and the requirement for originality within patent law.[44] The challenge is, while the IPR system seeks to balance the twin objectives of incentivisation and public benefit, public choice theory reminds that the public voice is often trumped by private voices.[45] As a corollary, private interests often reign supreme over public interests.[46]

The scholarship of Mark Rose implies the reason why private interests trump public interests in the IPR domain is an historical legacy resulting from the distinction between 'the fact of the public domain' and 'the discourse of the public domain'.[47] Drawing upon the copyright debates of the mid-eighteenth century, Rose argues that despite those debates giving rise to a robust rhetoric of copyright as property right, they failed to produce 'a legal discourse of public rights strong enough to balance the discourse of property rights'.[48] Rose goes on to state that this is 'a position which was sustained throughout the nineteenth century and which, by and large, still remains true today'.[49]

Rose's claim concerning copyright, coupled with the fact that the line between discovery and invention within patent law has become increasingly blurred as a consequence of contemporary scientific development, reminds that the in-built information commons mechanisms within the IPR system are not impermeable. As a corollary, it is necessary to contemplate methods and techniques we can rely upon to provide a stronger public interest foundation with respect to regulatory frameworks of the information environment. In accordance with principle 8 of Table 1.1 the allocation of rights and provision of standing to the information commons are critical in this regard. From an operational perspective, ICRs fulfil the public interest objective.

7.2.2.2 Boundaries of information commons are unstable

ICRs might be opposed because the boundaries of the information commons are inherently unstable and can morph depending upon temporal, geographical, individual and organisational considerations. As Deazley underscores, within the UK different information commons exists for different groups of people.[50] For instance in relation to copyright, librarians, teachers and those working in public administration can all speak of a different public domain. The matter is made more complex when geographical and temporal considerations are taken into account. It is even more complicated when copyright is contrasted with patents and so on and so forth.[51] Moreover, the information commons is not set in stone. As the IPR regulatory framework evolves so too do the boundaries of the information commons.[52] As Drahos reminds: '[t]he intellectual commons can be divided up in different ways according to place, time and content'.[53] Hence, there is some legitimacy to the argument that the information commons is unstable. Yet although defining boundaries of the information commons is inherently difficult the same is true with IPRs generally.[54] After all, in many respects the information commons is merely the mirror image of IPRs and other related restrictions within the information environment.[55] In this regard, with respect to copyright and the public domain, Deazley states:

> [T]he private domain of copyright and copyright's public domain necessarily share the same boundary – that which is not copyright protected is public

> domain and vice versa – and that the actual limits and extent of that which is copyright protected is no more readily identifiable and subject to coherent and complete articulation than that which is public domain. The boundary between the two is, and always will be, inherently unstable and unknowable, but that it is unstable and unknowable does not operate to conceptually discredit either phenomenon.[56]

Similar sentiments could be expressed with respect to patent law. If opponents of ICRs argue there is no value in formally creating ICRs because the information commons cannot be accurately defined, then we can point out that this too would be an effective argument against IPRs.[57] Furthermore, as IPRs and the information commons are to a large extent the mirror image of each other, by clarifying boundaries of the information commons, boundaries of IPRs also become more clearly defined. For instance in the US context section 102 of the Copyright Act defines elements that cannot be copyrightable and therefore potentially creates clearer boundaries to the scope of IPRs.[58] Likewise, in the UK and Europe there are lists of exclusions from patenting.[59] Such initiatives are embryonic examples of implicit statutory recognition of the information commons.[60] Attaching public standing rights to these IPR exclusions would be a useful starting point when seeking to enact ICRs. The formation of locally based 'information Environmental Defenders Offices' (iEDOs) would also be a fruitful development by supporting 'community policing' of ICRs.[61]

Along with statutory initiatives in the US such as s 102 of the Copyright Act, recent US cases such as *Golan v Holder* and *Mayo v Prometheus* both challenge courts, in differing respects, to better define parameters of the information commons.[62] So while it is true boundaries of the information commons are inherently unstable, the response is that this is also the case with IPRs. Moreover, statutory and common law mechanisms could be drawn upon to clarify both IPRs and ICRs.[63]

7.2.2.3 Information commons rights are too abstract

Stone's argument of providing rights to nature and by extension the creation of ICRs may initially seem abstract. However, these rights allocations become much less abstract when rights provided to other non-human entities such as corporations, universities or states are considered.[64] In each case agents speak on behalf of non-human entities. As Stone maintained in relation to the physical environment:

> It is not inevitable, nor is it wise, that natural objects should have no rights to seek redress in their own behalf. It is no answer to say that streams and forests cannot have standing because streams and forests cannot speak.

> Corporations cannot speak either; nor can states, estates, infants, incompetents, municipalities or universities. Lawyers speak for them, as they customarily do for the ordinary citizen with legal problems.[65]

Of course the idea of expanding rights to something (or someone) that has not yet received rights such as the information commons is often considered to be strange, frightening and/or laughable.[66] This is the history of rights expansion. Gandhi's retort serves as a reminder: 'first they ignore you, then they laugh at you, then they fight you, then you win'.[67] History abounds with examples whereby extension of rights to new entities or groups of citizens is seen to be unrealistic. Whether the subject is Indigenous peoples, women or nature, at each turn there has been considerable reluctance within both political systems and judicial systems to be the first mover. For instance, Indigenous peoples of Australia were only granted citizenship rights in 1949 and the right to vote in 1967.[68] Also, as Stone relays, in 1856 the US Supreme Court stated that African-Americans were a 'subordinate and inferior class of beings, who had been subjugated by the dominant race'.[69] Likewise, in the nineteenth century, the most powerful court in California indicated that the Chinese did not possess the right to testify against white men in criminal matters because they were 'a race of people whom nature has marked as inferior, and who are incapable of progress or intellectual development beyond a certain point'.[70] Further still, the first female in Wisconsin to seek the *right* to practise law was met with the following arguments:

> The law of nature destines and qualifies the female sex for the bearing and nurture of the children of our race and for the custody of the homes of the world … [a]ll life-long callings of women, inconsistent with these radical and sacred duties of their sex, as is the profession of the law, are departures from the order of nature; and when voluntary, treason against it … The peculiar qualities of womanhood, its gentle graces, its quick sensibility, its tender susceptibility, its purity, its delicacy, its emotional impulses, its subordination of hard reason to sympathetic feeling, are surely not qualifications for forensic strife. Nature has tempered woman as little for the juridical conflicts of the court room, as for the physical conflicts of the battle field.[71]

Although allocating rights to an abstract entity such as the physical environment or the information commons is inherently challenging, history indicates the challenge is not insurmountable.[72] An important aspect of this rights expansion is to lift the profile of an entity. This accords with Boyle's perspective concerning the need to 'invent the information commons'.[73] Indeed, as pre-empted by Boyle, consolidation over the last decade of public interest groups concerned with the information environment demonstrates the social and political conditions relating to the information environment are evolving along similar lines to the environmental movement of the 1970s and 1980s.[74] More recent political action relating to SOPA, PIPA and the Anti-Counterfeiting Trade Act (ACTA) also supports this viewpoint. The sentiments of Ramsay and Rowe concerning the profile of environmental issues over the last several decades provide scope for some optimism:

> Environmental issues have come to dominate public and private life to a degree unimaginable even thirty years ago. While last century specific environmental problems achieved great importance and prompted political and legislative action in the form of public health, town planning and building laws, these were often seen as extremely radical challenges to existing rights and expectations, especially those of landowners. Now, however, towards the end of the twentieth century, scarcely a day passes without at least some environmental or resource concern receiving media attention.[75]

When thinking about developments related to the physical environment we should remember that environmental law is not simply an invention of the court, the legislature or the law reform commission. Rather, environmental law has been instigated by a broad range of citizens acting outside those sites usually associated with law formation.[76] For example, unionists, factory managers, consumers, scientists and the media have all contributed to environmental regulatory frameworks.[77] When this truism is taken into account within the ICR context, Boyle's plea to unify the disparate interests of computer software engineers, librarians, parodists and biotechnologists becomes intensely pertinent. This strategy can be relied upon to coalesce commonality of interests within the information environment. Creation and maintenance of ICRs is one method of realising this 'commonality of interests' coalition.

7.2.2.4 Information commons rights foster a rights/no rights dichotomy

Another potential argument against ICRs is that the allocation of such rights would foster a 'rights/no rights' dichotomy. This would mean if information is deemed to fall outside the ambit of ICRs for one reason or another then that information may be fully subject to propertisation without qualification.[78] This risk is symbolised by the characterisation of the public domain as a space where there are *no rights* reserved.[79] Stone himself acknowledged this risk in relation to the physical environment. Indeed he has recently reviewed his earlier call for the environment to be accorded standing and thus recognition of legal rights.[80] To some extent this risk can be mitigated by reference to Cohen's depiction of the information commons as 'a complex topology layered over and under and around domains that are "private"'.[81] Also, in accordance with principle 6 of Table 1.1 concerning semicommons theory the allocation of property rights does not need to be a completely dichotomous proposition.[82] It is possible for property to be owned and un-owned at the same time. As stated by Cicero in his third book *On Ends* 'although the theatre is a public place, yet it is correct to say that the seat a man has taken belongs to him'.[83] Rights allocation can be nuanced to the extent that creation of ICRs does not equate to allocating all rights under the sun to the information commons. As Stone argued in relation to the physical environment:

> To say that the environment should have rights is not to say that it should have every right we can imagine, or even the same body of rights as human beings have. Nor is it to say that everything in the environment should have the same rights as every other thing in the environment.[84]

A central rationale of ICRs would be to create a point of leverage upon which to expand. In the first instance rights allocation would serve to foster a positive definition of the information commons. Pertinently, this is a project advanced by Dusollier with reference to the public domain at a Communia workshop in 2008:

> In legal regimes of intellectual property, the public domain is generally defined in a negative manner, as the resources in which no IP right is vested. This no-rights perspective entails that the actual regime of the public domain does not prevent its ongoing encroachment, but might conversely facilitate it. In order to effectively preserve the public domain, an adequate legal regime should be devised so as to make the commons immune from any legal or factual appropriation, hence setting up a positive definition and regime of the public domain.[85]

As was asked when introducing this chapter: If intellectual property is to be allocated rights why not also contemplate the allocation of rights to the information commons through creating and maintaining ICRs?

7.2.2.5 Private interests protect information commons

In further objecting to ICRs opponents might argue that in most instances public interest considerations relating to the information environment will coincide with private interests. According to this view relevant private parties will at least inadvertently speak on behalf of the information commons. As powerful corporations such as Google and IBM have a vested interest in protecting and conserving the information commons, at least in certain respects, public and private interests concerning the information environment might sometimes or even often coincide. Yet as stated by Vera Franz from the Open Society Institute: '[while] there often is an overlap between public interest and business interests ... [this] is not a permanent thing'.[86] Furthermore, as Stiglitz has underscored in relation to patents and the public goods provisioning problem, there is likely to be an under-investment with respect to private parties in challenging unjustified IPRs:

> When a firm gets a patent, it encloses the commons, making private what would otherwise be public; it receives a private return for obtaining a patent – regardless of whether the patent was or was not deserved. But when a firm challenges a patent, it creates a public good, because if it successfully challenges a patent, that piece of knowledge enters the public domain, where anybody can use it. Thus, challenging a patent is a public good. The result, of course, is that there will be an underinvestment in fighting bad patents, and an overinvestment in trying to get bad patents.[87]

It is not enough to make private interests natural guardians of public interests in relation to the information environment. Creating ICRs would enable and empower public citizens to have the opportunity to speak on behalf of the information commons in a similar vein to the manner in which environment law has been so constructed. There are both practical and rhetorical dimensions to this argument. We will discuss some of these considerations in the following chapter.

7.2.2.6 Other miscellaneous criticisms

The above list of possible criticisms and corresponding responses in relation to the call to create and maintain ICRs is not exhaustive. There are other objections which might be raised. Another example, being that ICRs rely upon 'the public' to speak on behalf of the information commons and defining notions of 'publicness', is inherently problematic.[88] A brief response here is that these challenges have been overcome or at least mediated in a host of different forums with respect to the physical environment. Yet further still, it might be argued, with reference to the scholarship of Chander and Sunder, that the creation of ICRs falls into the trap of idealizing the information commons as a 'lost Eden', which ultimately 'overshadows the fact that for centuries the public domain "has been a source for exploiting the labor [sic] and bodies of the disempowered"'.[89] The comeback in this regard is that there is a significant difference between romanticising the information commons on the one hand and seeking to allocate rights to it on the other.

Of course once we accept the information commons should be allocated rights and provisioned with standing through ICRs a subsequent question is: how might this project actually be realised? In accordance with principle 9 of Table 1.1 the following chapter suggests the theoretical foundation of ICRs is to be built upon rational truths, reasonable arguments and rhetorical imagination.

7.3 CONCLUSION

This chapter sought to address the question of whether the information commons should have standing. The question is principally rhetorical to the extent the chapter answers distinctly in the affirmative. Though the question explicitly relates to legal standing the perspective adopted within this chapter was that standing and rights are intimately intertwined. In this respect the chapter adopted ICRs terminology to refer to a governance tool which encompasses both legal standing and rights. We saw that ICRs represent a powerful contradistinction to IPRs. This is important because of the natural tendency of IPRs to 'create and defend property rights' rather than secure public benefit.[90] After outlining ICRs this chapter reinforced economic efficiencies of the information commons. While it is clear there are sound reasons to protect the information commons it does not follow the information commons will automatically be protected. This is why we need an information environmental governance framework. However, the framework cannot be operationalised without tools. It is here ICRs are most useful. After acknowledging the unorthodox nature of ICRs the chapter turned to countering possible ICR criticisms. Many of the arguments that can be mounted against ICRs might also apply to IPRs – one example being that the boundaries of the information commons are inherently unstable. The ultimate conclusion of this chapter is the information commons should be allocated rights and provisioned with standing by creating and maintaining ICRs. The next chapter advances this claim by exploring further methods of operationalising those aspects of the information environmental governance framework relating to the information commons.

8. Rational truths, reasonable arguments and rhetorical imagination

Philosophy makes progress not by becoming more rigorous but by becoming more imaginative.

Richard Rorty

8.1 INTRODUCTION

Chapter 7 advocated creation and maintenance of ICRs. In doing so considerable effort was spent addressing possible criticisms. This chapter seeks to move beyond 'straw men' ICR criticisms by building a positive springboard upon which to think and act. Realising explicit protection of the information commons through ICRs will rely upon a strategic combination of rational truths, reasonable arguments and rhetorical imagination.[1] We will see in this chapter the rational truths plea is founded upon the proposed information ecology discipline advanced in Chapter 6; the reasonable arguments submission correlates with the public trust doctrine as it might apply to the information environment; and the rhetorical imagination aspect of the chapter posits 'informational national parks' as one example of an imaginative device. Each criterion is ultimately directed at establishing the foundation for an ICR programme. This programme is couched within the broader construction of an integrated information environmental governance framework. While many ideas presented in this chapter may appear novel we will see that the chapter is actually built upon traditional understandings of the public domain and the public trust. Structurally, the chapter will be presented in three sections in accordance with the chapter title.

8.2 RATIONAL TRUTHS – INFORMATION ECOLOGY AND STANDING

Within the legal domain and elsewhere rational truths flow from a threshold level of technical expertise. With respect to the physical environment, ecological science along with civil society organisations have made significant contributions in this regard by establishing a body of 'objective expert knowledge', which can be relied upon by governments and courts.[2] The evolution of standing as it relates to the physical environment in Australia during the 1980s provides one site of reference for this claim.[3] It is at least partly because civil society advocates fashioned themselves as 'ecological experts' that these advocates have been able to secure standing in relation to environmental matters.[4]

In the landmark case of *ACF v Commonwealth* (1980) the High Court stopped short of providing standing to the Australian Conservation Foundation (ACF) because according to Justice Gibbs an 'intellectual or emotional concern' was not the type of interest that differentiated the ACF from other members of the public.[5] Despite the outcome, 'special damage' was stretched to include 'special interest in the subject matter of the action'.[6] This stretch was consolidated throughout the 1980s so that in 1989, when the ACF sought standing for a second time, the Federal Court was ready to grant it.[7] By the late 1980s in Australia the legal groundwork had been laid for the courts to begin recognising counter-ecological expertise of civil society organisations such as ACF. One specific example is the case of *ACF v Minister for Resources* (1989) where Justice Davies stated as a matter of relevance that '[p]ublic perception of the need for the protection and conservation of the natural environment and for the need of bodies such as the ACF to act in the public interest has noticeably increased, and is demonstrated by the growth of the ACF itself since the time of the 1980 ACF case'.[8]

In parallel to common law evolution, and largely as a consequence of agitation by civil society organisations during the 1970s and 1980s, many environmental legislative regimes in developed Western countries such as Australia began to facilitate and require input and comment from the public.[9] Section 123 of the Environmental Planning and Assessment Act 1979 (NSW) is exemplary. This section provisioned justification for courts to subsume rational truths of civil society organisations into their judgments. For instance, Justice Stein opened his judgment in *Oshlack v Richmond River Council* (1994) – a case concerning the habitat of koalas that may have detrimentally been affected by a residential subdivision – with reference to open standing provisions embedded within the statute:

> The notion of public interest litigation has been gaining ground in Australia over the last decade. The concept derives from principles of public law rather than private. The development springs from the increasing access of individual members of the public and groups to approach the courts and seek to

> enforce aspects of public law. This is particularly so in the area of environmental law where many New South Wales statutes include open standing provisions enabling 'any person' to seek to enforce breaches of the law.[10]

From this we can begin to posit that common law and statutory evolution, alongside the activities of information environmental civil society organisations, are all likely to contribute to a threshold level of information environmental technical expertise. This expertise will play an important role in building a body of rational truths. These truths can be drawn upon by information environmentalists when advocating protection of the information commons through information environmental governance framework initiatives such as ICRs.

Although rational truths are imperative when seeking to protect the information environment and/or information commons, alone these truths are unlikely to suffice. We will see information environmentalists also need to rely upon a combination of reasonable arguments and rhetorical imagination. These criteria will now be explored respectively.

8.3 REASONABLE ARGUMENTS – PUBLIC TRUST DOCTRINE

Thinking about the information commons through an ICR prism may seem novel but to a large extent ICRs are 'old wine in a new bottle'. ICRs are built upon traditional meanings of 'public domain' as it pertains to real property belonging to the state to be used for public purposes.[11] Furthermore, protection of the information commons has traditionally been a fundamental goal of intellectual property law.[12] Thus the allocation of rights to the information commons merely involves reframing age-old concepts, many of which have been alluded to or discussed previously. Examples include usufruct rights, positive community and *res communis*. Despite the traditional foundation of ICRs lawyers will need to be as bold and imaginative as those who convinced the Supreme Court in the US that a railroad corporation was a 'person' under the Fourteenth Amendment – a provision that was ultimately established to secure rights of freedmen.[13] From a macro perspective there are three possibilities when seeking a contemporary jurisprudential foundation for ICRs: (i) constitutional provision; (ii) legislative initiative; and/or (iii) common law evolution. Each of these possibilities can be explored through the application of the public trust doctrine to the information environment. Naturally, the first step in this process is outlining the 'public trust doctrine'.

The public trust doctrine evolved from Roman law concepts of public property, or more specifically the Justinian Code inherent within Byzantine law, whereby rivers, air and the sea were dedicated to the public and therefore incapable of private ownership.[14] The doctrine was to some extent codified within the Magna Carta and it was eventually adopted by most medieval European legal systems.[15] For instance there is clear evidence of the doctrine operating within eleventh-century French law.[16] A more modern version of the doctrine was embedded within the US Supreme Court Case of *Illinois Central Railroad v Illinois* 146 US 387 (1892) where the Court disallowed privatisation of navigable waters of Lake Michigan as these resources were regarded as being 'held in trust for the people of [Illinois]'. The Court stated:

> [The title to submerged lands] is a title different in character from that which the State holds in lands intended for sale. It is different from the title which the United States hold in the public lands which are open to preemption and sale. It is a title held in trust for the people of the State that they may enjoy the navigation of the waters, carry on commerce over them, and have liberty of fishing therein freed from the obstruction or interference of private parties.[17]

Inherent within *Illinois Central* is a basic principle – the public possesses certain rights in resources.[18] This principle limits the power of legislative representatives to alienate such resources. When the public trust doctrine is perceived in this way we can begin to think about how it might apply to the physical environment and information environment in turn.

8.3.1 Public Trust and the Physical Environment

The public trust doctrine was revitalised in the 1970s by Joseph Sax who argued the doctrine could be employed to protect the public's right to a healthy and sustainable environment.[19] The essence of Sax's argument was the public trust doctrine empowers courts to act on behalf of citizens to override unreasonable privatisation of natural resources carried out by government.[20] Contemporaneously some scholars have perceived the doctrine as a precursor of securing environmental rights as fundamental human rights.[21] The Earth Law movement adopts this approach in relation to the physical environment and the Access to Knowledge Treaty tends towards a parallel approach in relation to the information environment.[22]

Sax's plea concerning the public trust doctrine certainly did not go unheeded. By providing examples of at least 25 US jurisdictions, Lazarus has explicitly demonstrated renaissance of the public trust doctrine in US case law.[23] While the doctrine initially related to navigation, commerce and fishing it has since been extended to include wildlife and marshlands along with various recreational activities such as 'boating, hunting, bathing, taking shellfish, gathering seaweed, ... and passing and repassing'.[24]

By relying upon the public trust doctrine the judiciary has recognised what Rose has labelled 'inherent public property'.[25] This refers to property whereby citizens possess free and unimpeded access. According to Rose's analysis the crux of the public trust doctrine is 'to reserve for the public those properties that the public needs for travel, communication, commerce, and to some degree public speaking – that is, uses that connect people with one another and with the wider world and allow all to interact in a social whole'.[26] Within her scholarship, Rose suggests property related to either commerce or recreation tend to be traditional candidates of 'publicness'.[27] It is noteworthy the rights protected by the public trust doctrine are inherently collective in nature and are therefore held by persons as members of the public akin to the doctrine of *res communis*.[28] In this sense the rights are indivisible and inalienable from the public in line with the previous discussion of positive community in Part II (and principle 4 of Table 1.1).[29]

Practically speaking the public trust doctrine operates to ensure the state does not revoke the public's collective rights by trading them away and/or transferring them to private parties. The only exceptions laid down by the US Supreme Court to the general rule of inalienability is the state can only transfer public trust resources to private parties if they 'are used in promoting the interests of the public' or the transfer is made 'without any substantial impairment of the public interest'.[30]

8.3.2 Public Trust and the Information Environment

Just as the public trust doctrine has assisted in mobilizing the environmental movement through increasing the public awareness of each human being's entitlement to healthy natural ecosystems, it also has the potential to be employed with analogous effect in relation to the information environment.[31] Similarly to how air and water are implicitly held in a public trust, so too some information should also be held in a public trust given 'every individual has a social membership in the cultural ecosystem of the intangible public space'.[32]

Joseph Sax has come to recognise the implicit link between the public trust doctrine and the information environment when he argues that 'recognition that our accumulated knowledge and insight should be viewed as elements of a common heritage undergirds the basic premise of intellectual-property rules that govern patents and copyrights'.[33] Carol Rose has also pre-empted correlation between the public trust doctrine and the information environment by suggesting, along with property related to commerce and recreation, that property relating to free speech is a natural candidate for 'publicness'. This view was vindicated in *Hague v Committee for Indus. Organization* where the US Supreme Court invoked the doctrine to ensure 'streets and parks as the public fora for free speech activities are open to all'.[34] The Court further stated:

> Wherever the title of streets and parks may rest, they have immemorially been held in trust for the use of the public and, time out of mind, have been used for purposes of assembly, communicating thoughts between citizens, and discussing public questions. Such use of the streets and public places has, from ancient times, been a part of the privileges, immunities, rights, and liberties of citizens.[35]

The public trust doctrine is useful within the information environment context because many traditional public domain safeguards such as fair use are either side-stepped through TPMs or read down to accord with pure individual rights/interests at expense of the public interest.[36] In contrast to IPR maximalist tendencies the public trust doctrine tends to begin with a presumption in favour of 'public use, access and enjoyment'.[37] Hence if the doctrine were to apply to the information environment, and more specifically the information commons, the judiciary would be initially bound to provide sufficient consideration to public interest rather than a pure focus on individual interests within the information environment.[38] To a limited extent, evidence of this approach exists within present case law such that deployment of the public trust doctrine would simply strengthen a judicial tendency already evident (albeit only in restricted quarters). For example, the Canadian Supreme Court held in 2004:

> The fair dealing exception, like other exceptions in the Copyright Act, is a *user's right*. In order to maintain the proper balance between the rights of a copyright owner and users' interests, it *must not be interpreted restrictively* … 'Research' must be given *a large and liberal interpretation* in order to ensure that users' rights are not unduly constrained … 'Dealing' connotes not individual acts, but *a practice or system*. This comports with the purpose of the fair dealing exception, which is to ensure that users are not unduly restricted in their ability to use and disseminate copyrighted works. Persons or institutions relying on the … fair dealing exception need only prove that their own dealings with copyrighted works were for the purpose of research or private study and were fair. They may do this either by showing that their own practices and policies were research-based and fair, or by showing that *all individual* dealings with the materials were in fact research-based and fair.[39]

Accordingly the public trust doctrine affords opportunity of judicially recognising that the public dimension of the IPR system is not a tack-on or somehow incidental but rather foundational to the IPR system as a whole. Recognition of the public trust doctrine is not confined to the judiciary. Article 27 of the Pennsylvania State Constitution, for example, states in relation to the physical environment: 'Public natural resources are the common property of all the people, including generations yet to come. As trustee of these resources, the Commonwealth shall conserve and maintain them for the benefits of all the people.'[40] Exchanging 'informational' for 'natural' would exemplify the content of a public trust doctrine-inspired 'information environmental constitutional clause'. Of course reliance on such an Article would be dependent on fleshing out a range of issues, an example being the need to establish a clear contrast between 'public informational resources' and 'private informational resources'.

Once a clear dichotomy between public and private information resources is established an information environmental constitutional clause would serve substantive and procedural values of the information environment.[41] Substantive values relate to free flow of knowledge and information afforded to the public. Procedural values concern democratizing IPR policy through further engagement of public participation in shaping laws relating to information flow and usage. The substantive and procedural application of the public trust doctrine within the information environment context cements the link between 'public space' and IPRs. This is because copyright law mediates the manner in which citizens can legally make public use of their reason.[42] In other words, through copyright law the state provides exclusive ownership on expressions of communicative actions such as art, literature, movies, etc. In this way copyright law, as it has always done, filters who can use information and how. In doing so it strongly influences the degree of openness within the information environment.

An important function of an information environmental public trust doctrine would be to place a check on state power to allocate informational resources in an appropriate and reasonable manner. Just as the state cannot grant property rights to individuals that undermine reasonable use of certain physical resources by the public, so too the state should not be able to grant IPRs over informational resources purely for the benefit of private parties.[43] This approach is not completely new. To some extent it was adopted in *Sony Corp. of Am v Universal City Studios,* 464 US 17 (1984) at 429 where the Court stated: 'The monopoly privileges that Congress may authorize are neither unlimited nor primarily designed to provide a special private benefit. Rather, the limited grant is a means by which an important public purpose may be achieved.'[44]

Although a literal application of the public trust doctrine to the information environment may seem novel it is not without precedent. In *Eldred v Reno*, for instance, the plaintiffs argued:

> While copyright creates a present interest in the copyright holder, it simultaneously creates a future interest in the public. The Public Trust Doctrine holds that government may not transfer the public property of a commons into private hands in the absence of any public benefit in exchange. While this doctrine has traditionally been applied in the context of public lands, the same principle should apply to the reallocation of public rights in intangible property, such as copyright.[45]

In summarily dismissing the argument put forward by the plaintiffs, the US Columbian District Court in *Eldred v Reno* rejected the plea to extend the public trust doctrine to copyright by simply asserting: 'the public-trust doctrine applies to navigable waters and not copyrights'.[46] The Court went on to state: 'Insofar as the public trust doctrine applies to navigable waters and not copyrights, the retroactive extension of copyright protection does not violate the public trust doctrine'.[47] Regrettably when the case was appealed to the Supreme Court the plaintiffs abandoned the public trust argument.[48] Therefore at the present time there is scant judicial reasoning relating to extending the doctrine into the information environment. But despite *Eldred v Reno*, just as the Australian High Court adopted a different approach in 1989 than it did in 1980 in relation to granting ACF standing (as we saw above), there is undoubtedly scope for judicial evolution of the public trust doctrine as it concerns the information environment.[49] Key elements leading to judicial evolution of legal standing as it related to the physical environment were rational truths inherent within objective expert knowledge of ecologists, accompanied by rational truths of civil society organisations evidenced through broad-based support within the polity. These counter expert elements will also be important in the evolution of public trust governance for the information environment.[50]

In further applying the public trust doctrine governance of the information environment we can note two dominant themes that emerge within public trust case law: (i) fiduciary obligations and (ii) judicial review. The case of *Arnold v Mundy* 6 NJL 1, 71–78 (1821) 'marks the origin of the fiduciary aspect of public trust doctrine'.[51] According to this fiduciary aspect of the public trust doctrine an individual may abandon her private property but a public trustee cannot abandon public property.[52] Here it would seem that either the public itself possesses a property right in relation to public resources;[53] or in the alternate, the state owes a duty to the public to protect public resources.[54] In *National Audubon Society v Superior Court*, for instance, the Court stated:

> The public trust is more than an affirmation of state power to use public property for public purposes. It is an affirmation of the duty of the state to protect the people's common heritage of streams, lakes, marshlands and tidelands, surrendering that right of protection only in rare cases when the abandonment of that right is consistent with the purposes of the trust.[55]

When discussing the judicial review aspect of the public trust doctrine, Joseph Sax stated in his pivotal 1970 article 'public trust is not so much a substantive set of standards for dealing with the public domain as it is a technique by which courts may mend perceived imperfections in the legislative and administrative process'.[56] This point brings to light the nexus between the public trust doctrine and IPRs to the extent the doctrine confers upon courts judicial review powers to consider state decisions in allocating protected resources. If the information commons or those that purport to speak on behalf of it had standing, then citizens and/or civil society organisations could make use of this judicial review process. Relying upon aforementioned 'opposition systems' inherent within patent legislation, such as section 25(2) of the Indian Patent Act, is one possibility.[57] Another legislative option might be to legislate a 'statutory derivative action' similar to that found within the Australian Corporations Act 2001 (Cth).[58] Also of note within the judicial review setting of the public trust doctrine is that courts have demonstrated a judicial concern for 'low visibility decision making'.[59] This decision making occurs where critical resource allocation decisions are made without adequate notice or publicity. Such democratic considerations are important since, according to Sax, lack of consideration of the public interest leads to structural flaws in decision making.[60] This is particularly so in relation to substantive values of the resource in question and the procedural mechanisms employed to make decisions in relation to these resources.

Yet the question lingers as to how judicial review would apply within the information environment. With respect to the procedural issues, for example, the judiciary might examine whether adoption of IPRs adequately considers interests of the public. Accordingly, the relevant legislative body would be under a positive onus to invite information environmental civil society organisations such as Public Knowledge, Electronic Frontier Foundation, Creative Commons, Free Software Foundation and Knowledge Ecology International to submit their concerns about impacts of proposed laws on the information environment.[61] If the legislative body failed to engage with this process, courts could strike down the law.[62] Alternatively courts could order the legislature to review legislation by mandating public input into the legislative process so the legislation is tested against the wishes of an informed public.

While there is no doubt applying the public trust doctrine to the information environment holds promise as a practical jurisprudential method of supporting enactment and operationalisation of ICRs, Sax himself was at pains to avoid overstating the doctrine as it might relate to the physical environment. In particular, Sax has indicated a majority of the positive statements relating to the doctrine are *obiter dicta* and at most the doctrine suggests 'no grant may be made to a private party if that grant is of such amplitude that the state will effectively have given up its authority to govern, but a grant is not illegal solely because it diminishes in some degree the quantum of traditional public uses'.[63] Additionally, we have seen the approach was outright rejected in the US Columbia District Court case of *Eldred v Reno*. For these reasons and more it is imperative to explore alternative methods (beyond rational truths and reasonable arguments) of protecting the information commons. Deployment of rhetorical imagination is one possibility.

8.4 RHETORICAL IMAGINATION – INFORMATIONAL NATIONAL PARKS

Realising ICRs will require strategic use of rational truths and reasonable arguments. As was the case in the nineteenth century when advocates of the physical environment sought the creation and maintenance of national parks, rhetorical imagination is also imperative. Beyond James Boyle, the scholar Eva Wirten has drawn out the historical nexus between struggles to protect the physical environment and struggles to protect the information environment:

> The public domain, and to an even larger degree the commons, operate with and can be approached from a number of perspectives that all somehow relate to place and space, be they primarily natural or virtual, tangible or symbolic. And as new as the concerns of our contemporary digital environment are, the impetus behind the formation of the Electronic Frontier Foundation and the Creative Commons are not that different from what prompted the launch of the Commons Preservation Society in Britain in 1865.[64]

While this historical nexus between the physical environment and the information environment is slightly conjectural, it is clear rhetorical imagination plays an important role in shifting social and political conditions.[65] Such imagination in turn opens up opportunities for law to mediate between rational truths and reasonable arguments. For instance in the nineteenth century advocates of the physical environment relied heavily upon romantic rhetorical imagination to enliven understandings of and sympathies towards the natural world.[66] John Muir is an historical ecological personality who symbolises this approach.

Drawing upon inspiration from Emerson, Thoreau and others, Muir founded the Sierra Club in 1892 (which subsequently spawned the breakaway Friends of the Earth in 1969) so as to push for several 'national parks' along with general protection of California's coastal redwoods.[67] Muir was the central impetus behind Yosemite National Park and he fought hard to establish a system of national forests across the US.[68] In doing so Muir relied upon romantic rhetoric as a mechanism to connect with a bundle of psychic and spiritual aspirations within the populous relating to desires for authenticity and re-integration of self with the environment:

> Thousands of tired, nerve-shaken, over-civilised people are beginning to find out that going to the mountains is going home; that wildness is a necessity and that mountain parks and reservations are useful not only as fountains of timber and irrigating rivers but as fountains of life. Awakening from the stupefying effects of the vice of over-industry and the deadly apathy of luxury they are trying as best they can to mix and enrich their own little ongoings with those of Nature, and to get rid of rust and disease … some are washing off sins and cobweb cares of the devil's spinning in all-day storms on mountains.[69]

Romantic rhetoric is also present within Muir's attempts to tap into prevalent US 'rugged individualist' sentiments of that time:

> I pushed on southward toward a group of savage peaks that stand guard about Ritter on the north and west, groping my way; and dealing instinctively with every obstacle as it presented itself … In so wild and so beautiful a region was spent my first day, every sight and sound and inspiration, leading one far outside of himself, yet feeding and building up his individuality.[70]

The idea that one encounters divinity and one's own self among deep crevasses and mountain peaks of nature was a popular notion within Romantic writings from Wordsworth and Thoreau onwards.[71] It is noteworthy that Muir modelled his literary persona to a large extent on these writings.[72] In surveying historical literature relating to nature we see that such literature itself has played an important role in shaping the relationship between Western culture and the natural world.[73] For instance it was no coincidence Edith Nesbit's *Island of the Nine Whirlpools* (1899) partly mirrored Darwin's account of the *Beagle* voyages (1832–1836).[74] Within this context relating Taylor's perspective is useful:[75]

> In many fictional works of the Victorian era, nature was an essential and integral part of their overall *imaginative* structure. For those whom the famous geographer Alexander von Humboldt (1769–1859) acknowledged to be 'endowed with susceptibility' for natural beauty, read fiction alongside studies like natural theology, biology, (with its attendant disciplines of botany and zoology) and, eventually evolutionary science. In general terms, these studies described the natural world as a system of dependencies formed between species and between organisms and their surroundings. Thought about 'eco-systems', as they came to be known in the twentieth century, and the 'wild places' where they were most clearly observed, were seldom far from their thoughts about the dependence of humankind on other living beings and inorganic matter.[76]

Beyond fictional works, Thoreau's mostly non-fictional account of his nature wanderings around Walden Pond provided a powerful account of his observations as a field ecologist and his struggle to articulate relationships and responsibilities of humans to 'the actual condition of the place where we dwell'.[77] Thoreau's phrase 'in wildness is the preservation of the world' provided a neat catchphrase for the late nineteenth-century national parks movement.[78] As the nineteenth century progressed, alongside the Romantic rhetoric embedded within the literature of Thoreau, Muir and others, emerged a range of artistic techniques with respect to paintings, sketches, literature and photography. All of these techniques were geared towards preservation and conservation of the physical environment. Indeed, Muir went to great lengths to take landscape artists to 'typical alpine landscape' so the picturesque qualities of nature could be fully appreciated. One landscape notably appreciated by artists was the 'Sierra Crown', which Muir reflected upon after his first encounter with this terrain:

> Pursuing my lonely way down the valley, I turned again and again to gaze on the glorious picture, throwing up my arms to enclose it as in a frame. After long ages of growth in the darkness beneath the glaciers, through sunshine and storms, it seemed now to be ready and waiting for the elected artists, like yellow wheat for the reaper; and I could not help wishing that I might carry colors and brushes with me on my travels, and learn to paint, meanwhile I had to be content with photographs on my mind and sketches in my notebook.[79]

Similar to nature paintings and sketches, yet perhaps more powerful still, popularisation of the camera in the late 1800s served to transport landscapes to the human eye in a manner previously unthinkable.[80] This was true for many developed Western countries such as Australia and the US.[81] For instance, railway departments in New South Wales and Victoria were instrumental in 'selling' scenic and picturesque qualities of the Australian landscape through photographs and posters as part of their marketing campaigns.[82] This fostered the national parks movement through 'reinforcing and disseminating a romantic and desirable image of Australia's bushlands'.[83] Correspondingly in the US a series of pictures from Dinosaur Monument became the cornerstone of a political conflict where 'those who were moved to defend the place never saw it in person'.[84] As Purdy states: 'The use of pictures goes back to the beginning of this mode of preservation politics, and precedes it in the (strictly speaking) sublime landscape paintings and popular prints that prepared the cultural ground for it in earlier decades of the nineteenth century.'[85] The critical dispatch here is that advocates of the physical environment during the nineteenth century relied upon innovative rhetorical devices and techniques (i.e. rhetorical imagination) to shift social and political landscapes to change the way human beings interacted with nature.[86] The thoughts of Purdy are most insightful within this context:

> What distinguished Muir and his followers, and made them a lasting presence in political life, is that they developed from these literary refinements a concrete mode of encountering nature. Their vocabulary of aesthetic and moral response was keyed to specific features of the Sierra Nevada and their other favorite landscapes, and they built a sub-culture and social movement around those places and the feelings associated with them. The heart of their political program was to secure an American geography for this experience. They worked to ensure that American law dedicated large tracts of ground, such as Yosemite Valley, to the experience that they saw as the highest human relation to nature. Their success was practical, in helping to drive the massive reservations of public land for recreation from the end of the nineteenth century through the twentieth (and beyond). It was also ideological, or, perhaps better, imaginative ... [National parks] existed ... to make the Romantic way of meeting nature into real and widespread experience.[87]

As Purdy emphasises, the function of romantic rhetoric employed was best described as imaginative. While it is easy to dismiss rhetoric, entire political movements shaping the course of history have been built upon it. Rhetoric can foster a language and geography of experience that simply might not be possible otherwise.[88] In this regard a core aim of Stone's advocacy relating to standing and natural entities was less for legal reasons and more to contribute to 'a radical new theory or myth –

felt as well as intellectualised – of man's relationships to the rest of nature … [in which] we may come to regard the Earth … as one organism, of which Mankind is a functional part'.[89] Of course in many respects rhetoric is founded on imagination and like rhetoric, imagination is vital, particularly as it relates to the information environment.[90] After all, creativity and innovation are largely built upon the power of imagination.

As was the case in relation to the physical environment, rhetorical imagination will undoubtedly be important when seeking to change social and political landscapes of the information environment. To this end, when seeking to protect the information commons, a key rhetorical challenge is to counter negative perceptions of the information commons as merely a residual realm of undeserving material – a no-rights wasteland or 'dump on the outskirts of respectable culture'.[91] Boyle has advanced this perspective with respect to the public domain thus: '[O]ne of the main goals of those who are engaged in the public domain project is to "reify the negative": only if "it" has a name, an organizing concept, can it be part of the [IPR] discourse, and not its residue.'[92] We have already seen how the information commons plays a critical role in facilitating a healthy environment. For this reason the information commons must become an active protector of information, not just a passive accumulator.[93] As IPR discourse is yet to fully develop a vocabulary sufficient to express the imperative for brakes or checks on control of information by the private sector, the emergent notion of 'informational national parks' should be considered.[94] Citizens generally appreciate the rationale of national parks in the physical environment.[95] That is, national parks are generally perceived as positive physical spaces fostering the well-being of nature and human beings through the facilitation of nature-based respite and recreation. In this way, like ICRs, the rhetoric of informational national parks is an important tool of the informational environmental governance framework. The main rationale of this tool is to shift perceptions of the information commons from an 'information graveyard' to an 'information playground'.[96]

In developing informational national parks there are several issues we need to flesh out. In the first instance, differences between the physical environment and the information environment would need to be taken into account. In this regard, rather than perceiving informational national parks as a geographically separate space, the parks might be thought of as 'domains of accessible and usable knowledge'.[97] This perspective accords with Cohen's view that 'an affirmative legal conception of the common in culture that respects creative practice will not flow from reifying the "public domain" as such, but rather from adoption of an organizing metaphor that more clearly rejects formal and experiential separation'.[98] Over time, it will be necessary to address questions such as what information would fall within the ambit of informational national parks, and whether or not users of informational national parks need to pay.[99]

While there is scant scholarship that explicitly engages with either allocating rights to the information commons or the metaphorical creation and maintenance of information national parks, there are several subtle yet interesting references to parallel notions within contemporary IPR scholarship.[100] As already indicated, in David Lange's seminal article *Recognising the Public Domain* he submitted that 'recognition of new intellectual property interests should be offset today by equally deliberate recognition of individual rights in the public domain'.[101] Along with this claim Lange also suggests the public domain should be a 'valued sanctuary for unprotected materials' inferring a positive articulation of the public domain provides a powerful antidote to IPR maximalist ideology.[102] Other IPR scholars too, in their own distinct manner, have alluded to the need to preserve and conserve the information commons. For example Drahos discusses the significance of 'preservationist duties' with respect to the intellectual commons, suggesting 'duties of nurture' can be transposed.[103] Cohen alludes to the public domain in terms of a type of 'nature preserve' such that metaphorically one can visit 'rare creatures in their natural habitat' (although she did not necessarily advocate the metaphor);[104] and Samuelson's project of 'mapping the public domain' is partly based on the idea that to do so ensures the public domain becomes 'a terra cognita, a sanctuary, a refuge or a conservancy that the law ought to preserve and protect in the public interest'.[105] Furthermore, seemingly stemming from the information environmental work of Boyle and others, Kahle purportedly posed the following question in a recent workshop discussion: 'Is there room to establish the Yosemite Park of information in Europe?'.[106] Even more recently still, Severine Dusollier spoke of the need for a 'positively defined public domain' at the 2008 Communia Conference.

Though not yet fully developed, we are beginning to witness embryonic development of emergent information environmental tools such as ICRs and informational national parks within IPR scholarship. The information environmental governance framework outlined within this book proffers a guiding light for future developments in this regard.

8.5 CONCLUSION

The chapter moved beyond potential criticisms of ICRs (as discussed in Chapter 7) in order to explore a positive information environmental governance framework programme. We saw the advancement of ICRs is to be founded upon the strategic reliance on rational truths, reasonable arguments and rhetorical imagination. Principle 9 of Table 1.1 embeds this perspective. We also saw in this chapter the rational truths fundament is built on the information ecology discipline discussed in Chapter 6. The reasonable arguments imperative relies upon the public trust doctrine so as to provide a practical exemplar of jurisprudential reasoning that might be deployed within the ICR context. The rhetorical imagination criterion gave rise to the informational national park concept, which flows from the successful impact of romantic rhetoric inherent within the history of national parks. Since the information commons is a 'site of struggle' it follows the information commons will not automatically be protected even if it is an absolute fundament of the information environment. After all, while the physical environment is crucial to the future of *homo sapiens*, this fact alone has not always been enough to protect it. Preserving that which is essential often requires novel and innovative strategies. The broad range of artistic techniques relied upon in the 1900s to transport landscapes to the human eye is exemplary. A key function of Part III has been to consider how ecology informs struggles to protect the information commons. In the absence of a coherent information environmental governance framework, and accompanying tools such as ICRs and information national parks, the information commons is likely to face a Sisyphean battle during the twenty-first century.[107]

PART IV

Public choice theory

When respectively applying environmental analytical frameworks of welfare economics, the commons and ecology to the information environment, we have observed there are some natural correlations between the physical environment and the information environment. For instance, in each environment market failures operate to the detriment of those environments. Similarly, many of the tragedy of the commons concerns relating to the physical environment are mirrored through the tragedy of the anticommons as it relates to the information environment. And important ecological principles such as interrelationalism, resilience, diversity and modularity map to the information environment, providing both practical and theoretical guidance with respect to information environmental governance. Part IV highlights that public choice theory also sheds light on connections between the physical environment and the information environment.[1] Boyle underscored this nexus implicitly thus: 'In both environmental protection and intellectual property, the very structure of the decisionmaking process tends to produce a socially undesirable outcome. Decisions in a democracy are made badly when they are primarily made by and for the benefit of a few stakeholders, be they landowners or content providers.'[2]

Within this passage Boyle emphasises the important regulatory capture aspect of public choice theory. Yet public choice theory does not only speak to the power of incumbents to shape law in their favour, it also speaks to possible responses to counteract this incumbency. In this respect we can point out two limbs of public choice theory (i) rent seeking and regulatory capture, and (ii) overcoming collective action problems. After outlining the applicability of these two limbs of public choice theory to the information environment, Chapter 9 suggests leveraging social production as a complementary method of overcoming collective action problems. This claim is based on an intuition that collective action problems inherent within the information environment might be (partly) overcome through reliance upon economic efficiencies of social production. Chapter 10 will further draw out the efficiencies of social production with reference to constitutional economics. Beyond overcoming collective action problems, we will see in Part IV that social production holds the potential to counteract regulatory capture by fostering competitive tension between the productive forces. The proposed 'separation of (economic) power doctrine' is advanced within this context.

9. Public choice theory and social production

A map of the world that does not include Utopia is not worth even glancing at, for it leaves out the one country at which Humanity is always landing. And when Humanity lands there, it looks out, and, seeing a better country, sets sail. Progress is the realization of Utopias.

Oscar Wilde

9.1 INTRODUCTION

Although public choice theory is a relatively complex discipline, many of the lessons emerging from it are reasonably simple. As an example, concentrated interest groups are likely to have significant influence over regulatory frameworks. This regulatory capture lesson has been critical for the contemporary environment movement in developing strategies to counteract regulatory effects of concentrated interests. In this regard environmentalists have underscored two essential limbs to public choice theory. The first limb is concerned with the regulatory capture of concentrated power holders. This limb will be discussed mostly through the lens of rent seeking. The second limb relates to overcoming collective action problems. We will explore this limb with primary reference to civil society and the associated public sphere.

The chapter begins by discussing similarities and differences between welfare economics and public choice theory. We will then discuss the two limbs of public choice theory. In doing so, the idea of social production as a complementary method of overcoming collective action problems will be advanced. This discussion involves fleshing out the 'hardware-code-content' paradigm. The information process and allocative efficiency characteristics of social production will also be drawn out.

9.2 WELFARE ECONOMICS AND PUBLIC CHOICE THEORY

Part I of this book applied welfare economics to IPRs. This involved identification and analysis of market failures within the information environment and contemplating social net product analysis as it relates to the information environment. In Part IV public choice theory is applied to the information environment. In doing so we will see there are both similarities and distinctions between welfare economics and public choice theory.[1] Both disciplines are ultimately concerned with how the state makes political and economic decisions.[2] Yet the disciplines differ to the extent welfare economics concentrates on pathology of markets whereas public choice theory is ultimately concerned with pathology of politics.[3]

The differing focus of welfare economics and public choice theory stems partly from divergent views about the nature of government.[4] The welfare economics perspective assumes traditional economic views of a benevolent government where politicians seek to maximise economic welfare of citizens. In contrast, public choice theorists generally perceive governments more cynically as inefficient Leviathans that require enactment of competition and other microeconomic instruments so as to encourage efficient outcomes.[5] The solutions that each respective discipline put forth do not always satisfy concerns of the other. For instance, the Leviathan approach of Brennan and Buchanan – where politicians extract resources for themselves at the expense of voters – exemplifies how public choice models can lead to efficient policies that nonetheless fail to maximise social welfare.[6]

Perhaps because of the differing focus, welfare economics and public choice theory are useful complementary methods of analysing formation and administration of regulatory frameworks such as IPRs. In many instances social welfare concerns of welfare economics sit alongside efficiency concerns of public choice theory.[7] As the book has already traversed welfare economics in Part I, exploration of public choice theory awaits.

9.3 PUBLIC CHOICE THEORY AND INTELLECTUAL PROPERTY RIGHTS

Buchanan and Tullock initially discussed public choice theory in 1962 in their classic *The Calculus of Consent*.[8] The theory implies public decisions are likely to be detrimental when concentrated and well-organised groups with substantial, well-identified interests are pitted against diffuse groups with high information costs whose interests, while large in the aggregate, are individually small.[9] When applying the theory, political and economic inquiry often become bound together. For instance, legislative processes are seen as microeconomic systems such that political choice is largely influenced by efforts of individuals and groups to further their own interests.[10]

Neo-pluralism implicitly informs public choice theory to the extent the theory recognises that although power and influence are widely spread, the uneven nature of power distribution means dominant interests are able to capture primary decision-making processes.[11] Carl Schmitt has drawn upon power discrepancy by arguing modern political institutions have morphed from a site of deliberating public good to a space where powerful interest groups seek to negotiate and bargain for commercial arrangements of power distribution.[12] According to this view, it is the unparalleled wealth of resources that allows concentrated interests to penetrate the structure of democratic participation through their influence over the state and its representatives. As a corollary democratic participation tends to degenerate into an 'empty formality' at the expense of the public at large.[13]

The applicability of public choice theory in terms of how it illuminates the 'trade' that takes place between self-interested politicians, public officials and private interest groups (and the resulting detriment to the public interest) is evident in a variety of processes relating to both IPR formation and administration.[14] When concentration of economic power inherent within monopolies is analysed with reference to the IPR regulatory framework we can unpack public choice theory thus: (i) economic power facilitates the influence of concentrated interest groups; (ii) production is a key component of amassing economic power; and (iii) information is a critical aspect of contemporary production. According to this chain of reasoning concentrated economic interests attached to the information environment will have a significant influence over the regulatory framework of IPRs.[15] This influence in turn further facilitates centralisation of economic power.

We can see there is a self-reinforcing dimension to the regulatory capture limb of public choice theory because the greater the centralisation of economic power the more likely it is regulatory capture will occur. In other words the opportunity for concentrated interest groups to shape law in their favour becomes increasingly pertinent as economic power becomes more centralised.[16] As Hayek wrote: 'Whoever controls all economic activity controls the means for all our ends, and must therefore decide which are to be satisfied and which are not. This is really the crux of the matter.'[17] Building upon this reasoning, a broad range of IPR scholars have sought to rely upon public choice theory to argue IPR holders have a theoretically and practically disproportionate influence over IPR lawmaking.[18] The boldest articulations tend to suggest public choice theory pressures will exist wherever there are exclusive rights in information. Benkler's sentiments are exemplary:

> Our legislative process demonstrates a systematic imbalance in favor of the expansion and deepening of exclusive rights to information at the expense of the public domain. The imbalance exists because the benefits of such rights are clearly seen by, and expressed by, well-defined interest holders that exist at the time the legislation is passed. In contrast, most of the social costs – which are economic, social, political, and moral – are diffuse and likely to be experienced in the future by parties not yet aware of the fact that they will be affected by the extension of rights.[19]

Lessig proffers a slightly blunter prognosis:

> [I]t is an iron law of politics that the organized beat the unorganized and that the vested have interests that get organized over the unknown … The result is that the pressure in the existing system is biased in favour of the old. Policies get made to favour the old; the interest of the new simply has no voice.[20]

The significant influence concentrated economic interests have over IPR policy formulation is made explicit by applying public choice theory to the information environment.[21] Such an application accords with the traditional perspective of public choice theory, which focuses on the regulatory capture effect of rent-seeking activities. More contemporaneously, however, attention of public choice theory has shifted to the other side of the equation, being responses of disperse fragmented interests in overcoming collective action problems. That is, in applying public choice theory we must be mindful of the two limbs. The first, 'regulatory capture limb', which is grounded in rent-seeking analysis, underscores how acute concentrated interest groups stand to benefit from regulatory construction in their favour.[22] The second, 'collective action problem limb', highlights how the large number of disperse interests stand to lose from regulatory capture and how these interests are unlikely to do anything about this loss for a range of reasons often referred to as collective action problems.[23] We will now explore each of these limbs in more depth.

9.3.1 Rent Seeking and Regulatory Capture

When the activities of concentrated interest groups are analysed through the public choice theory lens it is evident that such activities often accord with rent seeking. This is to say concentrated interests will expend considerable resources pursuing capture of supra-normal returns.[24] Indeed economic theory suggests private parties are likely to disburse virtually the entire value of a benefit in order to capture it.[25] Lobbying for special legislative privileges is one common example of rent seeking.[26] Other legislative instruments that become captive to rent-seeking behaviour include tariffs, licence requirements and quotas.[27]

Somewhat ironically it is the rent-seeking behaviour the WTO framework seeks to diminish through the General Agreement on Tariffs and Trade (GATT) and the General Agreement on Trade in Services (GATS).[28] Yet at the same time TRIPS remains a central plank of this very same framework. In other words, the WTO trades off rent-seeking mechanisms such as tariffs, licences and quotas in return for the rent-seeking enabler of IPRs.[29] In this respect Drahos and Braithwaite suggest the link between free trade and IPRs is ultimately implausible.[30] This is because TRIPS is concerned with expanding monopoly rights within the context of a trade regime that is purportedly concerned with dismantling trade monopolies and removing artificial barriers to competition.

Much of the public choice theory analysis as to why rent seeking exists within political processes focuses on how political representatives are required to succumb to rent-seeking activities. A failure to succumb will lead to a lack of sufficient political support such that the politician 'will be driven from the political market through a classic Darwinian market process'.[31] As Tollison has argued, a corollary of this rationale is those who are willing and able to pay the most for legislation become beneficiaries of the resulting wealth transfer and those who are least able to object become (unwitting) bearers of the resulting burden.[32] The shorthand terminology allocated to this skewing process is 'log-rolling', which refers to the situation whereby political representatives have a tendency towards endorsing laws that support their own self-interest but yet at the same time undermine social welfare.[33]

While a variety of legislative instruments become subject to rent-seeking activities, Boyle and Benkler respectively argue it would be difficult to provide a more pure example of rent-seeking than those activities associated with IPRs.[34] As Benkler pithily muses:

> The economic returns to exclusive proprietary rights in information are highly concentrated in the hands of those who own such rights ... Monopoly is a good thing to have if you can get it. Its value for rent extraction is no less valuable for a database or patent-based company than it is for the dictator's nephew in a banana republic.[35]

Although rent-seeking behaviour is not isolated to IPRs, an abundance of rent-seeking activity does occur within the IPR context.[36] As Buchanan argues, the problem with establishing legal mechanisms that promote rent seeking such as IPRs is they generate 'social waste' by entrenching government regulation which cannot be eroded through market competition.[37] Fittingly the example provided by Buchanan of rent seeking is a patent monopoly on the sale of playing cards in medieval England.[38]

As will be recalled from Part I, monopolies spawn a number of costs, the most important being distributional costs.[39] As a monopoly is a state-sponsored right we might hope the public at large received corresponding benefits as a consequence of this right. However, rent-seeking activities that accumulate around state-sponsored rights such as monopolies mean a quid pro quo in relation to monopoly rights is not always forthcoming. This is one of the essential lessons of public choice theory. Lemley explains rent seeking as it relates to IPRs this way:

> The grant by the government of exclusive rights over inventions, like the grant of any government largess, inevitably attracts attention by those who would like to get their share of benefits from the government. In the intellectual property context, this 'rent-seeking' behavior takes two different forms. First, the fact that patents in particular are granted to the first to invent may lead to races to invent. Some have worried that this racing will lead to wasteful duplication of research effort [e.g. human genome project] ... Second, and more problematic, the very process of government granting rights over creations encourages creators to petition Congress to give them still more rights. This sort of legislative rent-seeking has proven to be a real problem in intellectual property, particularly in the copyright field, where Congress of late seems willing to give copyright owners whatever they ask for, at least as long as there is no large vested interest making demands on the other side. This rent-seeking is a cost of government-granted intellectual property rights.[40]

Although both forms of rent seeking within this passage are significant this book concerns itself mostly with Lemley's latter (second) rent-seeking process: 'the very process of government granting rights over creations encourages creators to petition Congress to give them still more rights'.[41] Clearly rent seeking is a significant contributor to IPR maximalist tendencies.

While rent-seeking activities are often directed towards formation of regulatory frameworks, a key lesson from applying public choice theory to the physical environment is the influence concentrated interest groups have over administrative aspects of regulation. A preliminary analysis of the regulatory effect of concentrated interest groups suggests regulation is unlikely to be forthcoming where vested interest groups prefer no regulation. Yet public choice theory paints a more complex picture, ultimately suggesting the more likely scenario is a relative abundance of regulation that is less effective than it otherwise could be.[42] Concentrated interest groups benefit from this scenario at the expense of the public at large.[43] The process manifests as a corollary of the popular idiom 'the devil is in the detail'.

As Dwight Lee has explained, more often than not, if public opinion strongly favours legislation of one form or another, well-organised groups are likely to 'get on board' and 'support' legislation that is inimical to their economic interests.[44] But once the legislation is passed the organised interests are likely to be unrelenting in their efforts to influence the day-to-day details of the legislation's implementation. In other words, even where motivation for the initial legislation is based on the public interest, it is concentrated economic considerations which produce special interest influence that ends up affecting its operation. The administrative aspect of rent seeking is particularly relevant to the information environment because many important policy decisions concerning IPRs are delegated to IPR administrative agencies. These agencies tend to bypass participatory processes of legislative decision making.[45] Thus a critical aspect of the regulatory capture limb of public choice theory is concentrated interests are afforded the opportunity to capture the very IPR administrative agencies designed to regulate them.

If there is any dormant doubt about the applicability of public choice theory, and more specifically rent seeking, to the IPR regulatory framework, the work of Drahos and Braithwaite in *Information Feudalism: Who Owns the Knowledge Economy?* proffers vital insights.[46] In this cogent work the authors offer a systematic account of how concentrated IPR interests triumph over numerous but fragmented informational concerns (particularly within the international trade framework context).[47] A crucial question stemming from this account is whether regulatory capture effect can be counteracted. Exploring the interaction between collective action problems and civil society organisations is one way of engaging with this inquiry.

9.3.2 Collective Action Problems, Civil Society and the Public Sphere

Collective action problems essentially encompass informational costs, organising costs and the free-rider problem.[48] Information costs are concerned with costs associated with an individual ascertaining the effects of an issue on her individual welfare.[49] Organising costs relate to identification of other similarly positioned individuals who will join in her quest for favourable legislation.[50] Information costs and organising costs are intimately interrelated. Both types of costs are accentuated by the fact that '[t]he probability that an individual's vote will be decisive in … [the legislative process] is effectively zero'.[51] Accordingly for a majority of citizens it is simply not worth becoming sufficiently informed in order to have an opinion on most issues, let alone to do anything about the outcome.

Alongside the information costs and organising costs, public choice theory highlights large collectivities are also systematically disadvantaged in the political process because they tend to be more affected by incentives to free ride. In this respect Olson has reinforced the second limb of public choice theory by focusing attention on what appears prima facie to be a relatively rudimentary insight: 'rational people with interests in common will, in many instances, be unwilling to act with others to advance these common interests'.[52] To be sure, as was implied in Part I, free riding is generally overstated as it relates to the capture of positive externalities within the information environment. Yet in the context of large collectivities with diffuse interests there is no doubt free riding creates significant organising obstacles.

Overcoming collective action problems lies at the heart of environmentalism. The typical approach of advocates has been to rely upon political organisation channelled through civil society organisations.[53] In this regard, the environmental movement has clearly underscored the two limbs of public choice theory by (i) highlighting the detrimental effect of allowing concentrated interests to influence environmental regulatory policy, and (ii) emphasising the need to overcome the collective action problems that compound this detriment.[54] By understanding the two limbs of public choice theory diffuse groups have been able to (partly) overcome collective action problems as they relate to the physical environment.

In applying the two limbs of public choice theory to the Australian environmental context several lessons can be extracted. For instance, although a proposed wood-chipping mill in Tasmania might affect a large number of people, opponents of this proposal are generally not as well organised as the company that plans to operate the mill. As a consequence of the organisational proficiency of the company we can reason that regulatory capture is likely to ensue.[55] A parallel lesson is the environmental movement will benefit from the functioning of a broad range of specialised civil society organisations such as Friends of the Earth, Greenpeace, The Wilderness Society, Launceston Environmental Centre, Tasmanian Conservation Trust, and Tasmanian Land Care Fund. All of these organisations work to sustain a coalition of people who attend rallies and donate money even when the particular issue does not directly affect them. In this way collective action problems can be (partly) overcome.

So to reinforce, a critical function of civil society organisations is channelling political activity that might otherwise fall dormant. Within the context of the physical environment, an important strategy has been to provide concerned citizens with an opportunity to 'outsource' their concerns to experts whose norms and pedigree they relate to.[56] In so doing, the information costs of the public are lessened as civil society organisations act as 'agents of citizenship' by collating the concerns of citizens.[57] Emphasising the pragmatics of this approach Goodie states that:

> No matter how strong our personal feelings may be on a matter of public interest, the limited time available for political action, after being a worker, parent, student, friend, carer or watching television, and our limited capacity to act effectively as individuals means that, for most of us, financial membership of an advocacy organization or signing a petition is the closest we will get to action on the issue we purport to care about.[58]

By leveraging these pragmatic considerations, professional civil society organisations have successfully provided conduits for the sum of individual concerns.[59] A critical task here is formulating socially palatable notions of collective interest which can in turn be registered by the state. Clearly this strategy is built upon an implicit understanding of public choice theory and the resulting institutional diversity stemming from this understanding.[60] In other words, by fostering institutional diversity it becomes possible to unify otherwise disparate issues and interests. This in turn progresses the 'battle for clarity' when seeking to overcome the neglect of media and decision makers.[61]

Seemingly, it is the success of civil society organisations to overcome collective action problems that inspired Boyle to argue information environmentalists should learn from those advocates seeking the conservation and preservation of the physical environment.[62] As we have seen throughout the book an important aspect of Boyle's plea is that information environmentalists must rely upon the analytical tools and perception of common interest so as to create a politics to protect the information commons.[63] Thus, the power of information environmentalism to unite becomes apparent – to bind a set of individual struggles 'over this chunk of the genome and that aspect of computer programs' into a more fundamental struggle concerning macro issues relating to the information environment and/or the information commons.[64] Within this context, at the dawn of the twenty-first century Boyle prophesied:

> Just as the duck hunter finds common cause with the bird-watcher and the salmon geneticist by coming to think about 'the environment,' so an emergent concept of the public domain could tie together the interests of groups currently engaged in individual struggles with no sense of the larger context.[65]

The prescient nature of Boyle's plea to establish a politics to protect the information commons has been confirmed over the past decade. A plethora of information environmental civil society organisations have continued to evolve and flourish. Kapczynski, in her exceptional exposition of the A2K movement, has powerfully advanced this perspective by referring to an abundance of examples where the information commons has united otherwise disparate groups.[66] As implied, over the last few decades information environmental civil society organisations such as the Electronic Frontier Foundation (EFF), the Free Software Foundation (FSF), Public Knowledge (PK) and Creative Commons (CC) have all emerged to fulfil different functions and niches in a similar vein to the institutional evolution within the environmental movement.[67] Kapczynski's analysis of A2K reinforces that those seeking to protect the information commons have adopted, either implicitly or explicitly, many of the political organisational lessons inherent within the environmental movement. That is, in a similar vein to environmental civil society organisations, information environmental civil society organisations have simultaneously sought to counteract regulatory capture and overcome collective action problems.

There is no doubt civil society organisations have successfully harnessed political activity in protecting the physical environment. Yet overall, the speed and extent of physical environmental degradation has continued apace.[68] Similar sentiments can be expressed in relation to civil society organisations seeking to protect the information environment and/or information commons: both the physical environment and the information environment continue to be subject to the forces of degradation.

Although it is beyond the scope of this book to articulate a full and complete catalogue as to why both the physical environment and the information environment continue to be subject to degradatory forces, one worthy consideration is the inherent risks involved in relying upon civil society organisations to successfully channel political activity.[69] According to Gramsci an important risk here is that much of contemporary civil society forms the 'outer earthworks' of the state and the market because the ruling class leverages civil society to maintain their 'hegemony' or dominance in society.[70] Somewhat paradoxically, in order to rely upon civil society organisations to challenge the hegemony of the state and the market, perhaps we need to transform civil society itself.[71]

Later we will reflect upon how social production might realise Gramsci's paradoxical civil society transformation. But before doing so, let us now briefly consider the eroding influence of mass communication on the public sphere. This is important because such erosion creates obstacles in transforming civil society. The first step in appreciating the eroding influence of mass communication is to recognise the relationship between civil society and the public sphere. Charney's perspective is useful here:

> The public sphere is where people can discuss matters of mutual concern as peers, and learn about facts, events, and the opinions, interests, and perspectives of others. Discourse on values, norms, laws, and policies generates politically relevant public opinion. These discussions can occur within various units of civil society (thus we can speak of multiple 'public spheres' or 'civil publics'). But there is also a larger public sphere that mediates among the various mini-publics that emerge within and across organisations of concerned citizens, and informal social networks in the conception of public opinion.[72]

Thus a healthy public sphere and the resulting communities of disagreement are fundamental to civil society. If such are absent public discussion becomes hopelessly one-sided and analytically useless, particularly so when concentrated interest groups dominate debate as democratic deliberation becomes divorced from what is rationally correct and rather tends towards a 'calculation of interests'.[73] Carpignano's assessment is acutely germane:

> The mass media today are the public sphere and … this is the reason for the degradation of public life if not its disappearance. Public life, the argument goes, has been transformed by a massive process of commodification of culture and of political culture in particular by a form of communication increasingly based on emotionally charged images rather than on rational discourse, such that political discourse has been degraded to the level of entertainment, and cultural consumerism has been substituted for democratic participation.[74]

Contemporaneously information environmentalists have reinforced this 'commodification of political culture' dynamic. Vaidhyanathan, for instance, has underscored the deleterious influence of mass communication on civil society by arguing that at the beginning of the twentieth century corporatisation of communication functions throughout nation-states had sapped the bourgeois public sphere of its deliberative potential and therefore much of its purpose.[75] Here, the Internet as a technological platform and the accompanying networked information economy as an organisation model of social production are often put forward as alternative springboards for transforming civil society.[76] In the process a parallel is drawn between the 'third space' that emerged in the West during the eighteenth century and the promising emergence of the Internet in the late twentieth century.[77] In the former era the third space served to mediate between domestic concerns and matters of state.[78]

Hence, despite, or perhaps because of the corporatisation of mass communication evident throughout the nineteenth and twentieth centuries, at the dawn of the twenty-first century the Internet has reignited Habermasian yearnings for rational discourse that has the potential to liberate.[79] The work of information environmentalists such as Benkler and Rheingold exemplify this optimistic interpretation of social production.[80] These scholars perceive the emergence of impressive and efficient organisational practices as an indication Habermasian notions might be realised in the form of digital signals and online democratic culture.

As Vaidhyanathan makes clear the Internet is not immune from the hegemonic forces of the state and the market.[81] Yet it is equally the case that the Internet has substantially facilitated the amplification of social production methods.[82] The end game is that social production is an important complement to the political activities of civil society organisations. This perspective is built upon the intuition that economic efficiencies of social production provide opportunities to overcome collective action problems inherent within the information environment.[83] An accompanying claim is social production provides scope to realise Gramsci's paradoxical civil society transformation. By further reflecting upon social production methodology (and associated economic efficiencies) we can contextualise this standpoint.

9.4 SOCIAL PRODUCTION

While social production is often thought of as a novelty, Benkler reminds such methods have been in operation since time immemorial.[84] The disciplines of science, law, education and music all provide examples of non-proprietary social production methodology.[85] Although the industrial model of production which dominated during the nineteenth and twentieth centuries tended to favour exclusivity, this is not so in relation to information production. As Benkler states, 'non-proprietary strategies have always been more important in information production than they were in the production of steel or automobiles'.[86] The crux is within the information production domain the social production methodology tends to trump.

In the next chapter we will contrast social production with state-, market- and firm-based production. For now social production remains front and centre. We can note this mode of production exhibits two critical traits. It is *commons based* and *decentralist.* Benkler implicitly alluded to these social production characteristics in the following passage:

> [I]n [*social*] *production*, we are seeing an avenue of resistance to the hierarchical exercise of economic power that does not flow through the state. More Kropotkin than Lenin, this source of *power in the hands of people networked together* is, I think, the single most attractive feature of the information commons.[87]

As social production is commons based the protection and nurturance of the information commons (as discussed in Part II) is an imperative of the social production mode. FLOSS, as a commons-based exemplar, relies intimately upon the commons on a philosophical and practical level.[88] Philosophically speaking, many FLOSS participants advocate a brand of positive community information commons; and practically speaking, the General Public License facilitates a type of privately ordered commons. Thus, aside from being a 'poster child' of social production, FLOSS also represents an innovative privately ordered method of fostering the information commons. In this way FLOSS implicitly underscores the intimate relationship between the information commons and social production. Obviously FLOSS is not the only contemporary social production exemplar which flows from the information commons. There are countless other commons-based social production examples embedded within the Internet, Wikipedia being the most commonly cited example.

Information commons-based initiatives such as FLOSS and Wikipedia are allocated a variety of labels including open source, peer production, crowd-sourcing, bazaar production and distributed creativity.[89] The latter notion is often attributed to Bill Nichols, although Yochai Benkler's *The Wealth of Networks* is perhaps the most important contemporary work relating to information commons-based production and related concepts.[90] Benkler defines commons-based production as 'radically decentralised, collaborative, and nonproprietary; based on sharing resources and outputs among widely distributed, loosely connected individuals who cooperate with each other without relying on either market signals or managerial commands'.[91] Social production is a subset of commons-based production because it not only focuses on how resources are managed (as per the commons) but also on how in fact users make decisions about what to do.[92] More specifically then, we can rely upon Benkler's description of social production as 'production systems that depend on individual action that is self-selected and decentralised, rather than hierarchically assigned'.[93]

Beyond being commons based, another vital attribute of social production is it relies on *decentralised*, micro level decision makers who are not bound to 'follow the signals generated by market-based, firm-based, or hybrid models'.[94] Within *The Wealth of Networks*, Benkler goes to some effort to flesh out the difference between centralisation and decentralisation. As Benkler explains, centralisation implies the separation of the locus of opportunities for action from the authority to choose the action that an agent will undertake.[95] On the other hand decentralisation implies conditions under which the actions of many agents cohere and are effective even though they do not rely on reducing the number of people whose will counts to direct effective action.[96] In the next chapter we will see how the centralisation/decentralisation dichotomy relates to planning, particularly in terms of who does it. For now, planning also provides clues as to the economic efficiencies of social production. These efficiencies can be fleshed out with reference to Benkler's hardware-code-content paradigm.

9.4.1 Hardware-code-content Paradigm

As Benkler stresses the practice of social production methods is 'not as a second best or a contingent remainder from the Middle Ages, but because at some things the non-proprietary [social] production system ... is simply better'.[97] There are some established criteria for determining whether social production methods can extend to the development of contemporary technologies beyond computer software (e.g. biotechnology or nanotechnology). The hardware-code-content paradigm discussed in Benkler's germinal article *Coase's Penguin, or, Linux and the Nature of the Firm* is particularly valuable in this regard.[98] The initial step within this paradigm is to divide the technology into layers.[99] The Internet, for instance, consists of three layers: first, *hardware*, which represents the machinery that facilitates the network; second, *code*, which facilitates the information travelling over the network; third, *content*, which is the actual information communicated.[100] In *The Future of Ideas*, Lessig discusses how these layers apply to various traditional modes of communication, such as Speaker's Corner in London, the arts, books and music.[101] In each area, the different layers, which may be either controlled or open, can be teased out.[102]

As Lessig argues, under Benkler's criteria, the best candidate for open source development is generally the *code* layer because code is usually 'modular', 'granular' and exhibits relatively 'low-cost integration'.[103] To extrapolate these characteristics, modularity relates to whether the project can be divided into asynchronous components. As discussed in Chapter 6 with respect to ecology and FLOSS, asynchronous components allow individuals to choose independently of each other what to contribute and when, which in turn maximises their ability to define the nature, extent and timing of their participation within a project.[104] This characteristic is critical since the self-direction of creative and intellectual input is essential within the context of social production. The modules must be fine grained, meaning each module is sufficiently small in terms of time and effort an agent must expend in order to produce a module. The number of people who are likely to participate in a project is inversely related to the size of the smallest-scale contribution necessary to produce a usable module. If the finest-grained contributions are relatively large, requiring significant investment of time and effort, the number of potential contributors diminishes. Consequently a significant proportion of the modules in a large-scale social production project must be relatively fine grained if the project is to be successful. The cost to integrate the modules must be lower than the value that the component adds to the project.

Therefore, when a project is modular, fine grained and exhibits relatively low-cost integration, social production may indeed have a comparative advantage over the alternate modes of production. The strength of the hardware-code-content paradigm is that it points to the conditions where social production may have a comparative advantage over other production modes. We will reinforce the comparative advantage characteristics of social production in the next chapter. For now, let us continue to explore the economic efficiencies of social production with reference to information processing and allocative efficiency.

9.4.2 Information Processing and Allocative Efficiency

As we have seen, social production is commons based and decentralist. It is also economically efficient, at least in discrete circumstances. Economic efficiencies of social production can be partly explained with reference to information processing and allocative efficiency.

All production modes rely upon some form of information processing.[105] This processing ultimately serves the function of lowering the uncertainty agents are confronted with when making economic decisions about the best course of action. Reducing uncertainty and costs associated with economic activity is fundamental, no matter how something is produced.[106] For instance, within market-based production the price mechanism is the method deployed to compare the relative value of alternate actions and therefore to reduce uncertainty. A critical function of price is it allows agents to (imperfectly) measure opportunity costs implicit within economic decision-making processes.[107] There is no doubt the price mechanism is useful. Yet Benkler highlights the imperfections of price by pointing to the relative homogeneity of law firm starting salaries as compared to the large variation in individual ability and motivational levels of law graduates.[108] The market is riddled with such discrepancies, which exemplifies the leaky nature of the price mechanism and (by extension) the leaky nature of the market.

Correspondingly, within the context of firm-based production, information processing is largely the domain of firm managers who rely upon property law and contractual arrangements to control both resources and people respectively. This control, however, is not without opportunity cost. By controlling resources via property law and commanding employees via contract, a boundary is set around the available set of resources and available agents. The boundary-setting effect limits the information flow available to managers. Hence, like the price system, hierarchical organisations are also an imperfect and leaky medium. This is because within a hierarchical organisation there is a host of 'lost information' concerning the factors of production that may have otherwise affected economic decision making.[109] In other words, a corollary of boundary setting (via property and contract) is that it becomes difficult to assess what other agents could have done with these same resources or what else these agents could have done with other resources. For the last several decades this dynamic has been appreciated by the knowledge-management movement within business schools, which has concerned itself with (among other things) how to moderate the leaky nature of managerial hierarchies.[110]

Recognising the leaky nature of both markets and firms is an important step in understanding why social production initiatives such as FLOSS and Wikipedia have been successful. Namely, social production has lower information opportunity costs when compared with markets or firms.[111] This is particularly the case where human intellect or creativity is a salient factor of production because of the self-identification nature of task allocation within social production. In many instances, self-identification is a more effective method of gathering and utilising information about 'who should be doing what' than a system that requires the allocation of tasks via contractual and proprietary specification.[112]

It is the decentralist nature of social production that influences the core question of 'who does what?' As it transpires, there are allocative efficiency gains to be had when individuals decide what they do and when they do it. An important part of this equation is the absence of private property. The crux of social production efficiency related to the *absence of private property* is that because social production relies on unbounded access of agents to resources and projects there are increasing economies of scale.[113] This is because the idiosyncratic characteristics of individuals means the overall productivity of a set of agents and set of resources will increase when there is an unbounded availability of agents and an unbounded set of projects. Even if in principle the decision maker has information as to who is the best person for a job given a particular set of resources and projects, the transaction costs involved in bringing that agent to bear on the project may be too great relative to the efficiency gain over the use of the resource by the next-best available agent who is within the boundary.[114] In short, a world whereby all agents can act effectively on all resources is likely to be more productive in creating information goods than a world in which firms divide the universe of agents and resources into bounded sets.[115] Thus, in a similar vein to information processing, the commons-based and decentralist characteristics of social production foster significant allocative efficiencies.

Social production will be further leveraged in the following chapter with reference to its ability to compete with alternate production modes. In doing so, we will see that social production can make an important contribution to operationalising the proposed separation of economic power doctrine (as per principle 12 of Table 1.1).

9.5 CONCLUSION

Public choice theory is intensely pertinent to regulatory frameworks relating to both the physical environment and the information environment. In the early days of public choice theory the key focus was the effect that concentrated interest groups had on regulatory frameworks. More contemporaneously, the theory has morphed to also consider how collective action problems might be overcome. The consolidation of environmental civil society organisations over the last several decades exemplifies this theoretical shift. Due to the success (albeit limited) of environmental civil society organisations, James Boyle and other information environmentalists have stressed the imperative of drawing upon lessons from the contemporary environmental movement. There is no doubt civil society organisations have had an important positive influence over physical environment regulatory frameworks. Yet the scale and extent of environmental degradation continues apace. Similar sentiments can be expressed with respect to the information environment and/or the information commons. We saw in this chapter there are significant risks in relying solely upon civil society organisations to save the day. This is why we should think of social production as a useful complementary method of overcoming collective action problems. Such an approach relies not so much on building a politic but rather upon the economic efficiencies of social production (such as information processing and allocative efficiency). In recognising the economic efficiencies of social production we can then start to think about its 'constitutional' effect within the broader political economic framework. Entertaining this possibility is a key function of the ensuing chapter.

10. Constitutional economics and the separation of (economic) power

One person with a belief is a social power equal to 99 who have only interests.

John Stuart Mill

10.1 INTRODUCTION

In the last chapter we began to see that social production can complement the political activities of civil society organisations. This perspective was based on the premise that while the political advocacy of information environmental civil society organisations is an important aspect of protecting the information commons, political organisation alone is unlikely to suffice. In this chapter we will observe that beyond overcoming collective action problems, social production can also be leveraged to operationalise the proposed separation of (economic) power doctrine. Economic efficiencies and comparative advantage of social production are critical here, as is the competitive tension between the alternate productive forces of the state, the market, the firm and society.

After outlining constitutional economics generally, the chapter will highlight the decentralising characteristics of constitutional constraints such as federalism and the separation of powers doctrine. The focus will then turn to contrasting the alternative production modes being state-, market-, firm- and social-based production. In the process, the concluding submission from the preceding chapter is reinforced: in discrete circumstances social production may surpass the advantages of alternate production modes.[1] In discussing the comparative advantage of social production we will see that such an advantage relies upon the fulfilment of two vital prerequisites (as per principle 10 of Table 1.1), being equitable access to (i) the information commons, and (ii) critical hardware infrastructure. Since the information commons has been discussed at length already (especially in Part II), the final aspect of the chapter will focus on equitable access to 'critical hardware infrastructure'.

10.2 SMALL-C CONSTITUTIONAL CONSTRAINTS AND SOCIAL PRODUCTION

Buchanan and Tullock published *The Calculus of Consent* in the early 1960s, giving rise to public choice theory. Yet it was not until the 1980s that the related notion of 'constitutional economics', being an offshoot of public choice theory, was formally coined. Although the 'constitutional economic' label only became part of the economic lexicon during the last several decades, in many respects, as Buchanan himself has acknowledged, the constitutional economic discipline is more closely aligned with the work of Adam Smith and the classical economists than its modern 'non-constitutional' counterpart.[2] In particular, constitutional economics accords with Adam Smith's moral philosophy perspective or more specifically the 'science of legislation', which is an academic enterprise blending economic, political, social, legal and philosophical viewpoints.[3]

Constitutional economics ultimately relates to *choice*. While most economic discourse is concerned with *choice*, constitutional economics seeks to shift the focus from the dominant preoccupation of economics being choice *within* constraints to a more macro perspective exploring choice *among* constraints.[4] In this respect, the attention of constitutional economics is on the rules that shape the framework in which the regular choices of economic and political agents are made.[5] A broad perspective of 'choice' and 'rules' is adopted such that individual decision making is said to affect the social order.[6] It follows that the advice of a constitutional economist is best directed at those who participate in constitutional change, rather than at political agents who act within a defined rule set.[7]

A key insight of Buchanan and Tullock's work was to focus on the core document – the Constitution – that establishes the rules and creates the institutions within which the political process operates.[8] The word 'constitutional' as it relates to constitutional economics is largely metaphorical. This is because, although the said discipline does occasionally emphasise the economic analysis of constitutional law, its main focus is to establish a broader research programme directing inquiry to 'the working properties of rules, and institutions within which individuals interact, and the process through which these rules and institutions are chosen or come into being'.[9]

In consolidating the distinction between the various uses of the word 'constitution' within constitutional economics, Brennan and Hamlin contrast capital-C Constitutionalism with small-c constitutionalism. Constitution in the capital-C sense relates to 'legal documents that seek to specify some aspects of the political and economic institutions of a political community'. In contrast, constitution in the small-c sense is deployed in a broader frame to include 'those things that constitute the social order'.[10] Obviously there is an overlap and interrelationship between capital-C and small-c constitutionalism. For instance within legal discourse the capital-C Constitution is considered to be an important manifestation of the *Grundnorm*.[11] This is because the Constitution determines the set of rules that govern political institutions and market interactions. Yet a Constitution rarely stands on its own in facilitating social order. A variety of constitutional mechanisms complement the 'core document'. Democratic elections, federalism and the separation of powers doctrine are the most obvious examples.

The constitution as perceived by Hayek is grounded in small-c constitutionalism. He believed that the 'core document' is a 'superstructure erected over preexisting systems of law to organise the enforcement of those systems'.[12] This *lex mercatoria* perspective of law is to be contrasted with the more widespread small-c conception of constitutionalism, which is based on the 'social contract' premise that a community has unanimously agreed on values and principles establishing constraints within which the community can act and markets operate.[13] This prevailing social contract viewpoint establishes a strong bind between discourse relating to the constitution and the contractarian approach that seeks to respond to the so-called Hobbesian state of nature.[14] According to the small-c social contract perspective, a critical function of a constitution is to militate against real or perceived Hobbesian state of nature insurgences through the embedment of property rights and other mechanisms that allow for social and market exchanges.[15] Inherent within this approach is the 'paradox of government'. Weingast underscored the paradox thus: 'The fundamental political dilemma of an economic system is this: A government strong enough to protect property rights and enforce contracts is also strong enough to confiscate the wealth of its citizen[s].'[16]

The follow-on question typically stemming from this paradox is: *Quis custodiet ipsos custodies?* Or, who guards the guardians? In other words, how does one constrain government? The answer is usually found in small-c constitutional constraints such as democratic elections, federalism and the separation of powers doctrine. Such mechanisms effectively serve to decentralise political power so as to place limits on how that power can be deployed.[17] Constitutional constraints such as federalism and the separation of powers doctrine were considered important hallmarks of the brand of liberal economic democracy advanced by the US Constitution framers in the eighteenth century. James Madison reflected the rationale for such constraints in *The Federalist No. 51* as follows:

> But what is government itself, but the greatest of all reflections of human nature? If men were angels, no government would be necessary. If angels were to govern men, neither external nor internal controls on government would be necessary. In framing a government which is to be administered by men over men, the great difficulty lies in this: you must first enable the government to control the governed; and in the next place oblige it to control itself. A dependence on the people is, no doubt, the primary control on the government; but experience has taught mankind the necessity of auxiliary precautions.[18]

The central claim of Madison was constitutional power must be decentralised so as to place inherent limitations on how that power can be operationalised. To this end, the essence of constitutional constraints is to militate against the old adage 'power corrupts and absolute power corrupts absolutely'.[19] It is decentralisation of power through constitutional constraints, which serves as an important means of disrupting the corruptive influence of power. If we lay aside postmodern Foucauldian conceptions, constitutional economics usually frames power in either vertical or horizontal terms.[20]

In relation to the vertical axis, power is to be decentralised within a federalist structure through division of power between the federal government and corresponding state governments. In this way a multi-level constitutional organisation is established by allocating legislation and taxation prerogatives to various levels of government.[21] In the Australian context, for instance, it is Section 51 of the Australian Constitution that outlines the powers of Federal Parliament (with the residual power lying with the respective State Parliaments). An important rationale of this division of power is to foster competitive tension *between* the Commonwealth Government and respective State governments to facilitate a self-enforcing mechanism to protect citizens from the central government.[22]

Correspondingly, *horizontal* power can be decentralised in a variety of ways within federalist liberal economic democracies.[23] One method is to establish a differing criterion for representation between two legislative branches (e.g. Lower House and Upper House). The rationale here being that the differing representational criterion nurtures competitive tension *within* the Federal Parliament.

Hence, at least theoretically, federalist liberal economic democracies such as the US and Australia decentralise power by fostering competitive tension *between* and *within* constitutional bodies.[24]

Beyond the differing criterion for representation between the two legislative branches, another complementary method of decentralising horizontal power is through the separation of powers doctrine. The application of this doctrine is obviously central to our present discussion. Locke alluded to the separation of powers doctrine during the Enlightenment by discussing the need to constrain the operation of law in order to protect the freedom of citizens.[25] In borrowing from the English constitutional model, Montesquieu further developed this aspect of Locke's thinking in *The Spirit of the Law* through his explicit promotion of the separation of power between the executive, legislative and judicial arms of governance.[26] In an often-quoted passage, Montesquieu stated:

> When legislative power is united with executive power in a single person or in a single body of the magistracy, there is no liberty, because one can fear that the same monarch or senate that makes tyrannical laws will execute them tyrannically ... Nor is there liberty if the power of judging is not separate from legislative power and from executive power. If it were joined to legislative power, the power over life and liberty of the citizens would be arbitrary, for the judge would be the legislator. If it were joined to executive power, the judge could have the force of an oppressor.[27]

While the separation of power between executive and legislature is not obvious in many Western liberal economic democracies, the separation between the executive and legislature (on the one hand) and judiciary (on the other hand) does remain a central tenet of most contemporary democratic frameworks. Naturally, a key objective of the separation of power is to decentralise political decision making. It is within this broad frame the decentralist nexus between constitutional economics and social production begins to unravel. This nexus can be elaborated in true constitutional economic form by considering how constitutional constraints such as the separation of power doctrine apply to the economic domain (rather than the political domain). That is, rather than considering the separation of power doctrine as a purely capital-C notion concerned with the formal separation of political power, what would happen if the separation of power doctrine was to be conceptualised through a small-c constitutional economic lens? One way to answer this question is to explore the proposed separation of (economic) power doctrine.

10.3 SEPARATION OF (ECONOMIC) POWER

Applying small-c constitutional economics to the information environment creates a springboard to discuss competitive economic tensions between the productive forces of the state, the market, the firm and society.[28] In doing so we arrive at the separation of economic power doctrine.

The relevant modes of production will be contrasted below. Before we do so, a further explanation of the relationship between competitive economic tension and the separation of powers doctrine is warranted. In the first instance it may seem that drawing a link between economic-based competition (as it concerns the productive forces) and the separation of powers doctrine is building a bridge too far. Yet deeper contemplation reveals that economic competition seeks to provide checks and balances within the economy in a similar vein to how the separation of powers doctrine provides checks and balances within the political system. As Long argues '[s]eparation of powers, like federalism and elective democracy, merely *simulates* market competition, within a fundamentally monopolistic context'.[29] The facilitation of competition between the various production modes serves to avert the threat of one or more of the productive forces obtaining disproportionate bargaining power.[30]

Although competition policy has traditionally been used as a micro-economic policy, and the separation of powers has traditionally been implemented within a capital-C frame, there is no inherent reason why both economic competition and the separation of powers doctrine cannot be operationalised through a small-c constitutional prism. This approach serves to simultaneously broaden the application of competition policy and the separation of powers doctrine. A core consideration then becomes how to foster a balance and tension between the main productive forces of the firm, the market, the state, and society at large.[31] Ultimately this small-c constitutional economic perspective seeks to separate power along the *economic* axis rather than the axis of *politics*.

A key rationale for this small-c constitutional economic approach is that during the past several decades power has tended to shift (within liberal economic democracies) from the public sphere to the private sphere.[32] Yet the legal and political structures have not evolved accordingly. In order to grapple with this power transition contemporary constitutionalism should, at least normatively speaking, recognise that jurisprudential issues within the private law domain (such as competition law, patent law, and copyright law) represent the fundamental public constitutional questions of the information age.[33] A question that follows from this approach is: How do the laws relating to competition and intellectual property concern the notion of 'free speech'? In the US, this question might be put in more specific terms: How does the private sphere inform the First Amendment?[34] Or, will the US Supreme Court inadvertently delve into civil society when determining the constitutionality of legislation such as the Copyright Act or the Patent Act?[35] In engaging with this type of questioning, Fitzgerald *et al* have suggested there needs to be a 'broader appreciation of the dynamic constitutive choices being made in adjudicating upon issues of interpretation of the private law'.[36]

Regardless of the specific outcomes of capital-C constitutional battles relating to the public and private sphere, social production may already be having a small-c constitutional effect in simultaneously transforming and consolidating the power of civil society. If this is true as is claimed, then we can further argue social production is contributing to the separation of economic power by competing with the state, the market and the firm. In order to progress this stance we must explicitly contrast the relevant modes of production.

10.3.1 Modes of Production

Production occurs through different means, or put another way, through different modes. For our purpose the most important modes are state-, market-, firm- and social-based production. Each mode represents an ideal to the extent that in reality production is often hybridised between the modes.[37] For instance throughout the last few decades, with a mixed history of success, there are many examples of Public Private Partnerships (PPP) where the state and the market work together to provision public infrastructure resources such as prisons, hospitals, roads and bridges.[38] Likewise within the context of the information environment the hybridisation of production is an important factor within social production models as evidenced by the collaboration between Creative Commons and Microsoft.[39] The business models of YouTube and Facebook and other such Web 2.0 websites also seek to aggressively leverage and monetise social production in its various shapes and forms. And of course social production initiatives such as Mozilla Firefox rely to some extent upon the firm as an organisational model.

Yet notwithstanding the somewhat fused nature of the alternate production modes, there are nevertheless distinguishing features that can best be analytically appreciated by contrasting the modes in their *ideal form*. In doing so, the unique characteristics of each mode of production can then be fleshed out. Reliance upon the political economic diagram in Figure 10.1 is useful here.

Just as each mode of production represents an ideal, the same can be said with respect to the corresponding political economic systems reflected in Figure 10.1. As we began to see in the previous chapter, a key distinguishing feature between alternate production modes is not planning per se but rather who does it.[40] In this regard the information-processing characteristics of the relevant production modes are significant. State-based production

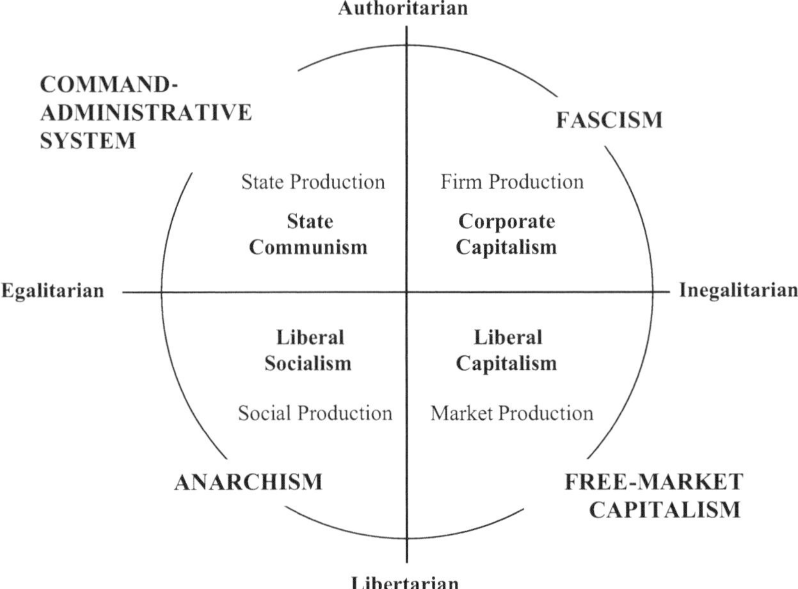

Source: Derived from Stilwell, F. (2000), *Changing Direction: A New Political Economic Direction for Australia*, Pluto Press, at 124.

Figure 10.1 Political economics of production

generally relies upon elected ministers and accompanying bureaucracies to make planning decisions; market-based production relies principally upon the price mechanism; firm-based production relies upon hierarchical managers; and social-based production relies upon decentralised and commons-fuelled self-selection methods.[41] Regardless of how each production mode plans, each mode is working towards the same end – to reduce uncertainty and costs associated with economic activity.[42] By contrasting these modes we can begin to see how the different modes fulfil different niches within the overall production landscape.

10.3.1.1 State production

State production is relatively self-explanatory being production engaged with by the state. Given the neoliberal reliance on Adam Smith, it is ironic he was one of the first to recognise the market sometimes fails in relation to public goods. To this end, Smith was a strong advocate of *state production* in overcoming the public goods market failure:

> [One] duty of the sovereign or commonwealth is that of erecting and maintaining those public institutions and these public works, which, though they may be in the highest degree advantageous to a great society, are, however, of such a nature, that the profit could never repay the expence to any individual or small number of individuals, and which it therefore cannot be expected that any individual or small number of individuals should erect or maintain.[43]

Along with the public goods already discussed in Part I, monetary currency and infrastructure provide further exemplars of public goods.[44] The state provisions these goods because they are generally subject to the public goods market failure.[45] Clearly the state is an important producer in its own right, especially in relation to infrastructure and the provision of essential services. But through their reliance on microeconomic techniques, public choice theorists often highlight that the creation of laws can also be seen as a form of state production.[46]

When the creation of law is perceived through the broader state production lens the dual function of state production – overcoming market failure and facilitating alternative modes of production – can be noted.[47] With respect to overcoming market failure we have already seen how the state is often accorded responsibility for establishing 'public institutions' and 'public works' so as to overcome public goods provisioning problems. Adam Smith explicitly endorsed this state function in *The Wealth of Nations*.[48] With respect to facilitating alternative modes of production the state can also overcome market failure by 'producing' regulation in order to influence economic activity. Pigou discussed this aspect of state production at length in *The Economics of Welfare*.[49] Perhaps the best way of understanding this second function is to contrast the perspectives of Adam Smith and Arthur Pigou with that of Ronald Coase.

10.3.1.2 Market production

The perspectives of Smith and Pigou – of relying upon state production (intervention) to overcome market failure – is to be contrasted with the view expressed by Coase in *The Problem of Social Cost*. In this work, Coase provided an oppositional perspective to Smith and Pigou by arguing the state should move away from the first function of state production and rather embrace the second function (as discussed above).[50] That is, in advocating the utility of the market, Coase argued the best way for the state to fulfil the first function of state production is to embrace the second function by establishing strong property rights and contract laws.[51] The reasoning goes that these laws facilitate market production, and market production in turn facilitates decentralised economic activity through price signals.[52] In other words, according to Coase's viewpoint, rather than relying upon the state, market failures such as externalities can be more effectively overcome by allowing economic agents to bargain within the marketplace. In this way Coase sought to demonstrate how the private bargaining of individuals in relation to costs and benefits of various economic activities counters the need for state production.

According to the Coase/Demsetz analysis it does not matter who has the relevant right to engage in a given economic activity because provided that transaction costs are low 'rearrangement will always take place if it will result in an increase in the value of production'.[53] While the externalities paradox discussed in Part I queried particular aspects of this Coasian/Demsetzian theory, the task here is to contrast the alternate production modes.

The chief contrasting feature between state- and market-based production is the planning agent. That is, as both state- and market-based production require planning, the difference between each mode is not planning per se but rather who does it.[54] Within state production it is obviously the state that dominates planning (i.e. relevant ministers and accompanying bureaucracies) whereas within the marketplace it is individual private agents who dominate. Accordingly when contrasting state- and market-based production the state generally represents a more centralised form of economic activity than the market.

Many of the characteristics employed to distinguish the state from the market are also relevant in distinguishing between the market and the firm. For this reason we will now turn to a discussion of firm production to consolidate the distinction between the market and the firm (and thereby the state and the market).

10.3.1.3 Firm production

Along with contrasting state- and market-based production the work of Coase is also significant when seeking to distinguish the market and the firm. We have already seen that the market is generally coordinated in a decentralised manner through price signals.[55] In contrast 'a firm is any hierarchical structure … in which economic activity is centrally coordinated through the authoritative decisions of managers or leaders'.[56] As with the distinction between the state and the market, the issue again is not planning per se but rather who does it.[57]

The best method of contrasting market- and firm-based production is to highlight those circumstances when one mode of production is advantageous over another. This was the core guiding aim of Coase's seminal article, *The Nature of the Firm*, when he asked the simple, yet profound, question of why it was that not all production throughout the world occurred within one giant firm.[58] To answer this question it is necessary to rely upon the theory of market exchange alongside the theory of the firm.[59]

Market exchange theory indicates that market transactions will generally be advantageous over intra-firm transactions as the firm becomes larger due to diseconomies of scale stemming from organisation, coordination and monitoring costs within a firm.[60] For example, depending upon the size of the firm, the market tends to be more efficient in monitoring performance because there is 'a high correlation between rewards and productivity'.[61]

On the other side of the ledger the theory of the firm indicates that firm-based production is generally more advantageous than market-based production in mitigating costs associated with contractual performance.[62] As indicated by Coase the size of the firm will be a key determinant in influencing how the costs inherent within the firm compare to the costs related to the market.

Coase goes to some length to distinguish between the firm and the market in *The Nature of the Firm* but for the present purpose the most relevant aspect of the distinction is the centralisation/decentralisation dichotomy. This dichotomy is also relevant with respect to social production.

10.3.1.4 Social production

Market- and social-based production both exhibit decentralist traits. Yet the production modes differ to the extent that social production does not rely upon the price signal. Instead, social production is founded upon a range of economic efficiencies flowing from information processing and allocative efficiency.[63] As we have seen, when a project is modular, fine grained and exhibits relatively low-cost integration, social production may indeed have a comparative advantage over the alternate modes of production. Social production is not always more effective than alternate production modes. Rather, where the factors of production include undeveloped ideas and unarticulated know-how (i.e. uncodified information) and where allocation of human creativity and/or intellectual input are relied upon as the engines of innovation, social production may in some instances surpass the advantages of states, markets and/or firms.[64]

The comparative advantage of social production means that social production can be leveraged to foster the small-c constitutional economic function of facilitating competitive tension within the 'production marketplace'.[65] Within this frame the key argument can be reinforced: social production holds the potential to decentralise economic power, which in turn operationalises the proposed separation of (economic) power doctrine.[66] In order for social production to realise the decentralising function of this doctrine, two vital prerequisites must be satisfied,[67] that is, equitable access to: (i) the information commons, and (ii) critical hardware infrastructure. In other words, just as market- and firm-based production are founded upon state-provisioned property rights and contract law, so too contemporary social production is premised upon the prerequisites of equitable access to the information commons and critical hardware infrastructure.[68]

As the information commons has already been discussed at length in Part II (and elsewhere) we will now, in finality, turn to a discussion of the critical hardware infrastructure imperative.

10.3.1.4.1 Critical hardware infrastructure In *The Second Enclosure Movement* Boyle implies that the question of whether social production can scale further into other domains outside of FLOSS is perhaps the wrong question.[69] Yet he continues:

> [T]here is a chance that a new (or old, but under-recognized) method of production could flourish in ways that seem truly valuable – valuable to free speech, innovation, scientific discovery, and the wallets of consumers, what William Fisher calls 'semiotic democracy', and perhaps, valuable to the balance between joyful creation and drudgery for hire.[70]

Boyle's lingering optimism concerning the 'scale-ability' of social production is seemingly founded, at least partly, on the promise of ensuring the inputs of information production are not locked away as a corollary of the second enclosure movement and related IPR maximalist impulses. In short, Boyle implies if IPR maximalist tendencies trump, then commons-based social production methods are likely to face an arduous battle.[71] Put another way, the information commons is a vital prerequisite of social production and the information environment generally. Interestingly, within this context, Boyle muses on a tangential point – innovation, and invention generally, requires 'hardware, capital investment, and large-scale real-world data collection – *stuff*, in its infinite recalcitrance and facticity'.[72]

In many respects the critical hardware infrastructure imperative alluded to by Boyle is as applicable for commons-based, social production as it is for market- and firm-based production.[73] Even traditional social production modalities such as science, law, education and music require a default level of critical hardware infrastructure.[74] Contemporaneously FLOSS simply would not have eventuated without broad-scale access to the critical hardware infrastructure of personal computing and telecommunication services.

Contrasting the development of computer software with other forms of modern technological innovation such as biotechnology is one means of exploring the role of critical hardware infrastructure as it relates to social production and accompanying questions of scale-ability. In this connection CAMBIA has been working on the application of social production methods to biotechnology for some time.[75] While it has undoubtedly had some critical successes, CAMBIA's open source biotechnology methods have not yet proliferated.[76] Presumably one of the obstacles to applying social production to innovations such as biotechnology is the capital-intensive nature of biotechnological processes and procedures. Although a computer operating system or software application can be developed with nothing more than 'a laptop, an Internet connection and a packet of Doritos', biotechnology development demands access to bio-informatic data, equipment and know-how far beyond the reach of a basement hacker.[77]

While biotechnological development presently remains more expensive than computer software development, this is mostly because the costs of building the necessary critical hardware infrastructure relevant to computer software development – such as the development of operating systems, the laying of fibre optic cables for fast cheap Internet connection and so on – have already been expended.[78] In biotechnology on the other hand, huge investments are still to be made.[79] In other words, the level and timing of critical hardware infrastructure development is one of the key reasons why there is a *social production disjuncture* when contrasting software development and biotechnology development. This point has explanatory power to the extent that the monopolistic firm-based production tendencies currently practised within biotechnology innovation are similar to those that occurred in the 1980s in relation to computer software development.[80] Figure 10.2 elucidates the importance of critical hardware infrastructure by contrasting the relative infrastructure development and accessibility in relation to computer software, biotechnology and nanotechnology.

When an industry resides below the social production continuum in Figure 10.2, the mode of production is likely to be dominated by monopolistic firm-based production tendencies. When infrastructure development and accessibility within an industry rises above the social production continuum, social production will become a feasible and

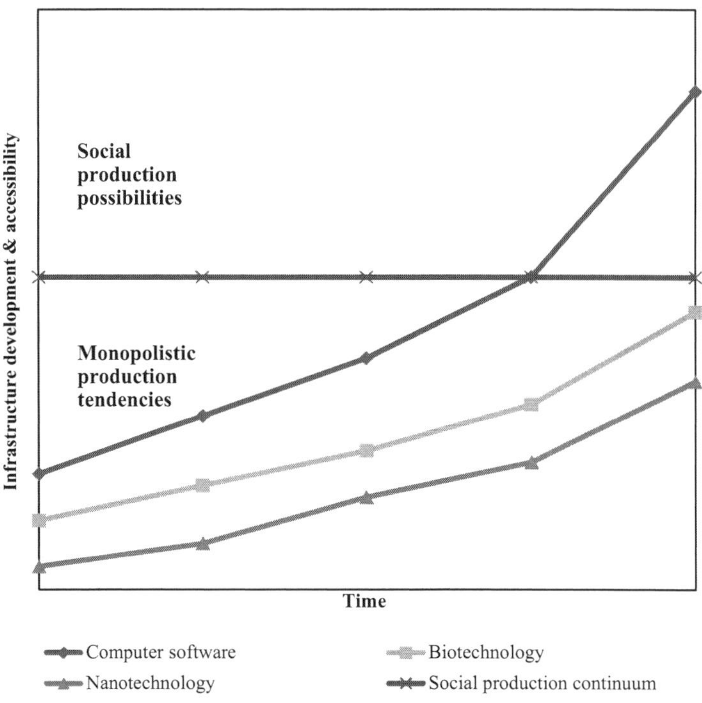

Figure 10.2 Critical hardware infrastructure and modes of production

desirable part of the overall production mix.[81] In the context of biotechnology, this diagrammatic dynamic is reflected in research undertaken by Graff *et al*, which states that by 1999 the top seven firms in the biotechnological industry, with reference to intellectual asset holdings, controlled three-quarters of patents on transformation technologies and genetic materials, together with close to 100 per cent of germplasm patents.[82] Similarly, in the survey of Agrobacterium-mediated transformation (a key enabling plant technology), of 27 key patents in the crucial 'vector' category, 26 were owned by three institutions; further, all of the patents on binary vectors (which largely supersede earlier vector technologies) were held by a single firm – Syngenta – that also held a dominant position in the 'dicot' category (which includes most commercially important crop plants).[83]

The crux is the history of information production has generally favoured monopolistic or oligopolistic firm-based production when hardware/infrastructure development resides below the social production continuum in Figure 10.2. Presumably this is because much post-Industrial Revolution production relating to information and culture has been modelled around a capital-intensive, industrial model where expensive physical capital has been the central organising principle.[84] This is true from the introduction of high-cost, high-volume mechanical presses, through to telegraph, telephone, radio, film, records, television, cable, and satellite systems.[85] At some point in time, however, as occurred in the computer software industry, the accumulation and accessibility of infrastructure reaches a critical mass. This in turn spurs the inversion of the capital structure of production (within at least some segments of an industry).[86] Although Figure 10.2 speculates that this tipping point may be some distance away in technologies such as biotechnology and nanotechnology, there is at the very least a tendency towards it. Carlson and Brent, for example, have indicated by some estimates the basic hardware required for molecular biology research may be within reach of individual hobbyists in developed countries and farmer collectives in developing countries within the foreseeable future:[87]

> [c]onsiderable information is already available on how to manipulate and analyse DNA in the kitchen. A recent Scientific American Amateur Scientist column provided instructions for amplifying DNA through the polymerase chain reaction (PCR), and a previous column concerned analysing DNA samples using home-made electrophoresis equipment. The PCR discussion was immediately picked up in a Slashdot.org thread where participants provided tips for improving the yield of PCR. Detailed, technical information can be found in methods manuals, such as Current Protocols in Molecular Biology, which contain instructions on how to perform almost every task needed to perform modern molecular biology, and which are available in most university libraries. More of this information is becoming available online. Many techniques that once required PhD-level knowledge and experience to execute correctly are now performed by undergraduates using kits ... DNA synthesis [is] becoming faster, cheaper, and longer, and it is possible that in ten years specified large stretches of sequence will be generated by dedicated machines. Should this capability be realised, it will move from academic laboratories and large companies to smaller laboratories and businesses, perhaps even ultimately to the home garage and kitchen.[88]

Once an industry surpasses the social production continuum reflected in Figure 10.2, it is likely that in a similar fashion to computer software development, social production becomes a feasible and desirable mode of production, at least within particular aspects of the 'code' layer of a given industry.[89] The scale-ability of social production is heavily dependent upon the cyclical position of a given technology and the related critical hardware infrastructure development phase. Though particular aspects of the computer software industry have surpassed the social production continuum (Figure 10.2) at least in certain geographies and contexts, there are many other technologies such as biotechnology and nanotechnology that await a similar tendency in the future.[90]

By way of deduction, when the two vital prerequisites of equitable access to (i) the information commons and (ii) critical hardware infrastructure, are satisfied, there will be discrete circumstances where social production can compete with alternate production modes. In doing so, social production serves to foster within the information environment the ecological governance principles discussed in Part III: resilience, diversity and modularity.[91] Social production also serves the small-c constitutional economic function of separating (economic) power.[92] In this way, social production and the accompanying separation of (economic) power doctrine become integral to the information environmental governance framework.

10.4 CONCLUSION

Constitutional economics is an offshoot of public choice theory, which is one of the four environmental analytical frameworks the book has applied to the information environment. Specifically, this chapter employed constitutional economics as a theoretical springboard to advance the claim that social production proffers an effective method of separating economic power within the information environment. Although constitutional economics and social production may initially appear to be strange bedfellows, a deeper analysis reveals they both relate to the role and function of (economic) power.

A preliminary application of constitutional economics leads to the 'paradox of government' and subsequent questions concerning who guards the guardians. The separation of powers is one formal capital-C Constitutional constraint employed to militate against the old adage that 'absolute power corrupts absolutely'. Undoubtedly the doctrine has played a critical function within liberal economic democracies throughout modern history. Yet the principle has generally been confined to the capital-C constitutional economic realm. The chapter argued there is a need to broaden the concept of the separation of powers doctrine within the small-c constitutional economic domain. Such broadening is ultimately concerned with expanding constituency of power considerations. In particular, it was argued that social production holds the potential to mediate economic power relations by fostering competitive tension between the primary productive forces of the state, the market, the firm and society. The state is not a neutral player here to the extent there are discrete prerequisites if social production is to realise small-c constitutional functions.

Just as the state facilitates the market and the firm through the creation and maintenance of property and contract, so too social production relies upon the state provisioning equitable access to the information commons and critical hardware infrastructure. In so doing, the state inadvertently facilitates competitive tension between the productive forces, which in turn fosters the small-c constitutional function of the separation of (economic) power doctrine as it applies to the information environment. The proposed doctrine is a critical component of the information environmental governance framework advanced within this book.

PART V

Conclusion

11. Control, alt, delete: Towards an information environmental governance framework

Doubt is not a pleasant condition, but certainty is absurd.

Voltaire

11.1 INTRODUCTION

A core task of the book has been to address the following research question: Is there utility in applying environmental analytical frameworks to Intellectual Property Rights (particularly copyrights and patents)? The answer to this question is yes. We have observed throughout the book how viewing the information environment through the lens of environmental analytical frameworks proffers important and unique insights for information regulation. These insights are best appreciated by reflecting upon the overall content of the book, which is the core focus of this concluding chapter.

Despite the various layers of complexity explored within the book, the application of each of the environmental analytical frameworks to IPRs can be surmised relatively succinctly. Applying welfare economics in Part I underscored the need to conduct a social net product analysis so the private and public costs and benefits of the IPR system are taken into account in the evaluation of whether IPRs foster creativity and innovation for the public benefit. Applying the commons to IPRs in Part II highlighted the significance of delineating parameters of the information commons and reconciling the information commons with private property dimensions of IPRs. The application of ecology to IPRs in Part III involved drawing upon a range of ecological governance principles such as methodological interrelationalism, resilience, diversity and modularity. These governance principles provided the springboard for a host of normative claims such as the creation and maintenance of an information environment ethic, Information Commons Rights and informational national parks. Finally, applying public choice theory to IPRs in Part IV involved promoting social production as a complementary means of countering IPR regulatory capture and overcoming collective action problems inherent within the information environment. In this way, social production serves to separate economic power.

After reinforcing the nature of information environmentalism, this chapter is structured in accordance with the book so that a brief summary of each of the four environmental analytical frameworks is forthcoming.

11.2 INFORMATION ENVIRONMENTALISM

Aside from answering the core research question, the book also sought to apply the four environmental analytical frameworks to IPRs with the view of building an information environmental governance framework. This framework is useful in fostering a language and geography of experience which can be used to advance the interests of the information environment (generally) and the information commons (specifically).[1]

Essentially, the information environmental governance framework advocated within the book has been built upon the following parallel understandings:

- The industrial model of production and consumption that has dominated since the nineteenth century has led to considerable environmental degradation.
- The contemporary environmental movement has had some success (albeit limited) in underscoring the failings of the industrial model of production and consumption by building an environmental movement which draws upon the analytical frameworks of welfare economics, the commons, ecology, and public choice theory.
- Many of the theoretical lessons synthesised within the contemporary environmental movement bear relevance to present struggles concerning the information environment.
- At the dawn of the twenty-first century the information age presents both opportunities and threats regarding the social fabric and the physical environment.[2]

Information environmentalism has been described throughout the book as a normative discourse that seeks to protect and nurture the information commons. We have seen how the information commons is a central unifying theme with respect to the application of the four environmental analytical frameworks. Due to inherent complexities of delineating the parameters of the information commons, the book discussed how the protection of the information commons will rely upon a variety of strategies, one of which is the allocation of rights and the provisioning of standing to the information commons via ICRs. In Part III we saw how the realisation of ICRs must be built upon a strategic combination of rational truths, reasonable arguments and rhetorical imagination.

A natural reply to information environmentalist discourse might be that the physical environment is much more significant than the information environment because without the physical environment human beings simply cannot exist. Yet as was stressed on several occasions, the dichotomy between the physical environment and the information environment is not so neat. The fundamental cause of the degradation of both respective environments flows from a failure of social and legal institutions to mediate an appropriate balance between private and public concerns.[3] The introductory chapter and Part I emphasised that of all the relevant contemporary institutions, the most important mediator between the private and the public is the institution of property.[4]

11.3 WELFARE ECONOMICS OF PROPERTISATION

While property definitions abound from Hobbes to Locke to Blackstone to Hume to Proudhon,[5] Benkler consolidates the private/public tension by describing property as a 'cluster of background rules that determine what resources each of us has when we come into relations with others, and, no less important, what "having" or "lacking" a resource entails in our relations with these others'.[6]

As we might imagine, given what is at stake, property validation throughout history has been riddled with contestation. Traditionally, monastic communities such as the Franciscans were particularly sceptical of propertisation, as were historical thinkers such as Winstanley, Rousseau and Proudhon.[7] More contemporaneously, 'environmentalists' such as Aldo Leopold argued that property often facilitates a dynamic whereby expediency trumps ethical concerns.[8] Leopold related these arguments to environmental degradation, indicating how property was often employed as a smokescreen to conceal or understate 'ethical considerations' complicit within the relationship between human beings and the physical environment.[9] Within the welfare economic context, these ethical considerations often manifest as negative externalities.

Building upon Leopoldian perspectives, it was argued throughout Part I that just as the expediency of property has served to conceal or understate ethical considerations (e.g. *terra nullius*) so too propertisation of the information environment often leads to the concealment or understatement of exclusivity costs that flow from relying upon property to overcome the market failures inherent within the information environment. The exclusivity costs related to propertising information discussed within Part I of the book include efficiency costs associated with the information paradox, administration costs stemming from the propertisation of public goods, externality costs arising from an externalities analysis, and distributional costs inherent within monopoly rights. At various times transaction costs and opportunity costs were also alluded to.

Part I stressed that the main reason why exclusivity costs are understated within IPR maximalist discourse is that IPRs are often construed in property terms rather than through the monopoly lens. The property bias of IPRs is why the benefits of propertisation frequently trump exclusivity costs flowing from monopolistic characteristics of IPRs. Within this context, the book advanced Pigou's welfare economic social net product analysis as a useful governance tool. Relying upon this tool assists in weighing up the private and public costs and benefits of the IPR system. It was also argued (especially within Part II of the book) the benefits of the information commons must be taken into account. The cost-benefit approach of IPRs is embedded within principle 1 of Table 1.1.

11.4 INFORMATION COMMONS AS POSITIVE COMMUNITY

Validation of information propertisation was partly explained in Part I through an overstatement of benefits and an understatement of costs in relation to IPRs. In Part II it was implicitly argued that validating theories of propertising information extend beyond Pigou's social net product analysis.

When Part II applied the commons analytical framework to the information environment, we saw that much IPR maximalist scholarship is built upon the concept of negative community (i.e. *res nullius*).[10] This concept stipulates that resources can generally be perceived as belonging to no one and are therefore unclaimed and for the taking. As a contradistinction IPR minimalists tend to adopt the positive community conception of the information commons, which is to specify that resources are considered to belong to everyone and therefore any use of such resources is required to be for the benefit of the public at large (i.e. *res communis*).[11]

While neither positive community nor negative community preclude ownership as such, the distinction is critical because it relates to how propertisation is validated within a given community and to what extent propertisation penetrates that community. Chapter 4 demonstrated how, generally speaking, a negative community conception of the commons leads to a deeper penetration of propertisation than a positive community conception. This is why principle 4 of Table 1.1 advocated the application of the positive community principle to the information commons.

As the information commons was a significant unifying theme within information environmentalism, in Part II the book went to some length to describe its parameters.[12] This task involved, among other things, discussing the similarities and distinctions between the intellectual commons and the public domain. Though the information commons was loosely conceptualised within the introductory chapter as the opposite of private property, a more nuanced perspective of the concept was forthcoming in Chapter 4 through a survey of the narrow and broad intellectual commons and the narrow and broad public domain. This survey drew on the premise that information environmentalism must seek to clarify the parameters of the information commons as far as is possible because the information commons cannot be protected unless there is some clarity about how it is delineated. In this respect the book adopted the terminology of the information commons as a bundling term encompassing both the intellectual commons and the public domain. The value of the information commons terminology stems largely from an appreciation of how the term is constituted.

The information commons is a critical component of information environmental discourse. However, the discussion of Hardin's tragedy of the commons in Chapter 5 emphasised how the commons can be perceived from a variety of different angles.[13] For instance, we saw the way in which the tragedy of the commons is often employed by IPR maximalists to support the proposition that all commons are tragic. In contrast, it was also stressed how not every commons situation falls into the trap of the commons dilemma.[14] In this context, Part II underlined that Hardin was initially relying upon tragedy of the commons discourse to support stronger state regulation with respect to pollution, based on the proposition that private incentives would lead firms to pollute their environment even against their own long-term interest.[15] Part II also highlighted that one of the main reasons why the tragedy of the commons occurs in the first place is because the cows are privately owned.[16] In this way, we can think of the tragedy of the commons as a 'tragedy of property', which was a sentiment reflected in Chapter 4 with reference to the tragedy of the anticommons.[17]

In seeking to move beyond the dichotomous positions flowing from tragedy discourse, Part II argued that when applying the commons analytical framework to the information environment, the commons as an explanatory construct must either be abandoned or alternatively we must find a method of reconciling commons rights with individual rights. The latter option was adopted. Despite IPR maximalist rhetoric concerning benefits of propertising information, exclusivity costs inherent within the IPR system are implicitly acknowledged by the system itself as evidenced by the leaky nature of IPRs. The requirement to disclose information about an invention as a quid pro quo for a patent right and fair use within copyright are both emblematic of such leaks. Hence, abandoning the commons within the context of the information environment is neither feasible nor desirable. To this end, Chapter 5 advanced the semicommons perspective by highlighting the benefits stemming from the dynamic interaction between private property dimensions of IPRs and the information commons.[18]

Obviously, the information commons is an important part of the information semicommons because without the information commons there is simply no information semicommons of which to speak. Yet how can we maintain the integrity of the information commons over time? Part III of the book turned to ecology in search for information environmental governance tools that might assist in nurturing the information environment (generally) and the information commons (specifically).

11.5 SOCIAL ECOLOGY OF INFORMATION ENVIRONMENTAL GOVERNANCE

Part III of the book reflected on several strands of ecology including ecological science, ecological ethics and interrelationalism. Chapter 6 primarily focused on the interrelational aspect of ecology, and more particularly methodological interrelationalism.[19] Such an approach was useful in overcoming both the 'individualist fallacy' inherent within IPR maximalist scholarship and the 'collectivist fallacy' inherent within IPR minimalist scholarship. The interrelational perspective and the accompanying systems theory also provided a useful foundation to advance the ecological governance principles of resilience, diversity and modularity.

Building upon the methodological interrelationalism perspective in Part III, one insight gained from applying ecology to social systems such as the information environment is the symbiotic relationship between empirical knowledge and governance principles.[20] That is, just as ecological science and related fields of knowledge such as interrelationalism and systems theory have evolved, so too have related governance principles relating to the physical environment. The precautionary principle provides one example in that it has developed alongside the development of empirical knowledge related to the physical environment.[21]

Exploring how the precautionary principle might apply to the information environment led to a discussion in Chapter 6 of practical initiatives such as information Environmental Impact Statements. Under this proposed iEIS process a patent holder, for instance, would be required, with respect to sensitive subsystems of the information environment, to submit an independently audited iEIS along with a patent application. Chapter 6 also sought to advance the discipline of information ecology being an empirically based information environmental discipline that would be akin to ecology as it relates to the physical environment. Normatively speaking, the role of information ecology would be to provide a foundation of empirical knowledge concerning the health and well-being of discrete systems within the information environment, and of the information environment as a whole.

Another argument within Part III was that information ecology would provide a foundation for informational environmental governance principles. This perspective was built upon Leopold's land ethic as it relates to the physical environment to the extent his ethic affected the general development of ecological governance principles (e.g. the precautionary principle). Through investigating how Leopold's land ethic might apply to the information environment, Chapter 6 argued that an information environmental ethic proffers a road map, which can in turn interact with the empirical evidence further developed by information ecology. The information environmental ethic was presented as follows:

A thing is right when it tends to preserve the resilience, diversity, and modularity of the information environment. It is wrong when it tends otherwise.

Naturally, an important aspect of advancing the information environmental ethic was to further explore the concept of resilience and the related notions of diversity and modularity.[22] While the private ordering mechanisms inherent within FLOSS proffered one effective method of applying resilience to the information environment, it was implicitly argued within Part III that there is also a role for the state in fostering resilience of the information environment. After all, IPRs are a state-sponsored monopoly. To this end, through blending the work of Christopher Stone and James Boyle, Part III argued for the creation and maintenance of ICRs.[23]

Within the ICR context, Chapter 7 put forward the following query: If intellectual property is to be allocated rights through IPRs, why not also contemplate the allocation of rights to the information commons through ICRs? An alternate framing of this inquiry, grounded in both the commons and ecology analytical frameworks, gave rise to the rhetorical question: Should the information commons have standing? This question was built upon similar inquiries advanced in the 1970s by American lawyers (such as Sax, Stone and Tribe) who sought to explore how the law symbolises and interacts with the inherent value of the physical environment.[24]

We saw in Part III that an important function of ICRs is to provide a counterbalance to private interest claims within the information environment so as to enable the public to speak on behalf of the information commons. In practical terms, opposition systems built into the patent legislation within many countries provide a tangible example of how ICRs could be operationalised. Establishment of locally based information Environmental Defenders Offices was also suggested as a useful institutional mechanism when seeking to operationalise ICRs.

As the notion of ICRs is somewhat unorthodox, Chapter 7 sought to debunk some of the potential criticisms from the outset. For instance, one argument that might be used to rally against ICRs is that boundaries of the information commons would be inherently unstable. As we saw in Chapter 4, it is indeed difficult to neatly define the information commons parameters. However, Chapter 7 highlighted how the boundaries of IPRs are also inherently unstable. Thus, if the argument that there is no value in the formal creation of ICRs because the information commons cannot be accurately defined were to be adopted, then this would also be an effective argument against IPRs.[25] Here, it was further argued the allocation of rights to the information commons is no more abstract than applying rights to corporations or states.

Although debunking possible criticisms of ICRs is vital, Part III suggested it is also imperative to build a positive ICR programme. Chapter 8 did so by relying upon a combination of rational truths, reasonable arguments and rhetorical imagination. In relation to rational truths, there is the need to develop a formal information ecology discipline that would build a body of 'objective expert knowledge'. Courts and governments, when making policy decisions with respect to the information environment, could in turn rely upon this knowledge. In relation to reasonable arguments, Chapter 8 suggested the public trust doctrine is an example of a jurisprudential mechanism providing a doctrinal foundation for ICRs. The rights protected by the public trust doctrine are inherently collective in nature. The rights are therefore held by persons as members of the public akin to the notion of positive community (i.e. *res communis*).[26] We saw that just as the public trust doctrine has assisted in mobilizing the environmental movement through increasing the public awareness of each human being's entitlement to healthy natural ecosystems, it also has the potential to be employed with similar effect in relation to the information environment.[27]

Alongside rational truths established through information ecology and reasonable arguments aided by the public trust doctrine, Chapter 8 contended that the creation and maintenance of ICRs must also rely upon rhetorical imagination. An example within this context is the notion of informational national parks, which drew upon the history of national parks within the physical environment.[28] John Muir was a key figure here because of the way in which he enlivened understandings of and sympathies towards the natural world.[29] We saw how rhetorical devices such as informational national parks might serve to shift perceptions of the information commons from an information graveyard to an information playground.[30]

Many of the claims advanced in Part III with respect to the ecology analytical framework had a strong normative dimension. Likewise, Part IV also had a strong normative foundation, particularly as it concerned social production.

11.6 SOCIAL PRODUCTION OF PUBLIC CHOICE THEORY

Part I of the book applied welfare economics to IPRs. Given welfare economics and public choice theory are both concerned with regulatory formation and administration, it is fitting that Part IV, being the final substantive aspect of the book, was concerned with public choice theory.[31] By applying public choice theory to IPRs the significant influence that concentrated economic interests have over IPR policy formulation was underscored.[32] Such influences most often manifest in the form of rent-seeking behaviour as concentrated interests will expend considerable resources pursuing the capture of supra-normal returns.[33] Although there are a variety of activities that fall under the rent-seeking banner, we saw in Chapter 9 how those activities associated with entrenching and expanding IPRs are pure rent-seeking exemplars.[34]

Public choice theory has tended to focus on the effect of the rent-seeking activities of concentrated interest groups on regulatory frameworks (i.e. regulatory capture). Yet the book stressed that public choice theory is also concerned with how disperse fragmented interests overcome collective action problems. Part IV explained that while the large fragmented interests stand to lose from the regulatory capture of the concentrated interests, collective action problems mean fragmented interests are unlikely to do much about it. Collective action problems are largely a corollary of informational costs, organising costs and the free-rider problem.[35] In Chapter 9 we saw how overcoming collective action problems has been a core focus of those advocating the conservation and protection of both the physical environment and the information environment. In doing so, the typical approach of advocates has been to rely upon political organisation channelled through civil society organisations.

As highlighted within Part IV, one obstacle flowing from the reliance on civil society organisations to secure the protection of the physical environment and/or the information environment is the corrosive influence of mass communication on civil society and the related public sphere. Here, the Internet as a technological platform, and the networked information economy as an organisational model of social production, is often touted by information environmentalists as a potential alternative pathway to secure the integrity of the information commons.[36] Chapter 9 argued that social production can be an important complement to the political organisation inherent within civil society organisations. The complement perspective was built upon the intuition that the economic efficiencies of social production, being information processing and allocative efficiency, partly map to the collective action problems inherent within the information environment.

The economic efficiencies of social production were further leveraged within Chapter 10 to stake the claim that social production holds the potential of decentralising economic power by competing with alternate production modes. In the process, it was suggested that social production facilitates the operation of the small-c constitutional economic function of separating economic power. A critical aspect here was the merging of the decentralist principles of social production with the small-c constitutional economic aspects of public choice theory. This was ultimately framed with reference to the question of who guards the guardians. The answer is found in small-c constitutional constraints such as elections, federalism and the separation of powers doctrine, all of which are geared towards the decentralisation of power.

It was conceded that drawing a nexus between economic competition as it concerns the productive forces and the separation of powers doctrine may initially appear overly speculative. But further exploration demonstrated how economic competition strives to provide checks and balances within the economy in parallel fashion to the way in which the separation of powers doctrine proffers checks and balances within the political system. To this end, a critical conclusion of Chapter 10 was that in order for social production to continue realising its decentralisation potential as per the proposed separation of economic power doctrine we must ensure equitable access to (i) the information commons, and (ii) critical hardware infrastructure.[37]

11.7 FUTURE RESEARCH

The work presented in this book is obviously not the final word on the evolving normative discourse of information environmentalism. Rather, a core ambition of the book was to make a contribution to the project of building an information environmental governance framework for IPRs. Such a framework is particularly useful when engaging with research contemplating the nexus between the physical environment and the information environment. Yet the utility of the framework is not limited in this regard. Information environmental governance also has broader applications for IPR-related research.

By way of finality, we will now briefly discuss some areas of the book that require further development. From the outset, the four chosen environmental analytical frameworks of welfare economics, the commons, ecology, and public choice theory do not necessarily fully encompass the entire theoretical foundation of the environmental movement. Rather, the four analytical frameworks provide a sound theoretical representation of environmentalism. Other scholars may wish to explore the application of alternate environmental analytical frameworks to the information environment.

A core claim of Part I was the need to engage in a social net product analysis of IPRs. This claim was largely theoretical in that an actual social net product analysis of IPRs was beyond the scope of this work. There is further research to be done here. For example, a social net product analysis could be relied upon to directly address the question of whether or not property is the optimum method of overcoming the various market failures within the information environment. Such an analysis would involve an attempt to quantify, or otherwise take into account, the efficiency costs, administration costs, externality costs and distributional costs associated with IPRs. Other exclusivity costs, such as transaction costs and opportunity costs, could also be explored within this context. Another line of inquiry pursued in Part I, which awaits further exploration, is determining exactly what externality costs flow from the externalities paradox as it concerns the information environment. Further still, the relationship discussed in Part I between price discrimination and IPRs, particularly with reference to TPMs, is also likely to be a fruitful line of inquiry.

Part II underscored that one of the obstacles in protecting and nurturing the information environment relates to challenges associated with defining the parameters of the information commons. By making use of the information commons definitional matrix presented in Chapter 4 there is scope for further refinement. Such refinement is an important component of 'inventing the information commons' as per James Boyle's plea. Although this book has made a contribution in this regard, clearly there remains further practical, theoretical and rhetorical work to be done. Part of this work may involve softening the dichotomy between private property and the commons. The tragedy of (ignoring) the information commons discussed in Chapter 5 is likely to be useful here. The social net product analysis is also beneficial within the semicommons context to the extent that such an analysis provides an effective method of taking into account private and public costs and benefits of the information semicommons.

In Part III, several normative claims were advanced in order to protect and nurture the information commons. Within this domain, there is still more work required. The book suggested the need to develop a formal information ecology discipline that would serve to build and systemise empirical knowledge relating to the information environment and/or the information commons. An information ecology textbook would be a useful starting point. Further development of practical initiatives discussed in Part III such as iEIS must be forthcoming. The information environment ethic submitted in Chapter 6 also requires further deliberation so as to ensure the ecological governance principles of resilience, diversity and modularity are indeed the most appropriate governance principles to advocate on behalf of the information environment. It would also be useful to further enrich the governance framework of ICRs. Just as there is an abundance of scholarship concerning IPRs, so too there is a need for ICR scholarship. The emergent rhetorical device of informational national parks is yet another topic discussed in Part III begging further research.

In Part IV a core claim was that social production provides a complementary method, alongside the political activities of civil society organisations, of overcoming collective action problems. More research is required to determine how well in fact collective action problems map to the economic efficiencies of social production. It was also suggested in Part IV that social production fosters the separation of (economic) power.

This broad claim invites contestation. It may be the claim overreaches. Further research and deliberation is therefore required to determine the veracity of the proposed separation of (economic) power doctrine. Social production may also rely upon much more than equitable access to the information commons and critical hardware infrastructure. If so, what are the other prerequisites underpinning social production? And how might these prerequisites relate to the proposed separation of (economic) power doctrine?

11.8 CONCLUSION

When James Boyle first advanced 'cultural environmentalism' in 1997, the idea there were strong correlations between struggles to protect the physical environment and the information environment was somewhat conjectural. Yet the prescient nature of Boyle's claims has been fortified by the passing of time. It has become clear there is an information environment that is the subject of political contestation and economic exploitation. Boyle was right to imply that environmentalism contained governance lessons for the information environment. The book has shown how the four environmental analytical frameworks – welfare economics, the commons, ecology, and public choice theory – provide the basis for extracting those lessons and principles of governance from environmentalism and applying them to the information environment. In doing so the book has contributed to building an information environmental governance framework. This framework can be used in seeking to protect the information environment (generally) and the information commons (specifically).

Throughout the book we have seen how the theoretical confrontations within the physical environment and the information environment ultimately relate to striking an appropriate balance between private and public concerns.[38] Property is a key factor in this equation because as Blackstone surmised 'property came first among institutions, and all else followed'.[39] Although the application of welfare economics to IPRs suggested the benefits of propertising information are overstated, a thorough social net product analysis may very well justify the application of property within the information environment, at least in some instances. But once private property is accepted as a social fundament, it then becomes necessary to think about how the parameters of private property and the commons are delineated, and how private property is to interact with the commons. It was here the book relied upon the application of the commons and ecology as a catalyst to support a range of normative information environmental governance framework devices. Examples include an information environment ethic, ICRs and informational national parks. These devices are useful in building a 'discourse of the information commons' to counteract the prevailing 'discourse of property rights'.[40]

The role of the information commons in facilitating a range of functions beyond creative and innovative activity was stressed throughout the book. For example, the information commons is a fundament of social production. In turn social production facilitates competitive tension between the productive forces of the state, the firm, the market and society. When the information commons is perceived through this broader chain of reasoning it becomes increasingly apparent that information environmentalists must continue to build and operationalise an 'information environmental governance framework'. The *raison d'être* of this framework is to protect and nurture the information commons. The book has strived to make a meaningful contribution to this ongoing project.

Notes

CHAPTER 1 NOTES

1. Boyle J. (1997), *A Politics of Intellectual Property: Environmentalism for the Net?*, 47 Duke Law Journal 87, at 113 [hereafter *A Politics of Intellectual Property*].
2. Ibid.
3. Carter A. (1999), *A Radical Green Political Theory*, Routledge. There are some similarities between the emergences of the Greens political party during the twentieth century, and the more recent development of the Pirate Party. For a general discussion about 'piratical ideology' in the digital age, see Allen-Robertson J. (2013), *Digital Culture Industry: A History of Digital Distribution*, Palgrave Macmillan, especially Chapter 6.
4. 'So-called' because the terminology of intellectual *property* rights is not without contestation. See, for example, Boldrin M. and Levine D. (2008), *Against Intellectual Monopoly Rights*, Cambridge University Press; Faunce T. (2012), *Global Public Goods*, in Chadwick R. (ed.), (2nd edition), *Encyclopedia of Applied Ethics*, Volume 2, Academic Press 523 at 526 (referring to IPRs as Intellectual Monopoly Privileges); Stallman R., *Did You Say 'Intellectual Property'? It's a Seductive Mirage*, available online at http://www.gnu.org/philosophy/not-ipr.html (cited 14 December 2012). Although the term 'intellectual property' was probably consolidated with the advent of the World Intellectual Property Organization in 1967, there are examples of much earlier usages of the term. For instance, see *Davoll v Brown*, 7 F. Cas. 197, 199 (C.C.D. Mass. 1845)(No 3662) (defining 'intellectual property' as 'the labors of the mind').
5. Okediji R. (2003), *The International Relations of Intellectual Property: Narratives of Developing Country Participation in the Global Intellectual Property System*, 7 Singapore Journal of International and Comparative Law 315, at 324–325; Yu P. (2007), *The International Intellectual Property Regime Complex: International Enclosure, the Regime Complex, and Intellectual Property Schizophrenia*, Michigan State Law Review 1, at 4–5. See also Luxemburg R. (2003), *The Accumulation of Capital*, trans. Agnes Schwarzchild, Routledge (discussing the relationship between Marx's idea of primitive accumulation and colonialism). For further references concerning the relationship between science and mercantile/colonial expansionism see Pyenson L. and Sheets-Pyenson S. (1999), *Servants of Nature: A History of Scientific Institutions, Enterprises, and Sensibilities*, W.W. Norton and Company, at 88–90. For a complementary point of view, see van Caenegem W. (2003), *Intellectual Property Law and the Idea of Progress*, http://epublications.bond.edu.au/law_pubs/170, at 243 onwards (tying the evolution of IPRs with the notion of 'progress').
6. Mitchell H. (2005), *The Intellectual Commons: Toward an Ecology of Intellectual Property*, Lexington Books, at 47 [hereafter *The Intellectual Commons*]. See also August R., Mayer D. and Bixby M. (2009), *International Business Law: Text, Cases and Readings*, 5th edition, Pearson, at 453 (where it is suggested that the first copyright was issued by the Duke of Milan in 1461); Mandich G. (1948), *Venetian*

Patents (1450–1550), 30 Journal of Patent Office Society 160 and Mandich G. (1960), *Venetian Origins of Inventors' Rights*, 42 Journal of the Patent Office Society 378, 380 (both cited in Drahos P. (2010), *The Global Governance of Knowledge: Patent Offices and Their Clients*, Cambridge University Press, at 91, footnote 1) [hereafter *The Global Governance of Knowledge*]. Also, Greenhalgh C. and Rogers M. (2010), *Innovation, Intellectual Property, and Economic Growth*, Princeton University Press, at 35 (arguing that the first formal European patent was granted in the City of Florence in 1426 to Brunellesci for a vessel to transport marble). Greenhalgh and Rogers also note at 35 that the first patent law was issued in Venice during 1474. Also, see Guellec D. and van Pottelsberghe B. (2007), *The Economics of the European Patent System: IP Policy for Innovation and Competition*, Oxford University Press.

7. Price W. (1906), *English Patents of Monopoly*, Houghton, Mifflin and Co., at 3; Rose M. (1993), *Authors and Owners: The Invention of Copyright*, Harvard University Press, at 10 [hereafter *Authors and Owners*] (stating that the 'first and most famous privilege was a monopoly on printing itself granted in 1469').
8. Mandich G. (1948), *Venetian Patents (1450–1550)*, 30 Journal of Patent Office Society 160 and Mandich G. (1960), *Venetian Origins of Inventors' Rights*, 42 Journal of the Patent Office Society 378, 380; Mitchell, *The Intellectual Commons*, at 47; Ricketson S. (1984), *The Law of Intellectual Property*, Law Book Co (Sydney), at 860–861; Drahos P. (1996), *A Philosophy of Intellectual Property*, Dartmouth, at 14 [hereafter *A Philosophy of IP*]; Drahos, *The Global Governance of Knowledge*, at 91 (see also Chapter 3 for a succinct history of patents generally).
9. Mitchell, *The Intellectual Commons*, Lexington Books, at 47; Drahos P. with Braithwaite J. (2002), *Information Feudalism: Who Owns the Knowledge Economy?*, The New Press, at 30 [hereafter *Information Feudalism*]; Prager F. (1944), *A History of Intellectual Property from 1545 to 1787*, 26 Journal of the Patent Office Society 711 at 734; Drahos, *The Global Governance of Knowledge*, at 91.
10. Mitchell, *The Intellectual Commons*, Lexington Books, at 46–47; see also Clement E. and Oppenheim C. (2002), *Anarchism, Alternative Publishers and Copyright*, Anarchist Studies, at 44.
11. Arber E. (ed.) (1950), *A Transcript of the Registers of the Company of Stationers of London: 1554–1640*, 1875–1894, Peter Smith, 5 vols, at 1: xxxi; Rose, *Authors and Owners*, at 12.
12. Patterson R. (1968), *Copyright in Historical Perspective*, Vanderbilt University Press, at 29; Walterscheid E. (1999/2000), *Defining the Patent and Copyright Term: Term Limits and the Intellectual Property Clause*, 7 J. Intell. Prop. L. 315 at 331–332, especially footnote 68; Mitchell, *The Intellectual Commons*, at 49; and Rose, *Authors and Owners*, at 12 (quoting the original being Arber E. (ed.), *A Transcript of the Registers of the Company of Stationers of London: 1554–1640*, 1875–1894 (n. 11), at 1: xxviii).
13. Mitchell, *The Intellectual Commons*, at 49; Rose, *Authors and Owners*, at 10–11.
14. Mitchell, *The Intellectual Commons*, at 49; Holdsworth W. (1924) [1937], *A History of English Law* (2nd edition), Sweet & Maxwell Ltd, at 362–363; Walterscheid E. (1999/2000), *Defining the Patent and Copyright Term: Term Limits and the Intellectual Property Clause*, 7 J. Intell. Prop. L. 315 at 333.
15. Mitchell, *The Intellectual Commons*, at 49.
16. Machlup F. and Penrose E. (1950), *The Patent Controversy in the Nineteenth Century*, 10(1) The Journal of Economic History 1, at 2.
17. For an interesting postmodern perspective of IPRs see Chon M. (1993), *Postmodern 'Progress': Reconsidering the Copyright and Patent Power*, 43 DePaul Law Review 97 [hereafter *Postmodern 'Progress'*]; Dent C. (2011), *Gray, Meticulous and*

Patently Documentary: Foucaultian Historical Methods and the Patent System, 47 Journal of Sociology 297.

18. Foucault M. (1969), *What is an Author?*, in Rabinow P. (ed.), *The Foucault Reader*, Pantheon at 108; Coombe R. (1998), *The Cultural Life of Intellectual Properties*, Durham NC, Duke University Press (arguing that according to the conditions of postmodernity, cultural consumption is increasingly understood as an active use rather than a passive dependence upon domination forms of signification). The postmodern standpoint partly accords with the views expressed in Benkler Y. (2006), *The Wealth of Networks: How Social Production Transforms Markets and Freedom*, Yale University Press at 127 [hereafter *The Wealth of Networks*] (arguing that there has been a fundamental shift away from 'passive' consumers to 'active' users as a corollary of the emergence of new technologies and markets). See also, Rimmer M. (2007), *Digital Copyright and the Consumer Revolution: Hands off my iPod*, Edward Elgar at 7 [hereafter *Digital Copyright*]; and Mitchell H. (2005), *The Intellectual Commons*, Lexington Books, at 140.
19. Mitchell, *The Intellectual Commons*, at 140; Rose, *Authors and Owners*, at 11.
20. See, for example, Hope J. (2008), *Biobazaar: The Open Source Revolution and Biotechnology*, Harvard University Press at 29 [hereafter *Biobazaar*]. See also *Commonwealth v John Fairfax & Sons Ltd* (1980) 147 CLR 39 (where the Australian government used the Copyright Act to censor information); Bell D. (1973), *The Coming of Post-Industrial Society*, Basic Books, at 15–18.
21. Birnhack M. (2006), *More or Better? Shaping the Public Domain* [hereafter *More or Better?*], in Guibault L. and Hugenholtz P. (eds), *The Future of the Public Domain: Identifying the Commons in Information Law*, Kluwer Law International at 81 [hereafter *The Future of the Public Domain*].
22. See, for example, Sell S. (2003), *Private Power, Public Law: The Globalization of Intellectual Property Rights*, Cambridge University Press [hereafter *Private Power, Public Law*].
23. This book adopts the terminology of 'information environmentalism' rather than 'cultural environmentalism'. The rationale for this approach is explained below.
24. Boyle, *A Politics of Intellectual Property* at 113.
25. See Benkler Y. (2010), *The Idea of Access to Knowledge and the Information Commons: Long-Term Trends and Basic Elements*, in Krikorian G. and Kapczynski A. (eds), *Access to Knowledge in the Age of Intellectual Property*, Zone Books, at 226–227 [hereafter *A2K in the Age of IP*].
26. Boyle J. (2003), *Foreword: The Opposite of Property?*, 66 (1 & 2) Law and Contemporary Problems 2003. As will be observed in Chapter 5, a more nuanced perspective can be forged through semicommons theory.
27. Drahos has argued that 'state property orders are extractive', especially for Indigenous peoples, in that property facilitates the large-scale, uncompensated extraction of assets to take place (i.e. the iron law of extraction). Drahos P. (2012), *Indigenous Developmental Networks and the Adaptive Management of Intellectual Property, Development, Creativity and Access to Knowledge in Pacific Island Countries*, RegNet ANU Canberra, 25 September 2012. Many scholars have discussed the notion of propertisation as it relates to information. For example, see Merges R. (1996), *Property Rights Theory and the Commons: The Case of Scientific Research*, Soc. Phil & Pol. Summer at 145, 146–147; Netanel N. (1996), *Copyright and a Democratic Civil Society*, 106 Yale L. J. 283 at 311–313; Samuelson P. (1989), *Information as Property: Do Ruckelshaus and Carpenter Signal a Changing Direction in Intellectual Property Law?*, 38 Cath. U. L. Rev. 365, 397–398; and Heverly R. (2003), *The Information Semicommons*, 18 Berkeley Technological Law Journal 1127.

28. As this reasoning applies to real property, see Rose C. (1986), *The Comedy of the Commons: Custom, Commerce, and Inherently Public Property*, 53 U. Chi. L. Rev. 711 at 723 [hereafter *The Comedy of the Commons*] (indicating that private property is not always efficient). Note that most commentators agree that 'basic research' should not be subject to propertisation, but distinguishing between 'basic research' and 'applied research' is fraught with difficulty (see, for example, Vaver D. (1990), *Intellectual Property Today: Of Myths and Paradoxes*, 69 Canadian Bar Review 98 at 117; Benkler Y. (2010), *The Idea of Access to Knowledge and the Information Commons: Long-Term Trends and Basic Elements* in Krikorian and Kapczynski (eds), *A2K in the Age of IP*, at 228–229 [hereafter *The Idea of Access to Knowledge and the Information Commons*] (discussing the 'productivity of the commons' and the 'counterproductive effects of property-mimicking regulations' such as IPRs).
29. Note that beyond 'cultural environmentalism', information environmentalism shares critical similarities with the Access to Knowledge movement. For a useful discussion concerning the relationship between information and knowledge, see Kapczynski A. (2010), *Access to Knowledge: A Conceptual Genealogy* [hereafter *Access to Knowledge*], in Krikorian and Kapczynski (eds), *A2K in the Age of IP*, at 45 (arguing that 'while information is certainly a pre-requisite in the generation of knowledge, acquisition of knowledge remains the ultimate goal'). See also, Benkler, *The Wealth of Networks*, at 313.
30. Lee I. (2001), *Culturally-Based Copyright Systems?: The U.S. and Korea in Conflict*, 79 Wash. U. L. Q. 1103, 1109; Cohen J. (2007), *Creativity and Culture in Copyright Theory*, 40 UC Davis L. Rev. 1151, 1165–1167; and Frischmann B. (2007), *Cultural Environmentalism and The Wealth of Networks*, 74 The University of Chicago Law Review 1083 at 1094, see particularly footnote 39 (discussing the broad nature of culture). For a differing perspective, see Frischmann B. (2012), *Infrastructure: The Social Value of Shared Resources*, Oxford University Press at 258 (arguing that the phrase 'information environment' potentially cleanses discourse of normative values).
31. See the Oxford Dictionary found at: http://oxforddictionaries.com/definition/english/information (cited 18/7/2012). Also, in reviewing Boyle's work, Mark Lemley argues that what ties together the various themes of Boyle's work is the analysis of 'information'. See Lemley M. (1997), *Romantic Authorship and the Rhetoric of Property*, 75 Texas Law Review 873 at 873–875.
32. The author is indebted to Professor Peter Drahos who inspired this definition by providing draft feedback on 18 September 2012. Throughout the book the information environment terminology is deployed in contradistinction to the physical environment. Also, the 'information environment' will generally be discussed in positivist terms, whereas 'information environmentalism' is primarily explored through a normative lens.
33. Although cultural environmentalism only entered the digerati lexicon in the past decade (see the proceedings of *Cultural Environmentalism @ 10* which can be found at (2007) 70 Law & Contemp. Probs. 1), the intellectual foundation of cultural environmentalism draws upon a rich tapestry of historical thought and action. That is, Jefferson, Franklin, Madison and Macaulay have all proved inspirational figures within the cultural environment. See Boyle, *The Public Domain* – providing a good overview of cultural environmental inspirational figures. Moreover, the first copyright can be traced to the Duke of Milan in 1481, and the Statute of Anne was enacted three centuries ago in 1709 (August R., Mayer D. and Bixby M. (2009), *International Business Law: Text, Cases and Readings*, 5th edition, Pearson, at 453).
34. Along with Creative Commons, another contemporary initiative includes the Science Commons: www.sciencecommons.org/about (cited 14 December 2012).

35. Boyle J. (1996), *Shamans, Software, and Spleens: Law and the Construction of the Information Society*, Harvard University Press at x [hereafter *Shamans, Software and Spleens*].
36. Boyle, *A Politics of Intellectual Property*, at 108.
37. Boyle J. (2003), *The Second Enclosure Movement and the Construction of the Public Domain*, 66 Law & Contemp. Probs. at 72–73 [hereafter *The Second Enclosure Movement*].
38. Ibid, at 52.
39. Boyle, *A Politics of Intellectual Property* at 108–109 (referring to the two analytical frameworks of ecology and welfare economics). While this is a useful starting point, this book seeks to expand the set of environmental frameworks to include 'the commons' and 'public choice theory'. This perspective is built on the prior work of the author including Cunningham R. (2010), *The Tragedy of (Ignoring) the Information Semicommons: a Cultural Environmental Perspective*, 4 Akron Intellectual Property Journal 1 [hereafter *The Tragedy of (Ignoring) the Information Semicommons*]; and Cunningham R. (2010), *The Separation of (Economic) Power: A Cultural Environmental Perspective of Social Production and the Networked Public Sphere*, 11 J. High Tech. L. 1 [hereafter *The Separation of (Economic) Power*].
40. As Boyle argues, what is lacking is a 'general framework, a perception of common interest in apparently disparate situations'. See Boyle, J. (2008), *The Public Domain: Enclosing the Commons of the Mind*, Yale University Press at 239 [hereafter *The Public Domain*]. More recently, Matthew Rimmer has suggested, in discussing the nexus between climate change and intellectual property, that '[t]here is scope for further theoretical work in this field, particularly in respect of cultural environmentalism'. See Rimmer M. (2011), *Intellectual Property and Climate Change: Inventing Green Technologies*, Edward Elgar at 398 [hereafter *IP and Climate Change*].
41. Purdy J. (2012), *Our Place in the World: A New Relationship for Environmental Ethics and Law*, Duke Law Journal (2012) at 22. Available at: http://scholarship.law.duke.edu/faculty_scholarship/2509 (cited 14 December 2012).
42. While James Boyle places great emphasis on authorial romance as a foundation of IPR maximalism, Mark Lemley argues that authorial romance does not fully explain the general expansionism of IPRs over time. Contrast, Boyle, *Shamans, Software, and Spleens*; and Lemley, *Romantic Authorship and the Rhetoric of Property*, at 887 (asking the question that if romantic authorship had explanatory power for IPR maximalism, then why is it that protection for works should change over time?).
43. Mitchell, *The Intellectual Commons*, at 148; Cohen F. (1935), *Transcendental Nonsense and the Functional Approach*, 35 Colum. L. Rev. 809, at 815 (arguing that the 'circularity of legal reasoning in the whole field of unfair competition is veiled by the "thingification" of property'). See also, Smith H. (2012), *Property as the Law of Things*, 125 Harvard Law Review 1691. The incentivisation arguments also encompass 'reward for labour' notions. In more formalised parlance, IPRs are usually built on natural rights (labour theory) and the utilitarian rationale (incentive theory). For further discussion see Derclaye E. (2012), *Eudemonic Intellectual Property: Patents and Related Rights as Engines of Happiness, Peace, and Sustainability*, 14(3) Vanderbilt Journal of Entertainment and Technology Law 495 at 497 [hereafter *Eudemonic Intellectual Property*]; and Ricketson S. (1992), *New Wine into Old Bottles: Technological Change and Intellectual Property Rights*, 10(1) Prometheus at 57–60 [hereafter *New Wine into Old Bottles*].
44. Boyle, *The Public Domain*, at xi (preface) (referring to a peanut butter and jelly sandwich patent in the US – although it was subsequently revoked). See also *Moore v Regents of the University of California* 793 P.2d 479 (Cal 1990), cert. denied, 111

S. Ct. 1388 (1991) discussed in Boyle J. (1992), *A Theory of Law and Information: Copyright, Spleens, Blackmail and Insider Trading*, 80 California Law Review 1413–1540 [hereafter *A Theory of Law and Information*] (referring to the ownership of Mr John Moore's spleen).

45. Aoki K. (1994), *Authors, Inventors and Trademark Owners: Private Intellectual Property and the Public Domain*, 18 Columbia VLA Journal of Law and the Arts 191 at 217.
46. Drahos P. (2010), *'IP World' – Made by TNC Inc*, in Krikorian and Kapczynski (eds), *A2K in the Age of IP*, at 198–202.
47. This argument was initially stated in *The Clothworkers of Ipswich*, 78 Eng Rep (1615) at 148 cited in Walterscheid E. (1999/2000), *Defining the Patent and Copyright Term: Term Limits and the Intellectual Property Clause*, 7 J. Intell. Prop. L. 315 at 323–324, footnote 29. But see also *Stewart v Abend* 495 US 207, 228 (1990) cited in Rimmer, *Digital Copyright*, at 29, footnote 35. See also, *Twentieth Century Music Corp. v Aiken*, 422 US 151, 156, 186 USPQ (BNA) 65, 67 (1975) (stating that the ultimate aim of copyright is to 'stimulate artistic creativity for the general public good'); and Harrison J. (2005), *A Positive Externalities Approach to Copyright Law: Theory and Application*, 13(1) Journal of Intellectual Property Law 1 at 3, footnote 4 [hereafter *A Positive Externalities Approach to Copyright Law*].
48. Vaver D. (1990), *Intellectual Property Today: Of Myths and Paradoxes*, 69 Canadian Bar Review 98, at 99. See also, Cunningham, *Tragedy of (Ignoring) the Information Semicommons*, at 7; Ricketson S. and Richardson M. (1998) (2nd edition), *Intellectual Property: Cases, Materials and Commentary*, LexisNexis Butterworths at 11; Hegel G. (1820) [1967], *Philosophy of Right*, T. Knox (ed. and trans.), Oxford University Press, at 44; Radin M. (1982), *Property and Personhood*, 34 Stan. L. Rev. 957; Locke J. (1690) [1988], *Two Treatises of Government – The Second Treatise*, Peter Laslett (ed.), Cambridge University Press, at 285–286; Gordon W. (1993), *A Property Right in Self-Expression: Equality and Individualism in the Natural Law of Intellectual Property*, 102 Yale L J 1533; Machlup F. and Penrose E. (1950), *The Patent Controversy in the Nineteenth Century*, 10 Journal of Economic History 1 (outlining four nineteenth-century justifications for the creation of patents, including but not limited to the rationale that inventors have a natural right to their invention and that justice requires that inventors be rewarded); Kase J. (1971), *Copyright Thought in Continental Europe: A Selected Bibliography*, William Hein & Co. at 8; Spector H. (1989), *An Outline of a Theory of Justifying Intellectual Property and Intellectual Property Rights*, 8 European Intellectual Property Review at 270; Ricketson, *New Wine into Old Bottles*, at 57.
49. Jaffe A. (1999), *The U.S. Patent System in Transition: Policy Innovation and the Innovation Process*, NBER Working Paper Series, August, at 24–26.
50. However, when the direction of an improvement to an invention is ambiguous, then licensing may not occur, and patents may in fact impede innovation. See Lessig L. (2002), *The Future of Ideas: the Fate of the Commons in a Connected World*, Knopf Doubleday Publishing Group at 205 [hereafter *The Future of Ideas*]; Mandeville T. (1996), *Understanding Novelty: Information, Technological Change and the Patent System*, Greenwood Publishing.
51. This perspective was relayed in Hurt R. and Schuchman R. (1966), *The Economic Rationale for Copyright*, American Economic Review at 421–432, quoted in Atkinson B. (2007), *The True History of Copyright: The Australian Experience 1905–2005*, Sydney University Press, at 9–10. See also Oddi S. (1987), *The International Patent System and Third World Development: Myth or Reality?* 63 Duke Law Journal 831 at 837–842 (surmising that '[d]espite the 500 year history of the patent system, it is still extremely difficult to ascertain whether a patent system actually results in a net social benefit to a developed country').

52. Lerner J. (2002), *Patent Protection and Innovation Over 150 Years*, working paper no. 8977, National Bureau of Economic Research, Cambridge (2002).
53. Ibid. See also Benkler, *The Wealth of Networks*, at 38–39.
54. Benkler, *The Wealth of Networks*, at 38–39. The difficulty of proving the correlation between IPRs and research and development is partly because of the difficulty of separating cause and effect. That is, IPRs may stimulate more investment, but countries that invest more in R&D may demand more protection. See, for example, Ingco M. and Nash J. (eds) (2004), *Agriculture and the WTO*, World Bank: Washington DC, at 254–256. The experience of the US and China specifically in relation to agriculture is thought provoking. The Chinese are one of the most advanced rice breeders in the world, even though historically they have not had any form of protection on new plant varieties. See van Wijk J. and Walter J. (eds) (1996), *Intellectual Property Rights and Agriculture in Developing Countries*, University of Amsterdam, at 25. On the other hand, in the US, protection led to an increase in improvement programmes for only two plant species. The rare studies that have been conducted in countries where the protection of vegetal breeding has existed for decades, like the US, show that this type of legal system had several consequences such as reduced information and genetic material exchange between the public sector and the private sector; a low stimulus impact on plant improvement; an increase in the price of seeds sold to farmers; and a diminished role of the public sector in plant improvement. See Al Brac de la Perriere R. and Seuret F. (2000), *Brave New Seeds: The Threat of Transgenic Crops to Farmers*, Pluto Press, at 95.
55. Drahos, *A Philosophy of IP*, at 15. Consideration of the network externalities or positive spillovers of information provide one explicit example whereby IPRs may indeed cause harm to the information environment. See, for example, Samuelson P. et al (1994), *A Manifesto Concerning the Legal Protection of Computer Programs*, 94 Columbia Law Review 2308, at 2375; Farrell J. (1989), *Standardization and Intellectual Property*, 30 Jurimetrics Journal 35, 36–38, 45–46 (discussing network effects).
56. Note that Justice Breyer is relying upon Rappaport E. (1998), *Copyright Term Extensions: Estimating Economic Values*, CRS Report for Congress. See also, Harrison, *A Positive Externalities Approach to Copyright Law*, at 28. Justice Breyer's view can be contrasted with the more traditional view within the US judiciary, exemplified by the following passage: 'the patent law is directed to the public purpose of fostering technological progress, investment in research and development, capital formation, entrepreneurship, innovation, national strength, and international competitiveness'. See *Hilton Davis Chem. Co v Warner-Jenkinson Co.*, 62 F. 3d 1512, 1536 (Fed. Cir. 1995) (Newman J concurring). Also, Derclaye, *Eudemonic Intellectual Property*, at 500–501.
57. Harrison, *A Positive Externalities Approach to Copyright Law*, at 28. The 'lottery argument' is also applicable with respect not just to the duration of an IPR but also whether a given work will be marketable immediately after it is released. The author is indebted to Dr Nic Suzor from the Queensland University of Technology for this point.
58. Towse R. (2001), *Creativity, Incentive and Reward: An Economic Analysis of Copyright and Culture in the Information Age*, Edward Elgar at 132–136 (discussing the fact that the copyright system tends to reward superstar artists at the expense of the rest); Zimmerman D. (2011), *Copyrights as Incentives: Did We Just Imagine That?*, 12 Theoretical Inquiries in Law 3, at 41; and Drahos with Braithwaite, *Information Feudalism*, at 185 (arguing that only a few benefit from the copyright monopoly system). The courts, the legislature and the literature all stress that the incentivisation arguments exist for the benefit of the public rather than for personal

benefit. For example, see Patterson L. and Lindberg S. (1991), *The Nature of Copyright: A Law of Users' Rights*, University of Georgia Press at 49; Pollack M. (2002), *Dealing with Old Father William, or Moving from Constitutional Text to Constitutional Doctrine: Progress Clause Review of the Copyright Term Extension Act*, 36 Loy. LA L. Rev. 337 at 382.

59. For a good summary of how incentivisation arguments pervade IPR discourse, see Derclaye, *Eudemonic Intellectual Property*, 495.
60. Patterson L.R. and Lindberg S. (1991), *The Nature of Copyright: A Law of User Rights*, University of Georgia Press, at 12–13 [hereafter *The Nature of Copyright*].
61. Price W. (1906), *English Patents of Monopoly*, Houghton, Mifflin and Co., at 154. In November 1601 a constitutional crisis ensued in England in relation to the bill entitled 'An Act for the Explanation of the Common Law in Certain Cases of Letters Patent'. See Cobbett W. (1806), *1 Cobbett's Parliamentary History of England* 925–30 (London) and Sir Simonds D'Ewes (1682), *Journal of All the Parliament During the Reign of Queen Elizabeth* 644–48 (London), both cited in Walterscheid E. (1999/2000), *Defining the Patent and Copyright Term: Term Limits and the Intellectual Property Clause*, 7 J. Intell. Prop. L. 315 at 322, footnote 23.
62. As we will see in Part III, authorial (inventive) romance and the accompanying incentivisation arguments related to IPRs are underpinned by a brand of 'methodological individualism' that generally succumbs to the 'individualist fallacy' by omitting relevant relational features of the information environment. This perspective is supported by Ricketson, *New Wine into Old Bottles*, at 56–57 (arguing that 'few, if any, intellectual creations are ever the unaided product of one person's mind, but rather … they represent the value-added component contributed by the so-called creator to information which is already in existence'). See also Kressel H. and Lento T. (2007), *Competing for the Future: How Digital Innovations are Changing the World*, Cambridge University Press, at 105 (discussing the overstatement of inventor romance, and how Edison was supported by a 'hand-picked research team', undermining the archetype image of a 'lone inventor'); and van Caenegem W. (2003), *Intellectual Property Law and the Idea of Progress*, http://epublications.bond.edu.au/law_pubs/170 at 238 (arguing that the economic justifications of IPRs fail to place creativity and innovation within a wider cultural and social context).
63. With respect to the dual objectives of the IPR system, note Breyer J's statement in relation to the Intellectual Property Clause within the US Constitution quoted above. This argument was initially stated in *The Clothworkers of Ipswich*, 78 Eng Rep (1615) at 148 cited in Walterscheid E. (1999/2000), *Defining the Patent and Copyright Term: Term Limits and the Intellectual Property Clause*, 7 J Intell. Prop. L. 315 at 323–324, footnote 29. See also, *Stewart v Abend* 495 US 207, 228 (1990) cited in Rimmer M. (2007), *Digital Copyright* at 29, footnote 35. See also, *Twentieth Century Music Corp. v Aiken*, 422 US 151, 156, 186 USPQ (BNA) 65, 67 (1975) (stating that the ultimate aim of copyright is to 'stimulate artistic creativity for the general public good'); Harrison, *A Positive Externalities Approach to Copyright Law*, at 3; and van Caenegem, *Intellectual Property Law and the Idea of Progress* (discussing the individualist nature of IPRs). The overarching theme is that the incentivisation arguments that prevail within IPR maximalist discourse must be counter-balanced with the public good. In relation to the issue that IPRs are granted to individuals rather than communities, there are of course examples of the collectivisation of rights such as the collecting societies. For a discussion in this regard see Ricketson, *New Wine into Old Bottles*, at 65 onwards. More contemporaneously, there are also some interesting examples of where the traditional knowledge of Indigenous peoples is recognised on a collective basis. For example, see Panama's Law No. 20 of 26 June 2002 where a special regime of IPRs was

established based on the collective rights of Indigenous peoples for the protection and defence of their cultural identity and traditional knowledge. See Correa C. (2010), *Access to Knowledge: The Case of Indigenous and Traditional Knowledge* in Krikorian and Kapczynski (eds), *A2K in the Age of IP*, at 242 [hereafter *Access to Knowledge*].

64. Anonymous (1735), 'A Letter to a Member of Parliament concerning the Bill now depending in the House of Commons, for making more effectual an Act in the 8th Year of the Reign of Queen Anne, entitled, An Act for the Encouragement of Learning, by Vesting the Copies of Printed Books in the Authors or Purchasers of such Copies, during the Times therein mentioned', document reproduced in Goldsmith's-Kress Library of Economic Literature, Segment 1: Printed Books Through 1800, Microfilm No. 7300 (Reel 430) cited in Rimmer, *Digital Copyright*, at 27, footnote 17. See also Judge C. (1934), *Elizabethan Book-Pirates*, Harvard University Press, at 86–87; Drahos with Braithwaite J., *Information Feudalism*, at 30; Drahos, *The Global Governance of Knowledge,* at 7, footnote 17 (arguing that just as copyright is a tax on readers, so too patents are a tax on consumers of technology); and Rose M. (2003), *Nine-Tenths of the Law: the English Copyright Debates and the Rhetoric of the Public Domain*, 66 Law and Contemporary Problems 75, at 83.
65. See Pine F. (1916), *The Autobiography of Benjamin Franklin*, Garden City, at 215–216; and Merton R. (1942), *A Note on Science and Democracy*, 1 Journal of Law & Political Sociology 115, at 123. Interestingly, Benjamin Franklin was instrumental in the creation of libraries.
66. Warshofsky F. (1994), *The Patent Wars*, Wiley, at 170, quoting Bill Gates.
67. Litman J. (1990), *The Public Domain*, 39 Emory Law Journal 965, at 965; and Ryan M. (2000), *Cyberspace as Public Space: A Public Trust Paradigm for Copyright in a Digital World*, 79 Or. L. Rev. 647, at 689 (relaying Aoki K. (1996) and arguing that: 'the baseline fallacies employed by neoclassical economic analysis have come to justify ever-increasing property rights in information'). Thus, see also Aoki K. (1996), *(Intellectual) Property and Sovereignty: Notes Toward a Cultural Geography of Authorship*, 48 Stan. L. Rev. 1293, at 1299 [hereafter *(Intellectual) Property and Sovereignty*].
68. Mitchell, *The Intellectual Commons*, at 149. One of the reasons that the Act of Anne (1709) was considered such a revolutionary statute was because it diminished the privilege system of the day and injected a public interest dimension. See Drahos, *A Philosophy of IP*, at 23, 54; and Patterson and Lindberg, *The Nature of Copyright*, at 29–31. Drahos suggests that it may be an artificial dichotomy to suggest that IPRs are either a reward for labour or a tool for encouraging creativity and innovation in the sense that there may be a variety of rationales for an 'intellectual commons' (see Drahos, *A Philosophy of IP*, at 60).
69. Mitchell, *The Intellectual Commons*, at 149. See also Rimmer, *Digital Copyright*, at 25 (highlighting the pretence that the main beneficiaries of the 1998 Copyright extensions in the US were artists and musicians, rather than multinational media companies who distributed and transmitted copyright works); Frye N. (1957), *Anatomy of Criticism: Four Essays*, Princeton UP, at 96–97 (arguing that the conventionality of literature is 'elaborately disguised by a law of copyright pretending that every work of art is an invention distinctive enough to be patented'); and Rose, *Authors and Owners*, at 3. Even as far back as the sixteenth century the author only ever had a 'cameo role' in the development of copyright. See Drahos, *A Philosophy of IP*, at 23, 99–100. This is because, at least under a Marxist analysis, IPRs are required to ensure that ruling interests retain and extend their control over critical aspects of the means of production being abstract objects (ibid at 100).

Similar arguments can also be cast in relation to patents and innovation. See, for example, Drahos with Braithwaite, *Information Feudalism*, at 16.

70. Drahos, *A Philosophy of IP*, at 101; Clement E. and Oppenheim C. (2002), *Anarchism, Alternative Publishers and Copyright*, Anarchist Studies, at 44; Rose, *Authors and Owners*, at 13 (arguing that 'despite the fact that book production was one of the most capitalistic of early industries, the book itself continued to be perceived as an object of mixed not absolute property, of collective not private enterprise'). According to a Hegelian analysis it is difficult to justify special treatment of the artist when it comes to validating property. See Hegel G. (1821), *Philosophy of Right*, Clarendon Press 1952 (1st edition) and reprinted 1967 at 68. See also Drahos, *A Philosophy of IP*, Chapter 4, especially at 81, 82; and Drahos with Braithwaite, *Information Feudalism*, at 32, 35 (arguing that trade agendas drove the process of copyright in the late 1800s rather than the interests of the author). The commonly used phrase 'the market place of ideas' exemplifies how readily information commodification is accepted within the modern era. See Schauer F. (1982), *Free Speech: A Philosophical Inquiry*, Cambridge University Press at 19–20; Birnhack M. (2003), *Copyright Law and Free Speech after Eldred v Ashcroft*, 76 S. Cal. L. Rev. 1275–1330; Birnhack, *More or Better?*, at 69; and Rimmer, *Digital Copyright*, at 26 (alluding to the marketplace of ideas).
71. Waldon J. (1993), *From Authors to Copiers: Individual Rights and Social Values in Intellectual Property*, 68 Chicago-Kent L. Rev. 841, at 841–887. See also Rose, *Authors and Owners*, at 13; Drahos with Braithwaite, *Information Feudalism*, at 32, 35 (arguing that trade agendas drove the process of copyright in the late 1800s rather than the interests of the author).
72. The root meaning of property stems back to Anglo-Norman texts in the 1180s to mean an 'attribute' or 'characteristic' of a person or thing. The secondary and less common usage of the word 'property' equated to a person's interest in having a thing. See, for example, Graham N. (2011), *Lawscape: Property, Environment, Law*, Routledge, at 26 [hereafter *Lawscape*]; and Aoki, *(Intellectual) Property and Sovereignty*, at 1333–1338 (linking romantic authorship and property rhetoric). Also, for an excellent description of how industrial information producer interests have shaped IPR debates with reference to property, see Sell S. (2002), *TRIPS and the Access to Medicines Campaign*, 20(3) Wisconsin International Law Journal, at 489–490 (maintaining that '[b]y wrapping themselves in the mantle of "property rights", [industrial information producers] suggested that the rights they were claiming were somehow natural, unassailable and automatically deserved').
73. For an interesting contemporary account concerning the relationship between colonialism and the commons see Atteberry J. (2010), *Information/Knowledge in the Global Society of Control: A2K Theory and the Postcolonial Commons* in Krikorian and Kapczynski (eds), *A2K in the Age of IP*, at 329 onwards.
74. Blackstone W. (1765) [1783], *Commentaries on the Laws of England*, cited in Rose, *Authors and Owners*, at 7. Blackstone also made the point that 'there is no foundation in nature or in natural law, why a set of words upon parchment should convey the dominion of land'. See Blackstone (1765) Book 2, Chapter 1, 2 cited in Drahos, *A Philosophy of IP*, at 3, footnote 7. See also Purdy J. (2010), *The Meaning of Property: Freedom, Community, and the Legal Imagination*, Yale University Press, at 1, footnote 1 [hereafter *The Meaning of Property*] (referring to this phrase as being 'almost Shakespearean in [its] familiarity'). Purdy refers to the accompanying text to that definition being: 'There is nothing which so generally strikes the imagination, and engages the affections of mankind, as the right of property; or that sole and despotic dominion …'. After Blackstone provided that definition, he then went on to state 'Pleased as we are with the possession, we seem afraid to look

back to the means by which it was acquired, as if fearful of some defect in our title'. See ibid, at 1, footnote 3.

75. Graham, *Lawscape*, at 17. See also Menell P. (2002), *Reunifying Property*, 46 St. Louis U. L. J. 599; Locke J. (1690) [1967], *Two Treatises of Government*, ed. Laslett, at 305–306. Many scholars have sought to give expression to the 'value judgments' inherent within property. For example, see Mitchell, *The Intellectual Commons*, at 127. However, cf Sun H. (2009), *Toward a Public Trust Doctrine in Copyright Law*, Cornell Law School Inter-University Graduate Student Conference Papers, found at http://scholarship.law.cornell.edu/lps_clacp/36/ (cited 27 April 2013) at 9 [hereafter *Toward a Public Trust Doctrine in Copyright Law*] ('having a private space is of essential importance for every human being to achieve self-development and flourishing'); Hegel G. (1820) [1991], *Elements of the Philosophy of Right*, trans. Nisbet, Cambridge University Press, at 41 ('the person must give himself an external *sphere of freedom* in order to have being as Idea'). Also, Boyle argues that 'property is perhaps the most important way in which we attempt to reconcile our desire for freedom and our desire for security'. See Boyle, *A Theory of Law and Information*, at 1458; and Singer J. (1982), *The Legal Rights Debate in Analytical Jurisprudence from Bentham to Hohfeld*, Wis. L. Rev. 975. See also, Liang L. (2010), *The Man Who Mistook His Wife for a Book*, in Krikorian and Kapczynski (eds), *A2K in the Age of IP*, at 277 (arguing that Locke's *Two Treatises of Government* was 'the most coherent argument linking theories of identity to property').
76. Smith A. (1759) [2000], *The Theory of Moral Sentiments*, Prometheus Books, at 87. See also, Purdy, *The Meaning of Property*, at 3. Also, Hont I. (2005), *Jealousy of Trade: International Competition and the Nation State in Historical Perspective*, Belknap, at 364 [hereafter *Jealousy of Trade*] (arguing that natural lawyers from the eras of Blackstone and Locke drew upon an 'innovative vision of property and exchange as the basic expressions of interdependence and the foundation of a society based on social-ability'). Hardin has argued that animal territoriality is the progenitor of property; and it may very well be that this territoriality trait underpins some aspects of the socially atomising effect of property. See Stone C. (1974), *Should Trees Have Standing? Toward Legal Rights for Natural Objects*, William Kaufmann Inc, preface, at xi–xii (Garrett Hardin) [hereafter *Should Trees Have Standing?*]. Lemley has also noted that some people argue that 'property ownership is hard-wired into our brains'. See Lemley M. (2004), *Property, Intellectual Property, and Free Riding*, Working Paper No 291, Stanford Law School, Hohn M. Olin Program in Law and Economics, at 8 [hereafter *Property, Intellectual Property, and Free Riding*]. Also, see Cohen J., *Overcoming Property: Does Copyright Trump Privacy?*, 2002 U. Ill. J. L. & Tech. Pol'y 375 at 379 [hereafter *Overcoming Property*] ('there is nothing which so generally strikes the imagination, and engages the affections of mankind, as the right of property'); Lastowka G. and Hunter D. (2004), *The Laws of the Virtual Worlds*, 92 Calif. L. Rev. 1, 36 [hereafter *The Laws of the Virtual Worlds*] (noting that even small children exhibit possessiveness over chattels); Pipes R. (1999), *Property and Freedom*, Alfred A. Knopf, at 65–86 (noting that animals and all human societies show the possessiveness instinct). Brennan and Buchanan argue that according to the rational choice theorist maxim it is safer to rely upon self-interest rather than virtue as the foundation for institutions, which is one reason why propertisation has become normalised. See Brennan G. and Buchanan J. (1985), *The Reason of Rules: Constitutional Political Economy*, Cambridge University Press [hereafter *The Reason of Rules*]. Also see Drahos, *A Philosophy of IP*, at 119.

77. Blackstone W. (1765–69) [1856], *Commentaries on the Laws of England*, Systematically Abridged and Adapted to The Existing State of the Law and Constitution with Great Additions, by Samuel Warren (2nd edition), Blackwood & Sons, at 418.
78. Stone, *Should Trees Have Standing?*, preface, at xii (Garrett Hardin). See also, Bentham J. (1820) [1975], *Theory of Legislation*, Trubner & Co, at 68 (where Bentham argues that property is 'nothing but a basis for expectation'); Fagundes D. (2009), *Crystals in the Public Domain*, 50(1) Boston College Law Review 139, at 146; Gray K. (1991), *Property in Thin Air*, 50 Cambridge Law Journal, 252, 259; Drahos, *A Philosophy of IP*, at 4 (arguing that 'the view that property is a thing is nowadays seen as quaint and false, or at least not helpful' and '[p]roperty is a contest for the control of objects that people need or want and sometimes upon which their very survival, either individually or as a group, depends') and at 19 (arguing that 'property is not a thing but a set of relations between people'). Also, see Coombe R. and Herman A. (2004), *Rhetorical Virtues: Property, Speech, and the Commons on the World-Wide Web*, George Washington Institute for Ethnographic Research, at 560 (referring to the work of Jack Balkin (1998) and the notion of property as a hegemonic meme). According to the critical realist perspective of property 'all private economic relations emerge re-described as relations of coercion'. See Purdy, *The Meaning of Property*, at 21, footnote 43, referring to Robert Hale (a realist property theorist). This critical realist perspective is also reflected in the social constructionist perspective of law. See, e.g., George A. (2012), *Constructing Intellectual Property*, Cambridge University Press, at 85–89 (discussing social constructionism generally).
79. Purdy, *The Meaning of Property*, at 21 (arguing that a complementary perspective of the self-reinforcing view of property is to recognise that property sets in motion market relations, which in turn affects the concept of value and the satisfaction of 'morally arbitrary and psychologically fungible preferences').
80. Locke J. (1689) [1988], 288.
81. It is perhaps the self-reinforcing aspect of property that provides a foundation for the defenders of property to equate the concept to something as substantive as an atom or molecule. See Stone, *Should Trees Have Standing?*, preface, at xi–xii (Garrett Hardin). Also note that Hegel believed that there is an 'absolute right' to appropriate 'things', albeit things equated to 'mental aptitudes, erudition, artistic skill' (see Hegel G. (1821) [1952], *Philosophy of Right*, at 44). Also, see Drahos, *A Philosophy of IP*, at 76 (discussing Hegelian perspectives).
82. Cohen, *Transcendental Nonsense and the Functional Approach*, at 814–817. See also, Drahos, *A Philosophy of IP*, at 204–205 (covering trademarks and proprietarianism). While trademarks were not initially based on incentivisation arguments, over time incentivisation has become a stronger justification. See Derclaye, *Eudemonic Intellectual Property*, at 505. Also, see *Pebble Beach Co v Tour* 18, I Ltd, 942 Supp. 1513, 1541–42 (S.D. Tex. 1996) (where the court held that 'even if a golfer in Texas could not be confused as to whether or not she was playing a hole on a trademarked course in California, confusion over whether the trademark's owner had endorsed a similarly designed hole constitutes trademark infringement'). Also, Lemley, *Romantic Authorship and the Rhetoric of Property*, at 899.
83. Locke J. (1690) [1821], *Two Treatises of Government – The Second Treatise*, Whitmore and Fenn, at 214 [para. 34].
84. Purdy, *The Meaning of Property*, at 42. While this book does not traverse the interrelationship between environmentalism, Indigenous rights/traditional knowledge, and IPRs, this is definitely a critical area of research that needs to be engaged with further.
85. Locke, *Two Treatises of Government – The Second Treatise*, at 219 [para 37]. Adam Smith also adopted a similar view with reference to Africa and the East Indies when

he discussed the 'need' to 'clear the natives' and 'extend the European plantations over the greater part of the lands of the original inhabitants'. See Smith A. (1776) [1965], *The Wealth of Nations*, Modern Library, at 599.

86. Darwin observes in *Descent of Man* that the history of the moral development of human beings has been a continual expansion of their 'social instincts and sympathies' cited in Stone, *Should Trees Have Standing?*, at 450 (referring to Darwin C. (1874), *Descent of Man* (2nd edition), John Murray Publishing, at 119, 120–121). Also, see Warren S. and Brandeis L. (1890), *The Right to Privacy*, 4 Harvard Law Review 193 (indicating that civilization has generally progressed from a concern for life and property to include spirituality, feelings and intellect); and Kropotkin P. (1902), *Mutual Aid: A Factor of Evolution*, William Heinemann (indicating that cooperation was a critical component of evolution). Kropotkin's perspective has been adopted by a host of contemporary IPR scholars including Benkler Y. (2011), *The Penguin and Leviathan: the Triumph of Cooperation over Self-Interest*, Crown Business; and Nowak M. (2011), *SuperCooperators: Why We Need Each Other to Succeed*, Simon & Schuster.
87. Leopold A. (1949), *A Sand County Almanac*, Oxford University Press, 1966 at 217 (emphasis added). See also, Stone, *Should Trees Have Standing?*, preface, at x–xi (Garrett Hardin).
88. Ibid. Leopold's view is to be contrasted with the view that property embeds ethics: 'as private rights and their supporting institutions evolve, incentives are created for individuals to behave cooperatively, ethically, and altruistically. On the other hand, institutions designed to produce involuntary transfers of wealth, and therefore, undermine the security of private property rights, also undermine the incentive to behave morally'. See De Alessi L. (2001), *Property Rights: Private and Political Institutions* [hereafter *Property Rights*] in Shughart, W. and Razzolini L. (eds), *The Elgar Companion to Public Choice*, Edward Elgar Publishing, at 36.
89. Stone, *Should Trees Have Standing?*, preface, at xi (Garrett Hardin). Obviously the relationship between human beings, the environment and property is complex. Numerous scholars have sought to discuss this relationship. Hardin, for instance, has argued that the concept of property is built upon an ingrained animal territoriality within human beings. See also Lemley, *Property, Intellectual Property, and Free Riding*, at 8 (noting that some people argue that 'property ownership is hard-wired into our brains'); Cohen, *Overcoming Property*, at 379 (stating that 'there is nothing which so generally strikes the imagination, and engages the affections of mankind, as the right of property'); Lastowka and Hunter, *The Laws of the Virtual Worlds*, at 36 (noting that even small children exhibit possessiveness over chattels); Pipes R. (1999), *Property and Freedom*, Alfred A. Knopf, at 65–86 (noting that animals and all human societies show the possessiveness instinct). Brennan and Buchanan argue that according to the rational choice theorist maxim it is safer to rely upon self-interest rather than virtue as the foundation for institutions, which is one reason why propertisation has become normalised. See Brennan and Buchanan, *The Reason of Rules*; and Drahos, *A Philosophy of IP*, at 119.
90. Leopold, *A Sand County Almanac*, at 240. A similar analysis can be engaged with based on James Lovelock's Gaia Hypothesis. For a discussion of this hypothesis see Kirk J. (2007), *Science & Uncertainty*, CSIRO Publishing, at 199–211.
91. For instance, property is central to the environmental changes that manifested when the English commons were enclosed and the lands of foreign countries were colonised. See Graham, *Lawscape: Property, Environment, Law*, at 6–7; and Chon, *Postmodern 'Progress'*, at 124. Also Giddens A. (1990), *The Consequences of Modernity*, Stanford University Press, at 18–19 noting that: 'The advent of modernity increasingly tears space away from place by fostering relations between

"absent" others, locationally distant from any given situation of face-to-face interaction. In conditions of modernity, place becomes increasingly phantasmagoric: that is to say, locales are thoroughly penetrated by and shaped in terms of social influences quite distant from them.' Leopold's land ethic will be revisited at length in Part III of the book when applying the ecology analytical framework to IPRs.

92. Graham, *Lawscape: Property, Environment, Law*, at 26; and Seipp D. (1994), *The Concept of Property in the Early Common Law*, 12(1) Law and History Review 29, at 69. However, contrast this perspective with Hegel, who argued that private property is a critical means in which personality comes into fruition. See Hegel, *Philosophy of Right*, at 44, cited in Drahos, *A Philosophy of IP*, Chapter 4. Interestingly, the root meaning of property stems back to Anglo-Norman texts in the 1180s to mean an 'attribute' or 'characteristic' of a person or thing. The secondary and less common usage of the word 'property' equated to a person's interest in having a thing. See Graham, *Lawscape: Property, Environment, Law*, at 26.
93. White L. (1967), *The Historical Roots of Our Ecological Crisis*, 155 Science 1203–1207.
94. Mitchell, *The Intellectual Commons*, at 110–111.
95. Ibid.
96. Ibid, at 117.
97. Hill C. (1973), *Winstanley: the law of freedom and other writings*, Cambridge University Press at 99.
98. Rousseau J. (1755) [1988], *Discourse on the Origin and Foundations of Inequality Among Men*, in Ritter A. and Bondanella J. (eds) (1988), *Rousseau's Political Writings*, Norton.
99. Guerin D. (2005) (ed.), *No Gods, No Masters: An Anthology of Anarchism*, trans. P. Sharkey, AK Press, at 55–56. Just as Proudhon argued that 'property is theft', so too some IPR scholars have argued that 'intellectual property is theft'. See, for example, Martin B. (1995), *Against Intellectual Property*, 21(3) Philosophy and Social Action 7.
100. Boyle, *The Second Enclosure Movement*, at 33–36.
101. Borch M. (2001), *Rethinking the Origins of Terra Nullius*, Taylor & Francis. For a critical perspective of the Australian High Court decision of *Mabo* and the *terra nullius* doctrine see Ritter D. (1996), *The 'Rejection of Terra Nullius' in Mabo: A Critical Analysis*, 18 Sydney Law Review 5.
102. One of the first appearances of the 'four-stages of history' perspective was Dalrymple J. (1758), *Essay Towards a General History of Feudal Property in Great Britain*, Millar. The primary source of this literature was likely Adam Smith's Edinburgh law lectures. See, Meek R. (1976), *Social Science and the Ignoble Savage*, Cambridge University Press, at 111–112. Regardless of the source, the four stages perspective was adopted by Blackstone onwards. See Blackstone, *Commentaries on the Laws of England*, at 246; and discussed more contemporaneously by Hont. See Hont, *Jealousy of Trade*, at 364.
103. Of course, the four stages of history lens is a stylised version of history (commonly found within colonial and imperial narratives of property). To be sure, there are many alternative methods of conceptualising the history of propertisation. One example is Benkler's discussion concerning the history of the shift from industrial to information economies. See Benkler, *The Idea of Access to Knowledge and the Information Commons*, at 218–219.
104. As Kent explained with reference to *Johnson v M'Intosh* 21 US 543, 8 Wheat 543 (1823), the specific 'destiny and duty of the human race' as it concerned the first American settlers was 'to subdue the earth, and till the ground'. See Kent J. (1826–1830) [1873], *Commentaries on American Law* (12th edition), at 386–387. Also, Purdy, *The Meaning of Property*, at 39, 61.

105. Reference to 'social contract' gives rise to a broad range of discourse stemming from the so-called 'contractarian philosophers' of Hobbes, Locke and Rousseau, who were among the first theorists to reconcile individual desires and choices with social and political outcomes. See, for example, Azfar O. (2001), *The Logic of Collective Action*, in Shughart and Razzolini (eds), *The Elgar Companion to Public Choice*, at 84. While property pre-empted the modern state, there is no doubt that the social contract arguments that underpin the state also tend to strengthen propertisation arguments. For coverage of the relationship between the state and property, see Avineri S. (1972), *Hegel's Theory of the Modern State*, Cambridge University Press.
106. Boyle, *Second Enclosure Movement.*
107. Chander A. and Sunder M. (2004), *The Romance of the Public Domain*, 92 California Law Review, 1331–1373, at 1356, especially footnote 133. This perspective also accords with the 'positive community' and 'negative community' descriptions discussed by Drahos, *A Philosophy of IP*, at 45–46, 57–59, 65–66, 68.
108. Ibid.
109. Ibid.
110. There are many other methods of discussing property validation. For example, in Part I of the book the Demsetzian perspective of property validation is explored at length.
111. Boyle, *The Second Enclosure Movement*, at 52.
112. Atteberry J. (2010), *Information/Knowledge in the Global Society of Control: A2K Theory and the Postcolonial Commons* [hereafter *Information/Knowledge in the Global Society of Control*], in Krikorian and Kapczynski (eds), *A2K in the Age of IP*, at 329. See also Liang L. (2010), *Beyond Representation: The Figure of the Pirate* [hereafter *Beyond Representation*], in Krikorian and Kapczynski (eds), *A2K in the Age of IP*, at 369–370.
113. Purdy J. (2012), *Our Place in the World: A New Relationship for Environmental Ethics and Law*, 62 Duke Law Journal 857. Available at: http://scholarship.law.duke.edu/faculty_scholarship/2509 (cited 14 December 2012) [hereafter *Our Place in the World*].

PART I NOTES

1. For literature that links property with economic efficiency see, for example, Demsetz H. (1964), *The Exchange and Enforcement of Property Rights*, 7 Journal of Law and Economics 11; Demsetz H. (1967), *Towards a Theory of Property Rights*, 57 American Economic Review 347; Manne H. (1975), *The Economics of Legal Relationships: Readings in the Theory of Property Rights*, West Publishing; Posner R. (1977), *Economic Analysis of Law*, Aspen Publishing.
2. See Buchanan J. (1989), *The Achievement and Limits of Public Choice in Diagnosing Government Failure and in Offering Bases for Constructive Reform*, in Buchanan J. (1989), *Explorations into Constitutional Economics*, Texas A & M University Press, at 24 (noting that '[t]heoretical welfare economics is properly labeled as a theory of market failure'). See also Greenhalgh and Rogers, *Innovation, Intellectual Property, and Economic Growth*, at xii, 18. Interestingly, Greenhalgh and Rogers discuss four market failures being public goods, positive externalities, under-investment stemming from uncertainty and large fixed costs, and duplication and excess costs stemming from competition. This book does not explore the issue of uncertainty as discussed by Arrow K. (1962), *Economic Welfare and the Allocation of Resources for Invention*, in *The Rate and Direction of Inventive Activity: Economic and Social Factors*, National

Bureau of Economic Research [hereafter *Economic Welfare*] but uncertainty is nonetheless acknowledged as a significant issue within the innovation context.

3. There are of course other market failures that this book does not seek to address. One example includes 'contract failure' discussed by Hansmann H. (1980), *The Role of Nonprofit Enterprise*, 89 Yale Law Journal 835. For an insightful account of market failure as it relates to IPRs, see Gordon W. (1982), *Fair Use as Market Failure: A Structural and Economic Analysis of the Betamax Case and Its Predecessors*, 82 Colum. L. Rev. 1600 [hereafter *Fair Use as Market Failure*].
4. Vera Franz has indicated that '[I]n the IP area ... the one biggest problem we currently have is actually a problem of market failure ... [S]o our work in the IP field is very specifically trying to address those market failures', quoted in Lee J. (2010), *The Greenpeace of Cultural Environmentalism*, 16 Widener Law Review 1, at 45, footnote 310.
5. Farina F. (2005), *Constitutional Economics I*, in Backhaus J. (2005) (ed.), *The Elgar Companion to Law and Economics*, Edward Elgar, at 186 (arguing that '[t]he theory of "market failures" explains the emergence in the last century of the "mixed" economy, a structure composed by private firms operating in the markets under regulations provided by public agencies, and public institutions devoted to allocative, stabilization and redistribution policies.'
6. Henry Smith's work, drawing upon an abundance of scholarship, provides a good theoretical foundation concerning costs related to IPRs such as opportunity costs and distribution costs. See, for example, Smith H. (2002), *Exclusion Versus Governance: Two Strategies for Delineating Property Rights*, 31 J. Legal Stud., S453 [hereafter *Exclusion Versus Governance*]. A useful summary discussion of the social costs associated with IPRs can be found in Blair R. and Cotter T. (2005), *Intellectual Property: Economic and Legal Dimensions of Rights and Remedies*, Cambridge University Press, chapter 2 generally. There are other costs that we will not consider. For example, there may be a range of unaccounted costs inherent within the information environment such as the *invasion of privacy* that stems from the propertisation of information by large Web 2.0 companies such as Facebook and Google.

PART I, CHAPTER 2 NOTES

1. A social net product analysis reflects to a large extent what has come to be known as a cost-benefit analysis. See, for example, Baumol W. and Oates W. (1975), *The Theory of Environmental Policy*, Cambridge University Press (capturing the essence of the environmental economic focus on market failures that began with Pigou in the 1920s but was consolidated during the 1960s and 1970s). See also, Yandle B. (2001), *Public Choice and the Environment*, in Shughart and Razzolini (eds), *The Elgar Companion to Public Choice*, at 593. For a discussion of neoclassical economics as it relates to copyright, see Netanel N. (1996), *Copyright and a Democratic Civil Society*, 106 Yale L. J. 283, at 314–321.
2. For an early cost-benefit analysis reference in relation to IPRs, see Ricketson, *New Wine into Old Bottles*, at 60. More contemporaneously, see Drahos P. (2010), *'IP World' – Made by TNC Inc* [hereafter *'IP World'*], in Krikorian and Kapczynski (eds), *A2K in the Age of IP*, at 198.
3. Smith A. (1776) [1965], *The Wealth of Nations*, Modern Library.
4. Stilwell F. (2012), *Political Economy: The Contest of Economic Ideas* (3rd edition), Oxford University Press; and Stilwell F. and Jordon K. (2007), *Who Gets What? Analysing Economic Inequality in Australia*, Cambridge University Press.

5. De Alessi, *Property Rights*, at 49 (acknowledging that the question of income distribution is ultimately an ethical issue).
6. Pigou A. (1952), *Economics of Welfare*, 4th Edition, Macmillan and Co, at 11, defined 'economic welfare' as 'that part of social welfare that can be brought directly or indirectly into relation with the measuring-rod of money'. In essence, welfare simply refers to wellbeing or happiness. See Nath S. (1973), *A Perspective of Welfare Economics*, Macmillan; Baumol W. and Wilson C. (eds) (2001), *Welfare Economics*, The International Library of Critical Writings in Economics 126, Volume II at 31 extracting Lange O. (1942), *The Foundations of Welfare Economics*, 10 Econometrica 215–228, at 215 (where it is stated that 'welfare economics is concerned with the conditions which determine the total economic welfare of a community'); Cowen T. (ed.) (2000), *Economic Welfare*, Critical Ideas in Economics (3), Edward Elgar, at 110; and Sen A. (1984), *The Living Standard*, 36 Oxford Economic Papers, Supplement, November, 74–90, at 74.
7. Baumol and Wilson (eds), *Welfare Economics*, Volume I at xvi–xvii. Interestingly, when Thorstein Veblen initially referred to the term 'neoclassical economics' in 1900 he was doing so in order to distinguish that school of thought from the welfare economic concerns of Alfred Marshall (among others) (Veblen, T. (1900), *The Preconceptions of Economic Science – III*, 14(2) The Quarterly Journal of Economics 240–269).
8. Adam Smith provided examples where self-interest can lead to profound damage, one example of which is within the teaching of religion where payment by results can lead to the self-interested promotion of 'superstition, folly and delusion' so as to 'excite the languid devotion of his audience'. See Smith A. (1776) [1811], *The Works of Adam Smith: The Nature and Causes of the Wealth of Nations*, Book V, Ch. I, Printed for T. Cadell and W. Davies et al., at 197. See also, Baumol and Wilson (eds), *Welfare Economics*, Volume I, at xxiii; see also xviii (concerning the moral philosophy of Adam Smith).
9. Ibid.
10. As a moral philosopher, Adam Smith was profoundly interested in matters of ethics (and religion). In this regard, the reference to the 'invisible hand' in the eighteenth century was likely to have been a reference to the 'hand of providence'. This had religious, or at the very least ethical, connotations. See Baumol and Wilson (eds), *Welfare Economics*, Volume I, at xix, citing Viner (1972) at 81–82. Drahos makes a similar point in relation to Locke in that the 'religious metaphysical scheme' that Locke was working within is often ignored. Accordingly, Locke's theories are often manipulated so as to provide a justificatory theory of IPRs (Drahos, *A Philosophy of IP*, at 48). Derclaye similarly argues that within the context of IPRs, ethical values were mostly discarded during the Enlightenment. See Derclaye, *Eudemonic Intellectual Property*, at 537. More generally on the notion of progress, see Lasch C. (1991), *The True and Only Heaven: Progress and its Critics*, Norton, at 59–60.
11. See, for example, Buchanan, *The Achievement and Limits of Public Choice in Diagnosing Government Failure and in Offering Bases for Constructive Reform*, at 33. Moreover, Smith demonstrated in other parts of *The Wealth of Nations* a deep distrust of the ethics of merchants and manufacturers in the context of resource allocation: '[p]eople of the same trade seldom meet together, even for merriment and diversion, but the conversation ends in conspiracy against the public, or in some contrivance to raise prices', Smith, *The Wealth of Nations*, at 129.
12. See, for example, Greenhalgh and Rogers, *Innovation, Intellectual Property, and Economic Growth*, at 33. For coverage of the 'non-objectionable' aspect of the monopolistic characteristics of IPRs, see Norman N. (1983), *Patent Law Revision: Some Economic Considerations*, 12 Australian Business Law Review, at 226. Of course, there is some contention about the monopolistic characteristics of IPRs in

light of the fact that IPR-related 'goods' are generally substitutable. For instance, see Ricketson, *New Wine into Old Bottles*, at 60 (contending that IPRs are 'not monopolies in the strict sense applied by economists').

13. McEachern W. (2012), *Economics: A Contemporary Introduction*, South-Western Cengage Learning, at 193.
14. Ibid.
15. The relationship between allocative efficiency and dynamic efficiency is not without controversy. For instance, Lemley counters the dominant position by arguing that IPRs can in fact decrease dynamic efficiency. See Lemley M. (2004), *Property, Intellectual Property, and Free Riding* (draft version – on file) at 37–39 (noting that innovation does not occur in a vacuum). Also, it is possible that some allocative efficiency gains might result from the creation of informational markets (e.g. licensing markets). Since these markets are built upon IPRs, it might be reasoned that discrete aspects of IPRs facilitate allocative efficiency. But the more prevalent aspect of IPRs is the monopoly characteristic, which theoretically exists to facilitate dynamic efficiency (not allocative efficiency). See also Frischmann B. (2012), *Infrastructure: The Social Value of Shared Resources*, Oxford University Press, at 163–164, where he alludes to the relationship between static efficiency and allocative efficiency.
16. Greenhalgh and Rogers, *Innovation, Intellectual Property, and Economic Growth*, at 3–4. The commonly used phrase 'the market place of ideas' exemplifies the contemporary acceptance of information commodification. See, for example, Schauer F. (1982), *Free Speech: A Philosophical Inquiry*, Cambridge University Press, at 19–20, cited in Birnhack M. (2003), *Copyright Law and Free Speech after Eldred v Ashcroft*, 76 S. Cal. L. Rev. 1275–1330; Birnhack, *More or Better?*, at 69; Rimmer, *Digital Copyright*, at 26 (alluding to the marketplace of ideas). Although note that the phrase 'marketplace of ideas' is properly attributed to Justice Holmes in *Abrams v United States*, 250 U.S. 616, 630 (1919).
17. Demsetz, *Toward a Theory of Property Rights*, at 348. Of course, 'the tension between wanting to encourage imitative conduct and wishing to prevent it leads in turn to a fundamental tension between markets and intellectual property' (Drahos, *A Philosophy of IP*, at 135, especially footnote 50).
18. Bork R. (1978), *The Antitrust Paradox: A Policy at War with Itself*, Simon and Schuster; Posner R. (2001), *Antitrust Law: An Economic Perspective* (2nd edition), University of Chicago Press; Lemley, *Property, Intellectual Property, and Free Riding*, at 21; and Drahos, *A Philosophy of IP*, at 5–6 (alluding to the intimacy between IPRs and markets).
19. Literature concerning the economic theories of Milton Friedman abounds. But the point here is that even Friedman admitted market failure (Friedman M. (1962), *Capitalism and Freedom*, University of Chicago Press). However, Friedman tended to rely upon 'government failure' as one method of diminishing market failure discourse. See, for example, Friedman M. and Schwartz A. (1963), *A Monetary History of the United States: 1867–1960*, Princeton University Press.
20. Salzberger E. (2006), *Economic Analysis of the Public Domain* in Guibault and Hugenholtz (eds), *The Future of the Public Domain*, at 31 (discussing market failures and IPRs).
21. Boyle, *Shamans, Software and Spleens*, at 35–42; Boyle, *A Politics of Intellectual Property*, at 96; Boyle, *The Public Domain*, at 40. Also, see Grossman S. and Stiglitz J. (1980), *On the Impossibility of Informationally Efficient Markets*, 70 American Economic Review 393–408. The efficiency costs usually relate to transaction costs, but there may be other unaccounted efficiency costs associated with propertisation of information. An important example is that of 'privacy costs'.

22. Some commentators have expanded the 'information paradox' to IPRs at large by referring to the 'paradox of intellectual property'. See, for example, Hugenholtz B. (2001), *Owning Science: Intellectual Property Rights as Impediments to Knowledge Sharing*, paper delivered at the second Communia Conference, Turin (29 June 2001) cited in Frosio G. (2012), *Communia and the European Public Domain Project: A Politics of the Public Domain* [hereafter *Communia and the European Public Domain Project*], in Dulong de Rosnay M. and Carlos de Martin J. (eds), *The Digital Public Domain: Foundations for an Open Culture*, OpenBook Publishers, at 18, footnote 59.
23. Mitchell H. (2005), *The Intellectual Commons*, Lexington Books at 159–160. Information can be considered a primary good in that it underpins the development of knowledge, culture and economic activity (see Drahos, *A Philosophy of IP*, at 171, 173 and Chapter 8 generally). Access to information is also critical in realising *justice* objectives. As Drahos (ibid) states at 175: 'Information is the primary good which citizens need in order to be able to make the abstract infrastructural principles of justice work in a concrete way in their daily lives.'
24. Grossman and Stiglitz, *On the Impossibility of Informationally Efficient Markets*, at 405; Arrow, *Economic Welfare*, at 618 (arguing that without IPRs too little information will be produced because producers of information will not be able to capture its true value); Fama E. and Laffer A. (1971), *Information and Capital Markets*, 44 J. Bus. 289, 295–297 (arguing that without property rights or some other way of protecting against public goods problems, too much information will be generated because some information will be produced solely to gain a temporary advantage in trading, thus redistributing wealth but not achieving greater allocative efficiency); and Hirshleifer J. (1971), *The Private and Social Value of Information and the Reward to Inventive Activity*, 61 Am. Econ. Rev. 561 at 570–572 (arguing that patent law may be either a necessary incentive for the production of inventions or an unnecessarily legal monopoly in information that overcompensates an inventor who has already had the opportunity to trade on the information implied by her discovery).
25. Boyle, *Shamans, Software and Spleens*, at 35–42; Boyle, *A Politics of Intellectual Property*, at 96; Boyle, *The Public Domain*, at 40; Grossman and Stiglitz (1980), *On the Impossibility of Informationally Efficient Markets*, at 393–408.
26. Grossman and Stiglitz (1980), *On the Impossibility of Informationally Efficient Markets*, at 405; Boyle, *A Politics of Intellectual Property*, at 96. Arrow indicates that the information paradox stems primarily from the uncertainty related to information. That is, it is uncertainty that leads to the commodification of information. See Arrow, *Economic Welfare*, at 614.
27. Boyle, *Shamans, Software and Spleens*, at 101. Informational asymmetry is an important source of competitive advantage within an imperfectly competitive market (e.g. Drahos, *A Philosophy of IP*, at 124). The reference to incentives within this passage relates to the public goods provisioning problem, which will be further discussed later in this chapter.
28. Grossman and Stiglitz, *On the Impossibility of Informationally Efficient Markets*. See also Boyle J. (2000), *Cruel, Mean, or Lavish? Economic Analysis, Price Discrimination and Digital Intellectual Property*, 53(6) Vanderbilt Law Review 2007, at 2013 [hereafter *Cruel, Mean, or Lavish?*].
29. Arrow, *Economic Welfare*, at 609.
30. Ibid, at 616–617 (where Arrow articulated this position by stating that 'in a free enterprise economy the profitability of invention requires a suboptimal allocation of resources'). However, Arrow also acknowledged that: 'Any information obtained … should, from a welfare point of view, be available free of charge … This ensures optimal utilization of the information, but of course provides no incentive for investment in research.' See ibid, at 616. Also, Greenhalgh and Rogers, *Innovation,*

Intellectual Property, and Economic Growth, at 19; and Boyle, *A Theory of Law and Information*, at 1452, especially footnote 94.

31. Arrow, *Economic Welfare*, at 616–617.
32. Hirshleifer J. (1971), *The Private and Social Value of Information and the Reward to Inventive Activity*, 61 Am. Econ. Rev. 561 at 572–573. See also, Boyle, *A Theory of Law and Information*, at 1452; and Fama and Laffer (1971), *Information and Capital Markets*, 44 J. Bus. 289.
33. One way of reframing IPR debates away from property and towards the monopoly characteristics of IPRs is to file complaints in competition tribunals. See Flynn S. (2010), *Using Competition to Promote Access to Knowledge*, in Krikorian and Kapczynski (eds), *A2K in the Age of IP*, at 465.
34. Arrow, *Economic Welfare*, at 618.
35. Merges R. (1994), *Of Property Rules, Coase, and Intellectual Property*, 94 Columbia Law Review 2655, at 2657–2658. Coase states this in Arrow, *Economic Welfare*, at 615. See also Hope, *Biobazaar*, at 71–72, referring to the work of Arrow. See also Drahos, *A Philosophy of IP*, at 180 (discussing the information paradox through a practical lens).
36. Merges, *Of Property Rules, Coase, and Intellectual Property*, at 2657–2658.
37. Ibid.
38. Salzberger, *Economic Analysis of the Public Domain*, at 28.
39. Koelman K. (2006), *The Public Domain Commodified: Technological Measures and Productive Information Use*, in Guibault and Hugenholtz (eds), *The Future of the Public Domain*, at 105–106; Chon, *Postmodern 'Progress'*, at 136 (implying that James Madison also grappled with the information paradox in his writings concerning IPRs) citing James Madison, 6 *The Writings of James Madison* 102 (Gaillard Hunt ed., 1906); and Bagdikian B. (1990), *The Media Monopoly* (3rd edition), Beacon Press, at 223. Note that James Madison stated that: 'A popular Government, without proper information, or the means of acquiring it, is but a Prologue to a Farce or a Tragedy; or, perhaps both. Knowledge will forever govern ignorance; And a people who mean to be their own Governors, must arm themselves with the power which knowledge gives.' See Letter from James Madison to W.T. Barry (4 Aug 1822) in *The Complete Madison* 337 (Saul K. Padover ed., 1953) cited in Boyle, *A Theory of Law and Information*, at 1437, footnote 52.
40. See, for example, Boyle, *Cruel, Mean, or Lavish?*, at 2032–2033. Arrow is more likely to refer to monopoly than property, but the point is that the 'veil of property' often subsumes the monopolistic characteristics of IPRs. Although Arrow indicates that patents were useful, he also argues that direct government investment in invention achieves better results. See, for example, Cheung S. (1986), *Property Rights and Invention*, 8 Research in Law & Economics 5.
41. See principle 6 of Table 1.1. This principle calls for the neutralization of the tragedy of ignoring the information semicommons as per Chapter 5.
42. Greenhalgh and Rogers, *Innovation, Intellectual Property, and Economic Growth*, at 3–4 (implicitly alluding to the tension between the public goods provisioning problem and positive externalities).
43. Litman J. (1990), *The Public Domain*, 39 Emory Law Journal 965, at 970; and Menell P. (1989), *An Analysis of the Scope of Copyright Protection for Application Programs*, 41 Stan. L. Rev. 1045, at 1059–1066 (discussing the application of the public goods problem in intellectual property).
44. Litman, *The Public Domain*, at 970.
45. Mitchell, *The Intellectual Commons*, at 40.
46. For a depiction of IPR maximalist tendencies generally see Ghosh S. (2004), *Deprivatizing Copyright*, 54 Case W. Res. L. Rev. 387, at 389; Litman J. (1989), *Copyright Legislation and Technological Change*, 68 Or. L. Rev. 275; and Lemley M.

(1994), *An Empirical Study of the Twenty-year Patent Term*, 22 AIPLA QJ 369. More specifically, for a description of the 1998 extension in the US see Rimmer, *Digital Copyright*, at 24–25; and Ricketson, *New Wine into Old Bottles*, at 64.

47. Ricketson, *New Wine into Old Bottles*, at 64.
48. By way of example, see *NBA v Sports Team Analysis & Tracking Sys Inc* 939 F. Supp. 1071 (S.D.N.Y. 1996), aff'd in part, vacated in part sub nom, *NBA v Motorola Inc* NO 96-7975, 1997 WL 34001 (2d. Cir. Jan 30, 1997) (where the National Basketball Association claims a property right in the scores of its games).
49. Heller M. and Eisenberg R. (1998), *Can Patents Deter Innovation? The Anticommons in Biomedical Research*, 280 Sci. 698, at 698–699 [hereafter *Can Patents Deter Innovation?*].
50. Drahos, *'IP World'*, at 201 (discussing the high costs associated with administering an IPR system, particularly with respect to IPR registration personnel required).
51. Faunce, *Global Public Goods*, at 523 (arguing that public goods are one of the most important conceptual battlegrounds for contemporary applied ethics); Greenhalgh and Rogers, *Innovation, Intellectual Property, and Economic Growth*, at 18 (discussing non-rivalry and non-excludability). Even though knowledge itself is intrinsically non-rival, within the commercial world the value of new knowledge can be rival (see ibid, at 19).
52. Lemley, *Property, Intellectual Property, and Free Riding*, at 30.
53. Arrow, *Economic Welfare*, at 614–616; Lemley, *Property, Intellectual Property, and Free Riding*, at 30.
54. Frischmann, *An Economic Theory of Infrastructure and Commons Management*, at 943–944; Lessig, *The Future of Ideas*, at 21; and Stiglitz J. (2008), *Economic Foundations of Intellectual Property Rights*, 57 Duke Law Journal 1693, at 1700.
55. Lemley, *Property, Intellectual Property, and Free Riding*, at 23–24. The depletion/congestion problem gives rise to a welfare economic distributional consideration in the sense that consumption by some agents may occur at the expense of other agents who do not obtain the opportunity to consume (e.g. Lessig, *The Future of Ideas*, at 21).
56. There are of course other relevant considerations in this respect such as distributional costs discussed in Chapter 3.
57. Not only are the axes of excludability and rivalry best perceived in spectrum terms, but also public goods as a whole should be observed in a similar light. For example, see Faunce, *Global Public Goods*, at 524 (contrasting 'basic public goods' such as roads or water infrastructure with 'higher order public goods' such as equity in the provision of medicines and health services, 'inherent public goods' such as clean air or accessibility to wilderness areas, and 'public policy public goods' such as public libraries). For an excellent diagram that includes 'exclusivity' on axis Y and 'market orientation' on axis X see Taubman A. (2010), *A Typology of Intellectual Property Management for Public Health Innovation and Access: Design Considerations for Policymakers*, 4 The Open AIDS Journal 4, at 10 [hereafter *A Typology of Intellectual Property Management for Public Health Innovation and Access*].
58. John Stuart Mill recognised the possibility of commodifying air as early as 1848 when he stated that 'if from any revolution in nature the atmosphere became too scanty for the consumption … air might acquire a very high marketable value'. See Mill J.S. (1848) [2004], *John Stuart Mill: Principles of Political Economy with Some of Their Applications to Social Philosophy*, Abridged, ed. Stephen Nathanson, Hackett Publishing Co., at 10. See also, Yandle, *Public Choice and the Environment*, at 590.
59. The commons analytical framework will be discussed at length in Part II. For further discussion of the parameters of exclusion, see Ostrom E. (1990), *Governing the Commons: The Evolution of Institutions for Collective Action*, Cambridge University

Press [hereafter *Governing the Commons*]. A key critique of Hardin's tragedy of the commons (discussed at length in Chapter 5) is that Hardin generally conflated open access and limited commons, treating all as open access. See Smith, *Exclusion Versus Governance*, 458.

60. Benkler, *The Wealth of Networks*, at 61, quoting Ostrom, *Governing the Commons*.
61. Ibid. See also, Benkler Y. (2003), *The Political Economy of the Commons*, IV(3) Upgrade 6, at 6.
62. Hughes J. (1988), *The Philosophy of Intellectual Property*, 77 Georgetown Law Journal 287, at 316. For a fuller explanation of 'Locke's commons' see Drahos, *A Philosophy of IP*, at Ch 3, especially 49 and 56.
63. Ibid.
64. Tully J. (1980), *A Discourse On Property*, Cambridge University Press, at 31. See also, Drahos, *A Philosophy of IP*, at 43 (discussing an inherent contradiction in Locke's perspective being that Locke did not address the issue of amassing non-perishable wealth in money or stock, but he did address the wastage of a bag of fruit that was not used). Also at 51 Drahos (ibid) argues that ideas can in fact spoil in the sense that their time span of useful application in many instances is limited.
65. Rose C. (2003), *Romans, Roads, and Romantic Creators: Traditions of Public Property in the Information Age*, 66 Law & Contemp. Probs. 89.
66. Hughes, *The Philosophy of Intellectual Property*, at 316. Also, Cunningham, *The Tragedy of (Ignoring) the Information Semicommons* (discussing non-exhaustability and non-rivalry characteristics of information).
67. Hughes, *The Philosophy of Intellectual Property*, at 314. A similar point is made in Liang, *The Man Who Mistook His Wife for a Book*, at 290 (arguing that 'we must always be generous with information and make gifts of our code, images, and ideas').
68. See, for example, Grotius H. (1625), *De Jure Belli Ac Pacis Libri Tres*, Kelsey F. (1964), Book II, Chapter 2, I cited in Drahos, *A Philosophy of IP*, at 3, footnote 9. Also, Yates J relies upon Grotiusian thinking in *Millar v Taylor* (1769) 98 ER 257 at 233.
69. Baumol and Wilson (eds), *Welfare Economics*, Volume III, extracting an excerpt from Pigou, *The Economics of Welfare*, at 184 (who in turn is citing Sidgwick H. (1887), *Principles of Political Economy*, Macmillan, at 406).
70. The lighthouse turns out to be of considerable interest to economists and others, both historically and contemporaneously. John Stuart Mill was one of the earlier thinkers to frame the lighthouse within the framework of public goods. See John Stuart Mill, *Principles of Political Economy*, in Robson J. (ed.) (1965), *The Collected Works of John Stuart Mill*, Vol III, at 968. More recently Coase indicated that a lighthouse was more closely aligned to club goods than public goods. See Coase R. (1974), *The Lighthouse in Economics*, 17(2) Journal of Law and Economics 357. However, much contemporary literature tends to affirm that the non-excludability aspect of the lighthouse generally accords with a public goods analysis. For example, see Van Zandt D. (1993), *The Lessons of the Lighthouse: 'Government' or 'Private' Provision of Goods*, 22(1) Journal of Legal Studies 47 (arguing that public involvement in the production and maintenance of lighthouses was much more substantial than Coase admits); and Bertrand E. (2006), *The Coasean Analysis of Lighthouse Financing: Myths and Realities*, 30 Cambridge Journal of Economics 389 (asserting that in reality the historical illustration conducted by Coase illustrates that the production system of lighthouses was mixed between public and private). For an even more contemporary example of lighthouse research, see Carnis L. (2011), *The Political Economy of Lighthouses* (unpublished – on file).

71. Coase, relying upon the words of Gilbert, hazards against authors relying on the lighthouse example to 'give artistic verisimilitude to an otherwise bald and unconvincing narrative'. See Coase, *The Lighthouse in Economics*, at 375, footnote 42 – citing Gilbert W., *The Mikado*, MacMillan & Co.
72. The public good characteristics of lighthouses have been well understood throughout history by philosophers such as J.S. Mill and economists such as A.C. Pigou (although more contemporaneously subject to considerable contestation from Chicago School property right advocates such as Coase). See, for example, John Stuart Mill, *Principles of Political Economy*, in Robson J. (ed.) (1965), *The Collected Works of John Stuart Mill*, Vol III at 968; Sidgwick, *Principles of Political Economy*, at 406; Arrow K. (1969), *The Organization of Economic Activity: Issues Pertinent to the Choice of Market Versus Nonmarket Allocation*, in US Cong. Jt. Econ. Committee, 91st Cong., 1st Session, The Analysis and Evaluation of Public Expenditures: the PPB System, vol. 1 at 47, 58 (arguing that 'it may be most efficient to offer the [lighthouse] service free'); however, cf Coase, *The Lighthouse in Economics* (arguing that the Trinity House structure of lighthouses in England demonstrates that in reality there were many lighthouses that were established through private production).
73. For similar questioning see Carnis L. (2011), *The Political Economy of Lighthouses*, at 6 (unpublished – on file).
74. Greenhalgh and Rogers, *Innovation, Intellectual Property, and Economic Growth*, at 24–26. The internalisation of positive externalities is an issue further advanced in Chapter 3.
75. Ibid, at 26 (summarising how this argument operates with respect to IPRs). According to this view, propertisation facilitates the functioning of the market.
76. Ibid.
77. Examples of social production as it relates to infrastructure stem from mutualism (e.g. the building of the 'Lion's Club road' in northern New South Wales, Australia) or subscription models that flow from community radio worldwide. For a nuanced perspective of how exclusivity and innovation interact see Taubman, *A Typology of Intellectual Property Management for Public Health Innovation and Access* (and the accompanying diagram).
78. Lemley, *Romantic Authorship and the Rhetoric of Property*, at 902. As Lemley states in footnote 158: 'Certainly, lighthouses are often privately owned. We could determine that a ship that benefits from the light provided by a lighthouse has infringed upon a property right of the lighthouse owner. We might even say that the lighthouse owner could protect its right with a property rule and obtain an injunction requiring the ship to run aground. But would anyone really argue that this was the *efficient* thing to do?'
79. Foldvary has indicated that current available technology solves, to a large extent, the problem of the public good. See Foldvary F. (2003), *The Lighthouse as a Private-Sector Collective Good* in Foldvary F. and Klein D. (eds), *The Half-Life of Policy Rationales: How New Technology Affects Old Policy Issues*, New York University Press, at 38–46.
80. Moreover, as Samuelson indicated: '[E]ven if the operators [of a lighthouse] were able – say, by radar reconnaissance – to claim a toll from every nearby user, that fact would not necessarily make it socially optimal for this service to be provided like a private good at a market-determined individual price. Why not? Because it costs society zero extra cost to let one extra ship use the service; hence any ships discouraged from those waters by the requirement to pay a positive price will represent a social economic loss – even if the price charged to all is no more than enough to pay the long-run expenses of the lighthouse. If the lighthouse is socially worth building and operating – and it need not be – a more advanced treatise can show how this social good is worth being made optimally available to all.' See

Samuelson P. (1964), *Economics: An Introductory Analysis* (6th edition), McGraw-Hill Book Co, at 151.

81. *Victoria Park Racing and Recreation Grounds Co Ltd v Taylor* (1937) 58 CLR 479.
82. Tarrant J. (2005), *What is Ownership?*, The University of Western Australia SJD Thesis, at 44 (unpublished – on file).
83. The administration costs is a theme further developed in Chapter 3 with respect to externalities.
84. See, for example, Drahos, *A Philosophy of IP*, at 15 (referring to China as an example of a society that achieved spectacular scientific and innovative outcomes without an IPR system).
85. Whether, as an empirical matter, this is the case has been the subject of debate. See, for example, Titmuss R. (1971), *The Gift Relationship: From Human Blood to Social Policy*, Allen and Unwin. Also, Arrow K. (1972), *Gifts and Exchanges*, 1 Phil. & Pub. Aff. 342. For helpful coverage of this debate, see Benkler Y. (2004), *Sharing Nicely: On Shareable Goods and the Emergence of Sharing as a Modality of Economic Production*, 114 Yale L.J. 273, at 321–324 [hereafter *Sharing Nicely*].
86. For insights on the interaction between technology and IPRs see generally Lessig, *Code 2.0*.
87. Landes W. and Posner R. (1989), *An Economic Analysis of Copyright Law*, 18(2) Journal of Legal Studies 325–363, at 326.
88. Boyle, *Cruel, Mean, or Lavish?*, at 2012.
89. Lessig, *Code 2.0*.
90. Rose, *The Comedy of the Commons*, at 711–712, 713.
91. Ibid, at 723. See also Scheiber H. (1984), *Public Rights and the Rule of Law in American Legal History*, 72 Cal. L. Rev. 217, at 221–227, 233–249.
92. Atteberry, *Information/Knowledge in the Global Society of Control*, at 329; Liang L, *Beyond Representation*, at 369–370.

PART I, CHAPTER 3 NOTES

1. Welfare economics has spawned a range of economic disciplines, the most important being ecological economics. While it would be possible to analyse IPRs from an ecological economic perspective, the underlying rationale of relying upon welfare economics is to expose the *hidden costs associated with the IPR system.*
2. Pigou, *The Economics of Welfare*.
3. Boyle, *Shamans, Software and Spleens*, at 35–36; Boyle, *A Politics of Intellectual Property*, at 97; Drahos, *A Philosophy of IP*, at 9 (where a similar point is made).
4. The privatisation of benefits and socialisation of costs perspective can be discussed using either a welfare economics lens, or a public choice theory lens. If the latter is adopted, Tullock has demonstrated that under any voting system that requires less than unanimous consent, the situation will manifest whereby the dominant strategy for any organised interest group will be to lobby for policies that provide large benefits to its members and spread the costs among everyone else. See Tullock G. (1959), *Problems of Majority Voting*, 67 Journal of Political Economy 571. Also, Van den Hauwe L. (2005), *Constitutional Economics II* in Backhaus (ed.), *The Elgar Companion to Law and Economics*, at 231.
5. The IPR system is leaky and therefore so too is the purity of this claim.
6. For example, since the 1950s life expectancy has increased by approximately 20 years. This is at least partly due to the spread of scientific and technical knowledge. See *World Report on Knowledge for Better Health: Strengthening Health*

Systems, World Health Organization (2004), available online: http://www.who.int/rpc/meetings/en/world_report_on_knowledge_for_better_health2.pdf (cited 12 April 2013).

7. Frischmann B. and Lemley M. (2007), *Spillovers*, 107 Columbia Law Review 257, at 267–268.
8. Demsetz, *Toward a Theory of Property Rights*, at 357.
9. Smith H. (2011), *Toward An Economic Theory of Property in Information*, in Ayotte K. and Smith H. (eds), *Research Handbook on the Economics of Property Law*, Edward Elgar, at 109.
10. Ibid.
11. Demsetz H. (1967), *Toward a Theory of Property Rights*, 57 Am. Econ. Rev. 347, at 350; Duffy J. (2005), *Intellectual Property Isolationism and the Average Cost Thesis*, 83 Tex. L. Rev. 1077, at 1080–1085 (discussing the requisite of balancing costs and benefits of property rights); Frischmann and Lemley, *Spillovers*, at 265.
12. Demsetz, *Toward a Theory of Property Rights*, at 348 ('every cost and benefit associated with social interdependencies is a potential externality'); Frischmann and Lemley, *Spillovers*, at 265.
13. Baumol W. (2002), *The Free Market Innovation Machine: Analysing the Growth Miracle of Capitalism*, Princeton University Press, at 5–6 [hereafter *The Free Market Innovation Machine*]; Frischmann and Lemley, *Spillovers*, at 266. Note that Demsetz has emphasised that his claims concerning the internalisation of externalities are normative, Demsetz H. (2008), *Frischmann's View of 'Toward a Theory of Property Rights'*, 4(1) Review of Law and Economics 347.
14. Frischmann and Lemley, *Spillovers*, at 267–268.
15. Harrison, *A Positive Externalities Approach to Copyright Law*, at 5–6. In discussing the need to align social and private costs Pigou asserted that 'no "invisible hand" can be relied on to produce a good arrangement of the whole from a combination of separate treatments of the parts. It is therefore necessary that an authority of wider reach should intervene to tackle the collective problems of beauty, of air and light, as those other collective problems of gas and water have been tackled', Pigou (1920), *The Economics of Welfare*, Macmillan, at 195 cited in Yandle, *Public Choice and the Environment*, at 593. Although Adam Smith alluded to the concept of externalities in *The Wealth of Nations*, it was A.C. Pigou's teacher, Alfred Marshall, who initially coined the 'externalities' term, albeit in a privately circulated publication. See Frischmann B. (2009), *Spillover Theory and Its Conceptual Boundaries*, 51 William and Mary Law Review 801, at 806. Also, Arrow K. (1970), *The Organization of Economic Activity: Issues Pertinent to the Choice of Market Versus Nonmarket Allocation* [hereafter *The Organization of Economic Activity*], in Havemand R. and Margolis J. (eds) (1970), *Public Expenditures and Policy Analysis*, Markham, at 59, 67 (defining externality as the absence of a functioning market).
16. Pigou, *The Economics of Welfare*, at 134; Coase R. (1960), *The Problem of Social Cost*, Vol. III The Journal of Law and Economics, October 1960, at 29. For an alternative description of externalities see Drahos, *A Philosophy of IP*, at 126.
17. Cornes R. and Sandler T. (1996), *The Theory of Externalities, Public Goods, and Club Goods* (2nd edition), Cambridge University Press, at 39–43; Meade J. (1973), *The Theory of Economic Externalities: The Control of Environmental Pollution and Similar Social Costs*, A. W. Sijthoff, at 15 [hereafter *The Theory of Economic Externalities*]; Arrow, *The Organisation of Economic Activity*, at 67; Frischmann B. (2006), *Evaluating the Demsetzian Trend in Copyright Law*, Paper 17 American Law & Economics Association Annual Meetings 2006, at 7.
18. Harrison, *A Positive Externalities Approach to Copyright Law*, at 10.
19. Ibid.

20. Arrow, *The Organization of Economic Activity*, at 67 (defining externality as the absence of a functioning market); Cornes and Sandler, *The Theory of Externalities, Public Goods, and Club Goods*, at 39–43; Meade, *The Theory of Economic Externalities*, at 67–68; Frischmann, *Spillover Theory and Its Conceptual Boundaries*, at 806; and Harrison, *A Positive Externalities Approach to Copyright Law*, at 10.
21. Ibid. It is true that a pharmaceutical company may consider 'positive externalities' that may flow to a competitor when considering corporate strategy. But as IPRs generally capture positive externalities, the relevant positive externality is most likely a property right.
22. See, for example, Greenhalgh and Rogers, *Innovation, Intellectual Property, and Economic Growth*, at 24–27.
23. Ibid.
24. Baumol and Wilson (eds), *Welfare Economics*, Volume I at xl–xli citing Sidgwick H. (1901), *The Principles of Political Economy*, 3rd Edition, London, and Nordhaus W. (1969), *Invention, Growth, and Welfare: A Theoretical Treatment of Technological Change*, MIT Press, at 39.
25. Alchian A. (1965), *Some Economics of Property Rights*, 30 II Politico 816; Lemley, *Property, Intellectual Property, and Free Riding*, at 23; Greenhalgh and Rogers, *Innovation, Intellectual Property, and Economic Growth*, at 24, 26; Lehmann M. (1989), *Property and Intellectual Property – Property Rights as Restrictions on Competition in Furtherance of Competition*, 20 International Review of Industrial Property and Copyright Law 33.
26. Gordon W. (2003), *Intellectual Property*, in Cane P. and Tushnet M. (eds) (2003), *The Oxford Handbook of Legal Studies* 617, at 622; Frischmann, *Spillover Theory and Its Conceptual Boundaries*, at 801.
27. Emphasis added. Harrison, *A Positive Externalities Approach to Copyright Law*, at 5–6 – in particular see references cited in footnote 13.
28. Baumol, *The Free Market Innovation Machine*, at 5–6; Frischmann and Lemley, *Spillovers*, at 266.
29. Note Cooter and Ulen summarise this idea: 'Granting exclusive property rights to the creator of an idea allows him or her to appropriate much of its social value'. See Cooter R. and Ulen T. (2000), *Law and Economics* (3rd edition), Addison-Wesley, at 128. See also Elkin-Koren N. and Netanel N. (2002), *The Commodification of Information*, Kluwer Law International, at 149.
30. Birnhack, *More or Better?*, at 75–76.
31. Kitch E. (1977), *The Nature and Function of the Patent System*, 20 J. L. & Econ. 265, at 276; and Kieff S. (2001), *Property Rights and Property Rules for Commercializing Inventions*, 85 Minn. L. Rev. 697, at 717.
32. Arrow, *The Organization of Economic Activity*, at 67 (defining externality as the absence of a functioning market); Harrison, *A Positive Externalities Approach to Copyright Law*, at 10; Frischmann, *Spillover Theory and Its Conceptual Boundaries*, at 806; Frischmann, *Evaluating the Demsetzian Trend in Copyright Law*; Cornes and Sandler, *The Theory of Externalities, Public Goods and Club Goods*, at 39–43; and Meade, *The Theory of Economic Externalities*, at 15.
33. Pearce D. and Sturmey S. (1966), *Private and Social Costs and Benefits: A Note on Terminology*, 76(301) The Economic Journal 152 (citing Pigou). If it makes more sense to the reader, the word 'benefit' can be substituted for 'product' so that Pigou's dictum reads 'social net benefit', but hereafter Pigou's traditional 'social net product' terminology is maintained.
34. The word 'informational' stems from Manuel Castells' discussion of the transition to the 'informational mode of development'. See Castells M. (2000), *The Rise of the Network Society* (2nd edition), Wiley-Blackwell, at 13–21, 30–31 and 225–226.

35. For an interesting application of the social net product analysis of IPRs as it relates to competition law, see Kaplow L. (1984), *The Patent-Antitrust Intersection: A Reappraisal*, 97 Harvard Law Review 9 (arguing that a cost benefit analysis should be used when determining whether competition law should apply to IPRs). For a more recent perspective, see Hovenkamp H., Janis M. and Lemley M. (2007), *IP and Antitrust: An Analysis of Antitrust Principles Applied to Intellectual Property Law*, Aspen Publishers, at 1–10.
36. Harrison, *A Positive Externalities Approach to Copyright Law*, at 17.
37. See principle 1 of Table 1.1. Also, Coase, *The Problem of Social Cost*. For further discussion of Coasian perspectives, see Lemley, *Property, Intellectual Property, and Free Riding*, at 10. Although Coase and Demsetz are often credited for the 'evolution of property rights' perspective, it is to a large extent based on Blackstonian ideas relating to property such that property is to prevent wasteful overuse of resources and encourage optimal investment. See Blackstone W. (1765), *Commentaries on the Laws of England*, Book II at 3–8. Also, Posner, *Economic Analysis of the Law*, at 30.
38. Frischmann, *Evaluating the Demsetzian Trend in Copyright Law*, at 15.
39. Demsetz, *Toward a Theory of Property Rights*, at 349.
40. Ibid, at 350–353.
41. The author is grateful to Professor James Grimmelmann who consolidated the author's Demsetzian understanding during a lunch at New York Law School in May 2012.
42. However, Demsetz did not necessarily refer to the equation in 'social net product' terms.
43. Harrison, *A Positive Externalities Approach to Copyright Law*, at 13–14.
44. Ibid, at 14.
45. Demsetz, *Toward a Theory of Property Rights*, at 349.
46. Ibid, at 348. See also Frischmann, *Spillover Theory and Its Conceptual Boundaries*, at 809; Drahos, *The Global Governance of Knowledge*, at 7 (arguing that 'the ideological appeal of property rights can sometimes obscure the cost when it comes to making decisions about whether or not to strengthen intellectual property rights'). Transaction costs are not just relevant to the question of property rights, but also have bearing on production decisions such that they will influence whether or not a firm engages with economic activity in-house or rather contracts out. See De Alessi, *Property Rights*, at 40.
47. Coase, *The Problem of Social Cost*, at 31. See also Hope, *Biobazaar*, at 39 (where she argues that transaction costs are higher the greater the number and complexity of negotiations needed to bring disparate rights together).
48. Coase, *The Problem of Social Cost*, at 31. In the IPR context, the main transaction costs relate to searching. See, for example, Hargreaves I. (2011), *Digital Opportunity: A Review of Intellectual Property and Growth*, Independent Report Commissioned by UK Government [hereafter *Digital Opportunity*], which discusses transaction costs with respect to IPRs at some length, positing at 13 that: 'In the patent world, a surfeit of property rights can mean that the transaction costs of acquiring permission to innovate or create new work is prohibitively high. Research shows that in certain technology fields this can cause a kind of gridlock with innovation delayed or even prevented' (footnote 16). Similar sentiments are expressed with regard to copyright at 13: 'In the copyright area transaction costs can create similar problems. Digital technologies have brought large reductions in the costs of copying … [etc]. This has the effect of making transaction costs around rights a much more significant element in the business equation and so, potentially, a likelier barrier to licensing and follow on innovation.' See also Merges, *Of Property Rules, Coase, and Intellectual Property*, at 2657–2660. Economists Graff,

Rausser and Small discuss the costs associated in the context of contracting for knowledge (cited in Hope, *Biobazaar*, at 41–51, especially footnote 36). See also, Drahos, *A Philosophy of IP*, at 125; Boyle, *Public Domain*, at 15 (discussing the seeking of permission as a transaction cost that ultimately fails to satisfy either the creator or the user); Boyle, *A Theory of Law and Information*, at 1453.

49. Hargreaves, *Digital Opportunity*, at 11, stating that 'the rewards to innovation can sometimes be boosted as effectively by cutting transaction costs as by strengthening rights'.
50. Hope, *Biobazaar*, at 64–66, especially footnotes 89 and 94. Also see the work of Drahos and Braithwaite where they argue that the high transaction costs related to IPRs may in fact be a deliberate strategy by IPR holders to keep potential competitors out of the market (Drahos and Braithwaite, *Information Feudalism*, Chs. 3 and 10). Although for a more optimistic perspective concerning the effectiveness of transaction costs on innovation see Merges R. (2001), *Institutions for Intellectual Property Transactions: The Case of Patent Pools*, in Dreyfuss R., Zimmerman D. and First H. (eds), *Expanding the Boundaries of Intellectual Property: Innovation Policy for the Knowledge Society*, Oxford University Press, 123–165, at 139. The high transaction costs inherent within IPRs is a critical issue because economic theory suggests that 'an important goal of a well-developed legal system is to promulgate rules that reduce the transaction costs facing privately contracting parties'. See Macey J. (1988), *Transaction Costs and the Normative Elements of the Public Choice Model: An Application to Constitutional Theory*, Yale Law School Faculty Scholarship Series, Paper 1734, at 472 [hereafter *Transaction Costs and the Normative Elements of the Public Choice Model*]. Also, Goetz C. and Scott R. (1985), *The Limits of Expanded Choice: An Analysis of the Interactions Between Express and Implied Contract Terms*, 73 California Law Review 261, at 266.
51. Calabresi G. and Melamed D. (1972), *Property Rules, Liability Rules, and Inalienability: One View of the Cathedral*, 85 Harvard Law Review 1089 [hereafter *Property Rules, Liability Rules, and Inalienability*].
52. Merges, *Of Property Rules, Coase, and Intellectual Property*, at 2664. Note that the initial construction of property/liability rules usually stems from Coase's well-documented farmer/rancher example, although Coase himself did not make the distinction. For further discussion, see Buchanan J. (1989), *The Coase Theorem and the Theory of the State*, in Buchanan (ed.), *Explorations into Constitutional Economics*, Texas A & M University Press, at 387–388.
53. Ibid.
54. Calabresi and Melamed, *Property Rules, Liability Rules, and Inalienability*, at 1106–1108.
55. Merges, *Of Property Rules, Coase, and Intellectual Property*, at 2655.
56. See principle 3 of Table 1.1 (supporting initiatives that foster the free-flow of information); and principle 4 (arguing for the application of 'positive community' to the information commons). Also, see Frischmann B. (2012), *Infrastructure: The Social Value of Shared Resources*, Oxford University Press.
57. Daily G. *et al* (2000), *Value of Nature and the Nature of Value*, 289 Science 395, at 395 (discussing the difficulties of valuing ecosystem assets and noting that '[o]ften, the importance of ecosystem services is widely appreciated only upon their loss'). See also Frischmann B. (2008), *Environmental Infrastructure*, 35 Ecology L Q 151, at 162; and Frischmann, *Spillover Theory and Its Conceptual Boundaries*, at 821, especially references cited in footnote 77.
58. Professor Tom Faunce discusses responses to this issue in 'planetary medicine' terms. See Faunce T. (2012), *Governing Planetary Nanomedicine: Environmental Sustainability and a UNESCO Universal Declaration on the Bioethics and Human*

Rights of Natural and Artificial Photosynthesis (Global Solar Fuels and Foods), in Weckert J. (2012), *NanoEthics*, Springer.

59. Stone, *Should Trees Have Standing?*, at 27 (footnote 82 omitted).
60. Explanations of ETSs abound elsewhere so will not be dealt with here. See, by way of one example, Ellerman D. (2007), *The European Union Emissions Trading Scheme: Origins, Allocation, and Early Results*, 1(1) Review of Environmental Economics and Policy 66.
61. Demsetz, *Frischmann's View of 'Toward a Theory of Property Rights'*, at 131; Frischmann, *Spillover Theory and Its Conceptual Boundaries*, at 814.
62. It is true, as will be discussed in Part II, that some externalities are deemed 'irrelevant'. But as we will see below, it is often the case that those externalities considered to be economically irrelevant have considerable impact upon the public. Environmental degradation is exemplary.
63. Carter A. (1999), *A Radical Green Political Theory*, Routledge, at 22–23.
64. See, for example, Dodgshon R. (1980), *The Origin of British Field Systems: An Interpretation*, Academic Press, at 53 (where it is argued that over time land law becomes more 'intense').
65. Demsetz, *Toward a Theory of Property Rights*, at 357.
66. Stone, *Should Trees Have Standing?*, at 27–28.
67. Daily G. *et al*, *The Value of Nature and the Nature of Value*, at 395 (arguing, in relation to the physical environment, that '[o]ften, the importance of ecosystem services is widely appreciated only upon their loss').
68. Drahos P. (2011), *Six Minutes to Midnight: Can Intellectual Property Save the World?* [hereafter *Six Minutes to Midnight*], in Bowrey K., Handler M. and Nicol D. (eds), *Emerging Challenges in Intellectual Property*, Oxford University Press, at 36–37.
69. Market failure can be thought of as the 'failure of a more or less idealised system of price-market institutions to sustain desirable activities or to estop undesirable activities'. See Bator F. (1958), *The Anatomy of Market Failure* LXXII Quarterly Journal of Economics 351–379, at 351.
70. Boldrin M. and Levine D. (2008), *Against Intellectual Monopoly*, Cambridge University Press. The monopolistic viewpoint is supported by the fact that the history of patent is founded upon the Statute of Monopolies, 1623, 21 Jac. 1, c. 3, or more specifically an exception to monopolies inherent within the said legislation, although note that Merges makes the point that IPRs are structured so as to stifle the power of political elites granting monopolies. See Merges R., *The Proper Scope of the Copyright and Patent Power*, at 47. Also, Hovenkamp H. et al. (2004), *IP and Antitrust* § 4.2 (arguing that IPRs usually do not confer market power for antitrust purposes).
71. The fact that IPRs can be categorised in a number of different ways was discussed in the introductory chapter. IPRs differ from real property in the sense that it is difficult to regulate on an *ex ante* basis since it is not possible to place a fence around intellectual property as can be done in the context of real property, although it should be noted that TPMs and other such examples discussed by Lawrence Lessig seek to make IPRs more compatible with the 'property' rule than the 'liability' rule (Lessig, *Code 2.0*). For these reasons and more, despite the fact that IPRs are conceived as a type of 'property', in some respects the actual practice relating to IPRs equates more to the liability rule than the property rule. For further discussion here, Drahos, *The Global Governance of Knowledge*, at 32 (arguing that contract is a 'more neutral starting point than property when we come to think about the nature of patents'). Also note the arguments of Yates J in *Millar v Taylor* (1769) 4 Burr. 2303, 98 ER 201 discussed in Drahos, *A Philosophy of IP*, at 27 where Drahos relays the arguments of Yates – as property is founded upon occupancy,

abstract objects cannot be occupied and therefore property rights in information are inconsistent with the general rules of property. For an example of scholarship treating IPRs as subsidy, see Bell T. (2003), *Author's Welfare: Copyright as a Statutory Mechanism for Redistributing Rights*, 69 Brooklyn L. Rev. 229.

72. Although there are strong arguments in favour of the view that 'an IPR establishes a state-sponsored monopoly' this position is contested. See, for example, Landes and Posner, *An Economic Analysis of Copyright Law*, at 361 (arguing that copyright does not actually confer monopoly power); Kitch E. (2000), *Elementary and Persistent Errors in the Economic Analysis of Intellectual Property*, 53 Vand. L. Rev. 1727, at 1734. Harrison associates copyright with subsidization thus: 'Copyright is ultimately about public goods, and in the context of many other public goods a general *subsidization* is necessary for the good or service to be produced at all'. See Harrison, *A Positive Externalities Approach to Copyright Law*, at 57. Also, Greenhalgh and Rogers, *Innovation, Intellectual Property, and Economic Growth*, at 53 (arguing that subsidies can complement IPRs within innovation policy).
73. The fact that IPR owners can escape pure market forces as they possess a monopoly right is subject to the qualification that informational goods may be substitutable. See, for example, Linde F. and Wolfgang G. (2011), *Information Markets: A Strategic Guideline for the i-commerce*, Hubert & Co., at 433; cf Ramello G. (2005), *Intellectual Property and the Market of Ideas*, in Backhaus (ed.), *The Elgar Companion to Law and Economics*, at 136.
74. Environmental Protection Authority (USA) (2010), *Guidelines for Preparing Economic Analysis*, Chapter 8, at 8–9 (yosemite.epa.gov/ee/epa/eerm.nsf/vwAN/EE…/EE-0568-08.pdf, *cited 22/10/2012). See also* Vaver, *Intellectual Property Today*, at 127 (asking: 'should society be concerned about the unequal distribution of intellectual property in the same way as it is concerned (or not concerned) about the unequal distribution of traditional property?').
75. Bansak C. and Starr M. (2011), *Distributional Costs of the Housing-Price Bust*, American University, No. 2011-04 (March), Working Paper Series, found at: http://www.american.edu/cas/economics/pdf/upload/2011-4.pdf (cited 7/2/2013).
76. Stilwell, *Political Economy*; Stilwell and Jordon, *Who Gets What?*; Rawls J. (1972), *A Theory of Justice*, Oxford University Press, at 4 (arguing that allocation and distribution are mediated through the definition of property rights); Drahos, *A Philosophy of IP*, at 178; and Vaver, *Intellectual Property Today*, at 128 (arguing that IPRs are 'part of our social and economic policy').
77. For a good overview of the social costs associated with monopoly, see Fisher F. (1985), *The Social Costs of Monopoly and Regulation: Posner Reconsidered*, 93 J. Pol. Econ. 410; and Tullock G. (1967), *The Welfare Costs of Tariffs, Monopolies and Theft*, 5 W. Econ. J. 224.
78. Cohen J. (1996), *A Right to Read Anonymously: A Closer Look at 'Copyright Management' in Cyberspace*, 28 Conn. L. Rev. 981; and Fisher W. (1988), *Reconstructing the Fair Use Doctrine*, 101 Harv. L. Rev. 1661, at 1239 and 1251 (discussing reliance on fair use to create transformative works).
79. Cohen, *A Right to Read Anonymously*; and Fisher, *Reconstructing the Fair Use Doctrine*, at 1239 and 1251 (discussing reliance on fair use to create transformative works).
80. The exclusivity issue is further discussed in Part II.
81. The distributional costs associated with price have been recognised for many centuries. For example, the Statute of Monopolies in the 1600s, which allowed for the granting of letters patent for inventions, stated that the patent 'be not contrary to the Laws nor mischievous to the State, by raising the prices of Commodities at home'. See An Act Concerning Monopolies, 21 Jac. I, c. 3 (1623) (Eng). See also, Shashikant S. (2010), *The Doha Declaration on Trips and Public Health: An*

Impetus for Access to Medicines, in Krikorian and Kapczynski (eds), *A2K in the Age of IP*, at 141 (arguing that 'price is literally a matter of life or death when a deadly disease is treatable').

82. Bork R, *The Antitrust Paradox*; Posner, *Antitrust Law*; Lemley, *Property, Intellectual Property, and Free Riding*, at 21.
83. Gordon W. (1997–1998), *Intellectual Property as Price Discrimination: Implications for Contract*, 73 Chi-Kent L. Rev. 1367.
84. Boldrin and Levine, *Against Intellectual Monopoly Rights.*
85. Gordon, *Intellectual Property as Price Discrimination.*
86. As Meurer argues: 'Economists have long understood that an optimal copyright policy balances the dynamic efficiency concerns relating to the incentives to supply works with the allocative efficiency concerns relating to access'. See Meurer M. (2001), *Copyright Law and Price Discrimination*, Boston University School of Law, Working Paper No 01-06, 4 June 2001, at 33.
87. Footnotes omitted. Gordon, *Intellectual Property as Price Discrimination*, at 1371. For further examples of price discrimination in copyright markets, see Meurer, *Copyright Law and Price Discrimination*, at 2–3 (especially footnotes 5 and 11).
88. Meurer, *Copyright Law and Price Discrimination*, at 2–3 (see footnote 5 in relation to copyright and price discrimination). Meurer indicates at 3 that price discrimination will only be feasible where '(1) the seller has market power, (2) the seller can somehow link prices to individual customers' preferences; and (3) customers cannot arbitrage away price differentials'. See also Tirole J. (1988), *The Theory of Industrial Organisation*, MIT Press, at 133–152.
89. Lessig, *Code 2.0.*
90. Monopoly is not a necessary precondition of price discrimination. See, for example, Meurer, *Copyright Law and Price Discrimination*, at 20–21; and De Alessi, *Property Rights*, at 47–48. However, in contrast, see also, Drahos with Braithwaite, *Information Feudalism*, at 34 (arguing that when patents are easy to obtain then the prices rise) and at 36–37 (discussing the role of parallel imports as a method of price discrimination); Gordon, *Intellectual Property as Price Discrimination*, at 1369 (arguing that 'intellectual property law operates by fostering price discrimination').
91. Price discrimination leads not only to costs, but also benefits. See, for example, Meurer, *Copyright Law and Price Discrimination*, at 1. Meurer argues that monopoly is not necessarily a prerequisite for price discrimination (at 4). Yet there is undoubtedly a correlation between market power and price discrimination, and since monopoly rights can assist in forging market power we can therefore claim that there is a meaningful correlation between monopoly rights and price discrimination practices, particularly in the context of the information environment.
92. Maskus K. (2000), *Parallel Imports*, Blackwell Publishers, at 1275.
93. Boyle, *Cruel, Mean, or Lavish?*, at 2021–2027.
94. Ibid. Interestingly many IPR minimalists actually espouse the benefits of price discrimination. For example, see Fisher W. (1998), *Property and Contract on the Internet*, 73 Chi-Kent L. Rev. 1203, at 1234–1240 (discussing the positive effects of price discrimination on the Internet) and at 1251–1252 (suggesting that although price discrimination creates high rents that allow an expansion of the fair use doctrine it also simultaneously maintains current levels of reward); Gordon W. (1992), *Asymmetric Market Failure and Prisoner's Dilemma in Intellectual Property*, 17 U. Dayton L. Rev. 853 (arguing that price discrimination can solve efficiency problems in discrete circumstances); and Netanel N. (1998), *Asserting Copyright's Democratic Principles in the Global Arena*, 51 Vand. L. Rev. 217, at 224, 322–329 (discussing exhaustion by sale and international price discrimination

and arguing that geographic price discrimination might open markets in developing countries that would otherwise be ignored by publishers, etc).

95. Market segmentation is a key aspect of price discrimination. Meurer, *Copyright Law and Price Discrimination*, at 23 (arguing that 'A price discriminator wants to disaggregate market demand and, to the extent possible, deal with each buyer as an individual').
96. The difficulty of defining price discrimination is one of the reasons why it can be challenging to differentiate between price discrimination and price differentiation. For a discussion of this issue, see Meurer, *Copyright Law and Price Discrimination*, at 2, including content in footnote 3. Even within the literature price discrimination and price differentiation are often bundled together without nuance. For example, see ibid, at 14 (discussing different qualities of software but yet referring to price discrimination within this context).
97. Boyle, *Cruel, Mean, or Lavish?*, at 2007, introductory quote, citing Dupuit J. (1962), *On Tolls and Transport Charges*, International Economic Papers No. 11, Elizabeth Henderson (trans), at 23.
98. Demsetz H. (1970), *The Private Production of Public Goods*, 13 J. L. & Econ. 293 (arguing that price discrimination may increase profit and allocative efficiency); Liebowitz S. (1986), *Copyright Law, Photocopying, and Price Discrimination*, in Palmer J. and Ozerbe R. (eds.), *Research in Law and Economics: The Economics of Patents and Copyrights*, JAI Press, at 181; Gordon, *Intellectual Property as Price Discrimination*, at 1369 (arguing that 'all intellectual property law operates by fostering price discrimination'); Meurer; Flynn, *Using Competition to Promote Access to Knowledge*, at 458.
99. Boyle, *Cruel, Mean, or Lavish?*, at 2032–2033. For a practical example relating to pharmaceutical drugs in India during the 1960s see Drahos with Braithwaite, *Information Feudalism*, at 66. Meurer argues that one of the reasons why IPR scholars have generally ignored price discrimination is the 'mistaken belief that discrimination has mostly positive effects on social welfare'. See Meurer, *Copyright Law and Price Discrimination*, at 1.
100. Pareto optimal results exist where a change in the allocation of resources leads to at least one individual being better off without making any other person worse off. When no such improvements can be made the situation is said to be Pareto optimal. Bator expounds this situation as follows: '[a] community is on its Paretian frontier if it is impossible to make anyone better off (in terms of his own ordinal preference function) without making someone else worse off' (Bator F. (1958), *The Anatomy of Market Failure*, LXXII Quarterly Journal of Economics 351–379, at 351). See also, Baumol and Wilson (eds), *Welfare Economics*, at 335–363. Pareto optimality does not necessarily equate to allocative efficiency since it is entirely possible for the information environment to be Pareto optimum but yet allocatively inefficient.
101. Meurer, *Copyright Law and Price Discrimination*, at 2, 6–8. Meurer notes that, contrary to expectations, IPR minimalists have generally had a relatively positive view on price discrimination (especially at 7 and 28). See also *ProCD Inc v Zeidenberg*, 86 F 3d 1447, 1449–50 (7th Cir. 1996), at 1449 where Judge Easterbrook indicated that price discrimination increases the surplus created by a transaction, which results in consumer welfare being either unaffected or improved.
102. In this context Boyle reinforces the well-known economic fact that: '*either* perfect competition or monopoly with perfect price discrimination will produce Pareto optimal results'. See Boyle, *Cruel, Mean, or Lavish?*, at 2026. Also, see Bork, *The Antitrust Paradox*; Posner, *Antitrust Law*; Lemley, *Property, Intellectual Property, and Free Riding*, at 21.

103. Maskus, *Parallel Imports*, at 1269–1283, 1275; Bork, *The Antitrust Paradox*; Posner, *Antitrust Law*; and Lemley, *Property, Intellectual Property, and Free Riding*, at 21.
104. Boyle, *Cruel, Mean, or Lavish?*, at 2025–2026.
105. Consumer surplus is the difference between the maximum price that consumers are willing to pay for a good or service and the market price that they actually pay for that good or service. See ibid, at 2025–2026.
106. See Netanel N. (1996), *Copyright and Democratic Civil Society*, 106 Yale L. J. 283, at 293, particularly footnote 32; Ryan, *Cyberspace as Public Space*, at 654; and Greenhalgh and Rogers, *Innovation, Intellectual Property, and Economic Growth*, at 12–13.
107. Distributional costs provide one reason as to why competition/anti-trust law commonly seeks to preserve consumer surplus by advancing competition over monopoly. See Lemley, *Property, Intellectual Property, and Free Riding*, at 21.
108. Cowen, *Economic Welfare*, at 96.
109. Cooter R. and Rappoport P. (1984), *Were the Ordinalists Wrong About Welfare Economics?*, XXII(2) Journal of Economic Literature 507–530, at 517. See also Flynn, *Using Competition to Promote Access to Knowledge*, at 458–461.
110. The correlation between distribution and the proper functioning of the market is largely lost in economic theories such as the Coase theorem in that 'income effects' and 'transaction costs' are generally ignored. See Coase, *The Problem of Social Cost*.
111. For a more technical discussion of the distributional effects of IPRs, see Flynn, *Using Competition to Promote Access to Knowledge*, at 457–462 ('The lesson is this: the more unequal the distribution of income is in a country, the more people will be excluded from the market ... when a monopoly practices profit-maximising pricing strategies for an essential good') (at 462). See also Boyle, *Shamans, Software and Spleens*, at 125. See also, Chander and Sunder, *The Romance of the Public Domain*, at 1353.
112. Boyle, *Shamans, Software and Spleens*, at 125 (footnotes 122 and 123 omitted). Note here the relationship between distributional costs and the appropriation of Traditional Knowledge.
113. Maskus, *Parallel Imports*, at 1278; Drahos with Braithwaite, *Information Feudalism*, at 36–37 (discussing the role of parallel imports as a method of price discrimination); Malueg D. and Schwartz M. (1994), *Parallel Imports, Demand Dispersion, and International Price Discrimination*, 37 Int'l. Econ. 167, at 191 (arguing that international price discrimination increases total surplus but harms US consumers).
114. See generally Sell, *Private Power, Public Law*; and Drahos with Braithwaite, *Information Feudalism*.
115. BigPharma purportedly spends more money on advertising and marketing than they do on research. See, for example, Stiglitz, *Economic Foundations of Intellectual Property Rights*, at 1713; Marc-Andre G. and Lexchin J. (2008), *The Cost of Pushing Pills: A New Estimate of Pharmaceutical Promotion Expenditures in the United States*, 5 PLoS Med. 29, at 29; Hope, *Biobazaar*, at 288 (arguing that providing public money to support open source biotechnology would be beneficial because more money than at present would be geared towards technology development as distinct from profits and marketing costs). See also, Pisano G. (2006), *Can Science Be a Business? Lessons from Biotech*, 84(1) Harvard Business Review 114.
116. Pisano, *Can Science Be a Business?*. See also, Hope, *Biobazaar*, at 98 ('less than 5 percent of worldwide expenditure for pharmaceutical research and development goes to finding treatments for diseases in developing countries'); and Shashikant, *The Doha Declaration on Trips and Public Health*, at 141 onwards.

117. Hope, *Biobazaar*, at 97 (outlining the nature of disease in Lesser Developed Countries).
118. Ibid, at 100–102 (relaying that 'about 800 million people in the world today are suffering from malnutrition, many of them farmers who cannot grow or sell enough food to make ends meet').
119. Harrison J. (2004), *Rationalizing the Allocative/Distributive Distinction in Copyright*, 32 Hofstra L. Rev. 853; Harrison, *A Positive Externalities Approach to Copyright Law*, at 7.
120. Liebowitz S. (2010), *Is Efficient Copyright a Reasonable Goal?*, 79 George Washington L. Rev. 1692, at 1693; and Litman J. (2004), *Sharing and Stealing*, 27 Hastings Communication and Entertainment L. J., at 31–32.
121. Tushnet R. (2009), *Economics of Desire: Fair Use and Marketplace Assumptions*, 51 Wm & Mary L. Rev. 513, at 515; Benkler, *The Wealth of Networks*, at 35; and Frischmann, *Spillover Theory and Its Conceptual Boundaries*, at 811 (stating that 'Although distributional considerations might warrant policies that aim to limit or promote [wealth] transfers, efficiency considerations do not').
122. Frischmann, *Evaluating the Demsetzian Trend in Copyright Law*, at 21; Drahos with Braithwaite, *Information Feudalism*, at 80; Kapczynski, *Access to Knowledge*, at 24.
123. Drahos and Braithwaite, *Information Feudalism*, at 167. See also Hope, *Biobazaar*, at 310; Brown M. (2003), *Who Owns Native Culture?*, Harvard University Press, at 104 (arguing that 'the for-profit nature of drug development … privileges the medical needs of the affluent over those of the poor').
124. Boyle, *The Public Domain*, at 2. See also, Taubman, *A Typology of Intellectual Property Management for Public Health Innovation and Access*, at 4–5.
125. Cohen J. (2006), *Copyright, Commodification and Culture*, in Guibault and Hugenholtz (eds), *The Future of the Public Domain*, at 157–158; Dinwoodie G. and Dreyfuss R. (2006), *Patenting Science: Protecting the Domain of Accessible Knowledge*, in Guibault and Hugenholtz (eds), *The Future of the Public Domain*, at 191 [hereafter *Patenting Science*]. For a sound discussion of the tensions related to 'cultural appropriation', see Coombe R. (1993), *Cultural and Intellectual Properties: Occupying the Colonial Imagination*, 16 Political and Legal Anthropology Review 8.
126. While acknowledging the 'dynamic efficiency' arguments associated with IPRs, this book stresses the nexus between allocative efficiency and the internalisation of positive externalities based on the premise that the IPR maximalist position emphasises the property characteristics of IPRs rather than the monopoly characteristics of IPRs.

PART II NOTES

1. As will be observed below, semicommons theory proffers a more nuanced perspective.
2. Boyle, *The Second Enclosure Movement*, at 52.
3. Litman, *The Public Domain*.
4. Van Houweling M. (2007), *Cultural Environmentalism and the Constructed Commons*, 70 Law & Contemp. Probs. 23, at 23.
5. Atteberry, *Information/Knowledge in the Global Society of Control*, at 329. See also Liang, *Beyond Representation*, at 369–370.

PART II, CHAPTER 4 NOTES

1. Heverly R. (2003), *The Information Semicommons*, 18 Berkeley Technology Law Journal 1127.
2. See principle 3 of Table 1.1.
3. Many challenge the idea that the propertisation of information should be accepted from the outset. For example, the first general principle of *The Public Domain Manifesto* is that 'the Public Domain is the rule, copyright protection is the exception'. See Frosio, *Communia and the European Public Domain Project*, at 25.
4. Davey and Zdouc refer to the three main WTO Agreements of GATT, GATS and TRIPS as the 'Bermuda Triangle'. See Davey W. and Zdouc W. (2003), *The Triangle of TRIPS, GATT and GATS*, in Cottier T. and Mavroidis P. (eds), *Intellectual Property: Trade, Competition, and Sustainable Development*, The University of Michigan Press, at 53.
5. Mitchell, *The Intellectual Commons*, at 112; Drahos, *A Philosophy of IP*, at 42 (discussing the tension between the ideas of Grotius and the ideas of Sir Robert Filmer, and inquiring 'How could natural law, which proclaimed the existence of a commons, lead to a state of private ownership?'). Also, Tully, *A Discourse on Property*, at 54 (discussing the fact that Locke constructed an argument within natural law that demonstrated that equality and the commons could coexist with individual appropriation and property rights).
6. Mitchell, *The Intellectual Commons*, at 112. Interestingly, Purdy argues that property itself was historically a useful way to mediate between public and private concerns since property seeks to reconcile 'individual freedom and social order'. See Purdy, *The Meaning of Property*, at 9.
7. Heidegger M. (1927) [1962], *Being and Time*, Blackwell Publishing. Of course, Heidegger was intimately involved with the Third Reich in Germany, espousing many of the ideas of Hitler. See Evans R. (2003), *The Coming of the Third Reich*, Allen Lane, at 419–422. With respect to Sartre, see Sartre J. (1949) [2008], *The Aftermath of War (Situations III)*, (trans. C. Turner), Seagull Books.
8. Interestingly, the view that private and public are complements is also the argument put forward by Ostrom, *Governing the Commons*. To some extent, the tension between the IPR maximalists and the IPR minimalists is a tension that corresponds with the private/public divide.
9. Arendt H. (1958), *The Human Condition*, University of Chicago Press, at 52–53.
10. Ibid.
11. As has been implied above, the risk of over-propertising information is that information can become siphoned off from the information commons, diminishing the quantity and quality of the 'in-between' that facilitates relations. For a discussion concerning the characteristics of quantity and quality of the 'in-between' as it relates to the public domain, see Birnhack, *More or Better?*. There has long existed a concern of the relationship between IPRs and information dissemination. For a historical judicial perspective see Yates J in *Millar v Taylor* 98 ER, at 229–250 cited in Drahos, *A Philosophy of IP*, at 23, footnote 56.
12. Aside from natural law theorists such as Pufendorf, the positive/negative distinction has also been relied upon by philosophers such as Isaiah Berlin with respect to freedom. See Berlin I. (1958), *Two Concepts of Liberty*, in Berlin I. (1969), *Four Essays on Liberty*, Oxford University Press.
13. Carr C. (ed.) (1994), *The Political Writings of Samuel Pufendorf*, Book IV: Chapter 4 – The Origins of Dominion (trans. Michael Seidler), Oxford University Press, at 185.
14. Locke, *Two Treatises of Government*, II, section 34.
15. Drahos, *A Philosophy of IP*.

16. Chander and Sunder, *The Romance of the Public Domain*, at 1356, especially footnote 133. The Chander and Sunder perspective also accords with the 'positive community' and 'negative community' descriptions discussed in Drahos, *A Philosophy of IP*.
17. Purdy, *The Meaning of Property*, at 41, stating that: 'In Locke's account, however, the proviso was annulled with the introduction of money, which, as a token of value, enabled owners to "store" great wealth without its spoiling. Money marked the juncture between a world where most goods are held in common until someone takes them for personal use and a world parceled out in rights of property' (footnote 73 omitted).
18. Rose, *The Comedy of the Commons*; Ostrom, *Governing the Commons*.
19. See Ostrom, *Governing the Commons*.
20. Ibid.
21. Drahos, *A Philosophy of IP*, at 57 citing Pufendorf.
22. Ibid.
23. Ibid, at 26.
24. Ibid, at 58. One of the key critiques of Hardin's tragedy of the commons (discussed below) is that Hardin generally conflated open access and limited commons. See Smith, *Exclusion Versus Governance*, at 458.
25. Drahos, *A Philosophy of IP*, at 58.
26. Ibid, at 25.
27. Ibid, at 46. The concept of usufruct is enshrined in the law in Canada and some parts of Europe, defined thus: 'The right of enjoying a thing, the property of which is vested in another, and to draw from the same all the profit, utility and advantage which it may produce, provided it be without altering the substance of the thing'. See La. Civ. Code Ann. Art. 533 cited in Gibson R. (1962), *Protection of the Widow: A Common Law View of Community Property*, 15 U. Fla. L. Rev. 143, at 143, footnote 4.
28. Drahos, *A Philosophy of IP*, at 57.
29. In this respect, Drahos (ibid) states at 26 that '[the negative] conception of community provides greater scope for individuals to acquire property through their labour, because the individual is trying to acquire something which, although open to all to acquire, does not belong to any one individual'. See, especially ibid, at 26, footnote 66.
30. Ibid.
31. Locke, *Two Treatises of Government – The Second Treatise*, at 217–219 [para. 37].
32. Drahos, *A Philosophy of IP*, at 64; and Tuck R. (1979), *Natural Rights Theories*, Cambridge University Press, at 62.
33. Drahos, *A Philosophy of IP*, at 64.
34. Ibid, at 66–67.
35. Ibid, at 65.
36. Ibid, at 67.
37. Ibid, at 66. Strategic behaviour can also be perceived through the lens of transaction costs. See Farina, *Constitutional Economics I*, at 187 (discussing 'The Hayek View').
38. Along with the public domain and the intellectual commons, the phrase 'information commons' will also be used, but this is further discussed below by way of synthesising the intellectual commons and the public domain.
39. Rahmatian A. (2011), *Copyright and Creativity: The Making of Property Rights in Creative Works*, Edward Elgar, at 113. Rahmatian acknowledges some nuances between the intellectual commons and the public domain. For instance, at 113 he argues that the intellectual commons includes works in which copyright subsists. Also, Rahmatian distinguishes his work from that of Deazley (discussed below) by

stating that the work of the former is 'abstract and conceptual' in contrast to the latter's work which considers 'issues of practical accessibility of work' – see footnote 75, at 113.

40. Bannerman S. (2009), *The Ins and Outs of the Public Domain: A Review Article*, 2(1) Global Media Journal – Canadian Edition 167–173, at 168 [hereafter *The Ins and Outs of the Public Domain*]; Benkler, *The Wealth of Networks.*
41. Ibid. The term *access* in this context may refer to technology usability or Internet connectivity. See Borgman C. (2000), *From Gutenberg to the Global Information Infrastructure: Access to Information in the Networked World*, MIT Press, at 5–57 [hereafter *From Gutenberg to the Global Information Infrastructure*]. Note, for example, that the Chander and Sunder definition of the *public domain* is principally based on *the commons* conception: 'resources for which legal rights to access and use for free (or for nominal sums) are held broadly'. See Chander and Sunder, *The Romance of the Public Domain*, at 1338.
42. Bannerman, *The Ins and Outs of the Public Domain*, at 168; Benkler, *The Wealth of Networks*. The term *access* in this context may refer to *technology usability* or *Internet connectivity*. See Borgman, *From Gutenberg to the Global Information Infrastructure*, at 5–57.
43. *The Australian Oxford Pocket Dictionary*, Oxford University Press, 1976. For further discussion concerning the commons see Lessig (2002), *The Future of Ideas*, Vintage, at 19–20; Rose C. (1994), *The Comedy of the Commons*, in *Property and Persuasion: Essays on the History, Theory, and Rhetoric of Ownership*, Westview Press, 105, 106 (noting that US legal doctrine has strongly suggested that some kinds of properties should not be held exclusively in private hands but instead should be open to the public or at least subject to public right of use). See also Pasquale F. (2005–2006), *Toward an Ecology of Intellectual Property: Lessons from Environmental Economics for Valuing Copyright's Commons*, 8 Yale J. L. & Tech. 79.
44. Lessig, *The Future of Ideas*, at 19–20.
45. Reichman J. and Lewis T. (2005), *Using Liability Rules to Stimulate Local Innovation in Developing Countries: Application to Traditional Knowledge*, in Maskus K. and Reichman J. (eds), *International Public Goods and Transfer of Technology Under a Globalized Intellectual Property Regime*, Cambridge University Press. For an interesting discussion of the 'liability rule' and its application to the contemporary commons, see Boyle, *The Second Enclosure Movement*, at 68, especially footnote 145. Also, note the perspective of Calabresi and Melamed discussed in Part I. See Calabresi and Melamed (1972), *Property Rules, Liability Rules, and Inalienability*.
46. See Lessig L. (2002), *The Architecture of Innovation*, 51 Duke L. J. 1783, at 1788.
47. Benkler, *The Political Economy of the Commons*, at 6.
48. Benkler, *The Wealth of Networks*, at 61–62.
49. Drahos, *A Philosophy of IP*, at 56; and Gadsden G. (1988), *The Law of Commons*, Sweet & Maxwell.
50. Drahos, *A Philosophy of IP*, at 56.
51. Ibid.
52. Ibid.
53. Emphasis added. Ibid, at 56. The historical fact that there was not always a right of access to 'the commons' by commoners and/or members of the public, reinforces an earlier claim that the commons is a culturally contingent concept, as emphasised by Carol Rose and Elinor Ostrom respectively. See Rose, *The Comedy of the Commons*; Ostrom, *Governing the Commons*. Also, Bonyhady T. (1987), *The Law of the Countryside: The Rights of the Public*, Professional Books, at 131 [hereafter *The Law of the Countryside*].

54. Benkler, *The Political Economy of the Commons*, at 6; Drahos with Braithwaite, *Information Feudalism*, at 210–211.
55. Boyle, *The Second Enclosure Movement*, at 62–63.
56. Drahos, *A Philosophy of IP*, at 55.
57. Ibid, at 54.
58. Bonyhady, *The Law of the Countryside*, at 131.
59. Cohen, *Copyright, Commodification and Culture*, at 127–129.
60. Guibault L. (2006), *Wrapping Information in Contract: How Does it Affect the Public Domain?* [hereafter *Wrapping Information in Contract*], in Guibault and Hugenholtz (eds), *The Future of the Public Domain*, at 89. See also Boyle, *The Second Enclosure Movement*, at 58; and Litman, *The Public Domain*, at 975.
61. Non-copyrightable and non-patentable subject matter was referred to as 'public property', 'common property' or '*public juris*' throughout the nineteenth century. See Lee E. (2003), *The Public's Domain: The Evolution of Legal Restraints on the Government's Power to Control Public Access Through Secrecy or Intellectual Property*, 55 Hastings L. J. 91–209, at 102; Ochoa T. (2002), *Origins and Meanings of the Public Domain*, 28 U. Dayton L. Rev. 215–266, at 258–259; and Guibault and Hugenholtz (eds) (2006), *The Future of the Public Domain*, at 125. The term 'public domain' is deployed 10 times in the case of *Singer Manufacturing Co v June Manufacturing Co* 163 US 169, 203 (1896). After this case the US courts began using the term more often, although they continued to use older terminology as well (see Cohen, *Copyright, Commodification and Culture*, at 126). The term 'public domain' became widespread in the US after the enactment of the Copyright Act (1909) as section 7 of that Act adopted the 'public domain' phrase.
62. *Singer Mfg. Co v June Mfg. Co.*, 163 US 169 (1896). See also, Hunter D. (2004–2005), *Culture War*, 83 Tex. L. Rev. 1105, at 1110.
63. *Singer Mfg. Co v June Mfg. Co.*, 163 US 169 (1896).
64. Boyle embraces both the narrow and broad definition of public domain when he defines it as 'material that is not covered by intellectual property rights' as well as 'reserved spaces of freedom inside intellectual property'. See Boyle, *Public Domain*, at 39. For a discussion of different definitions of the public domain generally, see Samuelson P. (2006), *Enriching Discourse on Public Domains*, 55 Duke L. J. 783; and Greenleaf B. and Bond C. (2013), *'Public Rights' in Copyright: What Makes Up Australia's Public Domain?*, 23 AIPJ 111 [hereafter *'Public Rights' in Copyright*].
65. Greenleaf and Bond, *'Public Rights' in Copyright*, at 112.
66. Ibid. Cohen argues that the terms 'public property', 'common property' or 'public juris' were the terms often deployed to describe material for which copyright or patent protection had expired along with material that was ineligible for protection from a definition perspective. See Cohen, *Copyright, Commodification and Culture*, at 130.
67. Frosio, *Communia and the European Public Domain Project*, at 5; and Samuelson P. (2003), *Mapping the Digital Public Domain*, 66 L. & Contemp. Probs. 147–171, at 148–151 (describing fair use, for example, as a 'contiguous territory' to the public domain).
68. Samuelson P. (2006), *Challenges in Mapping the Public Domain*, in Guibault and Hugenholtz (eds), *The Future of the Public Domain*, at 13.
69. Greenleaf B. and Bond C. (2013), *'Public Rights' in Copyright: what makes up Australia's public domain?*, 23 AIPJ 111 at 112.
70. Greenleaf and Bond, *'Public Rights' in Copyright*, at 117; Gordon, *Fair Use as a Market Failure*; and Salzberger, *Economic Analysis of the Public Domain*, at 27. For an interesting and relevant discussion of the interaction between compulsory licensing and 'green technology', see McManis C. (1998), *The Interface Between International Intellectual Property and Environmental Protection: Biodiversity and*

Biotechnology, 76 Washington University Law Quarterly 255 [hereafter *The Interface Between International Intellectual Property and Environmental Protection*]; and Derclaye E. (2008), *Intellectual Property Rights and Global Warming*, 12 Marquette Intellectual Property Law Review 263, at 282.

71. Benkler Y. (1999), *Free as the Air to Common Use: First Amendment Constraints on Enclosure of the Public Domain*, 74 NYU Law Rev. 354–445, at 358 [hereafter *Free as the Air to Common Use*]; Chander and Sunder (2004), *The Romance of the Public Domain*, 92 California Law Review, 1331–1373, at 1338; and Salzberger, *Economic Analysis of the Public Domain*, at 27.
72. A more technical definition of the public domain encompasses works in which copyright has expired due to the expiry of the copyright term. It might also include works that do not ever attract copyright protection, and those works over which the author has renounced all claims of copyright. See Greenleaf and Bond, *'Public Rights' in Copyright*, at 115, 122. The public domain is discussed more extensively below.
73. Bannerman, *The Ins and Outs of the Public Domain*, at 168.
74. Salzberger, *Economic Analysis of the Public Domain*, at 27; Birnhack, *More or Better?*, at 60.
75. Frosio, *Communia and the European Public Domain Project*, at 5; and Samuelson, *Mapping the Digital Public Domain*, at 148–151 (describing fair use, for example, as a 'contiguous territory' to the public domain).
76. Drahos, *A Philosophy of IP*, at 54–55; Deazley R. (2006), *Rethinking Copyright: History, Theory and Language*, Edward Elgar, at 109 [hereafter *Rethinking Copyright*] – see also figure 4.2 at 109 indicating that the intellectual commons is larger than the public domain.
77. Drahos, *A Philosophy of IP*, at 54–55.
78. Strictly speaking an unpublished work is copyrighted indefinitely. Hence, the interaction between an unpublished work and the public domain is somewhat more complex than presented. For a useful US case example on this issue, see *Harper & Row, Pubs. v Nation Enterprises*, 471 U.S. 539 (1985).
79. Drahos, *A Philosophy of IP*, at 55–56.
80. Bannerman, *The Ins and Outs of the Public Domain*, at 168.
81. Some scholars have argued that the commodification of computer software is an example of commodifying a contemporary language. See, for example, Bonaccorsi A. and Rossi C. (2003), *Why Open Source Software Can Succeed*, 32(7) Research Policy 1243, at 1248 (arguing that software is a 'common language'). Another example of the propertisation impulse is the deCODE genetics project, which seeks to achieve commercial control of the entire genome of Iceland (discussed in Mitchell, *The Intellectual Commons*, at 100).
82. Creative Commons website (www.creativecommons.org). See also Elkin-Koren N. (2006), *Exploring Creative Commons: A Skeptical View of a Worthy Pursuit*, in Guibault and Hugenholtz (eds), *The Future of the Public Domain*, at 330; and Loren L. (2007), *Building A Reliable Semicommons of Creative Works: Enforcement of Creative Commons Licenses and Limited Abandonment of Copyright*, 14 Geo. Mason. L. Rev. 271, at 274–76, 283–88 (arguing that CC licensed works are semicommons rather than commons and describing FLOSS and CC as social movements).
83. Drahos, *A Philosophy of IP*, at 55.
84. Deazley, *Rethinking Copyright*, at 110.
85. Drahos, *A Philosophy of IP*, at 49.
86. Although the information commons term is adopted, it is acknowledged that there may be instances where it is necessary to rely upon more precise terminology (e.g. the 'narrow public domain' or the 'broad intellectual commons').

PART II, CHAPTER 5 NOTES

1. See generally Hardin G. (1968), *Tragedy of the Commons*, 162 Science 1243.
2. Lessig, *The Future of Ideas*, at 22.
3. Hardin, *The Tragedy of the Commons*, at 1244. See also Lessig, *The Future of Ideas*, at 22. While the tragedy of the commons is often used in stylised form to advance arguments about the commons or otherwise, if Hardin's example is engaged with on a deeper level, it would seem, as Fennell suggests, that Hardin's commons factual is really an example of a semicommons in action because there is a commons grazing field interacting with privately owned cows. See Fennell L. (2009), *Commons, Anticommons, Semicommons*, Public Law and Legal Theory Working Paper Series, February 2009, at 19. Also, the negative commons, as discussed in Chapter 4, is inherent within Hardin's depiction of the tragedy.
4. Saunders T. (trans.) (1995), *Aristotle, Book II*, Clarendon Press, quoted in Ostrom, *Governing the Commons*, at 2.
5. Thornton H. (2005), *State of Nature or Eden? Thomas Hobbes and his Contemporaries on the Natural Condition of Human Beings*, University of Rochester Press. See also Ostrom, *Governing the Commons*, at 2–3.
6. Lloyd W. (1977), *On the Checks to Population*, in Hardin G. and Baden J. (eds), *Managing the Commons*, Freeman.
7. Clark C. (1976), *Mathematical Bioeconomics*, Wiley; Clark C. (1980), *Restricted Access to Common-Property Fishery Resources: A Game-Theoretic Analysis*, in Liu P. (ed.) (1990), *Dynamic Optimization and Mathematical Economics*, Plenum Press; and Dasgupta P. and Heal G. (1979), *Economic Theory and Exhaustible Resources*, Cambridge University Press.
8. Ostrom uses a variety of other examples including Sahelian famine: Picardi A. and Seifert W. (1977), *A Tragedy of the Commons in the Sahel*, 43 Ekistics 297–304; firewood crisis: Norman C. (1984), *No Panacea for the Firewood Crisis*, 226 Science 676; Thomson J. (1977), *Ecological Deterioration: Local-Level Rule Making and Enforcement Problems in Niger*, in Glantz M. (ed.), *Desertification: Environmental Degradation in and around Arid Lands*, Westview Press, at 57–79; acid rain: Wilson R. (1985), *Constraints on Social Dilemmas: An Institutional Approach*, 2 Annals of Operations Research 183–200; Mormon Church: Bullock K. and Baden J. (1977), *Communes and the Logic of the Commons* in Hardin and Baden (eds), *Managing the Commons*, at 182–199; US Congress overspend: Shepsle K. and Weingast B. (1984), *Legislative Politics and Budget Outcomes*, in Mills G. and Palmer J. (eds), *Federal Budget Policy in the 1980s*, Urban Institute Press, at 343–367; urban crime: Neher P. (1978), *The Pure Theory of the Mugger*, 68 American Economic Review 437–445; public sector/private sector relationships: Snidal D. (1985), *Coordination Versus Prisoner's Dilemma: Implications for International Cooperation and Regimes*, 79 American Political Science Review 923–947; Cyprus conflict: Lumsden M. (1973), *The Cyprus Conflict as a Prisoner's Dilemma*, 17 Journal of Conflict Resolution 7–32; all of which are quoted in Ostrom, *Governing the Commons*, at 3.
9. See case studies in part 2 of Bromley D. (ed.) (1992), *Making the Commons Work: Theory, Practice and Policy*, ICS Press [hereafter *Making the Commons Work*]. Also, Ostrom, *Governing the Commons*, Ch 3 generally; Ellickson R. (1991), *Order Without Law: How Neighbors Settle Disputes*, Harvard University Press [hereafter *Order Without Law*]; and Fennell, *Commons, Anticommons, Semicommons*, at 2.
10. Nonini D. (ed.) (2007), *The Global Idea of 'the Commons'*, Berghahn Books, at 1–2; Bannerman, *The Ins and Outs of the Public Domain*, at 170.
11. Ostrom, *Governing the Commons*, at 21.

12. Ibid. For an excellent overview of scholarship that discusses circumstances under which common property regimes are more efficient than individual property regimes, see Hess and Ostrom, *Ideas, Artifacts and Facilities*, at 118–121 (suggesting that scholars sometimes conflate resource classification with property right issues).
13. Ostrom, *Governing the Commons*, at 21. This description of strategic behaviour exemplifies the public choice theory scenario, which will be discussed in future research.
14. Benkler, *The Political Economy of Commons.*
15. Smith R. (1981), *Resolving the Tragedy of the Commons by Creating Private Property Rights in Wildlife*, 1 CATO Journal 439–468. See also Welch W. (1983), *The Political Feasibility of Full Ownership Property Rights: The Cases of Pollution and Fisheries*, 16 Policy Sciences 165–180 (at 171: 'the establishment of full property rights is necessary to avoid the inefficiency of overgrazing'). Along with allocative efficiency, the tragedy of the commons issue is often married to negative externalities. See Smith, *Exclusion Versus Governance* (arguing at 457: 'The Demsetzian account of the rise of property rights fits in well with the traditional story of the "tragedy of the commons"').
16. Rose, *The Comedy of the Commons*, at 712. Some have argued that the global financial crisis of 2007–2009 will lead to the taming of the privatisation tendencies that have gained currency since the 1980s. For a colloquial and distinctly Australian exposition of this claim, see Rudd K. (2009), *The Global Financial Crisis*, The Monthly (February), at 20–29. Yet there has been little evidence over the last several years of this 'taming process'.
17. Demsetz, *Toward a Theory of Property Rights*; Comaroff J. and Comaroff J. (eds) (2001), *Millennial Capitalism and the Culture of Neoliberalism*, Duke University Press. See also, Smith, *Exclusion Versus Governance*, at 457.
18. Of course, whether the creation of new markets leads to new externalities will depend partly upon how the property rights and corresponding markets are structured.
19. Drahos, *Six Minutes to Midnight*, at 33–34.
20. Carter, *A Radical Green Political Theory*, at 34.
21. Ibid.
22. Fennell, *Commons, Anticommons, Semicommons*, at 5. Beyond alluding to the semicommons quality of the tragedy of the commons, Fennell also highlights the issue of scale. Thinking about the role of scale inherent within the semicommons theory brings to the fore the question of what the appropriate mix is between private property and commons in relation to a given set of activities. As Fennell notes, this question gives rise not just to a consideration of a 'given set of activities', but also to the issue of timing – 'temporal semicommons'. That is, it may be that at a given time a specific piece of land should be held as private property, but at other times it should be held in common. See ibid, at 19. Fennell also makes the point that the arrangement described in the quote found in the body of the book is similar to a semicommons.
23. Heller M. (1998), *The Tragedy of the Anticommons: Property in the Transition from Marx to Markets*, 11 Harvard Law Review 621, at 624 [hereafter *The Tragedy of the Anticommons*]. See also, Heller M. (2008), *The Gridlock Economy: How Too Much Ownership Wrecks Markets, Stops Innovation, and Costs Lives*, Basic Books [hereafter *The Gridlock Economy*].
24. Frank Michelman is generally credited for introducing the anticommons concept. See Michelman F. (1982), *Ethics, Economics and the Law of Property*, 24 Nomos 3, at 6. See also, Ellickson R. (1993), *Property in Land*, 102 Yale Law Journal 1315, at 1322.
25. Heller, *The Tragedy of the Anticommons*, at 624.

26. Heller (2000), *Three Faces of Private Property*, 79 Or. L. Rev. 417, at 423–424; Heller, *The Tragedy of the Anticommons*, at 624–626.
27. Michelman, *Ethics, Economics and the Law of Property*, at 6. See also Hunter D. (2003), *Cyberspace as Place and the Tragedy of the Digital Anticommons*, 91 California L. Rev. 439, at 509–511.
28. Heller, *The Tragedy of the Anticommons*, at 627–660. See also Hunter, *Cyberspace as Place and the Tragedy of the Digital Anticommons*, at 509–511. More recently, Heller has suggested a number of methods by which the anticommons can be overcome, one example being patent pools. See Heller, *The Gridlock Economy*, at 73 (simultaneously arguing that while 'patent pools may be a good solution to gridlock in some circumstances', patent pools 'are [also] fraught with peril.').
29. Aoki K. (1998), *Neo-colonialism, Anticommons Property and Biopiracy in the (Not-So-Brave) New World Order of International Intellectual Property Protection*, 6 Indiana Journal of Global Legal Studies 11, at 29–30.
30. Hunter, *Cyberspace as Place and the Tragedy of the Digital Anticommons*, at 509–511.
31. Michelman, *Ethics, Economics and the Law of Property*, at 5–6; and Hunter, *Cyberspace as Place and the Tragedy of the Digital Anticommons*, at 509–511.
32. Heller, *Three Faces of Private Property*, at 424–425; and Hunter, *Cyberspace as Place and the Tragedy of the Digital Anticommons*, at 509–511.
33. Heller, *Tragedy of the Anticommons*, at 623–624, 628–633.
34. Ibid, at 659.
35. Hunter, *Cyberspace as Place and the Tragedy of the Digital Anticommons*, at 512.
36. Heller, *Three Faces of Private Property*, at 424; and Heller and Eisenberg, *Can Patents Deter Innovation?*, at 700–701.
37. Fennell, *Commons, Anticommons, Semicommons*, at 10.
38. Hope, *Biobazaar*, at 137; and Heller and Eisenberg, *Can Patents Deter Innovation?*.
39. Bookchin M. (1990), *Philosophy of Social Ecology: Essays in Dialectical Naturalism*, Black Rose Books, at 39, relaying Denis Diderot in *Jacques le Fataliste*.
40. Heller, *Tragedy of the Anticommons*, at 625–626; Heller, *Three Faces of Private Property*, at 424 ('Once an anticommons emerges, collecting rights into usable private property may prove to be brutal and slow').
41. Fennell, *Commons, Anticommons, Semicommons*, at 11.
42. Ibid.
43. See principle 6 of Table 1.1.
44. Lessig, *The Future of Ideas*; Perelman M. (2002), *Steal This Idea: Intellectual Property Rights and the Corporate Confiscation of Creativity*, Palgrave [hereafter *Steal This Idea*]; Rose, *Authors and Owners*; Heverly, *The Information Semicommons*, at 1130–1141; and Kapczynski, *Access to Knowledge*, at 31 (arguing that 'If so-called "real property" rights worked like copyrights, for example, the home you built would be turned over to the public some fifty to seventy years after your death').
45. Beckerman-Rodau A. (1994), *Are Ideas Within the Traditional Definition of Property?: A Jurisprudential Analysis*, 47 Ark. L. Rev. 603 (concluding that common law idea protection, trade secret law, and patent law are all property-based regimes predicated on the recognition of property rights in ideas).
46. Benkler Y. (2000), *From Consumers to Users: Shifting the Deeper Structures of Regulation Toward Sustainable Commons and User Access*, 52 Fed. Comm. L. J. 561 [hereafter *From Consumers to Users*].
47. The paradoxes inherent within the information environment facilitate the tension between the IPR maximalists and the IPR minimalists. In particular, the indeterminacy of IPRs with respect to information production adds fuel to the fire. As stated by Fritz Machlup in the famous study of the patent system in the US in the 1950s: 'If

national patent laws did not exist, it would be difficult to make a conclusive case for introducing them; but the fact that they do exist shifts the burden of proof and it is equally difficult to make a really conclusive case for abolishing them'. See Senate Subcomm. On Patents, Trademarks, and Copyrights, Senate Comm. On the Judiciary, 85th Cong., An Economic Review of the Patent System 55 (Comm. Print 1958), prepared by Fritz Machlup. See also, Penrose E. (1951), *The Economics of the International Patent System*, Johns Hopkins Press, at 40.

48. Heverly, *The Information Semicommons*, at 1143.
49. Contemporary initiatives such as FLOSS and CC provide the rationale to move the debate away from the historically based 'private use versus common use' dichotomy.
50. Hardin, *The Tragedy of the Commons*, at 1248; Heverly, *The Information Semicommons*, at 1144; Turner M. (1986), *English Open Fields and Enclosures: Retardation or Productivity Improvements*, 46 J. Econ. Hist. 669, at 688. *Cf* Allen R. (1982), *The Efficiency and Distributional Consequences of Eighteenth Century Enclosures*, 92 Econ. J. 937, at esp. 950–951; and Allen R. (1992), *Enclosure and the Yeoman*, Oxford University Press.
51. Grimmelmann J. (2010), *The Internet Is a Semicommons*, 78 Fordham L. Rev. 2799–2842, at 2801; Taubman, *A Typology of Intellectual Property Management for Public Health Innovation and Access*, at 11 (arguing, in the context of health provision and IPRs, that 'a bare dichotomy between public and private forms of management is likely to be insufficient to describe actual patterns of behaviour, or to guide future practical choices'); and Weinstock N. (ed.) (2009), *The Development Agenda: Global Intellectual Property and Developing Countries*, Oxford University Press, at x (arguing that '[t]he debate over IP and development has often been infused with ideological fervor. It has pitted a faith in the efficacy of markets against a belief in government as guarantor of social welfare').
52. Smith H. (2000), *Semicommon Property Rights and Scattering in the Open Fields*, XXIX The Journal of Legal Studies 131, at 131–132; Rose, *The Comedy of the Commons*, in *Property and Persuasion*; and Ostrom, *Governing the Commons*.
53. Smith, *Semicommon Property Rights and Scattering in the Open Fields*, at 131–132.
54. Although Henry Smith (ibid) refers to the semicommons as the dynamic interaction between private and common property uses, it is occasionally referred to as 'open access and restricted use' as per, for example, Levmore S. (2002), *Two Stories About the Evolution of Property Rights*, 31 Journal of Legal Studies 421–451.
55. Smith, *Semicommon Property Rights and Scattering in the Open Fields*, at 132.
56. Heverly, *The Information Semicommons*, at 1164.
57. Ibid.
58. The transaction costs that flowed from scattering in medieval times were represented by the time and effort for the shepherd and the private user to enact an agreement relating to the strategic grazing or enclosure of the flock. For further discussion see Heverly, *The Information Semicommons*, at 1164.
59. Smith H. (2000), *Semicommon Property Rights and Scattering in the Open Fields*, XXIX The Journal of Legal Studies 131 at 139. Some commentators have emphasised other reasons why the semicommons described by Smith evolved. For instance, diversification of risk has been another reason posited. See Fennell L. (2009), *Commons, Anticommons, Semicommons*, Public Law and Legal Theory Working Paper Series, February 2009 at 16.
60. There were no economies of scale for farming during this time period, but there were economies of scale to herding. See Smith, *Semicommon Property Rights and Scattering in the Open Fields*, at 134. Also, Heverly, *The Information Semicommons*, at 1165.
61. Smith, *Semicommon Property Rights and Scattering in the Open Fields*, at 134.

62. In relation to the costs of prohibiting strategic behaviour within the information semicommons, strategic behaviour can be exemplified from the perspective of information users or producers. Unauthorised copying and distribution of information goods exemplifies the strategic behaviour of users, whereas the strategic behaviour of producers is exemplified by anti-competitive behaviour known as tying whereby information producers require information users to purchase additional information (or non-information goods) so as to be granted legal access to desired information. For further discussion see Heverly, *The Information Semicommons*, at 1172–1173, 1175–1176.
63. Ibid, at 1169–1170.
64. Ibid, at 1171–1172. Of course, if one imagines a situation where IPRs were permanent and hermetic, then nothing would ever flow back into the information commons and it would therefore become less and less useful as a starting point. See Drahos, *A Philosophy of IP*, at 63 (deploying the evolution of scientific theories as an exemplar). In this context, Sir Hugh Laddie has said that 'the whole of human development is derivative'. See Deazley, *Rethinking Copyright*, at 113, citing at footnote 43, Laddie H. (1996), *Copyright: Over-strength, Over-regulated, Over-rated?*, European Intellectual Property Review 253, at 259. Also, Lemley M. (1997), *The Economics of Improvement in Intellectual Property Law*, 75 Texas L. Rev. 989. A similar point can be made in relation to patent law. See, for example, Merges R. and Nelson R. (1990), *On the Complex Economics of Patent Scope*, 90 Colum. L. Rev. 839; Scotchmer S. (1991), *Standing on the Shoulders of Giants: Cumulative Research and the Patent Law*, 5 J. Econ. Persp. 29.
65. See, for example, *Harper & Row Publishers Inc v Nation Enters.*, 471 U.S. 539, 547 (1985). Heverly discusses strategic behaviour from both the information producer perspective and the information user perspective. For example, '[a]nother method used to dissuade strategic behaviour from a legal perspective is the use of enforcement actions by information owners (i.e. where information owners bring lawsuits for the unauthorised use of information, common users may reduce their strategic behaviour)'. See Heverly, *The Information Semicommons*, at 1179. The focus in this book is on the strategic behaviour of information producers.
66. Heverly, *The Information Semicommons*, at 1179–1180, particularly footnote 140 where Heverly is discussing Smith, *Semicommon Property Rights and Scattering in the Open Fields*. See also Townsend Gard E. (2012), *Traditional Contours in Intellectual Property: Before and After Golan and Prometheus*, on file at 9, especially footnotes 26 and 27 [hereafter *Traditional Contours in Intellectual Property*] – referring to the case of *Eldred v Ashcroft* 537 U.S. 186 (2003) 239 F. 3d 372 at 219–220.
67. Heverly, *The Information Semicommons*, at 1164–1165.
68. Lessig, *Code 2.0*.
69. Heverly, *The Information Semicommons*, at 1164–1165; *cf* Lessig, *Code 2.0*.
70. Another method of framing the tension between producers and users is through the lens of freedom and control. For a useful account in this regard see Hui Kyong Chun W. (2006), *Control and Freedom: Power and Paranoia in the Age of Fibre Optics*, MIT Press.
71. Bentham J. (1791) [1995], *Panopticon*, in Bozovic M. (ed.), *The Panopticon Writings*, Verso, at 29–95.
72. Lessig (2006), *Code 2.0*, Basic Books.
73. See, for example, *Universal City Studios, Inc v Corley*, 273 F. 3d 429 (2d Cir. 2001) (holding that the DMCA anti-circumvention provisions prohibit circumvention of the DVD CSS). Also, Weatherall K. (2011), *IP in a Changing Information Environment*, in Bowrey K., Handler M. and Nicol D. (eds), *Emerging Challenges in Intellectual Property*, Oxford University Press, at 20 (discussing the modus operandi

of DVD CSS encoding); Drahos with Braithwaite, *Information Feudalism*, at 184. TPM protection ultimately had its origins in Article 11 of the WIPO Copyright Treaty, and was subsequently endorsed in Europe through the Information Society Directive A.6 and other countries such as the UK with the passing of the Copyright and Related Rights Regulations 2003 (SI 2003/2498). See also, Deazley, *Rethinking Copyright*, at 124–125.

74. Heverly, *The Information Semicommons*, at 1164. So-called 'illegal downloading' can be analysed through a variety of lenses. For example, although 'illegal downloading' is often equated to piracy and free-riding, economic analysis suggests that many people who download would not purchase the information in any case because of a lack of ability or willingness to pay. Also, as Foucault reminds, a form of resistance accompanies every power (e.g. Foucault M. (1991), *Discipline and Punish: The Birth of a Prison*, Penguin). In the information environment, downloading can be perceived as one form of resistance. See Krikorian, *Access to Knowledge as a Field of Activism*, at 75–78.
75. Rose, *The Comedy of the Commons*.

PART III NOTES

1. In particular, see Article 8(j) and Article 15 of the Convention on Biological Diversity (1992). While this book does not focus on the interface between the CBD and IPRs, it is undoubtedly a worthy area of future research. This is particularly in light of the fact that corporations from the EU, the US and Japan own approximately 77% of renewable energy patents. See Compendium of Patent Statistics 2008, OECD, 21 cited, in Drahos, *The Global Governance of Knowledge*, at 328, footnote 10. See also, McManis, *The Interface between International Intellectual Property and Environmental Protection*; Chander and Sunder, *The Romance of the Public Domain*, at 1366 (for a brief discussion of the CBD and IPRs); Kieff F. (2002), *Patents for Environmentalists*, 9 Washington Journal of Law and Policy 307; Phillips J. (2010), *Can IP Save the Day?*, 5(2) Journal of Intellectual Property Law and Practice 67; and Maskus and Reichman (eds), *International Public Goods and Transfer of Technology*; Wiener J. (2006), *Sharing Potential and the Potential for Sharing: Open Source Licensing as a Legal and Economic Modality for the Dissemination of Renewable Energy Technology*, 18 Georgetown International Environmental Law Review 277 at 294 (discussing correlations between open source licensing as it relates to computer software development and renewable energy technology); and Pogge T. (2010), *Poverty, Climate Change, and Overpopulation*, 38 Georgia Journal of International and Comparative Law 511, at 540 (supporting the notion of an 'Ecological Impact Fund' that would encourage green technology innovation 'by offering an alternative reward that is conditioned on the ecological benefit of their invention').
2. Gollin M. (1991), *Using Intellectual Property to Improve Environmental Protection*, 4 Harvard Journal of Law and Technology 193 (one of the earlier proponents of leveraging IPRs to improve environmental outcomes); Derzko N. (1996), *Using Intellectual Property Law and Regulatory Process to Foster the Innovation and Diffusion of Environmental Technologies*, 20 Harvard Environmental Law Review 3; Drahos, *Six Minutes to Midnight*; Derclaye E. (2009), *Patent Law's Role in the Protection of the Environment: Re-Assessing Patent Law and its Justifications in the 21st Century*, 40 Int'l Rev. Intell. Prop. & Competition L. 249; Ruse-Kahn H. (2011), *The Concept of Sustainable Development in International IP Law – New Approaches from EU Economic Partnership Agreements?*, in Kur A. and Mizaras V. (eds), *The Structure of Intellectual Property Law: Can One Size Fit All?*, Edward Elgar, at

338–339; Rimmer, *IP and Climate Change*, especially at 26–28 (citing a range of references concerning the nexus between IPRs and environmental preservation); and Gollin M. (2008), *Driving Innovation: Intellectual Property Strategies for a Dynamic World*, Cambridge University Press, at 333.
3. It is unclear whether the 'nothing quite as practical as good theory' notion should be traced to Kurt Lewin (the founder of social psychology) as per Lewin K. (1945), *The Research Center for Group Dynamics at Massachusetts Institute of Technology*, 8(2) Sociometry 126, at 129, or, in the alternate, John Dewey in accordance with his general pragmatist theories (e.g. Dewey J. (1938), *Experience and Education*, Kappa Delta Pi, at 12–22).

PART II, CHAPTER 6 NOTES

1. Cohen, *Copyright, Commodification and Culture*, at 141.
2. Kirk, *Science & Uncertainty*, at 205 (discussing the nature of feedback mechanisms within the context of James Lovelock's Gaia hypothesis). See also the principle formulated by Henry Le Chatelier in 1888: 'If a system at equilibrium is disturbed by a change in temperature, pressure, or the concentration of one of the components, the system will shift its equilibrium position so as to counteract the effect of the disturbance.' See Le Chatelier H. (1884), *Comptes Rendus* 99, at 786. For a contemporary scientific application of the Le Chatelier principle see, for example, Dasmeh P., Ajloo D. and Searles D. (2011), *Transient Violation of Le Chatelier's Principle for a Network of Water Molecules*, 8(2) J. Iran. Chem. Soc. 424.
3. Drahos, *Six Minutes to Midnight*. See also Rimmer, *Climate Change and Intellectual Property*.
4. Mitchell, *The Intellectual Commons*, at 98; Drahos, *Six Minutes to Midnight*. Interestingly, Rick Falkvinge, the founder of the Swedish Private Party, perceives the role of that political party as 'raising awareness about the border between public and private information'. See Kapczynski A. and Krikorian G. (2010), *Virtual Roundtable on A2K Politics*, in Krikorian and Kapczynski (eds), *A2K in the Age of IP*, at 383. Also, Sell S. (2010), *A Comparison of A2K Movements: From Medicines to Farmers*, in Krikorian and Kapczynski (eds), *A2K in the Age of IP*, at 392 (arguing that '[a]ll of the access campaigns share the goals of rebalancing the scales from private reward to public interest').
5. *Berkey v. Third Ave. Ry. Co.*, 155 N.E. 58, 61 (N.Y. 1926). For a similar comment by Justice Frankfurter, see *Tiller v. Atlantic Coast Line R.R. Co.*, 318 U.S. 54, 68 (1943). Also, see Hunter, *Cyberspace as Place and the Tragedy of the Digital Anticommons* (discussing the relationship between metaphor and law).
6. Boyle has written about the ideological dimensions of ecology with reference to the 'Naturalist Fallacy'. See Book Review: Boyle J. (1998), *Against Nature*, reviewing Macnaghten P. and Urry J. (1998), *Contested Natures*, TCS (found at http://law.duke.edu/boylesite/tls98nat.htm (cited 23/4/2013)). In many respects these tensions within ecology reflect older tensions within natural law discourse. For instance, Jeremy Bentham sought to reject natural law theory based on the notion that it is not possible to know the intentions of the creator. It is for this reason that Bentham ultimately rejected natural law and sought to promote utilitarianism. See Koepsell D. (2011), *Innovation and Nanotechnology: Converging Technologies and the End of Intellectual Property*, Bloomsbury Academic, at 162–163 [hereafter *Innovation and Nanotechnology*]. Buchanan also discussed the 'naturalist fallacy' in Buchanan J. (1990), *The Domain of Constitutional Economics*, Vol 1(1) Constitutional

Political Economy, on file, pages unnumbered (discussing how he has been criticised for fusing the positive/normative distinction).

7. For an insightful discussion of ecology and political ideology see Hayward T. (1995), *Ecological Thought: An Introduction*, Polity, at 189, arguing that a historical analysis of ecology and politics leads to the political philosophy of anarchism: 'A strong current of opinion maintains that ecological politics must in fact be a form of anarchism. Certainly, from a historical perspective, it seems to be the case that the most searching ecological questions were raised – long before questions of environment and ecology were of widespread public concern – by anarchists more than by thinkers of other political colours.' See also, Carter, *A Radical Green Political Theory*, at 105.
8. Finnis J. (2011), *Natural Law and Natural Rights* (2nd edition), Oxford University Press.
9. Odum E. and Barrett G. (2004), *Fundamentals of Ecology* (5th edition), Thomson, at 3.
10. Goodie J. (2006), *The Invention of the Environment as Legal Subject*, PhD (Murdoch University Western Australia), Unpublished (on file), at 15–16, 50, 55 [hereafter *The Invention of the Environment*]. See also, Rutherford P. (1999), *Ecological Modernization and Environmental Risk*, in Darier E. (1999), *Discourses of the Environment*, Blackwell, at 101–102; and Bates G. (2002), *Environmental Law in Australia* (5th edition), Butterworths, at 8–9.
11. *Collins Dictionary* (10th edition), (2009) – complete and unabridged.
12. Ibid.
13. Goodie, *The Invention of the Environment*, at 86. In many respects, it is *cultural values* that determine the contours of legal regulation. As Professor Eric Freyfogle observes, 'even … a nature-based land ethic requires a human translator to jump from the "is" of nature to the "ought" of human conduct … A community must draw its own lessons from nature and somehow translate its new values into legal form.' See Freyfogle E. (1995), *The Owning and Taking of Sensitive Lands*, 43 UCLA L. Rev. 77, 136. Also, Mahoney J. (2002), *Perpetual Restrictions on Land and the Problem of the Future*, 88(4) Virginia L. Rev. 739, at 759.
14. Bate J. (1991), *Romantic Ecology: Wordsworth and the Environment Tradition*, Routledge, at 40.
15. Pepper D. (1986), *The Roots of Modern Environmentalism*, Routledge, at 6.
16. Ibid.
17. Pepper Ibid, at 14–15, relaying Jeans D. (1974), *Changing Formulations of the Man–Environment Relationship in Anglo-American Geography*, 73(3) Journal of Geography 36–40. See also Nietzsche who deployed the metaphor of *windows* to describe the different realities in which the world could be viewed, (Kaufman W. (1950), *Nietzsche*, Princeton University Press, at 61). Also, Ortega y Gasset J. (1961), *Meditations on Quixote*, Norton, at 45 (arguing that ultimate reality itself was a perspective); and McAdam D., McCarthy J. and Zald M. (1996), *Introduction: Opportunities, Mobilizing Structures, and Framing Processes – Toward a Synthetic, Comparative Perspective on Social Movements*, in McAdam D., McCarthy J. and Zald M. (eds), *Comparative Perspectives on Social Movements: Political Opportunities, Mobilizing Structures and Cultural Framings*, Cambridge University Press, at 6.
18. Feyerabend P. (1975), *Against Method: Outline of an Anarchist Theory of Knowledge*, Humanities Press, at 15, 223 (arguing that science and myth overlap in many ways).
19. Kropotkin P. (1902) [1955], *Mutual Aid: A Factor of Evolution*, Extending Horizons Books.
20. Goodie, *The Invention of the Environment*, at 69.

21. Emphasis added. *Collins Dictionary* (10th edition).
22. Goodie, *The Invention of the Environment*, at 33–34.
23. Of course, since time immemorial Indigenous peoples have engaged in natural world inquiry. But the claim here relates specifically to 'Western scientific discovery'. Full respect and homage is paid to Indigenous epistemology concerning the natural world. For a good overview in this regard, see Bowrey K. (2011), *Indigenous Culture, Knowledge and Intellectual Property: The Need for a New Category of Rights?*, in Bowrey, Handler and Nicol (eds), *Emerging Challenges in Intellectual Property*, at 47, where it is argued: '[I]n relation to associated scientific knowledge, the modern notion of invention focused on the distinction between discovery and invention, with emphasis on the role of individual agency and legal-scientific forms of documentation. This approach has left Indigenous science as largely uncredited, with Indigenous knowledge undifferentiated, as part of Nature, to be discovered, translated and credited to expert biologists, botanists, anthropologists and ethnographers who have studied Indigenous communities.'
24. Taylor W. (2004), *The Vital Landscape: Nature and the Built Environment in Nineteenth-Century Britain*, Ashgate, at 24 [hereafter *The Vital Landscape*]. Also, see Chander and Sunder, *The Romance of the Public Domain*, at 1348 (explaining that many valuable contemporary drugs were 'invented' through reliance on the study of Indigenous remedies).
25. Goodie, *The Invention of the Environment*, at 33–34.
26. Ibid.
27. Bramwell A. (1989), *Ecology in the 20th Century: A History*, Yale University Press, at 61 [hereafter *Ecology in the 20th Century*]; Boughey A. (1971), *Fundamental Ecology*, Intext, at 5; and Pepper, *The Roots of Modern Environmentalism*, at 103–104.
28. Ibid.
29. Carter, *A Radical Green Political Theory*, at 82; Rutherford P. (1999), *The Entry of Life in to History*, in Darier E. (ed.), *Discourses of the Environment*, Blackwell, at 52–55.
30. Bramwell, *Ecology in the 20th Century*, at 4, cited in Goodie, *The Invention of the Environment*, at 50–51.
31. Pepper, *The Roots of Modern Environmentalism*, at 103–104.
32. Carter, *A Radical Green Political Theory*, at 82.
33. Bramwell, *Ecology in the 20th Century*, at 4; Boughey, *Fundamental Ecology*, at 5; Carter, *A Radical Green Political Theory*, at 19. Traditionally 'science' had a broader meaning than it does today, encompassing 'a whole body of regular or methodological observations or propositions ... concerning any subject of speculation ... a kind of knowledge or argument rather than a kind of subject'. See Williams R. (1976), *Keywords: A Vocabulary of Culture and Society*, Fontana, at 233 [hereafter *Keywords*]. Also, Chon, *Postmodern 'Progress'*, at 114.
34. Mokyr J. (2002), *The Gifts of Athena – Historical Origins of the Knowledge Economy*, Princeton University Press (explaining that propositional knowledge is knowledge about 'how to manipulate nature'); and Dolfsma W. (2005), *Towards a Dynamic (Schumpeterian) Welfare Economics*, 34 Research Policy 69.
35. Hont I. (2005), *Jealousy of Trade: International Competition and the Nation State in Historical Perspective*, Harvard University Press, at 173.
36. Purdy, *The Meaning of Property*, at 37, especially footnote 51 (implying that Pufendorf prescribed a form of economic organisation as an alternate to the social contract).
37. Carter, *A Radical Green Political Theory*, at 66–67.

38. Ibid, at 81. The methodological individualist perspective flows from the 'possessive individualism' notion coined by C.B. MacPherson. See MacPherson C. (1962), *The Political Theory of Possessive Individualism: Hobbes to Locke*, Oxford University Press.
39. Carter, *A Radical Green Political Theory*, at 82.
40. Ibid.
41. For an interesting discussion of how the 'principle of abundance' might apply to the information environment, for example, see Verzola R. (2010), *Undermining Abundance: Counterproductive Uses of Technology and Law in Nature, Agriculture, and the Information Sector* in Krikorian and Kapczynski (eds), *A2K in the Age of IP*, at 253 onwards.
42. Dryzek J. and Scholosberg D. (2005), *Debating the Earth: The Environmental Politics Reader*, Oxford University Press, at 92 [hereafter *Debating the Earth*] (discussing adaptive management and other ecological principles).
43. Boyle has argued that organisations that have coalesced around the protection of the information commons are similar in nature to Greenpeace, Environmental Defense Fund and, most relevantly, Environmentally Concerned Scientists. The call for 'information ecology' relies upon Boyle's thinking as a springboard. See, for instance, Boyle, *Second Enclosure Movement*, at 73.
44. Ricketson, S. (1992), *The Copyright Term*, 23(6) IIC 753–784. See also Rimmer, *Digital Copyright*, at 42–43.
45. The contemporary willingness of courts in the US to accept *amicus curiae* in relation to IPR cases has fostered a distinct site for relatively succinct empirically based submissions concerning IPRs. A useful example being in the case of *Eldred v Ashcroft* 537 US 186 (2003) where 17 prominent economists analysed the economic effect of the Sonny Bono Act. See, Rimmer, *Digital Copyright*, at 39–40. Also, the recent Hargreaves Report in the UK was steadfast in calling for empirical foundations with respect to IPR policy formulations. See Hargreaves, *Digital Opportunity*, at 3, 10, 16–17.
46. Cornish W. (2012), *Opening Session*, Intellectual Property Academics Conference 2012, National Wine Centre of Australia, 13 July 2012 (discussing the novelty of intellectual property textbooks when they emerged).
47. Haochen, *Toward a Public Trust Doctrine in Copyright Law*, at 21 (arguing that 'we cannot divide our cultural ecosystem into separated bits and pieces').
48. See, for example, Frischmann B., Madison M. and Strandburg K. (2010), *Constructing Commons in the Cultural Environment*, 95 Cornell Law Review 657.
49. Gunderson L. and Holling C. (2001), *Panarchy: Understanding Transformations in Human and Natural Systems*, Island Press [hereafter *Panarchy*].
50. Bohanes J. (2002), *Risk Regulation in WTO Law: A Procedure-based Approach to the Precautionary Principle*, 40 Colum. J. Transnat'l L. 323, at 330; and Stenzel P. (2002), *How the World Trade Organization Must Promote Environmental Protection*, 13 Duke Envtl. L. & Pol'y F. 1, at 42–43.
51. See, for example, G.A. Res. 37/7, U.N. GAOR, 37th Sess., Agenda Item 21, at (I)(21) U.N. Doc. A/RES/37/7 (1982) (referring to this principle for first time in so-called World Charter for Nature) and Ministerial Declaration of the Second International Conference on the Protection of the North Sea (Nov. 1987), at www.journals.cambridge.org/article_S0376892900016878 *(cited 23/4/2013).* See also Ministerial Declaration of the Third International Conference on the Protection of the North Sea (Mar. 1990), at http://www.seas-at-risk.org/1mages/1990%20Hague%20 Declaration.pdf (cited 23/4/2013). This manifestation of the precautionary principle is the most authoritative in that it is generally widely accepted and has been embedded in several more recent treaties, the most notable of which relates to the World Trade Organisation (although it is highly contested as to

whether the precautionary principle applies within the WTO framework). See Cunningham R. (2005), *The ABCs of GMOs, SPS & the WTO: a critical analysis of the Sanitary and Phytosanitary Agreement*, 9 SCU Law Review 19.

52. David Lange briefly traversed the idea of 'impact statements' when he argued that: 'If it is fair, as we seem to have decided in this century it is, to require the users of public lands to prepare impact statements as a condition of their use, then perhaps it is also fair to require similar assurances before we permit the outright appropriation of the territory of the creative subconscious'. See Lange D. (1981), *Recognizing the Public Domain*, 44 Law & Contemporary Problems 147, at 176.
53. While the iEIS process may seem novel, Kastenmeier and Remington put forth a corresponding idea in the mid-1980s when they advocated a responsibility for the state engaging in a 'political test' for new IP legislation that would include consideration of whether and how the legislation 'will enrich or enhance the aggregate public domain'. See Kastenmeier R. and Remington M. (1985), *The Semiconductor Chip Protection Act of 1984: A Swamp or Firm Ground?*, 70 Minn. L. Rev. 417, at 438–442. See also Cohen, *Copyright, Commodification and Culture*, at 133. Also, Faunce, *Global Public Goods*, at 525 (arguing that it is possible to merge a global public goods analysis with the United Nations Millennium Development Goals).
54. The Intellectual Property Laws Amendment (Raising the Bar) Act 2012 (Australian Commonwealth Government), Section 15, shifts the burden of proof to the patent holder via a 'balance of probabilities' test. An early example of informational environmentalists relying upon the Internet to secure access to 'sensitive information' was the Taxpayers Assets Project and the accompanying Crown Jewels Campaign, which successfully fought to ensure access to the best-known and most valuable USA federal databases. See Ress M. (2010), *Open-Access Publishing: From Principles to Practice*, in Krikorian. and Kapczynski (eds), *A2K in the Age of IP*, at 478–479. See also Haochen, *Toward a Public Trust Doctrine in Copyright Law*, at 35.
55. Peter Drahos has alluded to the need for 'external audits of patent quality'. See Drahos, *The Global Governance of Knowledge*, at 296.
56. Rutherford P, *Ecological Modernization and Environmental Risk*, at 116.
57. Ibid.
58. Beck U. (1999), *World Risk Society*, Polity Press, at 51.
59. Beck U. (1992), *Risk Society: Towards a New Modernity*, Sage Press, at 56–57.
60. Levine D. (2012), *Bring in the Nerds: Secrecy, National Security and the Creation of International Intellectual Property Law*, 30 Cardozo Arts & Entertainment Law Journal (discussing counter-reactions to SOPA and PIPA).
61. Lange D. (1981), *Recognizing the Public Domain*, 44 Law & Contemporary Problems 147, at 147 (arguing that '[t]he chief attribute of intellectual property is that apart from its recognition in law it has no existence of its own').
62. Of course, IPRs exist not just for private benefit but also for the benefit of the public. See *Computer Associates International Inc v Altai Inc*, 982 F 2d at 711 (1992) cited in Chon, *Postmodern 'Progress'*, at 110. Also, Sherman B. and Wiseman L. (2006), *Towards an Indigenous Public Domain*, in Guibault and Hugenholtz (eds), *The Future of the Public Domain*, at 260; Landes and Posner (1989), *An Economic Analysis of Copyright Law*; Salzberger, *Economic Analysis of the Public Domain*, at 40.
63. Mitchell, *The Intellectual Commons*, at 98. See also, Drahos, *Six Minutes to Midnight*.
64. There is scant scholarship concerning an 'information environmental ethic', but one journal article that alludes to the application of Leopold's land ethic to the

information environment is Verzola R. (2010), *Undermining Abundance: Counter-productive Uses of Technology and Law in Nature, Agriculture, and the Information Sector* [hereafter *Undermining Abundance*], in Krikorian and Kapczynski (eds), *A2K in the Age of IP*, at 268.

65. Leopold A. (1949), *A Sand County Almanac: And Sketches Here and There*, Oxford University Press, at 262.
66. Errington P. (1948), *In Appreciation of Aldo Leopold*, 12(4) The Journal of Wildlife Management 341–350.
67. For a useful history of environmental law, see Plater Z. (1994), *From the Beginning, A Fundamental Shift of Paradigms: A Theory and Short History of Environment Law*, 27 Loy. LA L. Rev. 981.
68. Note that the information commons is discussed in the plural rather than singular. This is because the information commons is made up of various subsystems that in turn interact with the information environment as a whole.
69. Walker B. and Salt D. (2006), *Resilience Thinking*, Island Press, at 1. See also, Rogers N. (ed.) (1998), *Green Paradigms and the Law*, Southern Cross University Press, at 104.
70. Ibid. Translating ecological understandings to the information environment, it is desirable to work towards a stable information system built upon the principle of diversity. Cohen seems to allude to this perspective implicitly in Cohen, at 1168. The author is grateful to Dr Nic Suzor for pointing out this aspect of Cohen's work.
71. Walker and Salt, *Resilience Thinking*, at 121. See also Levin S. (1999), *Fragile Dominion*, Perseus Books Group. Sometimes 'tightness of feedback' is discussed as a separate criterion, but in many respects feedback relates to modularity.
72. Walker and Salt, *Resilience Thinking*, at 121.
73. Rogers (ed.), *Green Paradigms and the Law*, at 104; Cohen, *Creativity and Culture in Copyright Theory*, at 1168; and Liang, *The Man Who Mistook His Wife for a Book*, at 277 (arguing that the IPR system 'threatens to destroy the diversity that marks our relation to the world of ideas and consequently our relation to others and to ourselves').
74. Kirk, *Science & Uncertainty*, at 175–176.
75. For an example of scholarship concerning the nexus between ecological diversity, agriculture and IPRs, see Verzola, *Undermining Abundance*, at 253–254.
76. Carson R. (1962) [1968], *Silent Spring*, Penguin, at 27.
77. Ibid.
78. Ibid.
79. Pepper, *The Roots of Modern Environmentalism*, at 104.
80. Ibid.
81. Ibid.
82. Pepper, *The Roots of Modern Environmentalism*, at 104. Fiona Macmillan has discussed the notion of diversity with respect to IPRs. See Macmillan F. (2007), *The Dysfunctional Relationship Between Copyright and Cultural Diversity*, 27 Quaderns Del CAC 101. See also Frosio, *Communia and the European Public Domain Project*, at 30; Pessach G. (2003), *Copyright Law as a Silencing Restriction on Noninfringing Materials: Unveiling the Scope of Copyright's Diversity Externalities*, 76 Southern California L. Rev. 1067–1104, at 1068; and Coombe R. (2003), *Fear, Hope, and Longing for the Future of Authorship and a Revitalized Public Domain in Global Regimes of Intellectual Property*, 52 DePaul L. Rev. 1181 (arguing that '[a] vibrant cultural public domain will also require consideration of means to maintain *cultural diversity* and ongoing dialogue across and between cultural traditions' (emphasis added)). Also, Deazley, *Rethinking Copyright*, at 130; and Halbert D. (2005), *Resisting Intellectual Property*, Routledge, at 39.
83. Pepper, *The Roots of Modern Environmentalism*, at 104.

84. Walker and Salt, *Resilience Thinking*, at 9.
85. Gunderson and Holling, *Panarchy*, at 7. See also Walker and Salt, *Resilience Thinking*, at 76–77.
86. Walker and Salt, *Resilience Thinking*, at 9.
87. Pepper, *The Roots of Modern Environmentalism*, at 104.
88. Walker and Salt, *Resilience Thinking*, at 9.
89. Ibid.
90. While a resolution of the inquiry as to the precise consequences of a homogeneous information environment lies beyond the scope of this book, it is a useful starting point for a future research project.
91. The dynamic between methodological interrelationalism, empirical knowledge and governance principles can perhaps be referred to as 'adaptive management'. See Dryzek and Scholosberg, *Debating the Earth*, at 92 (discussing adaptive management and other ecological principles).
92. Walker and Salt, *Resilience Thinking*, at 121.
93. Ibid.
94. Ibid.
95. Ibid. As Benkler explains, 'centralization' implies the separation of the locus of opportunities for action from the authority to choose the action that an agent will undertake; 'decentralisation', on the other hand, implies conditions under which the actions of many agents cohere and are effective despite the fact that they do not rely on reducing the number of people whose will counts to direct effective action. See Benkler, *The Wealth of Networks*, at 62–63.
96. Henry Smith refers to the former situation as 'information hiding'. See Smith, *Toward An Economic Theory of Property in Information*, at 109; and Walker and Salt, *Resilience Thinking*, at 121.
97. Within the information environmental context Verzola has contextualised the 'system failure' issue with reference to 'reliability'. See Verzola, *Undermining Abundance*, at 270.
98. In this context, note David Bollier's comments: 'I believe we are moving into a new kind of cultural if not economic reality. We are moving away from a world organized around centralized control, strict intellectual property rights and hierarchies of credentialed experts, to a radically different order. The new order is predicated upon open access, decentralized participation, and cheap and easy sharing.' See Bollier D. (2008), *The Commons as New Sector of Value Creation: It's Time to Recognise and Protect the Distinctive Wealth Generated by Online Commons*, remarks at the *Economies of the Commons: Strategies for Sustainable Access and Creative Reuse of Images and Sounds Online Conference*, Amsterdam (12 April 2008) cited in Frosio, *Communia and the European Public Domain Project*, at 14. See also, Zittrain J. (2006), *The Generative Internet*, 119 Harvard L. Rev. 1974 (arguing at 1977–78 that there is a need to foster 'principles that will blunt the most unappealing features of a more locked-down technological future').
99. James P. (2003), *Open Source Software: An Australian Perspective*, in Fitzgerald B. and Bassett G. (eds) (2003), *Legal Issues Relating to Free and Open Source Software: Essays in Technology Policy and Law* (Vol. 1) Queensland University of Technology School of Law, at 68.
100. The General Public License, which is the legal instrument that underpins FLOSS, is in many respects a privately ordered 'information commons' mechanism.
101. Benkler Y. (2002), *Coase's Penguin, or, Linux and the Nature of the Firm*, 112 Yale L. J. 381.
102. Lessig, *The Future of Ideas*, at 23–25.
103. Ibid, at 23–25, 92.

104. Nadan C. (2002), *Open Source Licensing: Virus or Virtue?*, 10 Tex. Intell. Prop. L. J. 349, at 353–363 [hereafter *Open Source Licensing*].
105. Ibid.
106. Raymond E. (1998), *The Cathedral and the Bazaar*, www.firstmonday.org/issues/issue3_3/raymond (cited 27/4/2013).
107. Ibid.
108. Nadan, *Open Source Licensing*, at 353–363.
109. Ibid. See also Natoli A. (1999), *Open Source Software*, 5 Multimedia & Web Strategist 2.
110. Fitzgerald B. and Fitzgerald A. (2004), *Intellectual Property in Principle*, Law Book Co, at 454.
111. Nadan, *Open Source Licensing*, at 353–363.
112. Ibid.
113. While modularity generally makes a system more stable, it is also the case that a system like Apple's App Store is highly integrated and centralised. This gives rise to interesting questions concerning the interface between centralisation of iTunes and the micro-ecosystem of diverse apps that it supports. This idea is to be credited to Dr Nic Suzor from the Queensland University of Technology.
114. Hess and Ostrom hazard against the dangers of centralization within the information environment in Hess and Ostrom, *Ideas, Artifacts, and Facilities*, at 136–137.
115. Vaidhyanathan S. (2004), *The Anarchist in the Library: How the Clash Between Freedom and Control is Hacking the Real World and Crashing the System*, Basic Books, at xi (arguing that the monopolistic tendencies of IPRs means that on the whole the IPR system tends to foster centralised governance structures).
116. Sell, *Private Power, Public Law*.
117. This book focuses on when the ecology framework works as opposed to when it does not work. However, it is acknowledged that work should also be done on when the ecology framework is not suitable to IPR application.

PART III, CHAPTER 7 NOTES

1. Pepper, *The Roots of Modern Environmentalism*, at 88–89.
2. Sax J. (1970), *The Public Trust Doctrine in Natural Resource Law: Effective Judicial Intervention*, 68 Mich. L. Rev. 471, at 478–489; Sun, *Toward a Public Trust Doctrine in Copyright Law*, at 8; Ryan P. (2004), *Application of the Public-Trust Doctrine and Principles of Natural Resource Management to Electromagnetic Spectrum*, 10 Mich. Telecomm. & Tech. L. Rev. 285, at 348 (pointing out that Sax's article is one of the most cited law review articles of all time – referring to Shapiro F. (1985), *The Most Cited Law Review Articles*, Cal. L. Rev 1540, at 1551–53).
3. Stone, *Should Trees Have Standing?*.
4. Tribe L. (1974), *Ways Not To Think About Plastic Trees: New Foundations for Environmental Law*, 83 Yale L. J. 1315 [hereafter *Ways Not to Think About Plastic Trees*]. See also, Purdy, *Our Place in the World*.
5. Purdy, *Our Place in the World*.
6. O'Riorday T. (1981), *Environmentalism*, Pion Books, at 5, 280. See also, Pepper, *The Roots of Modern Environmentalism*, at 88–89.
7. Rogers (ed.), *Green Paradigms and the Law*, at 21.
8. Ibid. Critical race theory underscores that rights will only be allocated when the power-holders have something to gain from such allocation. This point was alluded to in a paper delivered by Margaret Chon at ANU RegNet in September 2013. See Chon M. (2013), *Public-Private Partnerships in Global Intellectual Property*, ANU

RegNet Conference, Innovation, Creative, Access to Knowledge and Development in Pacific Island Countries, 24–25 September 2013.

9. Rogers (ed.), *Green Paradigms and the Law*, at 21.
10. Lange D. (1981), *Recognising the Public Domain*, 24 Law and Contemporary Problems, 147–181; and Frosio, *Communia and the European Public Domain Project*, at 4.
11. Mitchell, *The Intellectual Commons*, at 101; and Ryan, *Cyberspace as Public Space*, at 717–718 (arguing at 717 that 'we need a mechanism for exerting the influence of the public interest on the drafting process to ensure that copyright legislation does not unduly burden public access to copyrighted works'). See also Drahos, *The Global Governance of Knowledge*; Lemley M. et al. (2005–2006), *What to Do About Bad Patents?*, Regulation (Winter), at 10; and Fagundes D. (2009), *Crystals in the Public Domain*, 50(1) Boston College L. Rev. 139, at 157.
12. Mitchell, *The Intellectual Commons*, at 101. Also, Drahos, *A Philosophy of IP*, at 67 stating that '[t]hose who argue for an extension of intellectual property rights and link that extension to negative community may ultimately be suggesting a self-defeating strategy. The extension of intellectual property rights under conditions of negative community may provide individuals with strong incentives to act in non-preservationist ways when it comes to the intellectual commons.' See also Drahos, *A Philosophy of IP*, at 209 positing that 'the longer-term effect of proprietarianism in patent law will be that all kinds of abstract information previously in the public domain will fall into private ownership'.
13. Drahos with Braithwaite, *Information Feudalism*, at 204.
14. Ibid, at 203.
15. *Mayo Collaborative Services v Prometheus Laboratories Inc*, 132 S. Ct. 1289 (2012).
16. Section 25(2) of the Patent Act (1970) (India) gives the right to 'persons interested' to oppose patents in accordance with a process that is clearly outlined within the legislation. Recent Indian case law has demonstrated a willingness to broaden the term 'persons interested' within s 25(2). See the *Roche Valcyte Decision* (Chennai Intellectual Property Office). Also, for a good global overview of opposition systems see WIPO, *Opposition Systems*, Standing Committee on the Law of Patents, Fourteenth Session, Geneva, 25–29 January 2010 found at: www.wipo.int/edocs/mdocs/scp/en/scp_14/scp_14_5.pdf (cited 6/9/2012). For an insight into the European Patent Office opposition system see Rule 26 EPC Directive 98/44/EC. This Rule was discussed by Mr Enrico Luzzatto from the European Patent Office in the following presentation: Luzzatto E. (2013), *Traditional Knowledge and Patents: A Look at How the European Patent Office Deals with the Issue*, ANU RegNet Conference, Innovation, Creative, Access to Knowledge and Development in Pacific Island Countries, 24–25 September 2013. In particular, see Case 1 – Neem, Case 2 EP 02777223 (Pelargonium), and Case 3 EP 973534 (Hoodia). As patent offices are not investigative, the EPO relies upon others to come forward to inform the EPO of opposition. Most European countries have voluntary schemes concerning the geographical origin of biological materials, albeit Switzerland is one exception.
17. Flynn S. (2010), *Using Competition to Promote Access to Knowledge*, in Krikorian and Kapczynski (eds), *A2K in the Age of IP*, at 453, 455, 457. Also, see Frischmann B. and Waller S. (2008), *Revitalizing Essential Facilities*, 75(1) Antitrust Law Journal 1–2.
18. Litman, *The Public Domain*, at 977.
19. Mitchell, *The Intellectual Commons*, at 98; and Drahos, *A Philosophy of IP*, at 63 (deploying the evolution of scientific theories as an exemplar). Of course it could be argued that perpetual IPRs could be used to protect the public domain, particularly where FLOSS and CC licensing methods are used more extensively.
20. Mitchell, *The Intellectual Commons*, at 98.

21. Litman, *The Public Domain*, at 1000–1004. See Drahos, *A Philosophy of IP*, at 62 (arguing that in creating individuals tend to borrow and copy); Drahos with Braithwaite, *Information Feudalism*, at 2; and Woodmansee M. (1984), *The Genius and the Copyright: Economic and Legal Conditions of the Emergence of the 'Author'*, 17 Eighteenth Century Stud. 425, at 434 (explaining that in the late eighteenth century the common view was that 'an author was a mere craftsman transcribing ideas already in the public domain, and, by extension, an author's work was in the public domain as well'). Also, Ryan, *Cyberspace as Public Space*, at 694.
22. Van Houweling, *Cultural Environmentalism and the Constructed Commons*, at 23.
23. Rubenfeld J. (2002), *The Freedom of Imagination: Copyright's Constitutionality*, 112 Yale L. J. 1–60; Birnhack, *More or Better?*, at 60.
24. Bannerman, *The Ins and Outs of the Public Domain*, at 168. See also Wirten E. (2008), *Terms of Use: Negotiating the Jungle of the Intellectual Commons*, University of Toronto Press, at 6 (referring to Pamela Samuelson's 'thirteen public domains').
25. Guibault and Hugenholtz (eds), *The Future of the Public Domain*, at 1; and Van Houweling, *Cultural Environmentalism and the Constructed Commons*, at 23.
26. Cohen, *Copyright, Commodification and Culture*, at 139–140.
27. Lemley, *Property, Intellectual Property, and Free Riding*, at 27; *Festo Corp. v Shoketsu Knzoku Kogyo Kabushiki Co.*, 535 U.S. 722, 736 (2002) (a quid pro quo of patent rights is disclosure of the invention to the public); and Guibault, *Wrapping Information in Contract*, at 89. See also Boyle, *The Second Enclosure Movement*, at 58; Litman, *The Public Domain*, at 975.
28. Frischmann, *Evaluating the Demsetzian Trend in Copyright Law*, at 20; and Ramello G. (2005), *Property Rights, Firm Boundaries and the Republic of Science: A Note on Ashish Arora and Robert Merges*, 14(6) Industrial and Corporate Change 1195, at 1198.
29. Lemley, *Property, Intellectual Property, and Free Riding*, at 27, especially footnote 85.
30. Frischmann and Lemley, *Spillovers*, at 282, especially footnote 92.
31. Frischmann and Lemley, *Spillovers*, at 282; Frischmann, *An Economic Theory of Infrastructure and Commons Management*, at 1000–1003; and Kreiss R. (1995), *Accessibility and Commercialization in Copyright Theory*, 43 UCLA L. Rev. 1, at 14–20.
32. Frischmann, *Spillover Theory and Its Conceptual Boundaries*, at 812; Baumol, *The Free Market Innovation Machine*, at 121–123.
33. Harrison, *A Positive Externalities Approach to Copyright Law*, at 14.
34. Frischmann, *Evaluating the Demsetzian Trend in Copyright Law*, at 19–20. See also, Frischmann and Lemley, *Spillovers*, at 276.
35. Buchanan J. and Stubblebine W. (1962), *Externality*, 29 Economica 371, at 371, 373; Frischmann, *Evaluating the Demsetzian Trend in Copyright Law*, at 19; and Fennell, *Commons, Anticommons, Semicommons*, at 3.
36. Frischmann, *Evaluating the Demsetzian Trend in Copyright Law*, at 19; Fennell, *Commons, Anticommons, Semicommons*, at 3; and De Alessi, *Property Rights*, at 45.
37. Frischmann, *Evaluating the Demsetzian Trend in Copyright Law*, at 19.
38. Ibid. See also, Fennell, *Commons, Anticommons, Semicommons*, at 3.
39. Frischmann, *Evaluating the Demsetzian Trend in Copyright Law*, at 19–20. See also, Frischmann and Lemley, *Spillovers*, at 276.
40. Merges R. (1997), *The End of Friction? Property Rights and Contract in the 'Newtonian' World of On-line Commerce*, 12 Berkeley Technology L. J. 115; Frischmann, *Evaluating the Demsetzian Trend in Copyright Law*, at 25; Fisher, *Reconstructing the Fair Use Doctrine*, 1695; and Vaidhyanathan S. (2003), *Copyrights and Copywrongs: The Rise of Intellectual Property and How It Threatens*

Creativity, NYU Press, at 184 (arguing that it is good for a copyright system to be somewhat leaky).

41. Frischmann, *Evaluating the Demsetzian Trend in Copyright Law*, at 25.
42. See Principles 1 and 2 in Table 1.1.
43. See Principle 10 of Table 1.1; and Part IV (especially Chapter 10).
44. Indeed, Ginsburg J in *Eldred v Ashcroft* 123 S. Ct. 769 (2003) referred to the Supreme Court judgment in *Harper & Row* where the Court stated that the 'idea/expression dichotomy strike[s] a definitional balance between the First Amendment and the Copyright Act by permitting free communication of facts while still protecting an author's expression'. See also, Rimmer, *Digital Copyright*, at 32. The term 'public juris' was referred to in earlier cases to refer to instances where there was insufficient novelty. In such jurisprudence the court indicated that where there was insufficient novelty the 'invention' could not be patented because it had always belonged to the public. See, for example, *Thompson v Haight*, 23 F. Cas 1040, 1047 (SDNY) 1826; and *Wall v Leck*, 66 F. 552, 556 (9th Cir 1895) ('A principle, considered as a natural physical force, is not the product of inventive skill. It is the common property of all mankind.'); and *Carr v Rice*, 5 F Cas 140, 143 (SDNY) 1856) (invention 'previously in public use' is 'public property, and the law does not permit it to be appropriated, by means of a patent grant, to individuals'). Also see Cohen, *Copyright, Commodification and Culture*, at 130.
45. Cindy Cohen from the Electronic Frontier Foundation stated the organisation's viewpoint regarding copyright policy is that 'copyright ... [has] really gotten far out of balance' because 'the content industries have a very loud voice against the government ... [B]ut there's nobody there talking for ordinary people ...' (Interview with Cindy Cohen, Legal Director, Electronic Frontier Foundation, in S.F., Cal. 11 March 2008 cited in Lee J. (2010), *The Greenpeace of Cultural Environmentalism*, 16 Widener Law Review 1, at 56, footnote 388). See also Enjolras B. (2000), *Coordination Failure, Property Rights and Non-Profit Organisations*, 71 Annals Pub. & Cooperative Econ. 347, at 362 (arguing that Non Government Organisations provide spaces 'where "voice" is possible'); Boyle, *Politics of Intellectual Property*, at 110–112; and Karjala D. (2002), *Judicial Review of Copyright Term Extension Legislation*, 36 Loy. LA L. Rev. 199, at 232–233 (providing the CTEA as an exemplar of how individuals are generally ignored in the legislative process relating to IPRs).
46. The application of public choice theory to IPRs is the core focus of Part IV. Cohen, *Copyright, Commodification and Culture*, at 160; Rimmer, *Digital Copyright*, at 32. See also, Jaszi P. (1991), *Toward a Theory of Copyright: The Metamorphoses of 'Authorship'*, 2 Duke Law Journal 455, at 465–502; Drahos P. (1994), *Decentring Communication: The Dark Side of Intellectual Property*, in Campbell T. and Sadurski W. (eds), *Freedom of Communication*, Dartmouth, at 257; Rimmer, *Digital Copyright*, at 32; and Fagundes, *Crystals in the Public Domain*, at 144 (arguing that '[t]he poorly defined standards that separate fair uses from foul ones, or ideas from expression, or delimit the boundaries of works of authorship all make it difficult for individuals to know which cultural resources are proprietary and which are free for them to use').
47. Deazley, *Rethinking Copyright*, at 133.
48. Rose, *Nine-Tenths of the Law*, at 86.
49. Deazley, *Rethinking Copyright*, 133.
50. Ibid, at 131.
51. There is not necessarily one 'information common', but rather many 'information commons'. See, for example, Boyle, *The Second Enclosure Movement*, at 52 and 62. It is for this reason that ICRs refer to the plural of 'information commons' rather than the singular 'information common'.

52. Deazley, *Rethinking Copyright: History, Theory and Language*, at 115.
53. Drahos, *A Philosophy of IP*, at 57.
54. Deazley, *Rethinking Copyright*, at 131.
55. This does not mean, however, that if there were no IPRs there would be no information commons. Indeed, as Deazley underscores with respect to the public domain: 'absent any form of legal regulation, all works lie within the public domain (whether disclosed or not)' (Deazley (ibid) at 130). This is important because it reminds that the public domain is a concept that is contingent upon the broad parameters of history, culture and politics in the same vein as IPRs.
56. Ibid, at 131.
57. Ibid.
58. Guibault and Hugenholtz (eds), *The Future of the Public Domain*, at 350.
59. Greenhalgh and Rogers, *Innovation, Intellectual Property, and Economic Growth*, at 34–35. For example, see UK Patent Act of 1977 and European Patent Convention of 1973. Examples include scientific theories/mathematical models, aesthetic creations, animal or plant varieties, and methods of treatment and diagnosis.
60. Guibault and Hugenholtz (eds), *The Future of the Public Domain*, at 350.
61. The work of such an office might also overlap with efforts to protect Traditional Knowledge (TK) in the sense that often it is difficult to ascertain who has legal standing in relation to such knowledge. An example discussed in a World Intellectual Property Organization document involves a Solomon Islands (SI) chant inherent within a popular Deep Forest song. Who has standing in relation to the SI chant in this song? See WIPO, *Intellectual Property Issues and Arts Festivals: Preparing for the 11th Festival of Pacific Arts – Solomon Islands 2012*, at 10 (found at: http://www.acpcultures.eu/_upload/ocr_document/WIPO-SPC_IntellectProperty Festival Arts_2009.pdf (cited 2/5/2013)).
62. Townsend Gard, *Traditional Contours in Intellectual Property*, at 4; Ochoa T. (2011), *Is the Copyright Public Domain Irrevocable? An Introduction to Golan v Holder*, 64 Vand. L. Rev. En Banc 123; and Zimmerman D. (2004), *Is There A Right to Have Something to Say? One View of the Public Domain*, 73 Fordham L. Rev. 297.
63. With respect to the common law, David Lange has argued that 'in cases in which it appears sensible to recognise new (or doubtful) intellectual property claims, it will be appropriate for the court to explain what is not covered by the grant as well'. See Lange, *Recognizing the Public Domain*, at 176–177.
64. Rogers (ed.), *Green Paradigms and the Law*, at 21.
65. Stone, *Should Trees Have Standing?*, at 17.
66. Ibid, at 8–9.
67. Mahatma Gandhi cited in Meeker H. (2008), *Outsource Software Development and Open Source: Coming of Age in the 2000s*, 24 Santa Clara Computer & High Tech. L. J. 869, at 870.
68. Until 1949 all people residing in Australia were considered 'British subjects'. See Zappala G. and Castles S. (1998–1999), *Citizenship and Immigration in Australia*, 13 Geo. Immigr. L. J. 273, at 273. However, perhaps more importantly, it was not until 1967 that Aboriginal Australians gained the right to vote in Commonwealth elections. See Peterson N. and Sanders W. (eds) (1998), *Citizenship and Indigenous Australians: Changing Conceptions and Possibilities*, Cambridge University Press, at 119; and Attwood B. and Markus A. (1997), *The 1967 Referendum, or When Aborigines Didn't Get the Vote*, Aboriginal Studies Press.
69. Stone C. (1972), *Should Trees Have Standing? Toward legal rights for natural objects*, William Kaufmann Inc, at 6. See also, *Dred Scott v Standford* 60 U.S. 393 (1856).
70. Stone, *Should Trees Have Standing?*, at 6, citing *People v Hall*, 4 Cal. 399, 405 (1854).

71. Stone, *Should Trees Have Standing?*, at 7–8, citing *In re Goddell*, 39 Wisc. 232, 245 (1875).
72. Lange, *Recognizing the Public Domain*, at 177 (arguing that 'the public domain tends to appear amorphous and vague, with little more of substance in it than is invested in patriotic or religious slogans on paper currency').
73. Boyle, *A Politics of Intellectual Property*, at 113. Note that Boyle refers to the public domain rather than the information commons.
74. Ibid. See also, Boyle, *The Second Enclosure Movement*, at 73; and Kapczynski A. (2008), *The Access to Knowledge Mobilization and the New Politics of Intellectual Property*, 117 Yale L. J. 804, at 825–839.
75. Ramsay R. and Rowe G. (1995), *Environmental Law and Policy: Text and Materials*, Butterworths, at 2.
76. Goodie, *The Invention of the Environment*, at 19, 142. The production of law by a broad range of citizens applies not just to environmental law, but to law generally. See, for example, Sarat A. and Simon J. (2001), *Beyond Legal Realism? Cultural Analysis, Cultural Studies and the Situation of Legal Scholarship*, 13(35) Yale Journal of Law and the Humanities 1, at 21.
77. Goodie, *The Invention of the Environment*, at 19, 142.
78. Rogers (ed.), *Green Paradigms and the Law*, at 72. The claim that if information falls outside of ICRs then it may be fully subject to propertisation without qualification may seem paradoxical in the first instance in that the fundamental right allocated to the public domain would be the right *not to be subject to property rights*. Yet once it is recognised that property rights do not encompass all varieties of rights then the 'anti-property rights' of the public domain are internally consistent with the arguments made in this book. See also Fagundes, *Crystals in the Public Domain* (arguing that the demarcation of rights engenders a social welfare function of informing citizens as to what property they can make use of, and how).
79. Elkin-Koren N. (2005/2006), *What Contracts Cannot Do: The Limits of Private Ordering in Facilitating a Creative Commons*, 74 Fordham L. Rev. 375, at 389.
80. Rogers (ed.), *Green Paradigms and the Law*, at 72. See also Glendon M. (1991), *Rights Talk: The Impoverishment of Political Discourse,* Free Press, at 171 (discussing the issue of voluntarism in relation to conservation and Native American rights indicating that over the long term the voluntary approach is preferred over a rights-focused imposition of respectful behaviour that is imposed by the state with the accompanying use of coercive power); and Brown, *Who Owns Native Culture?*, at 231 (arguing that 'It is in the nature of rights to seek absolutes. Rights have a finality that silences debate and possibilities for negotiation').
81. Cohen, *Copyright, Commodification and Culture*, at 158 (referring to the public domain rather than the information commons); and Litman, *The Public Domain* (arguing that at its inception the public domain was little more than a highly useful fiction).
82. Cunningham R. (2010), *The Tragedy of (Ignoring) the Semicommons*, 4(1) Akron Intellectual Property Journal 1.
83. Grotius (1625), *The Law of War and Peace*, Of Things Which Belong to Men in Commons, Book 2, Chapter 2, 2.2.2.1, relaying Cicero's third book 'On Ends'. See also, Mitchell, *The Intellectual Commons*, at 73.
84. Stone, *Should Trees Have Standing?*, at 10–11.
85. Dusollier S. (2008), *Towards a Legal Infrastructure for the Public Domain*, paper delivered at the first Communia workshop, Turin, Italy (18 January 2008); and Frosio, *Communia and the European Public Domain Project*, at 4–5.
86. Lee, *The Greenpeace of Cultural Environmentalism*, at 35, footnote 248, referring to telephone interview with Vera Franz.

87. Stiglitz, *Economic Foundations of Intellectual Property Rights*, 1715. See also Vaver, *Intellectual Property Today*, at 118–119.
88. It might be argued, as Snidal does, that public goods are only public to the extent that it has been politically decided that they are: 'The political analysis of public goods problems is most appropriately viewed not as an analysis of the exchange of goods but as an analysis of authority between actors. The setting up of organizations or groups capable of imposing and enforcing property rights and collecting payments for centrally provided services is crucial to understanding how public goods (or, more correctly, quasi-public goods) are provided.' See Snidal D. (1979), *Public Goods, Property Rights and Political Organizations*, 23(4) International Studies Quarterly 532, at 564.
89. Chander and Sunder, *The Romance of the Public Domain*, at 1334–1335; Bannerman, *The Ins and Outs of the Public Domain*, at 169; and Liang, *Beyond Representation*, at 369 (arguing that 'the invocation of the commons is indeed a useful starting point in discussions of intellectual property regimes, but it would be incomplete if we did not acknowledge the histories of contestation, conflict, and violence that accompanied the first enclosure movement and its subsequent history').
90. For a common law example, see Pigeon J's dictum in *Burton Parsons Chemicals Inc v Hewlett-Packard (Can) Ltd* (1974) 17 CPR (2d) 97 at 106: 'inventors are not to be looked upon as Shylock claiming his pound of flesh'.

PART III, CHAPTER 8 NOTES

1. Goodie, *The Invention of the Environment*, at 160–161, 165; Mootz F. (1998), *Rhetorical Knowledge in Legal Practice and Theory*, 6 Southern California Interdisciplinary L. J. 491, at 576–584; Wickham G. (2000), *Foucault and Gadamer: Like Apples and Oranges Passing in the Night*, 76(2) Chicago-Kent L. Rev. 913, at 928–929, 937–941 [hereafter *Foucault and Gadamer*]; Edmond G. (2004), *Think Decisions: Expertise, Advocacy and Reasonableness in the Federal Court of Australia*, 74(3) Oceania 190–230 [hereafter *Think Decisions*]; Fitzpatrick P. (2001), *Modernism and the Grounds of Law*, Cambridge University Press; Anderson J. (2009), *Law, Knowledge, Culture: The Production of Indigenous Knowledge in Intellectual Property Law*, Edward Elgar, at 43 [hereafter *Law, Knowledge, Culture*]; and *Oshlack v Richmond River Council* (1998) 193 CLR 72, per Gaudron and Gummow JJ (especially paras 71–75).
2. Rutherford, *The Entry of Life in to History*, at 37. The role of expertise in the law is of particular note. See, Mitchell T. (2002), *Rule of Experts: Egypt, Technopolitics, Modernity*, University of California Press; and Rose N. (1993), *Government, Authority and Expertise in advanced Liberalism*, 22(3) Economy and Society 283.
3. In the context of standing and environmental law, the courts have been very careful to rely upon (so-called) objective rationale when subsuming public interest into the ambit of its legal authority. See, for example, *Oshlack v Richmond River Council* (1994) 82 LGERA 236 at 238. It is for this reason that in the case of *Right to Life Association (NSW) Inc v Department of Human Services and Health* (1995) 56 FCR 50; 28 ALR 238 there was a failure to successfully make the public interest claim within the standing context because the plaintiffs sought to rely upon a moral rationale rather than a scientific one. See Rutherford, *The Entry of Life in to History*, at 50–57.
4. Goodie, *The Invention of the Environment*, at 175–176.
5. *Australian Conservation Foundation Inc. v Commonwealth* (1980) 146 CLR 493.

6. Ibid, at 530. The willingness to expand the notion of 'special interest' was further consolidated in a string of Australian cases in the 1980s such as *Onus v Alcoa of Australia Ltd* (1981) 149 CLR 27; and *Ogle v Strickland* [1987] 13 FCR 306.
7. However, the Court did ultimately reject the standing of Harewood, who was simply a 'concerned citizen'. See *Australian Conservation Foundation Inc. v Minister for Resources* (1989) 19 ALD 70.
8. *Australian Conservation Foundation Inc. v Minister for Resources* (1989) 19 ALD 70 at 73. Indeed, during the 1980s, ACF (along with other environmental organisations) did become increasingly savvy and professional in their operations through a series of highly visible campaigns relating to nationally contentious environmental issues such as the damming of the Franklin River in Tasmania. For a useful synopsis in this regard, see Bonyhady T. (1993), *Places Worth Keeping: Conservationists, Politics and the Law*, Allen and Unwin.
9. Goodie, *The Invention of the Environment*, at 146–147.
10. *Oshlack v Richmond River Council* (1994) 82 LGERA 236 at 238. Justice Stein's judgment was overturned by the High Court with Justice McHugh dismissing the appeal of the 'concerned citizen' based on the rationale that the case was not in the 'public interest' and that in coming to a contrary view the trial judge was simply influenced by a 'social preference'. For useful commentary, see Goodie, *The Invention of the Environment*, at 166–167.
11. Guibault and Hugenholtz (eds), *The Future of the Public Domain*, at 5; Cohen, *Copyright, Commodification and Culture* (arguing that the initial American usage of the term 'public domain' referred to as yet unsettled lands in the Western US); Samuelson, *Challenges in Mapping the Public Domain*, at 19; Ochoa, *Origins and Meanings of the Public Domain*, at 246 (arguing that it was not until the early twentieth century that 'public domain' was used to represent IPR-free information resources). Indeed, cross-citation of patent cases in public lands cases and vice versa was common; and in fact the document that transferred title to land that was formally part of the physical public domain was also called a patent. See Cohen, *Copyright, Commodification and Culture*, at 130.
12. Boyle, *The Second Enclosure Movement*, Part II generally.
13. Stone, *Should Trees Have Standing?*, at 18, citing *Santa Clara County v Southern Pac. R. R.*, 118 U.S. 394 (1886).
14. Sun, *Toward a Public Trust Doctrine in Copyright Law*, at 8; Araiza W. (1997), *Democracy, Distrust, and the Public Trust: Process-based Constitutional Theory, the Public Trust Doctrine, and the Search for a Substantive Environmental Value*, 45 UCLA L. Rev. 385, at 395 [hereafter *Democracy, Distrust, and the Public Trust*] (quoting The Institutes of Justinian bk, 2, tit. 1, pts. 1–6, at 65 (J. Thomas trans., 1975)); and Ryan, *Cyberspace as Public Space*, at 696.
15. Bloch M. (1966), *French Rural History: An Essay on its Basic Characteristics*, University of California Press, at 183.
16. Ibid.
17. *Illinois Central Railroad v Illinois*, 146 US 387 (1892).
18. Ryan, *Cyberspace as Public Space*, at 697; Araiza, *Democracy, Distrust and the Public Trust*, at 396–397.
19. Sax J. (1970), *The Public Trust Doctrine in Natural Resources Law: Effective Judicial Intervention*, 68 Mich. L. Rev. 471, at 478–489 [hereafter *The Public Trust Doctrine in Natural Resources Law*].
20. Ibid, at 491–565.
21. Takacs D. (2008), *The Public Trust Doctrine, Environmental Human Rights, and the Future of Private Property*, 16 NYU Environmental L. J. 711, at 732–733. Note in particular the Ecuadorian initiatives to embed rights of nature in the Ecuador Constitution. See, for example, Arsel M. (2012), *Between 'Marx and Markets'? The*

State, the 'Left Turn' and Nature in Ecuador, 103(2) Tijdshrift voor economische en sociale geografie 150, at 150–151. Also, note that recently the Whanganui River in New Zealand has become a legal entity provisioned with a legal voice as a consequence of an agreement struck between the New Zealand government and the Whanganui River iwi. See http://www.nzherald.co.nz/nz/news/article.cfm?c_id=1&objectid=10830586 (cited 13/9/2012).

22. See, for example, Earth Law Center website: www.earthlawcenter.org (cited 3/5/2013). Also, parallel approaches can be found in Helfer L. (2007), *Toward a Human Rights Approach Framework for Intellectual Property*, 40 University of California Davis L. Rev. 6; Vadi V. (2008), *Sapere Aude! Access to Knowledge as a Human Right and a Key Instrument of Development*, 12 International Journal of Communication Law and Policy 345, at 350 (arguing that 'access to knowledge is a basic human right, and that restrictions on access ought to be the exception, not the other way around'); and Olwan R. (2011), *Intellectual Property and Development: Theory and Practice*, QUT PhD Thesis, submitted May 2011 under the supervision of Professor Brian Fitzgerald, unpublished, at 91.
23. Lazarus R. (1986), *Changing Conceptions of Property and Sovereignty in Natural Resources: Questioning the Public Trust Doctrine*, 71 Iowa L. Rev. 631, at 644, especially footnote 7 (naming a plethora of state cases involving the public trust doctrine); and Ryan, *Cyberspace as Public Space*, at 697.
24. Ryan, *Cyberspace as Public Space*, at 698; and *Town of Orange v Resnick*, 94 Conn 573, 578 (1920).
25. Rose, *The Comedy of the Commons*, at 713.
26. Ibid, at 774–781. See also Rose C. (1998), *Joseph Sax and the Idea of the Public Trust*, 25 Ecology L. Q. 351, at 359–360.
27. Rose, *The Comedy of the Commons*, at 774–781.
28. Rose C. (2003), *Romans, Roads, and Romantic Creators: Traditions of Public Property in the Information Age*, 66(1/2) Law and Contemporary Problems 89.
29. Sun, *Toward a Public Trust Doctrine in Copyright Law*, at 32, 35.
30. *Illinois Central Railroad v Illinois*, 146 US 387 (1892) at 452–453.
31. Chon, *Postmodern 'Progress'*; and Ryan, *Cyberspace as Public Space*. However, note that the application of the public trust doctrine to the information environment was ultimately unsuccessful in *Eldred v Reno* 74 F. Supp. 2d 1 (DDC 1999), aff'd, *Eldred v Reno*, 239 F 3d 372 (DC Cir 2001), aff'd sub nom *Eldred v Ashcroft*, 537 US 186 (2003).
32. Chon, *Postmodern 'Progress'*, at 102, referring to Sax, *The Public Trust Doctrine in Natural Resources Law*.
33. Sax J. (1999), *Playing Darts with a Rembrandt: Public and Private Rights in Cultural Treasures*, University of Michigan Press, at 3; and Ryan, *Cyberspace as Public Space*, at 711.
34. Sun, *Toward a Public Trust Doctrine in Copyright Law*, at 16, referring to *Hague v Committee for Indus. Organization* 307 US 496, 515 (1939).
35. *Hague v Committee for Indus. Organization* 307 US 496, 515 (1939). See also *Frisby v Schultz*, 487 US 474, 480 (1988) ('No particularised inquiry into the precise nature of a specific street is necessary; all public streets are held in the public trust and are property considered traditional public fora'). Also Ryan, *Cyberspace as Public Space*, at 702–703.
36. Lessig, *Code 2.0*, at 174–175.
37. In *re Water Use Permit Applications*, 94 Hawai'i 97, 142 (2000); *In re Waiolo O Molokai, Inc* 103 Hawai'i 401, 432 (2004); Brown C. (2006), *Drinking from a Deep Well: The Public Trust Doctrine and Western Water Law*, 34 Fla. St. U. L. Rev. 1, at 4.

38. As outlined in Chapter 7, balancing the public and private aspects of intellectual property is one of the core aims of IPRs.
39. *CCH Canadian Ltd v Law Society of Upper Canada* [2004] 1 SCR 339 at para. 48 (emphasis added), partly cited in Patry W. (2009), *Moral Panics and the Copyright Wars*, Oxford University Press, at 127.
40. Found at: http://sites.state.pa.us/PA_Constitution.html (cited 3/5/2013). See also, Klass A. (2006), *Modern Public Trust Principles: Recognizing Rights and Integrating Standards*, 82 Notre Dame Law Review 699; and Kirsch, M. (1997), *Upholding the Public Trust in State Constitutions*, 46 Duke L. J. 1169.
41. Sun, *Toward a Public Trust Doctrine in Copyright Law*, at 4.
42. For the idea of public use of reason see Habermas J. (1989), *The Structural Transformation of the Public Sphere: An Inquiry into a Category of Bourgeois Society*, Polity Press (T Burger trans.), at 27.
43. See, for example, *Matthews v Bay Head Improvement Association*, 95 NJ 306 (1984).
44. Cited in Carlisle C. (1993–1994), *The Audio Home Recording Act of 1992*, 1 J. Intell. Prop. L. 335, at 340, footnote 37.
45. *Eldred v Reno* 74 F. Supp. 2d 1 (D.D.C. 1999) (No 1:99CV00065), Second amended complaint found at: www.cyber.law.harvard.edu/eldredvreno/cyber/complaint_amd2.html (cited 3/5/2013). See also, Ryan, *Application of the Public-Trust Doctrine and Principles of Natural Resource Management to Electromagnetic Spectrum*, at 348.
46. 74 F. Supp. 2d at 3–4. See also, Ryan, *Application of the Public-Trust Doctrine and Principles of Natural Resource Management to Electromagnetic Spectrum*, at 348–349.
47. *Eldred v Reno*, 74, F. Supp. 2d 1 (DDC 1999) at 3–4.
48. See *Eldred v Ashcroft*, 537 U.S. 186 (2003). For further commentary, see Ryan, *Application of the Public-Trust Doctrine and Principles of Natural Resource Management to Electromagnetic Spectrum*, at 349.
49. This was a view adopted by Professor Anthony Falzone at the 20th Annual Intellectual Property Law & Policy Conference, 11–13 April 2012, Fordham University School of Law, New York, USA (informal discussion). Falzone was a legal representative in the Golan matter.
50. There is some evidence that the requisite 'broad based support within the polity' is amassing as symbolised by recent legislative initiatives in Australia such as the Lifting the Bar Bill along with the Private Members Bill floated by Melissa Parke. See http://www.abc.net.au/news/2012-05-14/mp-urges-labor-to-back-gene-patenting-overhaul/4010612 (cited 6/9/2012).
51. *Arnold v Mundy*, 6 N.J.L. 1, 71–78 (1821) cited in Ryan, *Cyberspace as Public Space*, at 696.
52. *State v Cleveland & Pittsburgh R.R.*, 94 Ohio St. 61, 80 113 NE 677, 682 (1916) cited in Sax, *The Public Trust Doctrine in Natural Resource Law*, at 486, footnote 46.
53. Ryan, *Cyberspace as Public Space*, at 696–697.
54. *In Re Complaint of Steuart Transp. Co*, 495 F Supp 38, 40 (1980); *National Audubon Society v Superior Court*, 33 Cal. 3d 419, 441 (Cal. 1983).
55. *National Audubon Society v Superior Court*, 33 Cal. 3d 419, 441 (Cal. 1983).
56. Sax, *The Public Trust Doctrine in Natural Resource Law*, at 509; and Ryan, *Cyberspace as Public Space*, at 699.
57. Section 25(2) of the Indian Patent Act (1970) gives the right to 'persons interested' to oppose patents in accordance with a process that is clearly outlined within the legislation. Recent Indian case law has demonstrated willingness to broaden the meaning of 'persons interested' within s 25(2). See, for example, the *Roche Valcyte*

decision (Chennai IPO) – decision on file. Also, for a good global overview of opposition systems see WIPO, *Opposition Systems*, Standing Committee on the Law of Patents, Fourteenth Session, Geneva, January 25–29, 2010 found at: www.wipo.int/edocs/mdocs/scp/en/scp_14/scp_14_5.pdf (cited 6/9/2012).

58. See Australian Corporations Act 2001 (Commonwealth), ss 236–237.
59. Araiza, *Democracy, Distrust, and the Public Trust*, at 398; Ryan, *Cyberspace as Public Space*, at 700.
60. Sax, *The Public Trust Doctrine in Natural Resource Law*, at 521–523.
61. The Peer to Patent project and the EFF's patent-busting project provide concrete examples of initiatives that already relate to this theoretical discussion. The author is indebted to Dr Nic Suzor from the Queensland University of Technology for this point. Also, see Rimmer, *Digital Copyright*, at 2–3, particularly footnotes 16–20 (discussing the organizational development of coalitions seeking to protect the public domain); and Drahos with Braithwaite, *Information Feudalism*, at 7–8, 16–17 (discussing the emergence of IPR activist coalitions in relation to health).
62. Schlozman K. and Tierney J. (1986), *Organized Interests and American Democracy*, Harper & Row. For an early example of a case relating to procedural fairness and the environment in the US see *D.C. Fedn of Civic Assns., Inc v Airis*, 391 F 2d 478 (DC Cir. 1968) (failure to hold public hearings) cited in Sax, *The Public Trust Doctrine in Natural Resource Law*, at 474, footnote 11 – see also 514; and Lee, *The Greenpeace of Cultural Environmentalism*, 16 Widener Law Review 1, at 3.
63. Sax, *The Public Trust Doctrine in Natural Resource Law*, at 486, 488–489.
64. Wirten E. (2006), *Out of Sight and Out of Mind: On the Cultural Hegemony of Intellectual Property (Critique)*, 20 (2–3) Cultural Studies 282–291, at 288; and Rimmer, *Digital Copyright*, at 5.
65. Goodie, *The Invention of the Environment*, at 160–161, 165; Mootz, *Rhetorical Knowledge in Legal Practice and Theory*, at 576–584; Wickham, *Foucault and Gadamer*, at 928–929, 937–941; Edmond, *Think Decisions*; Fitzpatrick, *Modernism and the Grounds of Law*; Anderson, *Law, Knowledge, Culture*, at 43; and *Oshlack v Richmond River Council* (1998) 193 CLR 72, per Gaudron and Gummow JJ [especially paras. 71–75].
66. There are parallels with romantic rhetoric as it relates to the physical environment, and the rhetoric associated with the preservation of the information commons. For instance, as Boyle states, cultural environmentalism is not just about lamenting the dark, but also lighting candles. Similar themes can be identified within nineteenth-century romantic rhetoric associated with the national park movement. That is, nineteenth-century Romantics such as Mill, Ruskin, Morris, Emerson, Thoreau, and Wordsworth were instrumental in celebrating authenticity, while also simultaneously rejecting the Enlightenment attitudes of the day – e.g. that humans could and should improve nature through reason, technology, science and economic liberalism – through their equivocation of industrialism (which they perceived as a detriment to morality, social order, human health and nature). See Pepper, *The Roots of Modern Environmentalism*, at 18, 76–77; and Chon, *Postmodern 'Progress'*, at 134–135 (arguing that two framers of the US Constitution – notably James Madison and Thomas Jefferson – provide a textual basis that links the Enlightenment to the postmodern 'Progress' project).
67. Opie J. (ed.) (1971), *Americans and the Environment: The Controversy over Ecology*, Lexington, cited in Pepper, *The Roots of Modern Environmentalism*, at 81–82. See also, Kirk, *Science & Uncertainty*, at 151.
68. Pepper, *The Roots of Modern Environmentalism*, at 81–82.
69. Muir J. (1898), *The Wild Parks and Forest Reservations of the West*, LXXXI Atlantic Monthly 15, at 15–16. See also, Pepper, *The Roots of Modern Environmentalism*, at 83.

70. Muir J. (1894), *The Mountains of California*, The Century Co., at 18.
71. Purdy, *Our Place in the World*, at 889; and Kirk, *Science & Uncertainty*, at 150–153.
72. Worster D. (2008), *A Passion for Nature: The Life of John Muir*, Oxford University Press, at 160–161, 226–227.
73. Kirk, *Science & Uncertainty*, at 150–153.
74. Taylor, *The Vital Landscape*, at 129.
75. Goodie, *The Invention of the Environment*, at 84–85.
76. Taylor, *The Vital Landscape*, at 125.
77. Thoreau H. (1888), *Walden, or Life in the Woods*, (Blake H. ed.), Houghton, Mifflin and Company, at 286.
78. Thoreau H. (1862) [2007], *Walking*, Arc Manor, at 26. See also, Pepper, *The Roots of Modern Environmentalism*, at 85–86.
79. Muir, *The Mountains of California*, at 22.
80. Purdy, *Our Place in the World*, at 925; Huth H. (1957), *Nature and the American: Three Centuries of Changing Attitudes*, University of Nebraska Press (1990), at 30–53.
81. For useful background information in relation to the emergence of national parks in the US, see Burns K. (2009) (Director), *The National Parks: America's Best Idea*, DVD documentary series, ISBN 978-0307268969.
82. Hutton D. and Connors L. (1999), *A History of the Australian Environmental Movement*, Cambridge University Press, at 76.
83. Ibid.
84. Purdy, *Our Place in the World*, at 925; Stegner W. (1955), *This Is Dinosaur: Echo Park Country and Its Magic Rivers*, Knopf.
85. Purdy J. (2012), *Our Place in the World: A New Relationship for Environmental Ethics and Law*, Draft (on file) at 53, footnotes 184–186 (especially footnote 186).
86. Purdy J. (2013), *Our Place in the World: A New Relationship for Environmental Ethics and Law*, 62 Duke Law Journal 857, at 867, 885 and 925.
87. Ibid, at 889 (author's emphasis).
88. Ibid, at 887.
89. Ibid, at 866.
90. Cobb E. (1977), *The Ecology of Imagination in Childhood*, Columbia University Press (arguing that imagination is also a critical component of protecting the physical environment).
91. Bollier D. (2008), *Viral Spiral: How the Commoners Built a Digital Republic of Their Own*, New Press, at 42. See also Frow J. (1998), *Public Domain and Collective Rights in Culture*, 13 IPJ 39–52; Sherman and Wiseman (2006), *Towards an Indigenous Public Domain*, at 260; Litman, *The Public Domain*, at 968; and Hunter, *Culture War*, at 1111 (arguing that the negative conception of the public domain has been common for some time, citing the US case of *Compo Corp v Day-Brite Lighting, Inc* 376 US 234, 237 (1964) as an example).
92. Boyle, *The Second Enclosure Movement*, at 69–74 (responding to Samuels E. (1993), *The Public Domain in Copyright Law*, 41 J. Copy. Soc'y USA 137–182, at 150, where he asked: what is gained by reifying the negative and imagining a 'theory' of the public domain?); and Birnhack, *More or Better?*, at 60.
93. Many involved in the NGO sector relating to the information commons often lament that they spend most of their time 'stopping bad things, rather than making good things'. See Lee, *The Greenpeace of Cultural Environmentalism*, at 47–48, especially footnote 333. Thus, by way of counterbalance, there is a need for rhetorical devices that support 'good things'.
94. Chon, *Postmodern 'Progress'*, at 130. Although national parks are generally state sponsored, there are examples of community-sponsored national parks as discussed

by Techera E. (2012), *Protecting Nature and Culture: Enhancing Legal Frameworks for the Protection of Natural Resources and Cultural Heritage in the Pacific*, ANU RegNet Conference: Innovation, Creativity, Access to Knowledge and Development in Pacific Island Countries, 24–25 September 2012 [hereafter *Protecting Nature and Culture*] (referring to the Samoan Fisher By-Laws and the Village Feno Act in the Solomon Islands, which empower the local community to establish by-laws that are in turn enforceable within state courts). Other examples include the Vanuatu Community Conserved Areas facilitated by the Environmental Management and Conservation Act. Conservation easements, as discussed at length by Molly Van Houweling, provide another option that might complement informational national parks. See Van Houweling M. (2007), *The New Servitudes*, 96 Geo. L. J. 885.

95. On 13 June 2012 the Australian Commonwealth Minister for Sustainability, Environment, Water, Population, and Communities, Tony Burke MP, used the rhetoric of national parks within the context of ocean conservation when he stated: 'What we've done is effectively create a national parks estate in the ocean'. See http://www.abc.net.au/news/2012-06-14/burke-announces-marine-parks-reserve/4069532?WT.svl=news1 (cited 14/6/2012).
96. Patterson L. and Lindberg S. (1991), *The Nature of Copyright, A Law of Users' Rights*, University of Georgia Press, at 2; Birnhack, *More or Better?*, at 60; and Lange D. (2003), *Reimagining the Public Domain*, 66 Law & Contemp. Probs. 463, at 470 (stating that the public domain is 'a place of refuge for creative expression … a place like home, where, when you go there, they have to take you in and let you dance'). As Boyle states: '[t]he public domain is not some gummy residue left behind when all the good stuff has been covered by property law. The public domain is the place we quarry the building blocks of our culture. It is, in fact, the *majority* of our culture. Or at least it has been.' See Boyle, *The Public Domain*, at 40. See also, Bannerman, *The Ins and Outs of the Public Domain*, at 168–169.
97. Cohen, *Copyright, Commodification and Culture*, at 157–158; Dinwoodie and Dreyfuss, *Patenting Science*, at 191.
98. Cohen, *Copyright, Commodification and Culture*, at 158.
99. While the resolution of these questions lies beyond the scope of this book, they provide a fruitful foundation for a future research programme. With respect to payment, in some countries the reproduction of works of art that have fallen into the public domain are subject to payment made to the state (i.e. *domain public payant*). Exemplary countries include Argentina, Bolivia, Cameroon, Hungary, Italy, Mexico and Uruguay. See Correa, *Access to Knowledge*, at 240.
100. Beyond the references forthcoming in the body of the book, there are examples of scholarship that draw the link between global public goods and national parks. For example, see Faunce, *Global Public Goods*, at 527.
101. Lange, *Recognising the Public Domain*; and Frosio, *Communia and the European Public Domain Project*, at 4.
102. See Lange, *Recognizing the Public Domain*; Lange, *Reimagining the Public Domain*, at 470; Boyle, *A Politics of Intellectual Property*, at 87–116; Samuelson, *Challenges in Mapping the Public Domain*, at 8; and Greenleaf and Bond, *'Public Rights' in Copyright*.
103. Drahos, *A Philosophy of IP*, at 64.
104. Cohen, *Copyright, Commodification and Culture*, at 136 (suggesting that 'the part of the public domain that contains the old and the archetypal is like a nature preserve, which one can visit to see rare creatures in their natural habitat'). Note, however, that Cohen does not necessarily advocate this approach as she believes that the public lands-based understanding of the public domain fares poorly as a metaphor when measured against the manner in which creative practice works – see ibid, at 137.

105. Samuelson, *Challenges in Mapping the Public Domain*, at 20.
106. See Guibault and Hugenholtz (eds), *The Future of the Public Domain*, at 351 (workshop discussion).
107. Boyle, *The Second Enclosure Movement*, at 48.

PART IV NOTES

1. For a good overview of the application of public choice theory to the environment, see Yandle, *Public Choice and the Environment*, at 590–592.
2. Boyle, *A Politics of Intellectual Property*, at 110.

PART IV, CHAPTER 9 NOTES

1. For instance, Buchanan denies the premise that there is a unique efficient allocation of resources as is sometimes claimed by welfare economists. For a discussion in this regard, see Farina, *Constitutional Economics I*, at 190.
2. Besley T. (2002), *Welfare Economics and Public Choice*, London School of Economics and Political Science, Unpublished, on file and found at: www.econ.lse.ac.uk/~tbesley/papers/welfpub.pdf (cited 6/5/2013); and Farina, *Constitutional Economics I*, at 200. Paul Samuelson once labelled public choice theory as 'welfare politics', underscoring the perceived interrelationship between welfare economics and public choice theory. See Samuelson P. (1954), *The Pure Theory of Public Expenditure*, 36(4) Review of Economics and Statistics 387, at 389. Also, see Buchanan, *Explorations into Constitutional Economics*, at 25.
3. Buchanan, *Explorations into Constitutional Economics*, at 25; Mitchell W. (2001), *The Old and New Public Choice: Chicago versus Virginia*, in Shughart and Razzolini (eds), *The Elgar Companion to Public Choice*, at 5 [hereafter *The old and new public choice*].
4. Generally speaking, welfare economics gravitates towards normative inquiry and public choice theory tends towards positivist inquiry. However, this positive/normative dichotomy as it relates to welfare economics and public choice theory is somewhat complex. See, for example, Buchanan J. (1989), *Constitutional Economics*, in Buchanan (ed.), *Explorations into Constitutional Economics*, at 57–58 (arguing that although constitutional economics tends to be positive in nature, it does offer potential for normative advice to the metaphorical member of the continuing constitutional convention); and at 58–59, stating that: 'Any positive analysis that purports to be of use in an ultimate normative judgment must reflect an informed comparison of the working properties of alternative sets of rules or constraints. This analysis is the domain of Constitutional Economics.'
5. Farina, *Constitutional Economics I*, at 200–201. See also, Wagner R. (1988), *The Calculus of Consent: A Wicksellian Retrospective*, in Rowley C. (1993), *Public Choice Theory, Vol III: The Separation of Powers and Constitutional Political Economy*, Edward Elgar, at 415–416; and Buchanan J. (1986), *Liberty, Market and State: Political Economy in the 1980s*, Wheatsheaf Books, at 23.
6. Besley, *Welfare Economics and Public Choice*, at 2 (according to the Leviathan approach politicians extract resources for themselves at the expense of citizens/voters); and Brennan G. and Buchanan M. (1980), *The Power to Tax: Analytical Foundations of a Fiscal Constitution*, Cambridge University Press.

7. According to Posner and Goetz, 'the economic analysis of law involves three distinct but related enterprises': (1) prediction of the effects of legal rules, (2) determination of the efficiency of legal rules, usually in order to recommend what the rules ought to be, and (3) prediction of what the legal rules will be. See Posner R. (1986), *Economic Analysis of Law*, Little, Brown and Company; and Goetz C. (1984), *Cases and Materials on Law and Economics*, West Publishing. David Friedman suggests that 'the first is primarily an application of price theory, the second of welfare economics and the third of public choice'. See Friedman D. (1987), *Law and Economics*, in *The New Palgrave – A Dictionary of Economics*, Vol III, at 144. Also see, White P. and Islam S. (2008), *Formulation of Appropriate Laws: A New Integrated Multidisciplinary Approach and an Application to Electronic Funds Transfer Regulation*, Springer, at 56; and Benson B. (2001), *Law and Economics*, in Shughart and Razzolini (eds), *The Elgar Companion to Public Choice*, at 547.
8. Buchanan J. and Tullock G. (1962), *The Calculus of Consent: Logical Foundations of Constitutional Democracy*, Michigan University Press. See also Chomsky N. and Herman E. (1988), *Manufacturing Consent: The Political Economy of the Mass Media*, Pantheon Books (arguing that the media radically distorts the flow of information at the behest of private commercial interests).
9. Public choice theory is exemplified by the following statement of the leader of the International Intellectual Property Alliance: 'The problem with the greens is they're not as united as we are.' See Drahos with Braithwaite, *Information Feudalism*, at 92.
10. Farber D. and Frickey P. (1991), *Law and Public Choice: A Critical Introduction*, University of Chicago Press, at 14–15.
11. Gray R., Owen D. and Adams C. (1996), *Accounting and Accountability*, Prentice Hall, at 37. See also, Foucault M. (1980), *Power/Knowledge* (Gordon C. ed.), Brighton. Foucault's perspective of power is presciently compatible with the networked society of the Internet age in that Foucault argued that power is 'exercised through a net-like organisation' (see ibid, at 91); and Trilling L. (1950), *The Liberal Imagination*, Viking, at xiv–xv (arguing that political (neo)pluralism requires a commitment to civil societies that are defined by distributed power and dynamic internal diversity).
12. Schmitt C. (1988), *The Crisis of Parliamentary Democracy* (E. Kennedy trans), MIT Press.
13. Ibid, at xviii and 6.
14. Duxbury N. (1997), *Trading in Controversy*, 45 Buff. L. Rev 615, at 621 (book review). See also, Ryan, *Cyberspace as Public Space*, at 706; Drahos with Braithwaite, *Information Feudalism*, Chapter 1 generally and 192–193 especially; Lemley M. (2000), *The Constitutionalization of Technology Law*, 15 Berkeley Tech. L. J. 529, at 532–534; Merges R. (2000), *One Hundred Years of Solitude: Intellectual Property Law, 1900–2000*, 88 Cal. L. Rev. 2187, at 2235–2236 [hereafter *One Hundred Years of Solitude*]; Samuelson P. (2004), *Should Economics Play a Role in Copyright Law and Policy?*, U. Ottawa L. & Tech J. 1, at 9–10; Sterk S. (1996), *Rhetoric and Reality in Copyright Law?*, 94 Mich. L. Rev. 1197, at 1244–1246; and Wu T. (2004), *Copyright's Communications Policy*, 103 Mich. L. Rev. 278, at 291–292.
15. For a discussion of the application of social contract to IPRs, see Drahos, *The Global Governance of Knowledge*, at 32. Also, Llewelyn M. (2005), *Schrodinger's Cat: An Observation on Modern Patent Law*, in Drahos P. (ed.) (2005), *Death of Patents*, Lawtext Publishing at 11, 56–59; and Benkler, *The Wealth of Networks*, at 268 (arguing that economic centralization and information production may not always correlate ad infinitum – the Internet in particular has exhibited the possibility of changing the equation).

16. The correlation between economic power and economic centralisation relies upon an 'institutional economics' perspective whereby 'power seems to be more broadly conceived of as something that shapes and creates markets rather than just something that is delivered through the pricing mechanism'. See Drahos, *A Philosophy of IP*, at 6–7, 159, 163. Also see, Commons J. (1934), *Institutional Economics*, Macmillan; Tool M. and Samuels W. (eds) (1989), *State, Society and Corporate Power* (2nd edition), Transaction Publishers. The abstract objects underpinning IPRs are a form of capital that facilitates the concentration of economic power, especially when the said objects concern resources like genes or seeds. See Veblen T. (1904) [1965], *The Theory of Business Enterprise*, Augustus M. Kelley, at 143.
17. Hayek F. (1944), *The Road to Serfdom*, Routledge, at 68, cited in Drahos, *A Philosophy of IP*, at 163.
18. Duxbury, *Trading in Controversy*; Ryan, *Cyberspace as Public Space*; at 706; Drahos with Braithwaite, *Information Feudalism*, at Chapter 1 generally and 192–193 especially; Lemley, *The Constitutionalization of Technology Law*, at 532–534; Merges, *One Hundred Years of Solitude*, at 2235–2236; Samuelson, *Should Economics Play a Role in Copyright Law and Policy?*, at 9–10; Sterk, *Rhetoric and Reality in Copyright Law?*, at 1244–1246; and Wu, *Copyright's Communications Policy*, at 291–292.
19. Benkler Y. (2003), *Through the Looking Glass: Alice and the Constitutional Foundations of the Public Domain*, 66(1/2) Law & Contemp. Probs. 173, at 196.
20. Lessig, *The Future of Ideas*, at 237.
21. For a discussion of the application of social contract to IPRs see Drahos, *The Global Governance of Knowledge*, at 32. See also, Llewelyn, *Schrodinger's Cat*, at 11, 56–59.
22. Buchanan and Tullock, *The Calculus of Consent*. See also Chomsky and Herman, *Manufacturing Consent* (where it is argued that the media radically distorts the flow of information at the behest of private commercial interests).
23. Buchanan and Tullock, *The Calculus of Consent*, at 46–48, 165–167, and 291.
24. Buchanan J. *et al* (1980), *Toward a Theory of the Rent-Seeking Society*, A & M University Press, at 294–295.
25. Indeed, Judge Posner has suggested that an interest group will find it efficient to expend up to $99.99 to obtain $100 of wealth transfer. See Posner R. (1975), *The Social Costs of Monopoly and Regulation*, 83 J. Pol. Econ. 807, at 812. See also Lemley, *Property, Intellectual Property, and Free Riding*, at 40–42 (especially footnotes 120–125).
26. Buchanan J. *et al*, *Toward a Theory of the Rent-Seeking Society*, at 40, 57, 68 and 117–118.
27. Boyle, *Cruel, Mean, or Lavish?*, at 2035; Litman J. (1987), *Copyright, Compromise and Legislative History*, 72 Cornell L. Rev. 857; and Benkler, *The Wealth of Networks*, at 319 (arguing that strong property rights aid the wealthy and that they led to increasing exclusive rights).
28. See generally Sell, *Private Power, Public Law*; Hope, *Biobazaar*, at 323; and Drahos with Braithwaite, *Information Feudalism*, at 11, 36–37 (arguing that IPRs are historically a 'protectionist weapon') along with 214 (stating that 'rent seeking through intellectual property rules brings with it high costs because included in those costs are the social costs that flow from not allowing knowledge to be freely available').
29. Drahos, *Six Minutes to Midnight*, at 36–37; Drahos with Braithwaite, *Information Feudalism*, at 84; and Shashikant S. (2009), *US Protectionism Increases Barriers to Climate-Friendly Technologies*, Third World Network, http://www.twnside.org.sg/

title2/climate/info.service/2009/climate.change.20090704.htm (cited 6/5/2013) (suggesting that the US legislative measures concerning IPRs and climate change are a form of protectionism).

30. Drahos with Braithwaite, *Information Feudalism*, at 196.
31. Macey, *Transaction Costs and the Normative Elements of the Public Choice Model*, at 490.
32. Tollison R. (1988), *Public Choice and Legislation*, 74 Va. L. Rev. 339, at 343.
33. Log-rolling is actually defined as 'the exchanging (buying or selling) of votes on specific issues by members of a legislative or other voting chamber'. See Rowley, *The Reason of Rules*, at 466. Tullock initially introduced log-rolling as an efficiency mechanism, but Rowley and other scholars have referred to the notion in derogatory terms. See Rowley C. (1988), *Rent Seeking in Constitutional Perspective*, in Rowley R., Tollison R. and Tullock G. (eds), *The Political Economy of Rent-Seeking*, Kluwer Academic Publishers; and Farina, *Constitutional Economics I*, at 190.
34. Benkler, *The Wealth of Networks*, at 319 (arguing that strong property rights aid the wealthy and that they lead to increasing exclusive rights); and Boyle, *Cruel, Mean, or Lavish?*, at 2035. See also, Litman, *Copyright, Compromise and Legislative History*.
35. Benkler, *The Wealth of Networks*, at 571.
36. Posner R. (2005), *Intellectual Property: The Law and Economics Approach*, 19(2) The Journal of Economic Perspectives, 57 at 59 (referring to the work of Arnold Plant (1934) in introducing the concept of 'rent seeking', although the term was not used in the first instance). Rent seeking is economically (and socially) troublesome because it results in several forms of deadweight loss. See, for example, Posner, *The Social Costs of Monopoly and Regulation*, at 812; and Macey, *Transaction Costs and the Normative Elements of the Public Choice Model*, at 478.
37. Drahos, *Six Minutes to Midnight*, at 36–37.
38. Ibid. For a discussion of *The Case of Monopolies* (1602) 11 Co Rep 84b, 77ER 1260 see Holdsworth, *A History of English Law*. See also, Drahos, *A Philosophy of IP*, at 30; and Fox H. (1947), *Monopolies and Patents: A Study of the History and Future of the Patent Monopoly*, University of Toronto Press.
39. Drahos, *A Philosophy of IP*, at 178; Drahos, *Six Minutes to Midnight*, at 36–37; and Rawls, *A Theory of Justice*, at 4 (arguing that allocation and distribution are mediated through the definition of property rights).
40. Lemley, *Property, Intellectual Property, and Free Riding*, at 40–42 (footnotes omitted). In relation to Lemley's first point, see Hope, *Biobazaar*, at 38, footnote 27 where Hope quotes John Sulston, one of the leaders on an international sequence collaboration who described the research atmosphere related to his project as one of mutual suspicion: 'Those who were working to map particular human genes either expected to secure patents on them, or were terrified that someone else would beat them to it.' This phenomenon is often referred to in the literature as a 'patent race' – see Greenhalgh and Rogers, *Innovation, Intellectual Property, and Economic Growth*, at 22, along with Chapters 6 and 11 generally.
41. Lemley, *Property, Intellectual Property, and Free Riding*, at 40–42 (footnotes omitted).
42. McChesney F. (1987), *Rent Extraction and Rent Creation in the Economic Theory of Regulation*, 16 J. Legal Stud. 101, at 103; Stigler G. (1971), *The Theory of Economic Regulation*, 2 Bell J. Econ. & Mgmt. Sci. 3, at 5–6.
43. Macey J. (1989), *Public Choice: The Theory of the Firm and the Theory of Market Exchange*, Yale Law School Faculty Scholarship Series, Paper 1748, at 49–50 [hereafter *Public Choice*].
44. Lee D. (1988), *Politics, Ideology, and the Power of Public Choice*, 74 Va. L. Rev. 191, at 197.

45. Macey, *Transaction Costs and the Normative Elements of the Public Choice Model*, at 513; and Drahos, *The Global Governance of Knowledge*.
46. Drahos with Braithwaite, *Information Feudalism*, Chapters 6, 10 and 11 generally. A concrete example is that 'whenever an important commercial asset such as Mickey Mouse or A. A. Milne's Winnie-the-Pooh threatens to fall into the public domain, because copyright protection is about to expire, ferocious lobbying takes place to extend the term of copyright protecting these assets'. See Drahos, *The Global Governance of Knowledge* at 177. Other scholars too have discussed the influence of corporate entities in shaping the IPR regulatory framework. For example, see Sell, *Private Power, Public Law*.
47. Drahos with Braithwaite, *Information Feudalism*, especially Chapter 6.
48. Buchanan and Tullock, *The Calculus of Consent*, at 46–48, 165–167.
49. Posner R. (1982), *Economics, Politics, and the Reading of Statutes and the Constitution*, 49 U. Chi. L. Rev. 263, at 263; Macey, *Public Choice*, at 46–47.
50. Ibid.
51. Becker G. (1983), *A Theory of Competition Among Pressure Groups for Political Influence*, 98 Q. J. Econ. 371, at 384–385; and Macey, *Public Choice*, at 46–47.
52. Olson M. (1965), *The Logic of Collective Action*, Harvard University Press. For a prescient, albeit brief, discussion of Olson's work as it relates to IPRs see Drahos, *A Philosophy of IP*, at 137–138.
53. Buchanan, *Constitutional Economics*, at 57–59, stating that: 'Any positive analysis that purports to be of use in an ultimate normative judgment must reflect an informed comparison of the working properties of alternative sets of rules or constraints. This analysis is the domain of Constitutional Economics.'
54. Buchanan and Tullock, *The Calculus of Consent*.
55. Azfar, *The Logic of Collective Action*, at 74 (arguing that 'the most visible collective action problem in today's world is the prevention of environmental degradation'). Azfar surmises (at 75) that 'the challenge is to design institutions that can elicit cooperation in protecting the environment without creating a world government'.
56. Boyle, *The Second Enclosure Movement*, at 72–73.
57. Edwald F. (1986), *Social Law*, in Teubner G. (ed.), *Dilemmas of Law in the Welfare State*, Walter de Gruyter at 50–52.
58. Goodie, *The Invention of the Environment*, at 150–151.
59. Edwald, *Social Law*, at 51.
60. For reference to the term 'institutional diversity' see Boyle, *Public Domain*, at 243, where Boyle refers to the term as meaning that various organisations have their own approaches to address issues relevant to the information commons movement.
61. Boyle J. (2007), *Cultural Environmentalism and Beyond*, 70 Law & Contemp. Probs. 5, at 18.
62. Ibid.
63. Ibid.
64. Boyle, *The Second Enclosure Movement*, at 72–73.
65. Ibid.
66. Kapczynski, *The Access to Knowledge Mobilization and the New Politics of Intellectual Property*, at 825–839; Krikorian and Kapczynski, *A2K in the Age of IP*, at 13 (where it is conceded that the label Access to Knowledge 'may not be the one that represents this new politics over time').
67. Kapczynski, *The Access to Knowledge Mobilization and the New Politics of Intellectual Property*, at 825–839. See also Lee, *The Greenpeace of Cultural Environmentalism*, at 3.
68. For a brief discussion regarding the speed and extent of environmental degradation, see: Azfar, *The Logic of Collective Action*, at 74–75.

69. See Kurtz L. (ed.) (2003), *Encyclopedia of Violence, Peace and Conflict*, Academic Press, at 269–278, See: http://www.sussex.ac.uk/Users/hafa3/cs.htm (cited 2/2/2010). There are other paradoxes inherent within civil society. For example, by relying on the work of Hegel, Drahos argues that 'the systems complexity of civil society, if unchecked, produces poverty at the same time that it produces luxury and wealth'. See Drahos, *A Philosophy of IP*, at 87. It is perhaps for this reason that Hegel argued that the ascendancy of civil society in relation to the state is ruinous (ibid, at 84–85).
70. Gramsci A. (1975), *Prison Notebooks*, Vol I, Columbia University Press, at 179. See also, Braithwaite J., Charlesworth H. and Soares A. (2012), *Networked Governance of Freedom and Tyranny*, ANU Press, at 129 [hereafter *Networked Governance of Freedom and Tyranny*] (arguing that 'it is possible for civil society to become an overwhelming source of domination', relying upon China's Cultural Revolution in the 1960s and the Ku Klux Klan in the US as exemplars).
71. Peter Drahos makes the point that 'civil society experiences an intellectual property consciousness' in that 'the vulnerability of abstract objects makes those elements of civil society most dependent on them put enormous pressure on the state to mint new forms of intellectual property protection'. See Drahos, *A Philosophy of IP*, at 85. Other scholars have argued that neoliberal economic ideology has generally triumphed over the political organisation strategies of both the environmental movement and the information environmental movement respectively. See Frow J. (2000), *Public Domain and the New World Order in Knowledge*, 10(2) Social Semiotics 173, at 182 (discussing the relationship between neoliberalism and the public domain).
72. Charney E. (1998), *Political Liberalism, Deliberative Democracy, and the Public Sphere*, 92(1) The American Political Science Review 97, at 98.
73. Schmitt, *The Crisis of Parliamentary Democracy*, at 5. For an exposition of responses to the 'calculation of interests', see Feher M., Krikorian G. and McKee Y. (eds) (2007), *Nongovernmental Politics*, Zone Books.
74. Carpignano *et al* (1993), *Chatter in the Age of Electronic Reproduction: Talk Television and the 'Public Mind'*, in Robbins B. (ed.), *The Phantom Public Sphere*, Minnesota University Press, at 97–98; and Ryan, *Cyberspace as Public Space*, at 714.
75. Vaidhyanathan S. (2007), *The Anarchist in the Coffee House: A Brief Consideration of Local Culture, the Free Culture Movement, and Prospects for a Global Public Sphere*, 70 Law and Contemporary Problems 205, at 205–206 [hereafter *The Anarchist in the Coffee House*].
76. Benkler, *The Wealth of Networks*, at 176–177. Drahos has also argued that 'networks are the best form of managing knowledge', *Indigenous Developmental Networks and the Adaptive Management of Intellectual Property*.
77. Vaidhyanathan, *The Anarchist in the Coffee House*, referring to Habermas.
78. A key enabler of the third space was a communicative revolution evidenced by the spread of literacy and the rise of cheap printing in Europe. As Habermas argued, the third space was virtually non-existent in Europe before the eighteenth century and by the closing of the nineteenth century it became subject to some considerable transformations. See Habermas J. (1962) [1989], *The Structural Transformation of the Public Sphere: An Inquiry into a Category of Bourgeois Society*, Polity; and Habermas J. (1992) [1996], *Between Facts and Norms: Contributions to a Discourse Theory of Law and Democracy*, Thomas McCarthy ed., William Regh trans., MIT Press. See also, Eisenstein E. (1979), *The Printing Press as an Agent of Change: Communications and Cultural Transformations in Early-Modern Europe*, Cambridge University Press.

79. There are a variety of critiques that can be directed at such Habermasian yearnings, including the fact that the public sphere which Habermas espoused was temporal and geographically specific – similar to Benedict Anderson's notion of 'imagined communities' – and therefore one needs to be exceptionally prudent when relating the public sphere to 'places' such as the Internet. See Anderson B. (1983) [1991], *Imagined Communities: Reflections on the Origin and Spread of Nationalism*, Verso. Also, disparities in wealth and accompanying lack of access to information technology create serious impediments to realising a Habermasian civil society. See Boyle, *A Theory of Law and Information*, at 1433 (footnote omitted). In particular, as Vaidhyanathan highlights, the Internet does not escape the hegemonic influence of the state and the market. See Vaidhyanathan S. (2005), *Remote Control: The Rise of Electronic Cultural Policy*, 597 Annals Am. Acad. Pol. & Soc. Sci. 1 [hereafter *Remote Control*]; and Vaidhyanathan, *Copyrights and Copywrongs*.
80. Benkler, *The Wealth of Networks*; Rheingold H. (2002), *Smart Mobs: The Next Social Revolution*, Perseus Publishing; and Rheingold H. (2000), *The Virtual Community: Homesteading on the Electronic Frontier*, MIT Press.
81. Vaidhyanathan, *Remote Control*; Vaidhyanathan, *Copyrights and Copywrongs*. See also Lessig L. (2004), *Free Culture: How Big Media Uses Technology and the Law to Lock Down Culture and Control Creativity*, Penguin; Boyle, *Shamans, Software, and Spleens*; Drahos and Braithwaite, *Information Feudalism*; Lessig, *The Future of Ideas*; Norris P. (2001), *Digital Divide: Civic Engagement, Information Poverty, and the Internet Worldwide*, Cambridge University Press (arguing that the 'digital divide' flows from the historical process of imperialist expansion of monopoly capital); and Atteberry, *Information/Knowledge*, at 345.
82. Ibid.
83. Of course, whether or not social production is a complement to the activities of civil society organisations depends upon further empirical research. Such works would seek to correlate the collective action problems with the economic efficiencies of social production.
84. Benkler, *The Wealth of Networks*, at 4; and Benkler, *Coase's Penguin, or, Linux and the Nature of the Firm*, at 383. See also, Schultz J. and Urban J. (2012), *Can Defensive Patent Licenses Prevent Threats to Open Innovation?*, Draft Only, unpublished, on file, at 15; Chesbrough H. (2003), *Open Innovation: The New Imperative for Creating and Profiting from Technology*, Harvard Business School Press; Chesbrough H. (2006), *Open Business Models: How to Thrive in the New Innovation Landscape*, Harvard Business School Press; Shirky C. (2008), *Supernova Talk: The Internet Runs on Love* (2008) available at http://www.shirky.com/herecomeseverybody/2008/02 /supernova-talk-the-internet-runs-on-love.html (cited 28/12/2010); and Shirky C. (2008), *Here Comes Everybody: The Power of Organizing Without Organizations*, Penguin.
85. Boyle, *The Second Enclosure Movement*, at 47.
86. Benkler, *The Wealth of Networks*, at 4.
87. Emphasis added. Benkler, *The Idea of Access to Knowledge and the Information Commons*, at 231.
88. See, for example, Sunstein C. (2006), *Infotopia: How Many Minds Produce Knowledge*, Oxford University Press [hereafter *Infotopia*]; Ghosh R. (ed.) (2005), *CODE: Collaborative Ownership and the Digital Economy*, MIT Press [hereafter *CODE*]; Shirky, *Here Comes Everybody*; von Hippel E. (2005), *Democratizing Innovation*, MIT Press; Hunter D. and Lastowka G. (2004), *Amateur-to-Amateur*, 46 William & Mary L. Rev. 951–1030; and Zittrain J. (2008), *The Future of the Internet – And How to Stop It*, Yale University Press.

89. Social production does not necessarily equate to commodification. For a discussion concerning the limits of commodification within the social context see Radin M. (1987), *Market-Inalienability*, 100 Harv. L. Rev. 1849, at 1870–1877.
90. Although Bill Nichols is often credited for creating the term 'distributed creativity', he is not necessarily associated with that phrase. Nichols B. (2000), *The Work of Culture in the Age of Cybernetic Systems*, Rutgers University Press; and Benkler, *The Wealth of Networks*. There are many other works. See, for example, Sunstein, *Infotopia*; Ghosh, *CODE*; Shirky, *Here Comes Everybody*; von Hippel, *Democratizing Innovation*; Hunter and Lastowka, *Amateur-to-Amateur*; Zittrain, *The Future of the Internet – And How to Stop It*; and Hope, *Biobazaar*, at 107 (referring to distributed creativity as 'bazaar governance').
91. Benkler, *The Wealth of Networks*, at 60.
92. Frischmann, *Cultural Environmentalism and The Wealth of Networks*, at 1111.
93. Benkler, *The Wealth of Networks*, at 60, 275–276, although some large-scale social production projects evolve hierarchical administration mechanisms. See, for example, Hope, *Biobazaar*, at 131.
94. Benkler, *The Wealth of Networks*, at 60.
95. Ibid, at 62–63.
96. Ibid.
97. Nelson R. (1959), *The Simple Economics of Basic Scientific Research*, 67 J. Pol. Econ. 297; Eisenberg R. (1996), *Public Research and Private Development: Patents and Technology Transfer in Government-Sponsored Research*, 82 Va. L. Rev. 1663, at 1715–1724; and David P. (1997), *From Market Magic to Calypso Science Policy*, 26 Res. Pol'y 229.
98. Benkler, *Coase's Penguin, or Linux and The Nature of the Firm*. See also Benkler, *Sharing Nicely*, at 381–382.
99. Benkler, *From Consumers to Users*, at 562–563; and Lessig, *The Future of Ideas*, at 23–25; Benkler, *Coase's Penguin, or Linux and The Nature of the Firm*.
100. Lessig, *The Future of Ideas*, at 23–25.
101. Opderbeck D. (2004), *The Penguin's Genome, or Coase and Open Source Biotechnology*, 18 Harvard J. of Law & Technology 167, at 170–171.
102. The different layers of technology is a topic that is definitely in need of further research, particularly within the domain of technological innovation as it relates to biotechnology and nanotechnology. While Lessig and Benkler have discussed the ideas below, Hope's work is also useful here. See Hope, *Biobazaar*, at 201–203.
103. Lessig, *The Future of Ideas*, at 23–25. However, in this regard, the content layer of Wikipedia is of some interest.
104. Ibid, at 23–25, 92.
105. Benkler, *Coase's Penguin, or, Linux and the Nature of the Firm*, at 408.
106. Hope, *Biobazaar*, at 107. See also Demil B. and Lecocq X. (2006), *Neither Market nor Hierarchy nor Network: The Emergence of Bazaar Governance*, 27(10) Organization Studies 1447; Williamson, *The Economic Institutions of Capitalism*; Williamson O. (1991), *Comparative Economic Organisation: The Analysis of Discrete Structural Alternatives*, 36(2) Administrative Science Quarterly 233; and De Alessi, *Property Rights*, at 33 (arguing that 'the basic economic choices are when, how, what, and how much to produce, who receives it, who bears the risk, and who decides').
107. Benkler, *Coase's Penguin, or, Linux and the Nature of the Firm*, at 408.
108. Ibid, at 409.
109. Ibid, at 410–411.
110. Brint.com, *What Is Knowledge Management?*, at http://www.brint.com/km/kmdefs.htm (cited 29/01/2010). See also, Eric Raymond's reference to the leaky nature of hierarchies, relaying the decentralist sentiments of Pyotr Kropotkin: 'Having been

brought up in a serf-owner's family, I entered active life, like all young men of my time, with a great deal of confidence in the necessity of commanding, ordering, scolding, punishing and the like. But when, at an early stage, I had to manage serious enterprises ... I began to appreciate the difference between acting on the principle of command and discipline and acting on the principle of common understanding. The former works admirably in a military parade, but it is worth nothing where real life is concerned, and the aim can be achieved only through the severe effort of many converging wills.' See Raymond E. (1998), *The Cathedral and the Bazaar*, 3(3) First Monday, March, http://firstmonday.org/htbin/cgiwrap/bin/ojs/index.php/fm/issue/view/90, (cited 29/01/2010).

111. Benkler, *Coase's Penguin, or, Linux and the Nature of the Firm*, at 412.
112. Ibid, at 414.
113. Ibid, at 406–407.
114. Ibid, at 415–416.
115. Ibid, at 422.

PART IV, CHAPTER 10 NOTES

1. Benkler, *Coase's Penguin, or, Linux and the Nature of the Firm*, at 381. For coverage of the term 'uncodified' see Cunningham, *The Separation of (Economic) Power*.
2. Buchanan, *Constitutional Economics*, at 57.
3. Van den Hauwe, *Constitutional Economics II*, at 223. See also Buchanan, *Constitutional Economics*, at 58–59 (discussing how Adam Smith was ultimately engaged in contrasting alternative institutional/constitutional structures, and as part of this comparative analysis it was imperative to offer an explanation of how markets operate in the absence of political directives).
4. Buchanan, *The Domain of Constitutional Economics*, at 2–3; and Brennan G. and Hamlin A. (2001), *Constitutional Choice*, in Shughart and Razzolini (eds), *The Elgar Companion to Public Choice*, at 117.
5. Van den Hauwe, *Constitutional Economics II*, at 223–224.
6. Brennan and Hamlin, *Constitutional Choice*, at 117.
7. Van den Hauwe, *Constitutional Economics II*, at 223–224.
8. Shughart and Razzolini (eds), *The Elgar Companion to Public Choice*, at xxx.
9. Buchanan, *The Domain of Constitutional Economics*, at 1 (relaying that 'Richard B. McKenzie introduced the term *constitutional economics* to define the central subject matter of a Heritage Foundation conference that he organised in Washington, D.C., in 1982'). See also Van den Hauwe, *Constitutional Economics II*, at 223.
10. Brennan and Hamlin, *Constitutional Choice*, at 117.
11. Hayek (1973), *Law, Legislation and Liberty: A New Statement of the Liberal Principles of Justice and Political Economy*, Routledge and Kegan Paul, at 134–135. See also, Kelsen H. (1978), *Pure Theory of Law: Legality and Legitimacy*, University of California Press; and Farina, *Constitutional Economics I*, at 191–192.
12. Rowley, *The Reason of Rules*, at 440.
13. Farina, *Constitutional Economics I*, at 188–189, 190.
14. Ibid, at 191–192.
15. Ibid. See also, Benson, *Law and Economics*, at 562.
16. Weinhast B. (1995), *The Economic Role of Political Institutions: Market-preserving Federalism and Economic Development*, 11 J. of Law, Economics and Organization 1, at 1.

17. Decentralisation was a critical dimension of the *modularity* ecological principle discussed in Part III with reference to resilience.
18. Shughart and Razzolini (eds), *The Elgar Companion to Public Choice*, at xxxi; *The Federalist Papers No. 51* (1787–1788), at 356.
19. For judicial authority to this effect, see *R v Davison* (1954) 90 CLR 353 at 380–381 (HCA) per Kitto J (pronouncing, in relation to the three branches of government, that: '… it is necessary for the protection of the individual liberty of the citizen that these three functions should be to some extent dispersed rather than concentrated in one set of hands …').
20. Farina, *Constitutional Economics I*, at 194.
21. Ibid, at 196.
22. Ibid, at 194–195.
23. Although Locke popularised the decentralisation of horizontal power during the Enlightenment, the idea can perhaps be traced back to ancient Greece.
24. Farina, *Constitutional Economics I*, at 194–195.
25. Ibid, at 194.
26. Cohler A. *et al.* (eds) (1989), *Montesquieu: The Spirit of the Laws*, Cambridge University Press, at 156–166 [hereafter *Montesquieu*]. See also Patterson F. (ed.) (1932), *The Works of John Milton*, Vol. V, Columbia University Press, at 132 (where it is argued that 'In all wise Nations the Legislative Power, and the judicial execution of that power have bin (sic) most commonly distinct, and in several hands: but yet the former supreme, the other subordinat'); and Rossiter C. (ed.) (1961), *The Federalist*, Mentor Books, at 322, relaying *Federalist Papers No. 51* where James Madison states: 'If men were angels no government would be necessary. If angels were to govern men, neither external nor internal controls on government would be necessary. In framing a government which is to be administered by men over men, the great difficulty lies in this: You must first enable the government to control the governed; and in the next place, oblige it to control itself. A dependence on the people is no doubt the primary control on the government, but experience has taught mankind the necessity of auxiliary precautions.' See also, Clark D. (2010), *Principles of Australian Public Law* (3rd edition), LexisNexis Butterworths, at 84. The work of John Locke is also often relied upon in this context. For example, see Laslett P. (ed.) (1965), *John Locke: Two Treatises of Government*, Mentor Books, at 410; and Farina, *Constitutional Economics I*, at 194.
27. Cohler, *Montesquieu*, at 157. This passage is also cited by Gummow J in *Grollo v Palmer* (1995) 185 CLR 348 at 393 (HCA).
28. Cox E. (2000), *Adding Ethics and Equity to the Economic Equation*, 82 Chain Reaction, Autumn, at 2–3, referring to the German academic Clause Offe.
29. Long R. (2008), *Market Anarchism as Constitutionalism*, in Long R. and Machan T. (eds), *Anarchism/Minarchism: Is a Government Part of a Free Country?*, Ashgate.
30. Farina, *Constitutional Economics I*, at 194–195.
31. Cox, *Adding Ethics and Equity to the Economic Equation*. A macro approach to competition policy concurs with the diversity principle advocated within the ecology chapter (with reference to resilience).
32. Fitzgerald B. *et al* (2002), *Internet and E-Commerce Law: Technology, Law and Policy*, Thomson Lawbook Co, at 25–27; Drahos with Braithwaite, *Information Feudalism*, at 3 (arguing that the power of states has been weakened by the forces of globalisation). Drahos and Braithwaite (ibid, at 11) inquire: '[why do states] give up sovereignty over something as fundamental as the property laws that determine the ownership of information and the technologies that so profoundly affect the basic rights of their citizens?'. See also, Drahos, *The Global Governance of Knowledge*, at 318–321 (implying that there is evidence to support the argument that the global private governance that underpins the international patent standards facilitates state

sovereignty erosion); Braithwaite, Charlesworth and Soares, *Networked Governance of Freedom and Tyranny*, at 291, arguing that '[T]he 2008 financial crisis was not caused by a failure of a tripartite separation of powers in the public sector, but by a failure of powers to be sufficiently separated within the private sector. More profoundly, there was a failure of public powers to be sufficiently separated from Wall Street power in enforcing regulations that required these culpable private powers to be separated.' See also, Brown W. (2005), *Neoliberalism and the End of Liberal Democracy*, in *Edgework: Critical Essays on Knowledge and Politics*, Princeton University Press, at 40, 46–53 (arguing that the market has become the dominant organisation principle of states, individuals and society).

33. Fitzgerald *et al*, *Internet and E-Commerce Law*, at 25–27.
34. Hamilton M. (2000), *Database Protection and the Circuitous Route Around the United States Constitution*, in Charles Rickett and Graeme Austin (eds), *International Intellectual Property and the Common Law World*, Hart Publishing; Benkler, *Free as the Air to Common Use*; Lessig L. (1999), *Code and Other Laws of Cyberspace*, Basic Books; Balkin J. (2004), *Virtual Liberty: Freedom to Design and Freedom to Play in Virtual Worlds*, 90 Virginia L. Rev. 2043; and Benkler Y. (2001), *Property, Commons and the First Amendment: Toward a Core Common Infrastructure*, found at www.benkler.org/WhitePaper/pdf (cited 6/5/2013) at 8. For established case law arguably in conflict with this view, see *San Francisco Arts and Athletics Inc v US Olympics Committee* 483 US 522 (1987); *Harper & Row Publishers Inc v Nation Enterprises* 471 US 539 (1985); *Zacchini v Scripps-Howard Broadcasting Co* 433 US 562 (1977); and *Eldred v Ashcroft* 537 US 186 (2003).
35. Fitzgerald *et al*, *Internet and E-Commerce Law*, at 25–27.
36. Fitzgerald B. (2005), *The Playstation Mod Chip: A Technological Guarantee of the Digital Consumer's Liberty or Copyright Menace/Circumvention Device?*, found at: http://www.law.qut.edu.au/staff/lsstaff/fitzgerald.jsp (cited 3/2/2009). An earlier and shorter version of this paper appears in 10 Media and Arts L. Rev. 89 (2005).
37. The hybridisation of production is reflected in the world at large in that the state, the firm, the market and society perform many complementary tasks. Indeed, '[t]heir complementary coexistence and relative salience as organizational forms for various social activities determine the allocation of resources in our society'. See Lee, *The Greenpeace of Cultural Environmentalism*, at 4. Professor Kathy Bowrey pointed this out to the author at the IP Academics Conference at UNSW in 2011. See also, Benkler, *The Wealth of Networks*, at 46–47; and Boyle, *Public Domain*, at 190.
38. See, for example, Koepsell, *Innovation and Nanotechnology*, at 161. Also, Chon, *Public-Private Partnerships in Global Intellectual Property* (where she argued that PPPs 'can do things that neither the states or markets can do …'). A quintessential PPP as it relates to IPRs is perhaps the 'complex operational interplay between public and private [as] illustrated in the highly topical instance of the patenting of BRCA1 and BRCA2 genes' as discussed in Taubman, *A Typology of Intellectual Property Management for Public Health Innovation and Access*, at 13. On one level the US Bayh-Dole Act (1980) also exemplifies the PPP approach in that the legislation was based on the assumption that 'governments are ill-suited and under-funded to undertake the management of IP that is required to bring an invention to the public in the form of a practical product, even where the underlying research is financed by the public purse' (ibid, at 15).
39. This hybridisation of production between society and the firm enables the addition of Creative Commons licensing information for works in popular Microsoft Office applications. With reference to this project, Lawrence Lessig enthused: 'We're incredibly excited to work with Microsoft to make that ability easily available to the hundreds of millions of users of Microsoft Office'. See Microsoft and the Creative Commons (2006), Microsoft and Creative Commons release Tool for Copyright

Licensing, 20 June cited in Rimmer, *Digital Copyright*, at 269. In the context of health, Taubman argues that 'a hybrid mix of forms of knowledge management will be employed along the full, extended pipeline of actual product development'. See Taubman, *A Typology of Intellectual Property Management for Public Health Innovation and Access*, at 11. For an excellent summary of the different hybridisation options with respect to IPRs, see ibid, at 12–13 and for a general discussion of PPPs as they relate to health and IPRs see ibid, at 17–22. See also Taubman A. (2004), *A Public-Private Management of Intellectual Property for Public Health Outcomes in the Developing World: The Lessons of Access Conditions in Research and Development Agreements*, Initiative on Public-Private Partnerships for Health Geneva; Rimmer, *IP and Climate Change*, at 329–332 (discussing GreenXchange, although note the critique at 332).

40. See De Alessi, *Property Rights*, at 34.
41. Benkler, *The Wealth of Networks*, at 60. Although note that some large-scale social production projects evolve hierarchical administration mechanisms. See, for example, Hope, *Biobazaar*, at 131; and Weber S. (2004), *The Success of Open Source*, Harvard University Press, at 185–189.
42. Hope, *Biobazaar*, at 107. See also Demil B. and Lecocq X. (2006), *Neither Market nor Hierarchy nor Network: The Emergence of Bazaar Governance*, 27(10) Organization Studies 1447; Williamson O. (1985), *The Economic Institutions of Capitalism*, Free Press; and Williamson, *Comparative Economic Organisation*; and De Alessi, *Property Rights*, at 33 (arguing that 'the basic economic choices are when, how, what, and how much to produce, who receives it, who bears the risk, and who decides').
43. Smith, *The Wealth of Nations*, Book 5, Chapter 1, Part 3, Of the Expence of Public Works and Public Institutions, cited in Hope, *Biobazaar*, at 132, footnote 52.
44. Azfar, *The Logic of Collective Action*, at 77–78.
45. Ibid.
46. Coupling the perspective that the creation of laws is a type of state production with Coasian/Demsetzian understandings of the market and the firm (discussed in Part I and further below), we can note that the state is much more likely to 'buy' office supplies externally but 'produce' foreign policy internally. See De Alessi, *Property Rights*, at 51.
47. While property is perhaps the most important law 'produced' by the state in the attempt to overcome the externalities market failure, many forms of regulation can in fact be perceived as 'internalising instrumentalities'. For instance, the fact that a careless driver must pay for the harm to the property of another exemplifies the internalisation of (negative) externalities within tort law. See Harrison, *A Positive Externalities Approach to Copyright Law*, at 5–6; and Buchanan J. and Faith R. (1989), *Entrepreneurship and the Internalisation of Externalities*, in Buchanan (ed.), *Explorations into Constitutional Economics*, at 406–407 (arguing that the law internalises these costs through a liability rule rather than a property rule). The property rule is one amongst a host of techniques that can be relied upon to internalise externalities. Other exemplars include the liability rule, regulation and taxation. A similar analysis could be applied to contract law and criminal law. See Stone, *Should Trees Have Standing?*, at 27.
48. Smith, *The Wealth of Nations*, Book 5, Chapter 1, Part 3, Of the Expence of Public Works and Public Institutions, cited in Hope, *Biobazaar*, at 132, footnote 52.
49. That is, Pigou would operationalise state intervention through the taxing (subsidising) of those who engage in negative (positive) externalities at a level that takes into account the external effects of the activity in question so as to align private and

social costs (benefits). See Frischmann, *Spillover Theory and Its Conceptual Boundaries*, at 808; Greenhalgh and Rogers, *Innovation, Intellectual Property, and Economic Growth*, at 24–25 referring to Pigou, *The Economics of Welfare*. See also Baumol and Wilson (eds), *Welfare Economics*, at 369–392, extracting Pigou A. (1912), *Wealth and Welfare*, Part II, Chapter VII, Macmillan and Co, at 148 (arguing that 'in certain cases, self-interest left to itself does not tend to bring about equality of marginal net products, and that, therefore, in these cases certain specific acts of interference with the free play of self-interest are likely, not to diminish, but to increase the national dividend'). Although compare a contemporary defence of the Pigouvian perspective written by Baumol W. (1972), *On Taxation and the Control of Externalities*, LXII(3) American Economic Review, June, 307–322; Baumol and Wilson (eds), *Welfare Economics*, at 81–96.

50. In relation to the Coasian perspective, De Alessi reminds: '[h]ow well the market works depends on the extent to which property rights are fully allocated, privately held and voluntarily transferable.' See De Alessi, *Property Rights*, at 33. Similar sentiments can be expressed in relation to the activities of firms.
51. Frischmann, *Spillover Theory and Its Conceptual Boundaries*, at 808, especially footnotes 27–31.
52. Hope, *Biobazaar*, at 108. Of course, IPRs allow a price to be put on information (e.g. Drahos, *A Philosophy of IP*, at 102).
53. Coase, *The Problem of Social Cost*, Vol. III, at 15.
54. In a market system, individuals make their own plans, implement them through voluntary exchanges, and bear the economic consequences. In central planning, government employees make the plans and implement them through coercion but do not bear the value consequences. See, De Alessi, *Property Rights*, at 34.
55. Hope, *Biobazaar*, at 108.
56. Ibid.
57. De Alessi, *Property Rights*, at 34.
58. Macey, *Public Choice*, at 43–44.
59. Ibid, at 43. See also, Greenhalgh and Rogers, *Innovation, Intellectual Property, and Economic Growth*, at 17, referring to the work of Pavitt K. (1984), *Sectoral Patterns of Technical Change*, 13 Research Policy 343–373 (discussing the variables as to when a firm would produce and when a firm would import via market production).
60. Macey, *Public Choice*, at 44.
61. Alchian A. and Demsetz H. (1972), *Production, Information Costs, and Economic Organization*, 62 Am. Econ. Rev. 778.
62. Macey, *Public Choice*, at 44.
63. Hope, *Biobazaar*, at 109. Although FLOSS is generally more decentralised than firm production, this is not without contention. See Weber, *The Success of Open Source*, at 63–64 (suggesting that Linux was created through a 'hierarchy of gatekeepers' who decide whether a piece of code is included within the software project).
64. Benkler, *Coase's Penguin, or, Linux and the Nature of the Firm*, at 381. For a discussion of the notion of 'uncodified' see Cunningham, *The Separation of (Economic) Power*.
65. To some extent, this idea is an extension of Janet Hope's perspective that seeks to 'flip markets in vice into markets for virtue'. See Hope J. *et al* (2008), *Regulatory Capitalism, Business Models and the Knowledge Economy*, in Braithwaite J. (ed.), *Regulatory Capitalism: How it Works, Ideas for Making it Work Better*, Edward Elgar, 59. Also, Chon M. (2012), *Law Professor as Artist: Themes and Variations in Keith Aoki's Intellectual Property Scholarship*, 90 Oregon Law Review 1251, at 1259.
66. See principle 12 of Table 1.1.
67. See principle 10 of Table 1.1.

68. In many respects, this perspective accords with the Samuelsonian idea of public goods: 'government provides certain indispensable *public* services without which community life would be unthinkable and which by their nature cannot appropriately be left to private enterprise.' See Samuelson, *Economics: An Introductory Analysis*, at 45.
69. Boyle, *The Second Enclosure Movement*, at 48.
70. Ibid, at 49. The term 'semiotic democracy' was first coined by John Fiske (1987), *Television Culture*, Routledge, but has since been relied upon by legal scholars such as William Fisher. See Fisher W. (2004), *Promises to Keep: Technology, Law and the Future of Entertainment*, Stanford University Press.
71. Boyle, *The Second Enclosure Movement*, at 48.
72. Boyle, *The Public Domain*, at 192.
73. In relation to commercial production Drahos states that 'the greater the role of abstract objects in capitalist production, the greater the production of the hardware of technology there needs to be'. See Drahos, *A Philosophy of IP*, at 112; and 'abstract objects are used to continue capitalism's obsession with ... the hardware of technology' (at 112–113). See also Benkler, *The Idea of Access to Knowledge and the Information Commons*, at 233–234 (arguing that 'effective agency in the domains of information and knowledge production requires access to material means, as well as to a knowledge commons'). For an interesting account of 'pirate infrastructure' in Nigeria see Larkin B. (2008), *Signal and Noise: Media, Infrastructure, and Urban Culture in Nigeria*, Duke University Press, at 218–219.
74. Also, for an analysis of the relationship between health and infrastructure see Taubman, *A Typology of Intellectual Property Management for Public Health Innovation and Access*, at 5 ('[a] comprehensive and realistic view of access to medication must, therefore, take account of the innovation process itself and *broader infrastructure needs*' (emphasis added)).
75. Jefferson R. (2007), *Science as Social Enterprise: the CAMBIA BiOS Initiative*, 1(4) Innovations: Technology, Governance and Globalisation 13.
76. For a brief discussion of the successes and failures of open biotechnology, see Joly Y. (2010), *Open Biotechnology: Licenses Needed*, 28 Nature Biotechnology 417. See also Rimmer, *IP and Climate Change*, at 336–339 (discussing the CAMBIA project); and Benkler, *The Wealth of Networks*, at 343–344. For a critique of CAMBIA see Nicol D. and Hope J. (2006), *Cooperative Strategies for Facilitating Use of Patented Inventions in Biotechnology*, 24(1) Law in Context, at 85.
77. Kevin Sweeney, *Open Source Biology Workshop* cited in Hope, *Biobazaar*, at 188.
78. Hope J. (2005), *Open Source Biotechnology*, PhD, Australian National University, at 184–185, 224 (unpublished manuscript, on file with author).
79. Ibid, at 223–224.
80. Wright S. (1998), *Molecular Politics in a Global Economy*, in Thackray A. (ed.), *Private Science: Biotechnology and the Rise of the Molecular Sciences*, The Chemical Sciences in Society Series, University of Pennsylvania Press, at 80–104.
81. For an interesting discussion of how 'pirate infrastructure' might relate to Lesser Developed Countries, see Liang, *Beyond Representation*, at 365–367.
82. Graff G. *et al* (2003), *Privatization and Innovation in Agricultural Biotechnology*, Agriculture and Resource Economics Update 6.
83. See Tzfira T. and Citovsky B. (2006), *Agrobacterium-mediated Genetic Transformation of Plants: Biology and Biotechnology*, 17 Current Opinion in Biotechnology, 147–154, found at: http://www.plantsci.cam.ac.uk/Haseloff/teaching/PlantSciPart1B_2006/reading/files/Tzfira2006.pdf (last cited 29/01/2010). See also Drahos, *The Global Governance of Knowledge*, at 12–14 (discussing the heavy concentration of patent ownership by a handful of multinational corporations).
84. Benkler, *Coase's Penguin, or, Linux and the Nature of the Firm*, at 377.

85. Ibid.
86. Ibid, at 341–342.
87. Hope, *Open Source Biotechnology*, at 184–185.
88. Carlson R. and Brent R. (2000), *DARPA Open Source Biology Letter*, Molecular Sciences Institute cited in Hope, *Open Source Biotechnology*, at 184–185 (unpublished manuscript, on file with author). Also cited in Hope, *Biobazaar*, at 198–199.
89. The social production process is not necessarily linear in that computer software was more open source based early in its development, but then certain parts of the industry were captured by commodification.
90. By the end of 2007 only 20% of the world's population was using the Internet. See UN, The Millennium Development Goals Report 2009, at 52, available online at: https://www.un.org/millenniumgoals/pdf/MDG_Report_2009_ENG.pdf *(cited 6/5/2013)*. This issue is addressed in passing by Benkler, *The Wealth of Networks*, but is referred to as a 'transitional problem' (at 236–237).
91. See principle 11 of Table 1.1.
92. See principle 12 of Table 1.1.

PART V, CHAPTER 11 NOTES

1. Purdy, *Our Place in the World*, at 887.
2. Boyle, *A Politics of Intellectual Property*, at 113.
3. Mitchell, *The Intellectual Commons*, at 98. See also, Drahos, *Six Minutes to Midnight*.
4. As we saw in Part I, the justification that often accompanies propertisation is the internalisation of externalities. For exemplary literature, see Landes W. (1981), *Lecture Notes in Economic Analysis of Law*; Knight F. (1924), *Some Fallacies in the Interpretation of Social Costs* 38 Q. J. Econ. 582; and Lehmann, *Property and Intellectual Property – Property Rights as Restrictions on Competition in Furtherance of Competition*, at 24.
5. See, e.g., Hobbes T. (1651) [1996], *Leviathan*, ed. R. Tuck, Cambridge University Press (explaining that property rights are the subject of sovereign discretion, but that the sovereign is bound to offer the citizens certain protections relating to property ownership such as providing a judicial system of resolution in matters concerning property conflict). See also, Mill J. (1859) [2003], *On Liberty*, ed. D. Bromwich and G. Kate, Yale University Press (casting property within the social contract context whereby freedom is traded in for certain securities stemming from impartial sovereign protection of property); Blackstone, *Commentaries on the Laws of England*, at 2 (defining property as the 'sole and despotic dominion which one man claims and exercises over the external things of the world, in total exclusion of the right of any other individual in the universe'); Hume D. (1744) [2006], *Moral Philosophy*, ed. S. McCord, Hackett Publishing Co., at 87–92 (advocating the pragmatic, but unnatural, view whereby property ownership is adopted as a means of dividing limited resources); and Proudhon P. (1840) [1970], *What is Property? Or An Inquiry in the Principle of Right and Government*, ed. G. Woodcock, Dover Publications, at 43–44 (making the important distinction between possession and property).
6. Benkler, *The Wealth of Networks*, at 143–144.
7. Mitchell, *The Intellectual Commons*, at 117; Rousseau J. (1755), *On the Causes of Inequality among Men*; and Guerin D. (2005), *No Gods, No Masters: An Anthology of Anarchism*, trans. P. Sharkey, AK Press, at 55–56.

8. Leopold, *A Sand County Almanac*, at 217; Stone, *Should Trees Have Standing?*, at x–xi (Garrett Hardin).
9. Ibid. Leopold's view is to be contrasted with the view that 'property embeds ethics': 'as private rights and their supporting institutions evolve, incentives are created for individuals to behave cooperatively, ethically, and altruistically. On the other hand, institutions designed to produce involuntary transfers of wealth, and therefore, undermine the security of private property rights, also undermine the incentive to behave morally.' See De Alessi, *Property Rights*, at 36.
10. Chander and Sunder, *The Romance of the Public Domain*, at 1356. The *res nullius* approach also accords with the 'negative community' description discussed by Drahos, *A Philosophy of IP*, at 45–46, 57–59, 65–66, 162.
11. Ibid. The *res communis* approach also accords with 'positive community' discussed by Drahos, ibid, at 57–58, 65, 68, 208.
12. See principle 5 of Table 1.1.
13. See generally Hardin, *Tragedy of the Commons.*
14. Nonini, *The Global Idea of 'the Commons'*, at 1–2; Bannerman, *The Ins and Outs of the Public Domain*, at 170. See also case studies in part 2 of Bromley (ed.), *Making the Commons Work*; Ostrom, *Governing the Commons*, especially chapter 3; Ellickson, *Order Without Law*; and Fennell, *Commons, Anticommons, Semicommons*, at 2.
15. Benkler, *The Political Economy of Commons*, IV(3) Upgrade 6.
16. Fennell, *Commons, Anticommons, Semicommons*, at 5 (especially footnote 16). Beyond alluding to the semicommons quality of the tragedy of the commons, Fennell also highlights the issue of *scale*. Thinking about the role of scale inherent within the semicommons theory brings to the fore the question of what the appropriate mix is between private property and commons in relation to a given set of activities. As Fennell notes, this question gives rise not just to a consideration of a 'given set of activities', but also to the issue of timing – 'temporal semicommons'. That is, it may be that at a given time a specific piece of land should be held as private property, but at other times it should be held in common. See ibid, at 19.
17. Frank Michelman is generally credited for introducing the anticommons concept as per Michelman, *Ethics, Economics and the Law of Property*, at 6. See also, Ellickson, *Property in Land*, at 1322; and Heller, *The Tragedy of the Anticommons*, at 624.
18. See principle 6 of Table 1.1. Lessig, *The Future of Ideas*; Perelman, *Steal This Idea*; Rose, *Authors and Owners*; and Heverly, *The Information Semicommons*, at 1130–1141.
19. Bramwell, *Ecology in the 20th Century*, at 4; Boughey, *Fundamental Ecology*, at 5; and Carter, *A Radical Green Political Theory*, at 19. Traditionally 'science' had a broader meaning than it does today encompassing 'a whole body of regular or methodological observations or propositions … concerning any subject of speculation … a kind of knowledge or argument rather than a kind of subject'. Also, see Williams, *Keywords*, at 233; Chon, *Postmodern 'Progress'*, at 114.
20. Dryzek and Scholosberg, *Debating the Earth*, at 92 (discussing adaptive management and other ecological principles).
21. Bohanes J. (2002), *Risk Regulation in WTO Law: A procedure-based approach to the precautionary principle*, 40 Colum. J. Transnat'l L. 323 at 330; and Stenzel P. (2002), *How the World Trade Organization Must Promote Environmental Protection*, 13 Duke Envtl. L. & Pol'y F. 1 at 42–43.
22. Walker and Salt, *Resilience Thinking*, at 1; Rogers (ed.), *Green Paradigms and the Law*, at 104.
23. Stone, *Should Trees Have Standing?*; and Boyle, *Politics of Intellectual Property.*
24. Sax, *The Public Trust Doctrine in Natural Resources Law*, at 478–89; Stone, *Should Trees Have Standing?*; Tribe, *Ways Not to Think About Plastic Trees.*

25. Deazley, *Rethinking Copyright*, at 131.
26. Rose, *Romans, Roads, and Romantic Creators*; and Sun, *Toward a Public Trust Doctrine in Copyright Law*, at 32.
27. Chon, *Postmodern 'Progress'*; Ryan, *Cyberspace as Public Space*. Note, however, that use of the public trust doctrine as it relates to the information environment has been deemed unsuccessful: *Eldred v Reno* 74 F. Supp. 2d 1 (DDC 1999), aff'd, *Eldred v Reno*, 239 F 3d 372 (DC Cir 2001), aff'd sub nom *Eldred v Ashcroft*, 537 US 186 (2003).
28. Chon, *Postmodern 'Progress'*, at 130. Although national parks are generally state sponsored, there are examples of community-sponsored national parks as discussed by Techera, *Protecting Nature and Culture* (referring to the Samoan Fisher By-Laws and the Village Feno Act in the Solomon Islands, which empower the local community to establish by-laws that are in turn enforceable within state courts). Other examples include the Vanuatu Community Conserved Areas facilitated by the Environmental Management and Conservation Act. Conservation easements, as discussed at length by Molly Van Houweling, provide another option that might complement informational national parks. See Van Houweling, *The New Servitudes*.
29. There are parallels with romantic rhetoric as it relates to the physical environment, and the rhetoric associated with the preservation of the information commons. For instance, as Boyle states, cultural environmentalism is not just about lamenting the dark, but also lighting candles. Similar themes can be identified within nineteenth-century romantic rhetoric associated with the national park movement. That is, nineteenth-century Romantics such as Mill, Ruskin, Morris, Emerson, Thoreau and Wordsworth were instrumental in celebrating authenticity, while also simultaneously rejecting the Enlightenment attitudes of the day – e.g. that humans could and should improve nature through reason, technology, science and economic liberalism – through their equivocation of industrialism (which they perceived as a detriment to morality, social order, human health and nature). See Pepper, *The Roots of Modern Environmentalism*, at 18, 76–77; and Chon, *Postmodern 'Progress'*. at 134–135 (arguing that two framers of the US Constitution – notably James Madison and Thomas Jefferson – provide a textual basis that links the Enlightenment to the postmodern 'Progress' project).
30. Patterson and Lindberg, *The Nature of Copyright, A Law of Users' Rights*, at 2; Birnhack, *More or Better?*, at 60; and Lange, *Reimagining the Public Domain*, at 470 (stating that the public domain is 'a place of refuge for creative expression … a place like home, where, when you go there, they have to take you in and let you dance'). As Boyle states: '[t]he public domain is not some gummy residue left behind when all the good stuff has been covered by property law. The public domain is the place we quarry the building blocks of our culture. It is, in fact, the *majority* of our culture. Or at least it has been' (2008: 40). See also, Bannerman, *The Ins and Outs of the Public Domain*, at 168–169.
31. Buchanan, *The Achievement and Limits of Public Choice in Diagnosing Government Failure and in Offering Bases for Constructive Reform*, at 25; and Mitchell, *The Old and New Public Choice*, at 5.
32. For a discussion of the application of social contract to IPRs see Drahos, *The Global Governance of Knowledge*, at 32.
33. Buchanan *et al*, *Toward a Theory of the Rent-Seeking Society*.
34. Boyle, *Cruel, Mean, or Lavish?*, at 2035; Litman, *Copyright, Compromise and Legislative History*; and Benkler, *The Wealth of Networks*, at 319 (arguing that strong property rights aid the wealthy and that they lead to increasing exclusive rights).
35. Benkler, *The Wealth of Networks*, at 46–48, 165–167.

36. Ibid. at 176–177. Drahos has also argued that 'networks are the best form of managing knowledge', *Indigenous Developmental Networks and the Adaptive Management of Intellectual Property.*
37. See principle 10 of Table 1.1.
38. Mitchell, *The Intellectual Commons*, at 98. See also, Drahos, *Six Minutes to Midnight.*
39. See Chapter 1 generally.
40. Deazley, *Rethinking Copyright*, at 133, referring to Mark Rose. Rose's quote refers to the 'public domain' rather than the 'information commons'.

Glossary

An important aim of this book is to foster 'a language and geography of experience' that can be used to advance the interests of the information commons. For this reason, a glossary of some of the key terms is useful.

Collective action problems: encompasses those costs associated with political organising. Examples include information costs and organising costs. The free-riding problem also falls within the ambit.

Cultural environmentalism: the original descriptor given to Professor James Boyle's claim that there are links, worthy of study, between the physical environment and the information environment.

Ecology: literally the study of life at home. Contemporaneously ecology encompasses three streams: (i) ecological science (the relationships between organisms), (ii) ecological ethics (the relationship between humans and the environment), and (iii) systems thinking (the relationship between organisms and their environment).

Exclusivity costs: includes efficiency costs, administration costs, externality costs and distributional costs. Commonly equated to the 'veil of property'.

Information commons: A bundling term that refers collectively to the intellectual commons and the public domain.

Information environment: those systems that relate to the processing, production, consumption, communication, distribution and diffusion of information.

Information environmental governance framework: the framework advanced within this book. In short, it refers to the application of welfare economics, the commons, ecology and public choice theory to IPRs (particularly copyrights and patents).

Information environmentalism: a normative discourse that seeks to protect the information commons by establishing an information environmental governance framework.

Intellectual commons: encompasses those abstract objects open to use. Can be divided into narrow and broad definitions (see Table 4.2).

IPR maximalism: IPR discourse that seeks the continued entrenchment and expansion of IPRs.

IPR minimalism: IPR discourse that seeks to challenge the continued entrenchment and expansion of IPRs and to underscore the benefits of the information commons.

Negative community: the state of affairs whereby resources belong to no one and are considered to be unclaimed and for the taking. Broadly equates to the concept of *res nullius*. Can be divided into inclusive and exclusive (see Table 4.1).

Positive community: the state of affairs whereby resources belong to everyone and therefore any use of such resources must be for the benefit of the public at large. Broadly equates to the concept of *res communis*. Can be divided into inclusive and exclusive (see Table 4.1).

Public choice theory: describes the effect that concentrated interests have on regulatory frameworks. Initially espoused by Buchanan and Tullock in their 1962 classic *The Calculus of Consent*.

Public domain: usually encompasses all types of public rights relating to the use of information. This broad definition can be contrasted with the narrow definition as per Table 4.2.

Rational truths: generally established with reference to a threshold level of technical expertise.

Reasonable arguments: generally founded upon sound and credible legal arguments.

Rhetorical imagination: innovative rhetorical methods that can be used to shift perceptions of a given perceived reality.

The commons: for joint use, shared, belonging to the community.

Tragedy of the anticommons: describes the situation where too many owners hold rights of exclusion, a resource is prone to under-use.

Tragedy of the commons: describes the situation where too many people have a privilege to use a resource and no one user has a right to exclude any other user, the resource is prone to over-consumption and depletion.

Tragedy of ignoring the information semicommons: describes the failure to take into account the dynamic interaction between private and public usages of information, which leads to inappropriate skews in IPR regulatory frameworks.

Veil of property: the concealment of exclusivity costs related to property.

Welfare economics: includes cost/benefit analysis that flows from choosing a particular economic pathway and/or regulatory framework.

'Poets are the unacknowledged legislators of the world.'
John Keats

Index